The Shaping of American Higher Education

Arthur M. Cohen

The Shaping of American Higher Education

Emergence and Growth of the Contemporary System

Jossey-Bass Publishers
San Francisco

Jossey-Bass books and products are available through most bookstores. To contact Jossey-Bass directly, call (888) 378–2537, fax to (800) 605–2665, or visit our website at www.josseybass.com.

Substantial discounts on bulk quantities of Jossey-Bass books are available to corporations, professional associations, and other organizations. For details and discount information, contact the special sales department at Jossey-Bass.

 Manufactured in the United States of America on Lyons Falls Turin Book. This paper is acid-free and 100 percent totally chlorine-free.

Library of Congress Cataloging-in-Publication Data

Cohen, Arthur M.
   The shaping of American higher education : emergence and growth of the contemporary system / Arthur M. Cohen.
     p. cm. — (Jossey-Bass higher and adult education series)
   Includes bibliographical references (p.   ) and index.
   ISBN 0-7879-1029-5 (hc. : alk. paper)
   1. Education, Higher—United States—History. 2. Universities and colleges—United States—History. I. Title. II. Series.
LA226.C66   1998
378.73—dc21   98-11854

FIRST EDITION
HB Printing 10 9 8 7 6 5 4 3 2

Contents

· ·

Preface

This book had its origins in the History of Higher Education course that I have taught for many years in UCLA's Department of Education. Few of the students who enroll each term have much prior knowledge of American history, and fewer still are aware of the roots of collegiate institutions. As the course evolved, it became apparent that it had to both encompass the entire scope of higher education since the Colonial Era and to set the developing colleges in the context of their times—all within the span of a ten-week quarter. Furthermore, the review of 350 years of continuous expansion in enrollments, staff, curriculum, finance, and all other aspects of the system had to be organized so that it would not overwhelm the students. The matrix described in the introduction to this volume has helped serve that purpose.

The book is useful as an overview for practitioners in all areas of higher education who can benefit from knowledge of the broad currents affecting their work. It can also be used as a text in a one-term or two-term course presented to students in any social science department at any level from freshman to graduate. It emphasizes the past fifty years because other texts have covered the earlier periods well. A complete course could be based on this book, or it could be coupled with one emphasizing the earlier eras and supplemented with additional readings on special topics and documentary sources.

The volume's chief contribution is its synthesis of the Mass Higher Education Era (1945–1975) and the Contemporary Era (1976–1998); most of the trends that had developed earlier matured during these periods. Contemporary periodicals, data collected by the National Center for Education Statistics, and a few essential books provided most of the information undergirding the work. Many examples from California are included because I have spent my entire academic career as a University of California professor and am therefore most familiar with that state. Also, several of the directions that American higher education has taken in the past fifty years first appeared there.

Many people helped to prepare the manuscript. Several students in the UCLA Graduate School of Education and Information Studies assisted. Erika Yamasaki took charge of the tables. Dan Zeidman reviewed legislation and court decisions affecting higher education in the past fifty years. Carol Kozeracki and Gwyer Schuyler, two of my doctoral advisees, contributed at every stage. They scanned books and articles, prepared the bibliography, gave careful readings to each draft, and provided their own perspectives. With people like these two coming into higher education, the system is in good hands.

Others also participated. Amy Pape transcribed the manuscript from audiotape. John Terrey, Burton R. Clark, and John Thelin reviewed an early draft and made helpful suggestions. I am grateful to them for sharing their expertise. The staff of the ERIC Clearinghouse for Community Colleges, headed by Tronie Rifkin, put the final draft together. UCLA provided a sabbatical leave so that I could give the project my full attention.

I owe a special debt to Florence B. Brawer, my wife, coauthor, and long-term collaborator in every area of my personal and professional life. She helped plan the book; she discussed ideas, reviewed drafts, criticized, and commended. I could not have undertaken the project without her encouragement, devotion, and support. This work is dedicated to her in total appreciation for the many years we have shared.

August 1998   Arthur M. Cohen
Los Angeles

The Author

Arthur M. Cohen has been professor of higher education at the University of California at Los Angeles (UCLA) since 1964. He received his B.A. (1949) and M.A. (1955) degrees in history from the University of Miami and his Ph.D. degree (1964) in higher education from Florida State University. He has been director of the ERIC Clearinghouse for Community Colleges since 1966 and has served on the editorial boards of numerous journals. He teaches courses in higher education history, system, and issues. His most recent book is *The American Community College* (3rd ed., 1996), coauthored with Florence B. Brawer.

The Shaping of American Higher Education

Introduction: A Framework for Studying the History of Higher Education

The foremost reason for reading the history of higher education is that it teaches appreciation for the power of tradition. Practically every aspect of contemporary higher education can be traced to the formation of universities in the latter part of the nineteenth century, and many to the colleges in the Colonial Era. Some aspects were present in the universities of medieval Europe. This stability of form effects a counterpoise quite familiar to anyone who has attempted to modify any aspect of an institution.

Reading history is thus essential for those who would reform higher education. Publications and presentations calling for completely revising governance, teaching, and funding appear frequently. An industry of innovation is apparent. But it must be satisfied with small victories: an occasional new course requirement, modified student admissions practices, changed patterns of faculty recruitment. More than that the system successfully resists, co-opts, or absorbs—eventually changing but with the glacial majesty befitting a venerable structure.

The basic questions in higher education have been debated since colleges began. What shall be taught? Who shall learn it? Who shall pay for it? Each question impinges on the others. Each is grounded in the history of the institution. Curriculum, faculty selection and review, student entry and progress, and institutional funding are perennial issues. Today's problems are related to yesterday's practices.

The system has its own momentum, its own well-trodden paths. How has it evolved? And to what degree?

The history of higher education is taught in most graduate programs that prepare practitioners for positions in postsecondary institutions. Sometimes it is presented as a self-standing course; often it is submerged in courses on higher education administration, system, or issues. Several reviews have presented course syllabi and specialized reading lists (Miller and Nelson, 1993; Goodchild and Stanton, 1987; Thelin, 1986) that reveal a chronological approach. Students are taught about colleges in the Colonial Era and then led through the founding of the American nation on into the present. The basic textbooks also are so arrayed. Rudolph's *The American College and University* (1962), Brubacher and Rudy's *Higher Education in Transition* (1976), and Lucas's more recent *American Higher Education: A History* (1994) begin by showing how European forms undergirded the establishment of colleges in Colonial America. They then carry the story forward. The document compilations by Hofstadter and Smith (1961) and those in the *ASHE Reader* (Goodchild and Wechsler, 1997) also follow a chronological pattern. Geiger's 1998 outline divides the chronology into ten eras.

Most syllabi and textbooks also take a topical approach, pointing out how the types of students attending colleges changed, working conditions for the faculty were modified, the curriculum expanded beyond the original liberal arts, the institutions grew in number, patterns of governance were modified, and finance shifted toward the public treasury. These topics are often supplemented by subtopics of interest: the rise of women's colleges, education for African Americans, intercollegiate sports, training for the professions.

Various events are noted throughout the texts. The founding of certain types of institutions—state colleges, graduate and professional schools, and junior colleges for example—may be accorded separate sections. Legislation, including the Morrill Acts and the Servicemen's Readjustment Act, is given space along with important court decisions such as the Dartmouth College case, which protected institutional independence. The courses and texts also show how certain trends have been pervasive: access for more students, vocationally oriented curricula, secular governance, and state-level coordination of higher education.

Organization of the material is critical in an area as broad as the history of higher education. The theme should be wide enough to display the sweep of topics, trends, and events from the beginnings of colleges in the American colonies. But the presentation must ensure that the topics are not confounded; at the same time, it is important to avoid a restrictive approach that emphasizes a few topics to the exclusion of others.

This book's approach is to define trends and events chronologically under topical headings, showing interrelationships among them. A *trend* is a long-term movement that points in a consistent direction. An *event* is a specific occurrence that marks the progression of a trend. A *topic* is a cluster of trends and events. An *era* is a chronological distinction marked by a number of events.

Thus a matrix is suggested, with topics and trends on one axis and eras on the other. The events are noted within the categorical divisions that are formed. Exhibit I.1 displays such a layout—the one that forms the plan for this text.

Each of the topics illustrated has at least one major trend associated with it. Many of the tendencies have lengthy histories. The institutions have grown steadily larger and adopted more varied purposes and specialties. The trend for higher education's enrollments has been in the direction of greater access for the American population; ever-increasing numbers of eighteen-year-olds and of older adults have been matriculating. The faculty have moved steadily toward professionalization. Curriculum has become more directly related to workforce entry, as one occupational group after another has begun demanding additional years of schooling for its initiates. Governance has tended toward broader systems and a diminution of church-related control. Finance has become ever more dependent

Exhibit I.1. Trends and Events in American Higher Education.

Eras	I Colonial 1636–1789	II Emergent Nation 1790–1869	III University Transformation 1870–1944	IV Mass Higher Education 1945–1975	V Contemporary 1976–1998	Trends
Topics						
Societal Context						Expanding nation and economy; increased demands and expectations
Institutions						Diverse; multipurpose
Students						Access
Faculty						Professionalization
Curriculum and Instruction						Vocational and varied
Governance and Administration						Secular; larger units
Finance						Public funding
Research and Outcomes						Individual mobility; societal and economic development

on public funds. Higher education's outcomes have been directed increasingly toward producing trained manpower, enabling people to move out of the social class into which they were born, and conducting scientific research that yields useful products and processes.

Not all topics show such distinct trends. The context varies as public perceptions reflect contemporary societal concerns. In general, the expectation that higher education will contribute to economic growth has found its way into the mainstream of public thought. But the belief that it can or should ameliorate social problems or that access for everyone should be pursued at any cost is affected by the short-term mood of the nation, its media, and its national administration.

The five eras reflect the evolution of the trends. In the Colonial Era, 1636–1789, the college form was established on Old World models. The Emergent Nation Era saw hundreds of small colleges established and the beginnings of access for different types of students. In the University Transformation Era, 1870–1944, the research university made its appearance, faculty professionalization took a leap forward, and the role of the state expanded. The Mass Higher Education Era, 1945–1975, was marked by greater size and number of institutions, augmented student access, and an increasing reliance on federal funding. The era since 1976 has seen a flattening of the growth in faculty professionalization, in new institutional openings, and in public per capita funding, while state-level governance and reliance on tuition has grown.

For several of the topics, major events cluster around the cleavage lines separating the eras. The year 1790 marked the beginning of a rapid expansion in number and type of institutions. The first state colleges and the first technical institutes were formed shortly thereafter, and the curriculum was opened well beyond the liberal arts to include a broader array of emphases. Within a few years on either side of 1869, the Morrill Land Grant Act was passed, graduate study was introduced along with colleges for African Americans, and the first sizable philanthropic donations were given to establish universities. The year 1945 marked the opening of the Mass Higher Education Era because the Servicemen's Readjustment Act, the President's Commission on Higher Education report, and the formation of the National Science Foundation all occurred around then. The beginning of the Contemporary Era in 1976 was notable less for major events than for a shift in the trends noted earlier.

This book accords approximately equal emphasis to each of the eight topics. But the eras are treated differentially. Because other works have covered the years prior to World War II rather completely, this book devotes only 40 percent of its total to those eras: 10 percent each to the Colonial and Emergent Nation Eras and 20 percent to University Transformation Era. Most of the work discusses trends and events of the past fifty years, from the beginning of the Mass Higher Education Era to the late 1990s.

The book is less a history than a synthesis. Several general history books from McMaster (1909) to Jordan and Litwack (1994) were consulted relative to the societal context for the period prior to 1945, but no attempt was made to uncover new information regarding debatable issues. A rich literature traces social reform, the background and effect of immigration policies, sources of the expansionist mentality in the nineteenth century, the oppression of Native Americans, economic, social, and political issues related to slavery, and so on. As Nash, Crabtree, and Dunn (1997) have documented, all have been reinterpreted repeatedly, with no lasting consensus reached or expected. Controversies also persist over most major events within higher education: whether the Dartmouth College case of 1819 truly altered relations between states and private institutions; who was most influential in Congress's passing the Morrill Act of 1862; the extent to which the Civil War retarded the development of higher education in the South; the importance of various collegiate forms that were tried early in the twentieth century; which institutions deserve the lion's share of credit for preserving general education—to name only a few. Thorough treatments of each of these issues are available elsewhere.

This work traces higher education's first three centuries by synthesizing prevailing views without iterating the debates over motives, causes, or prime movers. It recounts the story of the early eras only to establish a background to the past fifty years for readers unfamiliar with the ways higher education developed. It centers on what was and what is, with a minimum of what ought to be. However, biases do appear throughout; absolute objectivity is an impossible conceit.

Not all of postsecondary education is treated here. People always have learned outside the formal system; apprenticeships, ateliers, and academies have been prevalent throughout history. Today corporate classrooms, distance learning, proprietary schools, and virtual universities surround the core enterprise and involve millions of learners. But this work considers primarily the sector that the National Center for Education Statistics calls higher education and that most people mean when they say they went to college.

A few books are indispensable for a rounded view of the history of higher education. Rudolph (1962) reviewed numerous single-college histories, anecdotal accounts of college life, and reviews of collegiate functioning to produce *The American College and University*—a detailed account of colleges in the eighteenth and nineteenth centuries. The transformation of the university has been documented in several basic texts. Bledstein's *The Culture of Professionalism* (1976) traces one of the pillars on which the university system was built. Veysey's *Emergence of the American University* (1965) carries through the conversion of colleges and the development of new universities. Geiger's two-volume account of the research function, *To Advance Knowledge* (1986b) and *Research and Relevant Knowledge* (1993), analyzes how the growth of research stimulated and was itself furthered by universities from the nineteenth century through the Contemporary Era.

College outcomes have been considered from many perspectives. Bowen's *The Costs of Higher Education* (1980) displays various ways of analyzing costs, and his *Investment in Learning* (1977)

traces individual and societal benefits as revealed in numerous studies of college outcomes. The effects of college on individual students are reviewed by Feldman and Newcomb (1969), Pascarella
and Terenzini (1991), and Astin (1977). Kaplin's reviews of court
decisions and legislation affecting higher education have appeared
in three editions entitled *The Law of Higher Education* (1980, 1985,
and, with Lee, 1995). His succinct summaries reveal how every
aspect of the college is embedded in a legal structure.

Since the 1960s the National Center for Education Statistics
(NCES) has conducted numerous surveys of higher education students, faculty, curriculum, and finance, primarily through the Higher
Education General Information Survey (HEGIS) and its successor,
the Integrated Postsecondary Education System (IPEDS). Many of
the NCES compendia appear annually: *Digest of Education Statistics*,
Condition of Education, and *Projections of Education Statistics* are essential for contemporary reviews. The center's occasional reports on faculty, distance education, international comparisons, and subtopics
detailing special curricula and student types are also useful. All its
databases are searchable on-line at [http://nces.ed.gov].

The complexities of higher education at the end of the twentieth century defy depth of understanding in every area. However, the
era-topic-trend organization of this book effects a useful mnemonic.
It also enables the reader to learn about each topic throughout history by scanning the corresponding section in each era. In other
words, the trends in student access can be followed by reading the
third section in each of the five chapters, trends in faculty professionalization by reading the fourth, and so on. This cross-sectional
approach can be especially useful for people who want to follow a
preferred topic. Those who learn better by comprehending the system in its entirety for each chronological era can follow the sequence
chapter by chapter in the context of its time. Either way the importance and beauty of a system that every young adult must either take
advantage of or consciously reject should be apparent.

• •

1

Establishing the Collegiate Form in the Colonies: 1636–1789

Three characteristics of the English colonies in America most affected their development. First was the settlers' determination to form a way of life different from the governmental and familial rigidities they had left in Europe. Second was the land—the limitless horizons for which dissidents and new immigrants could reach whenever they tired of their previous stations. Third was the religious spirit of the time—Protestantism and Anglicanism newly separated from Catholicism and continually reforming, yielding variations in patterns of observance from deism (later Unitarianism) to fervent sects devoted to emotional worship.

Societal Context

Table 1.1. shows a statistical picture of the conditions surrounding American higher education in the Colonial Era.

The distance from Europe contributed to shaping the course of development, as the colonists built their own society with varying degrees of oversight from the parent country. Although explorers and immigrants had been arriving in the Western hemisphere for more than one hundred years, no lasting English settlement occurred until the beginning of the seventeenth century. Under British sovereignty, Virginia, the first colony, was settled in 1607, and all but one of the colonies were formed by the end of the

Table 1.1. Statistical Portrait of the Colonial Era, 1700–1789 (Estimates).

	1700	1789
Population	250,000	3,800,000
Number of students enrolled in higher education	150	1,000
Number of faculty (professors and tutors)	5	133
Number of institutions	2	9
Number of earned degrees conferred	15	200

Source: Rudolph, 1962; Snyder, 1993.

century. Georgia, the last of the original thirteen, was settled in 1732. As a result of the variant leadership, climate, and modes of settlement and subsequent immigration, each colony differed from the others.

Immigrants from England and from continental Europe quickly populated the Atlantic seaboard from New England to the Carolinas. Early on there were conflicts among the colonists based on religious convictions; the Puritans of the first migrations were challenged by new immigrants seeking religious freedom and by dissidents from within the original settlements. But a growing number came for profit-making purposes or to make new lives for themselves. The late 1600s marked the development of commercial agriculture for export. This growing industry was accompanied by a rising need for workers; hence there was an enormous increase in the number of slaves brought to the colonies.

Whereas the seventeenth century was characterized by an influx of English families, adventurers, and indentured servants, along with Africans who were brought unwillingly, in the eighteenth century sizeable numbers of Germans, Scots, and Irish arrived. From around 250,000 in 1700, the colonial population quadrupled by midcentury and increased by as much as 30 to 40 percent each decade thereafter. The settlements were widespread; Boston, the largest city, had 7,000 people in 1700, and by the end of the era only three cities had as many as 10,000. The more Europeans, the greater the need for land, hence the onerous displacement of the native peoples as the immigrants conquered the wilderness.

For most of the settlers, the New World represented a chance for a new start. Some came as servants who had escaped prison and bought their passage by promising to work for the plantation owners for a number of years after arrival. Others were disinherited children who saw greater promise in a continent where land was cheap and a farm and family could be built anew. The desire for religious freedom brought groups from England and the Continent during an era of religious turmoil and conflict.

In their social and cultural context, the colonies were decidedly English. For a half-dozen generations after the founding of Jamestown and the landing at Plymouth Rock, they retained the characteristics of the motherland. The Germans brought their own language and customs, but the colonial laws, dress, culture, religion, professions, government, and child-rearing and educational practices were modeled on English forms. However, the years in America effected modifications in all areas of life. Some were necessitated by the challenge of living in a land where the wilderness and potentially hostile natives lurked just outside the settlements. Others were shifts in thinking, as a unique American consciousness took shape. Distance from the mother country, reckoned in terms of the several weeks that it took for messages to pass between England and the American seaboard, allowed for new ideas in religious observance and acculturation of the young to take shape.

Religion and the churches are worthy of a special note because they were so close to the daily life and thought of the colonists. Anglicanism and various Protestant sects dominated seventeenth-century England, hence the English colonies as well. The Bible was the major text, often the only book in the home. God and the devil were real to believers. As the Salem witchcraft trials demonstrated, people could be possessed, have occult powers. Good and evil, the forces of light and darkness, were tangible qualities. The New England Puritans had fled the dictates of the high church of the home country and its links with the crown. They abhorred the idea of a theocracy, but the secular states they established had strong ties to their churches and in some areas of social control were more rigid than those they had left.

By the middle of the eighteenth century, European concepts of the Enlightenment and deism modified thought. Many of the leaders born in the first half of the century—Washington, Jefferson, Franklin—adhered to rationalist ideas, read political philosophy that espoused the rights of man, had less attachment to organized religious observance. To them, the Bible was not revelation but a text. Reaction against the eighteenth-century Enlightenment came with a religious backlash known initially as the Great Awakening, dating from around 1750 and reappearing subsequently under different identifiers. This religious fervor led to the continual splintering of established churches into various sects.

The major peculiarity of the North American continent—its limitless land—influenced the way the colonies and eventually the nation developed. The country was large enough to allow for continual reformation in all aspects of colonial life. New forms of religious observance and fresh ideas in everything from the building of settlements to child rearing could emerge in the vast spaces available. The boundless horizons affected family life. The general outlook, especially in the New England colonies, was that everyone should live in family units. But the restless son, chafing under the domination of parents who might have little patience with a rebellious child, could always strike off on his own. The frontier, new opportunities, a different environment always beckoned. In a land where cash was scarce, a child had little reason to hope for an inheritance, but although nearby farm land was not free, the frontier was ever expanding and a young man could work his way into a homestead of his own. Accordingly, a sense of optimism grew. The sons could expect to have more wealth than their fathers; the hope of doing better than one's parents was realistic. There were few barriers to those who wanted to make the move. A young man could become a professional person even if his father was a farmer. Roles for women were more limited; most opportunities other than domestic service as wife, maid, or older-generation assistant were still in the future.

The geographic openness of the land was reflected also in the way people could reinvent themselves. There were few restrictions on entering the professions. The lawyers, physicians, and theologians occasionally attempted to control entry into their professions, but in few communities was anyone eager to examine the credentials of a newly arrived practitioner; public licensing was seldom seen. Apprenticeships were the major form of access to the professions. A lawyer could take a young person to read with him, and that person could hang up a shingle and enter practice at any time. In medicine a few physicians tried to form groups to judge who was entitled to call himself a doctor, but apprenticeships and the subsequent opening of practice were not regulated. According to Handlin and Handlin (1971), "Only one colony, New Jersey, in 1772, actually limited by law the right of anyone to assume the title of Doctor" (p. 39). Clergymen were both preachers and teachers, and congregations tended to value those who were schooled. Numerous preachers ascended to the pulpit without formal schooling, but "university graduates who could hurl about quotations in the original Hebrew and Greek and loftily demonstrate their superior familiarity with Scripture enjoyed a strategic advantage" (Handlin and Handlin, 1971, p. 43). Teaching required no specific preparation; anyone who could read and write could show others how to do it.

The development of literacy did not depend on schooling. Today's children are exposed to language on television, billboards, magazines, newspapers, even the promotional material on cereal and toy boxes; regardless of the emphasis in their homes, they are surrounded by words. But although the colonists in the coastal cities saw books and newspapers, many who were living on the margins of civilization had little association with print other than in the family Bible. Their familiarity with ideas came through words delivered by a preacher or itinerant peddler. For the vast majority of young people, the family was the source of education in social mores, morality, and ways of behaving. Under the circumstances, the extent of literacy is remarkable. Their orthography was crude, but the colonists were more familiar with language than were their European social-class counterparts.

The American Revolution was born as the colonists gained a sense of uniqueness. Strung along the Eastern seaboard from Massachusetts to Georgia, oriented to the sea across which the immigrants had come, the colonists saw England as the mother country. All the main towns were on bodies of navigable water, and most of the commerce was waterborne trade among the colonies themselves, the English colonies in the West Indies, and Britain. The reasons for the American Revolution have been discussed countless times. Was it commercial interests? Blundering by the English rulers? A by-blow of the French-British rivalry? The revolution has gained particular status as a mythic quest for freedom from oppression by the crown. Taking a cynical view of the latter reason, the contemporary Samuel Johnson (Bate, 1975) said, "How is it that we hear the loudest yelps for liberty among the drivers of negroes?" (p. 193). Most of the colonists had no trouble holding compartmentalized notions of freedom—one for themselves, another for their slaves and servants. Views of parity were further stratified to account for what were perceived as natural differences among wealthy and poor and men and women. The "all men are created equal" phrase in the Declaration of Independence proved rather a qualified statement—one that was to be debated and reinterpreted countless times throughout the new nation's history.

Institutions

The nine colleges that were organized in the colonies were modeled on educational forms that had been developed in Europe over the prior five hundred years. This development has been traced well by Rashdall (1936) and, more recently, by Lucas (1994). One incipient university form was organized by groups of students who established their own organizations and assemblies, employing the faculty, deciding on how they would spend their funds, and setting rules governing the courses of study, examinations, and awarding of degrees. Such institutions were organized as early as the twelfth century in Italy and subsequently in Spain, Portugal, and central Europe. The curriculum included the classical writers along with studies in the liberal arts and natural science. They awarded bachelor's degrees and, if a graduate wanted to stay on for another year or two, the master's. A teaching license would be awarded somewhere between receipt of the bachelor's and the master's. The student-led institutions also established rituals surrounding graduation, including academic robes and commencement exercises.

A second type of European institution developed within the church. Allied closely with the priesthood, these institutions were dedicated to training clergymen. Their curriculum was based in church doctrine with students learning the words of doctrinal authorities and principles of theology. They were professional schools operated by and for the purposes of the centralized church. The University of Paris exemplified the form.

In retrospect, the threads of the colonial colleges and of higher education subsequently were apparent in both groups. The institutions incorporated the conceptual precision that would later lead to empirical investigation, the use of ancient texts as enhancing intellectual curiosity, and humanistic thought that led toward secularized study. The elements of all the institutional types can be found in higher education today. However, at the time of the founding of the colonial colleges, the pattern of curriculum and faculty-student relations stemming from church-related institutions was most prominent. The European universities were lagging in the development of science, and the colonial institutions had little to do with science until the end of the era. The students and the faculty had no say in governance matters; authority ran from the institution's board of governors to the college president. Curriculum centered on classical texts and the foundations of Christian doctrine. The humanities, as studied in classical writings as literature and the fine and performing arts, had to await a later day. Similarly, experimental science as an area of inductive inquiry could not emerge until scientists freed themselves from reliance on doctrine and prior authority and from the search for universal truths as revealed in classical writings.

The eighteenth-century Enlightenment did not have an immediate effect. The anticlerical ideas that were filtering into the thinking of Europeans from French and English philosophers to literate laypeople were slow to penetrate the universities. Gradually however, the idea of the university as the seat of all learning came to fruition in Oxford and Cambridge. And gradually across the continent, the university as an agent of the state was being born. Still, science as a path to understanding through experimentation and verification was developing outside the universities and remained there well into the nineteenth century. Except for theologians, few scientists, philosophers, or leading thinkers were working within the formal higher education structure in Europe or in the English colonies.

The colleges in the American colonies were modeled on an amalgamation of ideas and forms coming from Europe, but they emerged in their own way. Boorstin (1991) comments that the colonists settled the continent before they had a system for dealing with it. Hence they had to reinvent governmental and educational forms as they went along. The idea of lay governing boards was transplanted from Scottish universities and the curriculum and residential pattern from Cambridge. None of the colleges followed the continental pattern of students in charge of the institution, and none was strictly controlled by a dominant church. They all developed around notions of acculturating the young, passing on the wisdom of the classics, and preparing people not only for service as clergymen but as public servants as well.

Around 130 university-trained men were in the first generation of immigrants to Massachusetts Bay Colony. Thirty-five were graduates of Emmanuel College, Cambridge, and when they established Harvard they followed the Emmanuel pattern. Control was to be in the hands of church elders; curriculum was similar to Cambridge curriculum, and the residential pattern was suited for shaping immature youths. The college centered on teaching, not on the advancement of learning, and saw no contradiction in preparing young people to take their place as public officials and as ministers in a community where church and state were closely aligned. Because any institution could constitute itself as a college and grant the degrees that it chose, Harvard began awarding degrees even before it was legally incorporated.

The colleges formed in the other colonies followed the Harvard pattern but with some major distinctions. Soon after Virginia was settled, the colony received a grant of land for college purposes from the crown, but the College of William and Mary did not open until after it received a royal charter in 1693. The college was to prepare clergymen for service in the Anglican church, civilize the Indians, and prepare civil servants. Scottish influences were seen in the development of William and Mary, as its control was established in a board of trustees representative more of laymen than of church officials.

The combination of church influence blended with lay control became the pattern. There was a link between the established churches and the teaching of morality or the good life, and as new churches were formed, the colleges came along with them so that the young could be instructed in proper conduct. Each of the colonies was founded by "a considerable infusion of men who had received in the European universities a liberal culture, which they desired to reproduce on these shores" (Ten Brook, 1875, p. 17). Dartmouth and Yale were formed by Congregationalists—spin-offs from the Massachusetts Puritans. The dominant religious groups in the other colonies formed their own institutions: the College of

New Jersey, later Princeton, by the Presbyterians; the College of Rhode Island, later Brown, by the Baptists; Queen's College, later Rutgers, by the Dutch Reformed church; and King's College, later Columbia, by the Anglicans (but with a strong minority of other religions represented on its first governing board). The College of Philadelphia, later Pennsylvania, was the most decidedly nonsectarian of the colonial institutions.

Much has been written about these institutions; each has its own history, which Rudolph (1962) summarized well. In general they consolidated trends coming from England and Scotland. College governance, finance, faculty-student relations, curriculum, and instructional practices were all codified in this era, so that when hundreds of new colleges were founded after the formation of the United States, they followed the model even as their emphases shifted. Although they were connected with the churches, the colleges were not as much religious as educative, founded to produce a learned people. They would train clergymen, and because most clergymen were community leaders, they would prepare statesmen. Trow (1988) traced other reasons for establishing colleges: the idea of perpetuating a civilized society in frontier communities; the growing need for better-trained people not only in law, medicine, and theology but also in commerce and navigation; community pride; and idealism and philanthropy on the part of community leaders. The absence of any restraining political force helped. There was no centralized government to establish standards. Each colony was free to set its own rules, and although each college resembled the others because of the power of imitation, the institutions were free to develop in idiosyncratic patterns. The colonists could have sent their young to England for university schooling, and many did, but the trip was long and perilous and the expense was great. Coupled with the desire to build communities with strong religious orientation and to fit youth for public employment in the civil state, the colleges developed indigenously. They followed Harvard, the first, but Harvard never set rules for the others.

The ease with which religious sects formed as splinters from existing churches also influenced the development of higher education in the colonies. Rivalry between religious sects certainly played a part, as a half-dozen different church groupings were represented among the nine colonial institutions. Each of the colleges had a church connection, although two of them were effectually interdenominational. Church influence was never absolute, and a tradition of lay governance was established early on.

If the colleges were not needed to prepare people for professions, the impetus for their founding must be sought elsewhere. In general the colonists wanted to build communities that integrated religion with society, and religion depended on an educated laity. They needed institutions to assist in acculturating the young, and the notion of civilizing the Indians was not far from the surface. Furthermore, the college brought prestige to communities that needed to show that they were centers of civility, not merely rude outposts. The desire to build unified communities with strong religious orientation was powerful, and the belief that civil government needed educated leaders was prominent as well. Not only ministers but also civil servants were to be the product of the colonial institutions. For all these reasons the colonists built colleges—only three prior to the middle of the eighteenth century but six more between then and the founding of the nation. As few as they were, they effected lasting public perceptions of what a true college should be.

Toward the latter part of the Colonial Era the religious orientation waned, and the idea of a civil community centered on principles of morality and public service, apart from an established church, grew. The colleges (see Table 1.2) emphasized public service, acculturation of the young, and the civil community. Benjamin Franklin ([1749] 1931) detailed these purposes in his *Proposals Relating to the Education of Youth in Pensilvania,* in which he outlined the institution that would become the University of Pennsylvania. The college would center on the education of youth for the purpose of supplying qualified men who would serve the

Table 1.2. The Nine Colonial Colleges.

Original Name	Current Name	Year Established	Primary Religious Affiliation
Harvard College	Harvard University	1636	Puritan
College of William and Mary	College of William and Mary	1693	Anglican
Yale College	Yale University	1701	Congregationalist
College of Philadelphia	University of Pennsylvania	1740	Nonsectarian
College of New Jersey	Princeton University	1746	Presbyterian
King's College	Columbia University	1754	Anglican
College of Rhode Island	Brown University	1765	Baptist
Queen's College	Rutgers, the State University of New Jersey	1766	Dutch Reformed
Dartmouth College	Dartmouth College	1769	Congregationalist

public with honor. These youth would be prepared in writing, drawing, arithmetic, geography, and history, including natural history and the history of commerce. The rector would be a learned man, a correct and pure speaker and writer in English, and would have tutors serving under him. The scholars and students would live together and keep their bodies sound through frequent exercise. The English language would supersede Latin as the tongue of instruction. All would center on the good life for the students and the betterment of the community without reference to church doctrine. Here was the foundation of the institution that could sustain all the best purposes of the other colleges without reliance on doctrinal connection. William Smith, who published a similar plan for a college based on a broad curriculum, became the College of Philadelphia's first leader. More than any other colonial institution it seems to have presaged the institution that epitomized the American college.

Students

Few young people in the American colonies went to college. Either they had no need to go, or college was not accessible to them. College purposes and curricula did not match the interest and aspirations of most of the youth. Few families had the cash to pay the tuition, low as it was, and support their children through a course of study. They more likely depended on their sons for assistance on the farm or in the family business. Except in New England, education was not compulsory even in the lowest grades, hence there was no groundswell of demand for further study; few students attended school past the primary years.

College as an avenue of career preparation had limited appeal because few careers depended on further study. All the crafts and trades, as well as farming and business, could be learned through imitation or apprenticeships. The incipient professions—law and medicine—were learned in similar fashion. Only theology demanded some further schooling, and even there, most of the preachers were not college trained. As for the girls, they could learn all they needed to know from their mothers initially, then from their husbands.

Enrollments were small. By the end of the Colonial Era scarcely one in one thousand colonists had been to college. The total number of resident students at any of the colonial colleges was usually less than one hundred, and the graduating classes could be numbered in single digits. Harvard, the largest college, graduated sixty-four students in 1771, but it was well out in front of the others. Rudolph (1977) notes, "Not until 1759 did the handful of colonial colleges graduate, among them, more than a hundred young men in any one year" (p. 25). Some of the wealthier families, especially in New England, sent their children to the mother country for their higher education, but even adding those into the college-trained population, the numbers remained consistently small.

The careers followed by those who had been to college give an indication of the purposes for which students attended. Most became either ministers, physicians, teachers, lawyers, public servants, or a combination of these. However, their numbers were so sparse that they did not form alumni groups or otherwise interact with each other in terms of the institution they had attended. They were likely to associate in the literary societies formed in Boston and Philadelphia that enlisted members from any college in America or England, or from none.

The paucity of public schools meant that most of the young people who had any formal training studied with tutors—educated people who would take on a few students as a means of supplementing their own livelihood. In Virginia the planters' sons sometime boarded with preachers who would provide instruction in English grammar, Latin, mathematics, and natural science. Meriwether Lewis commented that finding a place with tutors was not easy because the rudimentary schools that they operated could house only a few pupils at a time. He had to stay away from home for long periods of time so that he would not lose his place as a student in the home of a person who was teaching him English grammar and arithmetic (Ambrose, 1996). Lewis's experiences as a member of a plantation-owning family were typical; most students were sons of land-owning families or of professionals. A few were from the families of artisans or tradesman; very few were from among the owners of small farms.

College life was designed as a system for controlling the often exuberant youth and for inculcating within them discipline, morals, and character. Each student was to attend the lectures and tutorials, obey the rules, and avoid the company of base people. Yale issued a set of rules describing the rigor with which the college expected its students to attend to a way of life: "No Student of this College Shall attend upon any Religious Meetings either Public or Private on the Sabbath or any other Day but Such as are appointed by Public Authority or Approved by the President. . . . If Any Student shall Prophane the Sabbath by unnecessary Business . . . or makeing any Indecent Noise or Disorder . . . He Shall be punished . . . . No Student Shall walk abroad, or be absent from his Chamber, Except Half an hour after Breakfast, and an hour and an half after Dinner" (Dexter, 1896, pp. 4–5). Further regulations described penalties, fines, or, at the ultimate, expulsion, for swearing, cursing, blaspheming, playing cards, singing loudly, associating with disorderly people, and the like. The freshmen were also obliged to go on errands if so instructed by students in superior classes. There were no provisions for grievance proceedings.

The family that sent its youngster to the college expected that the institution would take charge of the boy's life. Frequently the fourteen- or fifteen-year-old had already been identified by his parents as being in need of some greater discipline than a father or mother could provide. The colleges were truly to act as surrogate parents and to enforce behavior that the boy's parents might not have been able to instill. Youngsters who could not accept the form of discipline that the college imposed might be sent home.

The admissions requirements imposed by the colonial colleges further limited the number of students who could attend. Harvard required that the applicant be able to speak Latin verse and prose and to decline Greek grammar. At William and Mary an applicant was to be at least fifteen years old and to have studied Latin and Greek in the college's preparatory section if he had not attained a working knowledge of the classical languages previously. Admissions requirements at Yale were the same as at Harvard; students were to be "skilful in construing and grammattically resolving both latine and greek authors and in making a good and true latine" (Broome, 1903, p. 28). The only real change in admissions requirements all the way into the end of the era was when Yale added an understanding of arithmetic in 1745 along with "Sufficient Testimony of his Blameless and inoffensive Life" (p. 30). Princeton added arithmetic to its requirements in 1760; King's College began in 1754 with requirements in Latin, Greek, and arithmetic.

There were no written admissions tests. Students were examined orally by the college president or the tutors. Students were sometimes exempt from one or another requirement, especially because all the colleges needed students and could not afford to adhere too strictly to their written statements. Most of the books in use were written in Latin, hence knowledge of that language was certainly to be expected. But the colleges that required their students to converse exclusively in Latin were considerably less successful in enforcing the rule. Broome (1903, p. 23) cites a record of a visitor to Harvard in 1680 who found the students hardly able to speak a word of Latin. However, Latin was used on formal occasions.

Patterns of student life, some of which persisted well into the University Transformation Era, were set in the colonial colleges. The right of upperclassmen to haze freshman; college responsibility for student conduct; the residential nature of the institution, with students expected to obey rules set down by the college authorities; pranks played on faculty by students; punishment for mischief making—all the elements of adolescence displayed by boys living in isolated communities were present. The rules of conduct typically were those found in a monastery or a reform school run by a religious order.

Rudolph (1962) summarizes the formation of what became a particular way of combining living and learning: "The collegiate way is the notion that a curriculum, a library, a faculty, and students are not enough to make a college. It is an adherence to the residential scheme of things. It is respectful of quiet rural settings, dependent on dormitories, committed to dining halls, permeated by paternalism. It is what every American college has had or consciously rejected or lost or sought to recapture" (p. 87). He rationalized this form of community by pointing out that in the Colonial Era the population was so scattered that for colleges to develop they had to form their own communities. But he also points out: "By the time that the colleges in Philadelphia and New York were under way, the collegiate pattern was not a necessity, for there were cities. But by then what had been a necessity had become a tradition" (p. 88). Although young people living together led to excesses such as rowdiness, it continued to be justified as the best arrangement for maintaining control over the developing adolescents, merging the extracurriculum with the formal program, enhancing relationships among all the people involved, and in the more recent vernacular, merging cognitive and affective growth. Belief in the virtue of the isolated community persisted. "Supporting this belief was the attachment of the American people to an agrarian myth, to a view of the world that saw the land as the source of virtue and as the great moving force in history" (Rudolph, 1977, p. 95). Nice to have a myth that fits the landscape.

Faculty

Throughout the era, the teaching profession was struggling to be born, but there were too few faculty to form a critical mass of like-minded colleagues. Most faculty were tutors, typically recent graduates who were awaiting positions as ministers. They received little pay and might have been thankful for subsistence. Early on, the college president and the two or three tutors who served at his pleasure taught all the subjects to all the students. Subsequently, professors began to specialize in various subjects and nascent academic disciplines.

A review of the leading colleges reveals the situation. The president of King's College hired a tutor in 1755 and a professor two years later; the three taught the entire curriculum. Queen's College opened with one tutor in 1771 and employed another even before appointing a president; one tutor left, but the other taught all the classes and, in 1773, organized a student literary society. William and Mary had a total of ten professors over a forty-year span. Five principal masters teaching natural philosophy, moral philosophy, oratory, languages, and mathematics served the College of Philadelphia.

Yale and Harvard, which were older and larger, employed a combination of tutors and professors. Between 1702 and 1789, approximately four tutors a year worked at Yale; their tenure was typically three years. A Professorship of Divinity was endowed in 1746. Harvard had six professorships endowed between 1721 and 1783: Divinity, Mathematics and Natural Philosophy, Hebrew and other Oriental Languages, Rhetoric and Oratory, Anatomy and Surgery, and Theory and Practice of Physics. In addition a total of about sixty-three tutors were employed from 1643 on; all were Harvard graduates. The president and professors lived in their own houses, but the tutors, who were not allowed to marry, lived at the college and monitored the students twenty-four hours a day.

The idea of college teaching as a profession developed gradually and at different times in the early colleges. But none of them entertained the European idea that faculty constituted a corporate body possessing authority, privilege, and functional independence. Finkelstein (1983) conceptualizes academic careers as having three strands: disciplinary, institutional, and external. Until the middle of the eighteenth century the academic disciplinary strand had virtually no effect, and there was not much to the faculty member's involvement with the institution from the standpoint of autonomy, permanent appointments, and other elements of making a career. Toward the end of the eighteenth century, the institutional aspect of the academic career took form as a permanent faculty made up of professors appeared. However, the external career—the consultations with government and industry—was more than a century in the future.

Both professors and tutors tended to come from professional families; their fathers were in law, medicine, or the ministry. Faculty acted both as instructors and as custodians responsible for student behavior. The tutors usually taught all subjects to a single class, whereas the professors taught in a particular subject, often one in which they had some postbaccalaureate training. The relative permanence of the professors was another distinguishing characteristic; a professor might plan a career at a single institution, but few tutors remained at a college long enough to see their class through to graduation. In a few cases a tutor was promoted to professor; in most, the professor was appointed from the outside.

The low wages paid to tutors and professors set a pattern that persisted until the second half of the twentieth century. The faculty were similar to clerics in that they were expected to teach for the privilege of affiliating with the college. Unlike lawyers or physicians who expected to be paid for their ministrations, faculty were more like volunteers engaged in public service. Few social institutions, except churches, could command that type of loyalty. At any rate, for some, tutoring and attempting to shape young people had more appeal than the drudgery of farming.

Curriculum

In his foreword to Rudolph's 1977 book, *Curriculum: A History of the American Undergraduate Course of Study Since 1636*, Clark Kerr offers a definition of curriculum as "nothing less than the statement a college makes about what, out of the totality of man's constantly growing knowledge and experience, is considered useful, appropriate, or relevant to the lives of educated men and women at a certain point of time" (p. xxi). Whether curriculum is defined as a set of courses or the totality of experiences that the college designs for its students, it is always rationalized as being practical. The curriculum responds to society and in turn shapes society, sometimes lagging, sometimes leading.

Curriculum is directed toward acculturating young people—their character formation, preparation for careers, access to society, language, and manners. Over time and among institutions the emphasis on one or a combination of these purposes shifts. Except for the rarest of programs, learning for the sake of learning has not been used as a curriculum rationalization. Practicality and usefulness, whether for building a sense of accomplishment among the students or equipping them to obtain certain jobs or make more money, have been the goals; curriculum always has purpose.

The definition of what is practical shifts from era to era. A knowledge of rhetoric, classical scholarship, and the Bible was occupational preparation for lawyers, ministers, and statesmen in the Colonial Era. Science and mathematics entered the practical curriculum toward the end of the era, as many of the students prepared for commercial careers. Colleges do not change curriculum readily. The drawback of having a stable curriculum with only minor changes is seen when students begin using the college for purposes other than those for which it was designed, and the curriculum does not shift rapidly enough. If the college curriculum is designed to turn out clergymen or public servants, for example, and businessmen come out of the college, has something gone wrong with the curriculum? Or has society changed its mind? By the end of the Colonial Era the defenders of classical studies were hard put to justify their favored curriculum, as proportionately fewer graduates entered the clergy. But those studies persisted through several additional generations.

The colonial curriculum did not rest on vast numbers of courses. A few courses, required for all students, sufficed. The curriculum has since expanded dramatically, not necessarily because of the expansion of knowledge (a justification often placed on the overblown college catalogue of our times; there was much to be learned in the Colonial Era as well). But several forces acted to keep the colonial curriculum restricted: there were few students, as most young people entered society through learning outside the colleges; study was not for the purpose of advancing knowledge but for preserving what was already known; few occupations demanded specific preparation; and the colleges were dominated by religious organizations with a limited view of the scope of knowledge.

Principles of scientific inquiry were slow in penetrating the curriculum. Meriwether began his 1907 text by saying, "To-day science dominates our schools. Our colonial ancestors studied and taught in an atmosphere of religion which they had inherited from the middle ages. For centuries the pedagogic aim had been to point the road to Heaven" (p. 13). Education was a matter of authority; truth was derived from omniscience; individuality or creativity was not part of the plan. The classics and biblical texts dominated the curriculum throughout the Colonial Era because they proceeded from a well-organized base.

The classics could be justified as practical training for all careers. Because apprenticeship was the mode of training that led people toward every occupation, those who went to college would expect to advance in the higher reaches of the professions that they had entered through academic apprenticeship. A knowledge of rhetoric and Greek and Latin could certainly be justified as useful for practitioners in law and medicine as well as theology. No one was required to go to college to enter professional practice, and occasional efforts to restrict access to the professions had little effect. The label of practicality, then, was as easy to justify as it was difficult to prove. None of the professions demanded content examinations; modern foreign languages were no more or less useful than

Greek, Latin, and Hebrew; chemistry had no more or less practical relevance than rhetoric.

The curriculum in the colonial colleges was a direct import from Europe with little modification until the latter half of the eighteenth century. Rudolph (1977) traces it to both the Renaissance and the Reformation, whereas Lucas (1994) takes it back to the Roman Empire and the library and scholarly enclave at Alexandria. From the Renaissance the colleges taught Greek and intended to bring their charges toward adopting the role of gentlemen and scholars. Medicine and theology were the vocational studies of the time. From the Reformation the colleges took the study of Latin in preparation of the clergy. Both movements had been incorporated in Cambridge, where young men were prepared not only for the clergy and scholarship but also for public service. "Emmanuel at Cambridge, a Puritan foundation, was the model for Harvard; Queen's at Oxford was the model for William and Mary" (Rudolph, 1962, p. 24). Additional imports were the four-year baccalaureate and the names for the freshman, sophomore, junior, and senior classes, along with the organization of curriculum into courses with finite time blocks and the notion of a master or teacher who would dictate to his charges.

The curriculum derived from the seven liberal arts: grammar, rhetoric, logic, astronomy, arithmetic, geometry, and music. These seven subjects did not encompass everything that was known in Greece and Rome or even the curriculum as it was taught in the schools of the time, but they did appeal to the medieval church, not least because they were especially suited to the intellect and to spiritual concerns, as differentiated from the mundane or secular. Butts (1939) traced the codification of the seven liberal arts to the Roman scholar, Varro, in the second century B.C. Along with Lucas (1994), Rashdall (1936), and others, he tracked the development and modification of this essential curriculum form from its earliest days through the medieval church, the Reformation, and on across the Atlantic.

What is noteworthy is the way liberal arts studies were adapted to religious purposes, modified to add various forms of philosophy and ethics, and prescribed for all who would count themselves among the learned. At Oxford the four-year baccalaureate program included grammar, arithmetic, rhetoric, logic, and music. Students who would go on to the master's degree would read prescribed books in geometry, astronomy, and philosophy—the latter including physical science, ethics, and metaphysics. Thus the tradition of a prescribed curriculum was set before the American colonies had been founded.

Tracing curriculum in any precise form is difficult because the meaning of course names changes. Arithmetic, logic, physics, and philosophy were all present in the colonial curriculum, but content in those areas was different from the areas of learning into which those studies evolved. Latin in the seventeenth century was studied as a medium of communication, whereas by the eighteenth century it had been transformed into drill in composition and grammar. Science was certainly not as it is currently construed: an inductive process that involves discovering knowledge through theory building, hypothesis testing, and experimenting. Notes left by teachers of science in the Colonial Era show how painfully they attempted to straddle the worlds of observation and reliance on doctrine. They explained weather, the senses, and the elements such as air and water deductively, with a combination of rude observation and a heavy reliance on prior teachings. By the middle of the eighteenth century, Harvard had various types of apparatus for teaching science, including scales, pulleys, rulers, mirrors, and cylinders—the equipment found in a middle-school classroom two centuries later. Science teachers could demonstrate the force of gravity, a vacuum, and the rotation of the planets; thus the capacity for showing how experimentation and observation could yield understanding was present and undoubtedly used. Appliances to measure sound and electricity were meager, but space, time, and optics were well covered. Meriwether (1907) notes, "Of the scientific attitude as it is cultivated to-day, of cold, dispassionate study of nature without the lingering flavor of authority or of religion, our colonial ancestors knew nothing" (p. 224).

Barriers to a common curriculum across institutions stem from the earliest days of the colleges. Each college staff thinks it has a unique approach because of the special predilections of the teachers, students, and community from which they come. However, there is much imitation in curriculum formation. The two forces—uniqueness and imitation—are constantly at odds. But regardless of whether the colleges imitated or went their own way, the curriculum in the colonial colleges was serious. No frivolous courses decorated the catalogues with promises of divertissements for the young people. They went to college and they were expected to study. What happened on their own time may have been frivolous, but the college demanded rigorous involvement with what the masters felt was appropriate for students. Rudolph (1977) reports that "the official catalogue of the Yale library in 1734 listed the works of Shakespeare, Pope, and Spenser under the heading, 'Books of Diversion'" (p. 25).

A view of the colonial curriculum is available in the earliest schedule printed by Harvard, around the year 1638. It shows classes laid out from Monday to Saturday for students in the first, second, and third year of their studies. The first year included logic, physics, rhetoric, divinity, and the history and nature of plants, along with Greek etymology and Hebrew grammar. In the second year the students were presented with ethics, politics, and Greek prose and dialectics, along with a continuation of rhetoric, divinity, and plant taxonomies. The third year introduced them to arithmetic, astronomy, and geometry while they perfected their composition in Greek (Meriwether, 1907, p. 52). Although Harvard started with a three-year program, by 1654 it had adopted a four-year plan.

Yale modeled its curriculum on that of Harvard, and William and Mary picked up elements of that curriculum but added more science and mathematics. However, the College of Philadelphia

(later the University of Pennsylvania) laid out a three-year curriculum in 1756 that deviated somewhat. There, students studied
more arithmetic, including algebra; more science, including architecture, mechanics, optics, and astronomy; more natural science,
including both plant and animal history; more chemistry. Such
innovations as studies in navigation, surveying, civil history, law
and government, and trade and commerce were brought in as well.
Even so, students were expected to follow classical and rhetorical
studies with Greek and Latin literature at the core. And disputation was still important; the plan shows afternoons of the third term
for seniors held aside "for composition and declamation on moral
and physical subjects" (Snow, 1907, p. 71).

The other colonial colleges, all founded in the thirty years prior
to the revolution, kept the study of the classics and the Bible but
added modifications of their own. Most of the changes were in the
direction of natural philosophy and greater emphasis on mathematics. William and Mary was the first to establish a professorship
in science, and by the end of the era all the colleges had professors
of mathematics and natural philosophy or physics. Ethics became
an important area of study. It had been present from the start in
courses in moral philosophy, which were central to the study of
divinity, but as the Colonial Era progressed, the importance of reason and human nature began to supplant biblical studies. Ethics
courses, often taught to seniors by the president of the college,
included elements of science and religion; all were concerned with
questions about the right conduct for people to follow. Ethics had
to be defended continually against those who contended that faith
and religious texts pointed the way to proper conduct. Still, the
writings of modern philosophers such as John Locke were incorporated into the courses, and by the end of the era a professorship in
moral philosophy had been endowed at Harvard.

Evolution of the curriculum continued as King's College in New
York opened with a distinctive bent toward commerce. Soon after
the revolution, Jefferson, an alumnus and member of the board of

visitors, tried to reorganize the College of William and Mary by abolishing the professorships in divinity and adding medicine, natural history, and modern languages to the curriculum. His plan even included the introduction of electives, but it had only limited success. Throughout the era the champions of science fought continually against the religious orientation to which college founders and their successors had adhered. Plans for complete curriculum reorganization were usually defeated, and those who would introduce new studies would have to wait until separate professorships could be established. Then, as later, the disputes centered on what courses of study should be required of all students.

A view of curriculum in the Colonial Era shows, above all, how the colleges were struggling to break away from the influence of the church and adherence to the classics. Literature and history were introduced even at Harvard. Logic was studied as a key to understanding the scriptures but evolved so that it became more readily applied to human affairs. The early studies of science were dominated by recourse to authority; the works of Aristotle were scanned for reference to physical phenomena. As the era progressed, however, the teachers of science became more ready to base their curriculum on observation and experimentation. Languages that were studied as a way of learning literature and philosophy evolved so that they became objects of study in their own right. By the middle of the eighteenth century the classics were still at the core of the collegiate experience, but the study of political philosophy and science in the form of astronomy, mathematics, physics, chemistry, and geology was present in all the institutions. The establishment of professorships in the various disciplines revealed how the curriculum was splitting. Yale had both apparatus for teaching science and a professor of divinity, suggesting that the college leaders recognized the necessity for separating these areas of thought.

Throughout the era, issues of freedom of thought and the value of experience over authority were at the heart of the curricular battles. The Scottish universities had been reforming themselves throughout the eighteenth century and were becoming influential on the form of the colleges in the colonies. They had begun assigning specific subjects to professors, thus laying the foundation for academic specializations. They were also breaking away from the idea of a prescribed curriculum, with each student studying the same subjects, and they were adding scientific studies. William and Mary had been founded as an Anglican institution, but because its first president had come from the University of Edinburgh, its curriculum was never as strict as that in the New England institutions. The first provost at the College of Philadelphia was also influenced by the Scotch; he had attended the University of Aberdeen. The very idea that curriculum had to be justified as being for practical use effected other changes. At King's College and the College of Philadelphia, navigation, geology, the study of government, and mathematics was central. It pushed divinity and the classics to the side. A broader curriculum that tended away from a primary reliance on deductive reasoning was emerging.

Instruction

Methods of instruction are central to studies of curriculum. Not only what is taught but how it is taught is at the core of the collegiate experience. Complete descriptions of teaching methods are not available, but the pedagogy of the time can be pieced together from reports of students describing their experiences in the classes, the rules governing instruction, and the reminiscences of the tutors.

Grammar was learned through memorization and analogical reasoning. Classifications of words, paradigms for declension and conjugation, and syntactic structures had to be learned by heart. Long passages or even the complete speeches of celebrated orators were assigned to students who then had to repeat them. More advanced students were required to compose their own orations. The study of rhetoric included training in the finding of suitable subject matter, arranging a declamation, memorizing material, and developing the style and form of delivery. The students might construct their own speeches by taking extracts from the texts they were using. Education in rhetoric balanced reading and memorization with composition and performance.

Until the latter part of the era few textbooks had been written especially for college teaching. The tutors lectured, the students gave recitations, and readings were assigned in whatever books the college was able to acquire for its small library. Some of the professors gave laboratory demonstrations, and a few may have used a Socratic method. The paucity of books made the tutors and eventually the professors primary. The president lectured as well. When textbooks did appear they reflected ideas of the Enlightenment; written in English, they were thus subversive of Latin as the language of instruction.

Each of the colleges had a library, often with the core collection donated by a local book collector. Except for Harvard's twelve thousand volumes, the holdings averaged around two thousand. Most of the books were reprints of classical texts. Shores (1966) calculated the average annual rate of accessions to be less than one hundred volumes, some funded by student fees. The risk of fire or water damage was high.

Although much instruction, especially in the early years, was in Latin, few students spoke it outside of class. Most could no more speak Latin than can contemporary students who have studied a year or two of a modern foreign language speak readily in that language. Writing in Latin was similarly difficult for the students. The students may have been expected to read classics in the original, but translation guides in English were usually available. Students were supposed to be able to translate from Greek to Latin to Hebrew to English and so on, but few could do more than parrot the passages in the various languages. A professorship in Hebrew was established at Harvard in 1764, but "by 1775 the subject was almost extinct at Yale" (Meriwether, 1907, p. 108).

Scholasticism, a medieval philosophy centering on traditional teachings and doctrines, undergirded instruction that valued arguments based on authority. An archaic form of pedagogy, disputation clashed with the notion of experimentation and free inquiry as ways of discerning knowledge, but it held on throughout the era, possibly because it was popular, fitting the enthusiasms of young boys who may have seen it as verbal fighting in the classroom. Argument from authority, vehement rhetoric, and declamations all blended with the boyish desire to harangue in ringing terms. (Today we would call it an in-your-face method.) The intention was to see who could argue most convincingly.

What wonderful questions they argued: "Can the rite of baptism be performed with air, sand, or earth; with beer, fishbroth, rosewater as well as with water? What is the interior structure of Paradise? Why did Adam eat an apple instead of a pear?" (Meriwether, 1907, p. 231). Harvard demanded two disputes a week from students in the first three classes and one a week from the seniors. Disputation was even part of the entrance examination. The rules were carefully spelled out in great detail, specifying exactly how the adversaries should conduct themselves.

As the Colonial Era wore on, the disputation topics moved toward societal issues: "Is civil government absolutely necessary for men? Does a college education incapacitate a man for commercial life? Is the voice of the people the voice of God?" (Meriwether, 1907, p. 239). Science also fell into the list of topics: "Is the starry heaven made of fire? Is the earth the center of the universe? Were the aborigines of America descended from Abraham?" (p. 249). And so on through physiology ("Does the heart make blood?") and law ("Is extortion becoming a lawyer?") and ethics ("Is matrimony necessary to the safety of the state?") (p. 250). Student debates were featured in graduation ceremonies. A characteristic exercise was to give a thesis to two students who would apply their powers of deduction to establish its validity. Such topics as "prudence is the most difficult of virtues" would be brought forward, with the graduating students putting on a show at commencement time.

The reliance on a pedagogy centering on scholasticism grew steadily weaker throughout the era as students began studying empirical methods. Astronomy changed as students began studying the Copernican system, wherein the earth spins on its axis and the planets revolve around the sun, instead of the Ptolemaic system in which the earth was thought to be the center of the universe. But the old methods of learning from authority died hard and could be observed for more than a century after experimental science entered. Furthermore, the scholastic method was based on the rigor of logic and a reliance on rhetoric—two ways of organizing and displaying learning that served well for their time.

Gradually the new pedagogy of experiments and experimental evidence became prominent. Descartes, Bacon, Newton, Locke, and Hume were being studied. The colleges now had telescopes and other scientific apparatus. Mathematics evolved to become a foundation for surveying and navigation. Early experiments with electricity were conducted. By the end of the era the philosophy of experience and experiment had pushed scholasticism quite to the side; if not for the religious tradition it would have disappeared even earlier. Instruction was being carried on in English, and even at Harvard and Yale—the colleges that clung to Latin the longest—the ancient language had weakened its hold on students and faculty alike. Latin would have disappeared completely except that many of the available books were written in Latin. Instruction in Hebrew was no longer required, and consequently the language was used only at ceremonial occasions.

The classics survived, and even though science was clearly in the ascendancy at the end of the era, Greek and Latin texts were still being studied. The rationale for reading those texts had shifted. Studying the classics in the original Greek and Latin had replaced the texts emanating from the church. The humanists were the progressives of the time, arguing against strictly religious studies. They held sway through much of the era, even as engineering, navigation, and modern foreign languages were being introduced. The evolution of curriculum in the Colonial Era is shown in the change from a curriculum based on church doctrine, to one based on secular humanism revealed through Greek and Latin texts, to one in which science replaced divine revelation as the ultimate standard. Each in its time had been justified as practical: the teachings of authority represented orthodoxy and were necessary to bring young people into understanding Church doctrine and to leading a blameless life; humanistic studies, classical Greek, and Latin were necessary to demonstrate how the Protestant churches had broken from medieval orthodoxy and were certainly important for people who would display the garb of erudition; science was the foundation of engineering, hence necessary for people who would go into the emergent professions; study of language and literature would well fit the incipient statesmen and lawyers. Faith in the power of science, the reformation of social institutions, and belief in the intrinsic goodness of man were making their mark.

Governance

The governance of colonial institutions foreshadowed issues of governance in higher education throughout its history. The colleges were founded with a combination of public and private control, with a tilt toward the latter; the extent of influence by the lay board and the members appointed by the colonial court or legislature was always an issue. Similarly, the extent of control to be exerted by the board of trustees, as contrasted with the members of the college community itself, was always in question, although the board was certainly in control of all the important issues. The dominant president dates from the Colonial Era—a president appointed by the board and responsible to it alone.

These governance features came about because of the time when the colonial colleges were established and the peculiarities of the English colonies in America. In Europe the universities had evolved from self-governing groups of teachers and students or from within a court or church hierarchy itself. In the self-governing institutions, the masters and students received charters similar to those granted to the medieval guilds. The university properties and management were quite modest. But in the colonies there was no class of faculty, masters, teachers, or professors to organize its own institutions. The colleges founded in the Colonial Era were governed by outsiders— boards of overseers that were made up of clergymen or magistrates. The only teacher represented in the governing body was the president, and even he served at the pleasure of the board. Subsequently, when the colleges were incorporated, the notion of adding faculty as members of a governing body was raised. However, the faculty were never in a position of power and certainly far from having self-governing status. The combination of lay boards of trustees, strong presidents, a weak professoriate, and the absence of a central ministry of higher education throughout American history served to perpetuate the governance patterns that were established early on.

A short review of the governing principles in some of the colonial institutions serves to illustrate the nature of governance. The General Court (that is, the legislature) in the Massachusetts Bay Colony agreed to establish Harvard and in 1639 arranged for a committee of overseers to be the initial governing body. Members of this committee included the governor, deputy governor, and treasurer of the colony as well as three magistrates and six ministers. The overseers were not actually a governing board but were subject to the General Court, which itself hired the first president of the institution. This president taught the entire curriculum on his own and presided over the first graduation with no explicit authority until the General Court granted a college charter in 1650.

Under the charter a corporation consisting of the president, fellows, and treasurer was formed. As a corporate body it had the right to self-succession and to hold property, appoint other officers within the institution, and be exempt from taxes. However, the corporation exercised its rights only in the presence of the counsel and consent of the overseers who, after 1642, included the colonial governor and deputy governor along with the college president, nine assistants of the court, and nine pastors and teachers from adjoining towns. Thus, although Harvard had two governing boards—one a lay group, the other comprising the college's administrators and faculty members—the lay board was clearly the controlling group.

The College of William and Mary, organized in Virginia toward the end of the seventeenth century, took a slightly different form. Virginia was a royal colony dependent on officials in London, and the colony itself was dominated by plantation owners, many of whom did not rank public education as a high priority. In 1691 the head of the Anglican church in Virginia traveled to London and, on behalf of the Virginia assembly, petitioned the bishops for a grammar school and a college. James Blair returned to Virginia with a charter authorizing eighteen Virginia gentlemen to act as college trustees. This board, whose members were called visitors, would be augmented by additional members nominated by the general assembly. The visitors were authorized to draw statutes for the college and to arrange for their own successors. They also were to form a corporation made up of the college masters. But the board of visitors could elect members of the corporation and in effect had far greater authority over the faculty than had been the tradition in European universities. Like the lay board at Harvard, William and Mary's lay board had ultimate power with the corporation subordinate to it.

The third colonial college, Yale, was formed by the Congregational ministers in Connecticut. The Connecticut General Court appointed ten clergymen as trustees to organize the institution. They were given the power to manage the funds and property, to appoint the college rector and officers, and to grant degrees or licenses. The 1701 charter thus established a college operating without the direct participation of secular officials, even though the General Court promised to grant an annual sum to sustain the institution.

Toward the middle of the eighteenth century the trustees were incorporated as "The President And Fellows Of Yale College" under a charter that gave the General Court the right to inspect the college laws and to disallow those they considered improper. The charter upheld the ultimate authority of the General Court but also guaranteed the college's autonomy within certain limits. Because the ten trustees were still church ministers, the charter reaffirmed the original intention of the college planners to protect the established religion by keeping the secular authorities away from direct governance.

The charter of Rhode Island College, later Brown, similarly gave authority to a governing board that was made up of clergymen but had an ecumenical tone. The Baptists were a majority of the board, but positions were reserved also for Quakers, Congregationalists, and Episcopalians. The president was to be a Baptist. The Baptists dominated, not because they were the official religion of Rhode Island but because they outnumbered the other sects and were the original sponsors and chief supporters of the institution. The Rhode Island charter also stated that there should never be a religious test administered to anyone wanting to teach in or attend the college. Accordingly, the college developed as a blend of religious ecumenicalism with a strong tilt toward single-sect dominance in the governing board and in the person of the president.

The College of New Jersey, later Princeton, was organized under a charter granted by the king and approved by the colonial legislature. It advocated religious freedom, specifying that the masters and students be from any religious denomination. The trustees were required to take an oath of loyalty to the king and were entitled to receive land and funds from which they could draw their salaries and pay the president, tutors, and college officers. The trustees were responsible for employing the staff and were authorized to award degrees. Staff included not only the president but also tutors, professors, a treasurer, a clerk, an usher, and a steward.

Benjamin Franklin's plan for organizing the College of Philadelphia was not followed exactly, but it is notable for what it says about governance powers and the detail with which it specified institutional functions. The college was not to be church based but was to be formed by collecting money from a group of subscribers who would then choose trustees; the trustees in turn adopted a constitution. The plan thus provided for the formation of an institution without seeking permission from any outside governmental authority. It specified everything from tuition to the appointment of faculty and the president, from plans for a library to rules for the deportment of students, from the management of funds to salaries to be paid to the staff. The trustees were to have power over all those functions and would also engage people who would teach modern foreign languages, writing, mathematics, and natural and "mechanical" philosophy (Franklin, [1749] 1931, p. 29). Franklin's plan also provided for a variant curriculum with one program based on Latin and Greek, another on English. Here then was an early acknowledgment of the importance of having both traditional and modern programs in the same institution.

The colonial institutions reflected the social organization within the colonies: a major religion or combinations of sects; reliance on a legislative body for at least initial if not continuing control through appointing trustees; and funding to be derived from a combination of donations or subscriptions and legislative appropriations, supplemented by whatever tuition they could collect from the students. Some colleges received royal charters, and others began with charters issued by the colonial authorities. In three of the institutions—Harvard, William and Mary, and Brown—a dual governing structure was established in which the lay board of trustees shared power with an internal group of college fellows consisting of the president and members of the faculty. In the other six colleges the lay board had authority over all functions. The influence of organized religion was evident in the composition of the lay boards. Several of the charters provided for trustees to be drawn from certain religious denominations, but none required that control remain in the hands of the founding denominations. Only three specified that the college president be a member of a particular religious group.

Perhaps most in contrast to European institutions, the American college president was the unquestioned authority. He was the liaison between members of the college and the governing board and was responsible for all college operations. Most of the presidents were ministers who taught classes, raised money, recruited and disciplined students, and presided over all college functions. Much of their energy was devoted to ensuring that the college had enough students and funds to sustain itself. Many were homegrown; Harvard had six presidents in its first fifty years, four of whom were alumni of the institution. Many of the presidents of other colleges had been trained in Scotland, including the founding leaders of William and Mary, the College of Philadelphia, and the College of New Jersey.

Whether or not one religious denomination was dominant in a colony, the colleges tended to emphasize interdenominational freedom. Harvard, William and Mary, and Yale had been founded with an emphasis on preparing ministers, but in their original charters several of them mentioned the importance of interdenominationalism: "those of every Religious Denomination may have free and Equal Liberty and Advantage of Education in the Said College" (Princeton), and "all the members hereof shall forever enjoy full, free, *absolute, and uninterrupted* liberty of conscience" (Brown) (Hofstadter and Smith, 1961, pp. 83, 135). As Herbst (1981) notes, "It was a case where the religion of the people rather than of the sovereign determined the religion of the college" (p. 46).

In summation, regardless of whether the colleges were established indigenously or by the granting of a royal charter, the concept of the lay board of governors was part of the system. In the subsequent history of college governance, the major change was that the social composition of boards shifted as clergymen were replaced by businessmen and politicians. Even though the faculty subsequently gained a measure of self-governance, taking charge of curriculum and admissions requirements, they never gained more than token representation on the boards of trustees. And when the first state universities were organized soon after the formation of the United States, their governance followed the pattern established previously: lay boards were responsible for fiscal matters and for appointing a president answerable to the board who would manage the day-to-day affairs of the institution. The main difference in the state institutions was that church influence on the governing board and curriculum was abolished. Otherwise, these institutions functioned quite as did their private predecessors.

Finance

How could the colleges sustain themselves? In general they depended on voluntary contributions and on combinations of funds coming from various other sources. Funds were received from sponsoring church groups, from subscribers or private donors, and from governmental bodies. This combination of public and private financing led Rudolph (1962, p. 13) to coin the term *state-church colleges* to describe Harvard, William and Mary, and Yale, which were the first three.

Harvard received money from the Massachusetts General Court, including a tax levee and a donation of land. The court also assigned revenues from the Charlestown Ferry; years later when the ferry was replaced by a toll bridge, Harvard continued to receive revenue from it. The college itself was named for the Reverend John Harvard, who contributed money and what was then a sizable library of four hundred books. In the latter years of the seventeenth century, more than half of Harvard's annual income was provided by the government, less than 10 percent from tuition.

When William and Mary was chartered in 1693 the Virginia legislature awarded funds to it from a tax on tobacco and from export duties on furs. Subsequently, monies from a tax on peddlers were granted to it. As additional evidence of legislative support, the students were granted immunity from taxes and military service.

Exemption from taxes and military service was granted also to students at Yale as a way of making the college more attractive to the young people it was trying to enroll. The Connecticut General

Court also donated special funds from time to time. The institution was named in honor of Elihu Yale, who donated goods that yielded an endowment of around five hundred pounds, a goodly sum at a time when fifty or sixty pounds might support the entire staff for a year.

The College of New Jersey (Princeton) and Queen's College (Rutgers) did not receive regular financial support from the legislature, although they and the other colleges that were formed in the middle of the eighteenth century might appeal for ad hoc donations from time to time. Legislative support was capricious anyway because when a colonial assembly became dissatisfied with a college, it might reduce or omit an annual appropriation. Still, the colonies had a hand in assisting most of the institutions—some by donations of land, which they had in surplus. And the colonies helped in other ways, such as by granting permission for the colleges to operate lotteries.

The College of Philadelphia received funds from individual subscribers to get it started. Around four hundred pounds total was pledged per annum for the first five years by twenty-five donors, Benjamin Franklin among them. Even so, in most of the colonies substantial donations were hard to attract, and the colleges had to depend on student fees for their survival. A family that could afford to send its sons away to school could usually also spare some money for tuition. Fees, room, and board ranged from ten to fifty pounds, at a time when a journeyman mechanic earned fifty pounds per year and a prosperous attorney from two hundred to three hundred pounds. Obviously, college was not for the sons of the poor. However, few students were expelled if they could not pay the tuition; the notion of work-study was in place early on.

Thus the pattern of funding from multiple sources was established. Philanthropy—regular or occasional support from legislative bodies, tuition, and individual college fundraising efforts—played a part. None of the colonial colleges were well endowed; the pattern of trying to raise money continually, of spending all that could be raised, and of living in genteel poverty continued well into the future of practically all the colleges in the nation.

Outcomes

The few extant colleges with their small numbers of students—a minuscule portion of the population—were certainly less influential than the churches of the era, but some effects are apparent. These include career preparation, individual mobility, assistance in child rearing, the idea of the institution as an archive, and such intangibles as community pride.

Career preparation is especially notable in two areas: preparation for the ministry and for public service. Although many graduates became neither ministers nor public servants, a high proportion entered those callings. In the early years of Harvard and Yale, more than half their graduates became ministers, a percentage that dropped to about one-third by the end of the Colonial Era. Although this group did not account for the majority of the people who took up pulpits, it was a force because many of the alumni returned to the institution as tutors while they were awaiting reassignment and because ministers who had been college trained were often selected for the most prestigious church positions. The college function of preparing students for the ministry dropped as a percentage of the whole as new colleges were opened and new programs were added, but it remained significant; as late as the Civil War, 20 percent of the Yale graduates were ministry-bound.

The graduates of the other colonial institutions were less likely to enter the ministry. A record exists of the progress of students at King's College, which admitted between six and eleven young men in each of its early years. Few of those students completed the course of study; they went into business or into the army; they left because of illness or transferred to other institutions. One student "after three years went to nothing" (Schneider and Schneider, 1929, p. 244). These different career outcomes reflect the different orientation of King's, as well as some of the other institutions that had less stringent church affiliations than Harvard and Yale.

A sizable proportion of graduates became influential in public service. Fewer than five thousand people graduated from the nine colonial colleges during their entire period of existence, but twenty-five of the fifty-six signers of the Declaration of Independence and thirty-one of the fifty-five members of the Constitutional Convention were lawyers, along with ten of the first twenty-nine U.S. senators and seventeen of the first sixty-five congressmen. Not all the lawyers had graduated college, and some had been trained in England, but in an era when the colleges awarded approximately one bachelor's degree per year per twenty-five thousand people, their influence was well out of proportion to their size. Five of the first six presidents of the United States were college trained—the two Adamses at Harvard, Jefferson and Monroe at William and Mary, and Madison at Princeton. Several justices of the Connecticut Supreme Court were Yale graduates. William and Mary produced the first president of the Continental Congress, the principal author of the Declaration of Independence, a delegate to the Constitutional Convention, several senior officers in the Continental Army, a chief justice, a governor of Maryland, the first governor of Virginia, and several early congressmen. This suggests not only the importance of the early colleges but also that the nation was founded by an educated minority whose writings evidenced their dedication to classical and contemporary political philosophy.

The graduates who entered civil service, the ministry, or other activities, were similar in many respects. The distinction between one profession and another or between people in the professions and those who were managing estates or businesses was not nearly as clear as it would become later. The curriculum was not distinguished by barriers between academic disciplines. Young men stud-

ied the liberal arts along with science, classics, and classical languages. On a continent where social and professional roles were not
rigidly differentiated, the manner of preparing people for particular
callings was not differentiated either.

People had to be versatile. Men prepared for the ministry often
entered public service or managed estates. Most changed vocations
as opportunity or circumstances beckoned. The colleges prepared
learned men, using a liberal arts curriculum that was considered the
best preparation for people who would take their place in any walk
of society. Specialized curriculum for any endeavor was slow to
develop. A curriculum centering on rhetoric, the classics, and grammar was useful for ministers, lawyers, or statesmen, all of whom frequently embellished their arguments with quotations from the
ancients. The importance of rhetoric alone cannot be discounted
as an essential for politics and the pulpit.

Individual mobility was enhanced through college attendance.
The colonial institutions brought the young person into society in
a fashion similar to the function that later institutions sustained.
At issue was the proper way of rearing children. Could a family raise
sons with all of the necessary skills and connections that an aspiring member of the elite should have? Many could not, and they
depended on a college to properly prepare their sons.

The early colleges created several arrangements to acculturate
their charges. The living quarters included tutors as male role models and, because the students lived together, peer pressure was
strong. Students met others who could help them with social connections; a sample of students from Princeton, Philadelphia, and
King's suggests that around one-fourth of them married sisters of
classmates or daughters of trustees or college presidents. These personal connections led also to beneficial apprenticeships as the students met professional people who helped them connect with the
proper physicians or attorneys with whom they might study (Vine,
1997). Elaborate graduation ceremonies were another way that students connected with the community. Commencement exercises

were a rite of passage, and the new colleges that were formed at the latter part of the Colonial Era all had rules about conducting the ceremonies written into their charters.

The colonial colleges were only marginally connected with the advancement of knowledge. They did serve as archives because they had libraries and because their curriculum tended to perpetuate knowledge. But they were far from being centers of scholarship and research. Nor was there much interaction among professors at different institutions; more likely, the discussions about scientific research or philosophy took place in learned societies such as the Boston Philosophical Society and the Philadelphia-based American Philosophical Society. Various other specialized societies were formed outside the colleges in the Colonial Era; prominent among these were marine societies in Boston and Salem.

The colleges continually strived to demonstrate their value to the broader community. They petitioned repeatedly for public funds and wrote into their charters or regulations promises that they would fit young people for public employment. Certainly the colleges were valuable because of the status that was gained by someone who became conversant with the classics. Communities took pride in the number of erudite people among them. Even though the degree was not required for any particular vocation, a community with a number of college graduates serving as teachers, ministers, lawyers, and members of the town council was considered to be of high social status. Liberal education had a connection with community mores.

Thus the colleges provided an avenue of mobility for young men, prepared ministers and public servants, and assisted in the formation and maintenance of an elite group of public servants at a time when there was no specialized training for government, teaching, librarianship, or medical practice. Overall they served as symbols of community pride; an institution distinguished a civilized community from an unlettered settlement in the wilderness.

2

The Diffusion of Small Colleges in the Emergent Nation: 1790–1869

Several events occurred around the time the nation was formed that separated the Colonial Era from the Emergent Nation Era. Most notable were the opening of the West—punctuated by the treaty ending the revolution in 1783 and the Louisiana Purchase twenty years later—the rapid organization of dozens of new colleges in the newly acquired territories, and the establishment of the first state colleges soon after the Constitution was ratified.

Societal Context

Table 2.1 shows a statistical picture of the conditions surrounding American higher education in the Emergent Nation Era.

Table 2.1. Statistical Portrait of the Emergent Nation Era: 1790–1869 (Estimates).

	1790	1869
United States population	3,929,214	38,558,000
Number of students enrolled in higher education	1,050	61,000
Number of faculty	141	5,450
Number of institutions	11	240
Number of earned degrees conferred	240	9,200

Source: Herbst, 1981; Snyder, 1993.

The opening of the West marked the new nation. In the latter years of the British hegemony, the colonists were forbidden to settle the lands over the mountains. But as soon as the British were expelled and even before the Treaty of Paris in 1783 had specified that the Northwest Territories be ceded to the new nation, population moves toward the West were under way. By the time of the second national census in 1800, 1 million of the 5.3 million Americans were living west of the Appalachians.

Soon after the turn of the century, the Louisiana Purchase in 1803 nearly doubled the size of the nation. By 1820, 2.5 million people lived in the West, and by 1830, 3.5 million, accounting for 37 percent of the entire population of the United States. Gaining Florida, Texas, and Oregon, along with the territory ceded by Mexico in 1848, added so much territory that nothing stopped a single person or a family from going West and making a new start. The acquisition of new territory and a sense of optimism fed on each other.

The nation became conscious of itself as an American people, integrating waves of European immigrants. Many newcomers, especially the Irish Catholics, suffered from discrimination, but only the African Americans remained apart as a completely separate group, sharing in neither the bounty nor the optimism of the expanding nation. Their status as slaves marked the entire era, from their being noted in the Constitution as three-fifths of a person for purposes of apportionment, to the pattern by which new states were brought into the union, to the continuing intersectional rivalries that culminated in the Civil War.

The nation was one politically but its sections developed separately. The emphasis on manufacturing in the North and agriculture in the South had begun in the Colonial Era, as Virginia's economy centered on tobacco and the economies of the New England and mid-Atlantic states centered on fishing, shipping, and manufacturing. By 1810 the United States was producing more than $125 million worth of manufactured goods per year, most of them

in the Northern states. In the decade of the 1820s, in Massachusetts alone, the output of the textile mills rose more than tenfold.
During the same decade cotton production in the South more than
doubled, as farmers and plantation owners moved into the fertile
lands of Alabama and the Mississippi Delta. Exports of agricultural
products were high, with cotton supplanting in value the colonial
crops of tobacco, rice, and indigo.

The ties binding West to Northeast grew stronger each year as
the main railway lines ran between those sections. People and institutions followed the tracks. By the middle of the century, the tele-
graph and the railroad had become so widespread that for the first
time in the history of civilization, people and ideas could move
faster than an animal could carry them. Other elements in the
nation's infrastructure were growing. The Bank of the United States
was founded, along with a national currency, a post office, copyright
law, and patent and bankruptcy laws. Rivalry with Europe and the
vast amount of land to be developed turned the nation inward. At
the same time, rivalry between North and South was accelerating.
One section was building cities, being populated by waves of European immigrants, expanding its industry. The other was building its
agricultural capacity, exporting its products, and coalescing its
thinking around slavery—its peculiar institution.

The growth in power of the federal government was limited by
the determination of the Southern states to maintain their independence. Even so, the federal government helped develop canals
and railroads by giving land to private agencies. Canal construction
was further enhanced by the Army Corps of Engineers, formed in
1824. Although contemporary capitalists like to claim that free
enterprise built the nation, around 70 percent of the cost of the
canals and 30 percent of the cost of the railroads was advanced by
federal and state governments. The government was land rich; the
value of its public lands was probably greater than everything that
was owned in the private sector; certainly that was true after the
Louisiana Purchase. The movement of population to the West was

enhanced by the government's selling off its lands in small pieces or, more often, in large tracts to speculators who would in turn sell small freeholds. Eventually, with the passage of the Homestead Act in 1862, millions of acres were simply given away to anyone who would settle on them.

The early nineteenth century was notable for expansion not only in population, territory, and manufacturing but also for the continued evolution of forms of religious observance. Any alliance between church and state had been written out of the federal Constitution; Article VI said that no religious test shall ever be required as a qualification for any office. And the First Amendment to the Constitution said that Congress shall make no law respecting an establishment of religion. The states wrote similar provisions into their constitutions, although in a few states where a single church was dominant, the separation took a little longer. Despite the dominance of Puritanism in New England in the Colonial Era, by the time the nation was founded, the largest denominations were the Anglicans, Presbyterians, and Congregationalists.

Church membership grew, from around one in fifteen people at the beginning of the era to one in seven at the end of it. And church affiliations shifted around so that among the Protestants, the Methodists and Baptists were the most prominent after the middle of the century, followed by the Presbyterians, Congregationalists, and Lutherans. The Episcopal church, successor to the once-prominent Anglicans, had fallen to eighth place. Catholicism, fueled by new congregants each time a ship arrived bearing immigrants from Ireland or Central Europe, became the largest single denomination by the end of the era.

Not only did church membership increase but the splintering of denominations into various sects spawned numerous new churches, especially in the West. As the people moved over the mountains, the bonds they had with their prior cultural institutions, organizations, and churches broke down. Religious multiplicity became the norm, and church membership became fluid, with people joining different sects depending on where they moved and their feelings of comfort with a group. The fractionated churches had an additional effect; because many of them were based on emotional appeals and literal readings of the Bible, they retarded general understanding of scientific discoveries, especially the theory of evolution. Most of the colleges formed during the era, and all of those formed by religious sects, were slow to build modern science into their curricula.

Social reform movements grew all through the nineteenth century. Groups calling for the abolition of slavery became ever more vocal. A temperance movement spread, along with activities to ameliorate child labor and conditions in prisons and mental institutions. Agitation for expanding the years of compulsory schooling built, varying in strength from locality to locality and state to state. The United States government remained essentially aloof from the support of schooling at any level, although it founded a military academy and naval academy and supported the Smithsonian Institution, another type of educational structure.

Overall, the conflict between North and South, resting on different views of proper national policy toward agrarian or manufacturing interests and held to a boiling point by the pro- and antislavery advocates, dominated the era. Any act of Congress was judged on whether it seemed to enhance or retard the spread of slavery. The idea of Manifest Destiny—that the United States was ordained to spring from the Eastern seaboard to the Pacific Ocean—could not be held back, and eventually questions of whether and how far slavery should spread into the new territories triggered the armed conflict between the sections.

One of the myths that was furthered during the era was the idea of individual betterment and its concomitant, free enterprise. People can be more prosperous than their parents; an expanding economy almost mandates that they gain more wealth. People can move out of the class or social status into which they were born. They can join any occupational group that they choose. The less government interference with the person's drive for self-improvement, the better. This myth holds that the West was settled by people acting on their own. It neglects the reality of government donations of land and sizable subsidies for the railroad and canal builders. The dark side of the myth is that if all people have the opportunity of bettering themselves, anyone who does not is a failure. Those who do not advance beyond the station into which they were born must have something wrong with them. And because that is too much for most individuals to accept, the tendency to blame outside forces grows, fueling disaffection sometimes with "the rich," at other times with "the government."

In summation, the period from 1790 to 1869 was characterized by territorial expansion that, except for a few islands, brought the nation to its current size; by continually more strident intersectional rivalry culminating in armed conflict; by social reform movements; and by optimism that encouraged speculation, entrepreneurship, and the growth of businesses, churches, and educational institutions of every stripe.

Institutions

Hundreds of colleges were formed in the three-quarters of a century following the founding of the nation. In the first twenty years alone, twice as many colleges were opened as had been organized in the entire Colonial Era. By the 1860s well over 500 colleges had been established, and between 210 and 250 were still functioning. Questions about the number of institutions are difficult to answer because of the nature of the data. When speaking of the founding of an institution, do we use the charter date, the year classes were first offered, or the year the first degree was awarded? What about colleges that were chartered and never opened or those that provided classes but never awarded degrees? Herbst (1981), who has studied the founding of colleges in this era extensively, lists fifty-two degree-granting institutions chartered between 1636 and 1820. He traces also the various name changes and reorganizations that most of the colleges endured and points out how some of them were chartered and never opened, others closed before awarding any degrees, and still others have no data indicating whether or not the college was still in existence in 1820.

Imprecise definition adds to the question of numbers. The name *college* might be applied to an academy, technical institute, professional school, specialized training center, atelier, seminary, or group of apprentices studying with a practitioner. This plethora of institutional forms foreshadowed the contemporary pattern of postsecondary education, which includes technical schools, adult learning centers, junior and community colleges, graduate centers, and research institutes, in addition to liberal arts colleges and comprehensive and research universities. How many "colleges" are in the nation today?

The great flurry of institution building occurred for several reasons. The distances between settlements were great. The splintering of religious denominations continued, and each sect had to have its own college. In each newly formed community, town boosters felt they needed a college to legitimate their settlement. The field was open for philanthropic groups, churches, and community developers. But the overriding reason has to be the general feeling of expansiveness that swept across the United States in the first few generations after independence. The English colonies had served more than 150 years of apprenticeship, as it were, strung along the Eastern seaboard. When the West opened, the population expansion was so great and the attitude of conquering the continent so strong that the nation reached for the frontiers. High immigration fueled the growth. And the attitude was that everything was open, everything could be built, conquered, accomplished. Crossing the mountains and reaching for the Pacific included taking your institutions with you, if not in the first generation, surely in the second. The desire to imitate older communities was strong.

The colleges were formed without any superordinate agencies attempting to impose order. Accreditation was far in the future. Some colleges attended primarily to disciplining young people whose families could not control them. Others provided supplements to apprenticeship programs. Some had special vocational programs; others centered on the professions of engineering, law, and the ministry. As Jencks and Riesman (1968) note, "Hundreds of colleges owed their existence to the energy and dedication of a single man who felt a call to found a college and was able to rally a few supporters for his cause" (p. 3). Proselytizing by the established Eastern institutions was a powerful force. Princeton and Yale especially sent alumni, religious zealots, and evangelists westward to establish Christian colleges. This desire to spread the faith carried with it the patterns of curriculum, instruction, and governance that had been established during the Colonial Era.

The religious groups were most vigorous in establishing institutions. As the various denominations grew and splintered, more colleges were formed and each competed for students. Whereas in 1810 more than 85 percent of the enrollment was in colleges formed by three denominations—Congregational, Presbyterian, and Episcopal—by 1860 the share of the enrollment enjoyed by colleges under those auspices had declined to one-half, with the Baptists, Methodists, Catholics, and other denominations along with state institutions making up the difference (Burke, 1982, p. 87). The spread of colleges included a few that were formed for women. The first teacher-training schools appeared; one was founded in Vermont in 1823. Municipal colleges appeared, in Cincinnati in 1819 and in New York in 1847.

In the absence of regulations it was easy to form colleges. Any group could solicit funds, write a declaration of principle, obtain a business license, employ a few reasonably learned people, and open for instruction. As long as they could attract a steady trickle of tuition-paying students and collect enough donations to pay the staff and buy food and firewood, they could sustain the enterprise.

Much depended on the entrepreneurial skills and persuasiveness of the organizers. Most of the schools were continually on the edge of bankruptcy.

The federal government enhanced the free and open market in two major ways: first, through the conspicuously absent mention of education in the Constitution and the failure to form a national ministry of education or a national university and, second, through the Supreme Court's decision in the Dartmouth College case of 1819, in which corporations were held to be inviolable. Even though the first six presidents supported the idea of a national university, and four of them sent requests to Congress for that purpose, it was never established. The arguments in favor of a national university suggest what it might have been. In 1788 Benjamin Rush published a proposal for a federal university that would prepare young people for public life, going so far as to say that after the university had been in existence for thirty years, only its graduates should be appointed to federal office. Washington mentioned a national university in his first and last messages to Congress saying that it would promote national unity and, by concentrating resources, be able to employ the best professors. He too saw the institution as having as its primary objective the study of the science of government. President Madison asked Congress to develop an institution that would expand patriotism and strengthen the national government. In President Monroe's administration, a congressional committee endorsed a national university, saying that because there was a surplus in the treasury and plenty of land that could be allocated to it, such an entity should be built. The committee concluded that the undertaking was within the power of Congress to legislate, but many members of Congress, along with President Monroe, believed that a constitutional amendment would be necessary; the House voted against such an amendment. Had a national university been established it would have had a marked effect on higher education. It would have served as a beacon, setting standards for curriculum, degrees, professorial qualifications, and possibly even for college admissions. Without it, colleges developed capriciously, free to choose the patterns manifest in the more prestigious institutions. Absent a national ministry of education, the principle of anything goes guided their development.

The Dartmouth College case also affected the development of institutions. The point at issue was whether the state of New Hampshire would be allowed to reform Dartmouth College according to a bill passed by the legislature. The rationale for proposing such changes was that the college had been established as a private corporation designed to benefit the public, hence the public should be able to guide its operations. The counterargument was that once a charter had been granted, the state could not abridge or revoke it. The United States Supreme Court in 1819 held that the original colonial charter served as an inviolable contract. Even though education was a public matter, the teachers were not public officers, and donations given to the college were not public property subject to the caprice of the legislature. The basic proviso was that once a corporation had been established, it had a right to manage its own affairs, hold property, and exist indefinitely. The decision in effect gave a license to any church or philanthropic group to apply for a corporate charter and organize itself under a self-perpetuating board of trustees without fearing that the state would intervene by appointing trustees, rescinding the charter, or otherwise jeopardizing the autonomy of the institution, regardless of the extent to which the college might offend the sensibilities of state officials. Not only the colleges but any church or private corporation was protected from capricious legislative interference operating apart from rules of due process.

The federal government's refusal to shape higher education by creating a national university and the Supreme Court's limiting state power over private colleges, "constituted a kind of license for unrestrained individual and group initiative in the creation of colleges of all sizes, shapes, and creeds" (Trow, 1989, p. 12). And so the race was on, and colleges were founded in every state. Before the

Civil War, forty-three were established in Ohio, forty-six in Tennessee, fifty-one in Georgia, eighty-five in Missouri. Most suffered from financial failure, unfavorable location, fire, or dissensions among faculty, president, and trustees and failed to survive. But enough did so that the type and character of institutions remained as varied as the communities in which they were located, the purposes for which they were founded, and the groups that established them.

The states became prominent in establishing institutions as the principle of state support to higher learning gradually emerged. Vermont chartered a state college in 1791—the same year that it entered the union. In Tennessee an act was passed for the promotion of learning, even while the state was known as Franklin in 1785. While Kentucky was still part of Virginia in 1780, the legislature offered eight thousand acres of land for a publicly supported institution. Georgia and North Carolina also chartered state colleges before the turn of the nineteenth century. Michigan's first public university was organized while the area was still a territory. In all, state universities were formed in seventeen states during the era. The biggest problem was finding money. Most of the states awarded land. Dartmouth had been endowed with 44,000 acres; Maine gave 115,000 to Bowdoin. However, the sale of lands yielded little. Typically the university supporters would have to return to the legislature time and again to petition for more funds. It took a couple of generations before most of the states had sufficient income and legislative desire to support public colleges of any stature.

The federal government also helped state colleges get started by awarding land. The contract for the sale of 750,000 acres negotiated in 1787 between a congressional committee and the Ohio Company included a proviso that "two complete townships . . . be given perpetually for the purposes of an University . . . so that the same shall be of good land, to be applied to the intended object by the legislature of the state" (Peters, 1910, p. 40). Manasseh Cutler, a principal in the Ohio Company, modeled the institution that became Ohio University on his alma mater, Yale. Although it did not open until 1809, it was effectually the first educational institution endowed by Congress.

The colleges tended to be exceedingly weak—underfunded, too small to support a broad curriculum, too poor to pay their staff more than a subsistence wage, and in many cases, too marginal even to survive. Hofstadter (1952) comments, "The census of 1840 showed that there were 173 colleges which shared 16,233 students or an average of 93 students per college; the figure reached 120 by 1860. It can be left to the imagination what kind of a faculty could be supported by 93 students or fewer" (p. 119). The colleges were hardly agencies of social integration. They drew their board members and their funds from those whose interests they promised to serve. They were not as influential in defining American life as their supporters might have hoped, probably playing a smaller role than the churches did.

Because of the great number of struggling colleges, each had to promise something to attract students. This was the beginning of the era of brochures and catalogues pointing out the special features of the institution, usually depicted as sitting on the brow of a hill with an expanse of landscape around it, sending the message that one's child would be safe from the evil influence of the city. Each college claimed that its alumni went on to superior positions in society. Each pointed to the erudition of its president and tutors. Each touted the virtues of student life, the associations that students would make, the benefits they would carry with them. All such assertions were based on anecdotal data; a group running a separate professional school or specialized institute might have some follow-up information, but a liberal arts college was hardly in position to make reliable claims. Boasting that graduates obtained moral virtue could go only so far. The schools that trained for particular skills were on sounder footing in a nation that valued commerce and money-making vocations. Nonetheless the allure of social prestige and particular sets of manners remained strong. Although many colleges foundered for lack of support, others were able to sustain their liberal-arts-based curriculum, claiming all the while that young men and women were the better for having experienced it.

In summation, the growth and spread of institutions was typically American: no restrictions, try anything, graft new ideas on old. European influence was sporadic. Instruction in French had been offered as early as 1779 at Columbia, and French-style arts and sciences academies had been founded. French influence was seen also in the formation of the University of the State of New York in 1784, an institution that would supervise all branches of higher education in the state, even while doing no teaching or degree granting of its own. Jefferson's model for the University of Virginia with no attachment to the church reflected the teachings of the French philosophers. However, the flirtation with French ideas died out because of opposition to French liberalism and because of the rise of the German universities. Both French and English higher education had essentially neglected science, while the Germans placed maximum emphasis on it.

As the era moved toward its close the German universities more and more became models for the college system. Professorships in numerous branches of science and the arts were established, and the professors were expected to conduct research and to bring the fruits of their investigations into their teaching. Although only a few hundred American students had traveled to German universities by 1850, a sizable proportion of them returned to become professors at American colleges. The more the colleges pursued science, the more they looked to Germany. The German universities tended also to attract major thinkers, while in France and England few of the intellectual leaders were associated with the colleges. The German universities were also early in expecting the Ph.D. as evidence of preparation for teaching at a time when the English institutions were not even offering advanced studies. Across the United States, science and research, along with advanced training— the German model—was appended to preexisting English boarding schools for adolescent boys.

Several attempts were made to establish universities apart from the colleges, but they were not successful. The colleges that developed as specialized institutions—the engineering schools and military academies—were professional schools, not graduate- or research-based schools. Although professors of medicine were seen at the University of Pennsylvania and at King's College during the Colonial Era, in the early nineteenth century many colleges of medicine were established on their own. A number of religiously controlled Midwestern schools attempted to start agricultural programs in the 1840s and 1850s but without much success. A professor at a college in Illinois proposed the idea of an industrial university that would serve agricultural, mechanical, and industrial workers of the state, but conservative traditions kept that from getting off the ground. Still, experimentation was everywhere, and with the hundreds of colleges opening and closing and trying different ideas to attract support, the variety in institutional type that was to become the hallmark of higher education was present.

Students

The trend toward access was marked by a broadening of the student base. The era opened with around 1,000 students, all white males. It ended eighty years later with 63,000 students, including some women and a few African Americans. The median age of students at entry changed. In the early 1800s, between one-third and one-half of the entrants were younger than age seventeen, but by the 1850s the ratio of younger matriculants had declined to around 15 percent. People from more varied backgrounds began attending. Even in the old-line institutions in the East, students from the lower and middle classes far outnumbered those from wealthy families. Tuition charges were sufficiently modest so that students from all but the most destitute families could attend. The $90 per year charged by Columbia was quite the exception. Tuition was $55 at Harvard, $40 at Princeton, $33 at Yale, and from $25 to $40 at most other institutions. Although the colleges had supplemental charges for room and board, they all had provisions whereby students could work out a portion of their expenses.

The student-growth numbers look impressive until they are placed against the growth in the American population. The nation began with about 3.9 million people; by 1860 the population had expanded eightfold to 31.4 million. Furthermore the students were spread across many more colleges; hence, the institutions remained small, with most of them proud if they could boast as many as 100 students. The number of bachelor's degrees awarded remained at around 50 per 1 million of the total population until around 1820 when it began a gradual climb. Overall, the ratio of students to the number of eighteen-year-olds in the population hovered at or below 2 percent in the first two-thirds of the nineteenth century and did not increase substantively until after the universities came on the scene.

Public secondary schools were slow in developing, hence the students applying to college came from private academies, Latin grammar schools, proprietary schools, and private tutors. A few well-qualified students skipped the freshman year, often comprising a remedial sequence, and entered as sophomores. During the latter part of the era preparatory schools expanded, growing fourfold between 1860 and 1870. Although the high schools were not organized especially for preparing students who wanted to go to college, their net effect was to elevate the desire for more schooling and to hold the younger students away from college so that the median age of entrants increased.

At the start of the era the admissions requirements typically included arithmetic in addition to Latin and Greek. Algebra was specified in many of the prestigious Eastern institutions toward the middle of the century, and English grammar entered the list of admissions requirements as well. By the time the University of Michigan opened in 1841, geography had been added and history was included at Harvard in 1847. By the end of the era, one or another college was requiring "geography, English grammar, algebra, geometry, ancient history, physical geography, English composition, and United States history" (Broome, 1903, p. 46). The list of subjects generally required for admission masks the specialized requirements that grew as the colleges added programs. But most of the colleges did not strictly enforce the requirements. They needed the students and could not be too particular about whom they matriculated.

The early nineteenth century was marked not only by changes in residential patterns but also in notions of child rearing. There was a steady migration to the cities as people left the farms to find opportunity in the expanding factories. This was accompanied by a dramatic rise in choice of occupations and in differentiation of economic opportunities available. In preindustrial society, children provided parents with a form of social security, but the early nineteenth century saw increasing numbers of young men becoming more independent and moving away from their parents.

Within the colleges this youthful independence often translated into raucous behavior. The hazing of younger students by upperclassmen, harassment of instructors, and various forms of youthful hedonism were accentuated by the sequestered, residential pattern that led to student subcultures in every institution. Battles between students and faculty and attendant efforts at disciplining the rowdy young were reported frequently. In the Colonial Era students with grievances could only leave the college as a way of gaining recourse, but subsequently both formal and informal groups bound the young people together into a self-aware student body.

College discipline revealed an obsession with order. The concept of *in loco parentis* does not accurately describe the disciplinary measures the colleges attempted to install because most of them were considerably more stringent than parents would have prescribed. The students were rebellious at every turn, refusing to inform on their peers, using the ideas of human rights to establish the notion that being a student was a limited status and that faculty rules could go just so far. The colleges issued lists of rules, but the students reacted from their own perspective. They declared independence even while accepting the hierarchical nature of college organization. The colleges could go only so far in demanding order. They needed the students, and even when the administration threatened suspension or expulsion, the students were willing to take the risk because losing students was costly to the institution. The future president James Buchanan entered the junior class at Dickinson College in 1807 but was so disobedient that at the end of his first year, the principal of the college wrote to his father that the boy would not be welcomed back. A member of the board intervened, and he was received for his senior year, graduating in 1809. In 1851 he was an intermediary between the Dickinson College students and the faculty after the entire junior class had been dismissed for mischievousness and insubordination. Even well-established colleges like Harvard, which occasionally resorted to expulsions, had to reinstate most of their rebels.

Whether the students were reacting against overly strict disciplinary efforts by the president and faculty or whether the restlessness of youths who were expected to lead monkish lives directed the young people toward unruly behavior can be argued either way. But not all students were miscreant, and not all colleges were places of rebellion. The students in state colleges and smaller Midwestern institutions, especially those closely affiliated with a church, were more conforming. Coming from families of more modest income they tended to be industrious and goal-directed. They had little excess money to spend, and they were more likely to be working to help defray the costs of attending colleges than they were to be engaged in mischievous behavior. Nonetheless many students at the older institutions continued their prankish behavior, careless attitude toward studies, and disrespect for professors. The colleges were central to the development of a culture of adolescence.

Although the colleges at one time might have been places where families sent their unruly boys to be disciplined, the purposes of college-going and the social strata from which the students came had broadened so that the repressive rules seem to have outlived their necessity. In general, the colleges presented the students with a form of daily living quite in contrast to their home life. Their residence halls were spartan—little different from military barracks. Their meals were served in dining halls, with students required to be deferent to upperclassmen and tutors. In most institutions morning prayers and Sunday chapel attendance were mandatory. Typically, there were no infirmaries, and when a contagious disease hit, many were affected. A young person who maintained enrollment for a full four years had to have a strong constitution.

The Eastern colleges had many dedicated students as well as mischievous ones. As evidence of students' pursuit of higher learning, they formed literary clubs, debating societies, and other groups suggesting a seriousness of purpose. These student societies, most with Greek names, date from the middle of the eighteenth century. By the end of the Colonial Era, chapters of Phi Beta Kappa had been organized at William and Mary, Harvard, and Dartmouth. By the early years of the nineteenth century such organizations had been formed in well over a dozen institutions: Philologian (Williams), Dialectic (North Carolina), Adelphic (Union), Athenaean (Bowdoin), and Phoenix (Hamilton), to name a few. They provided a home for students who wished to study beyond the curriculum provided by the college and a fraternal organization for those who wished to associate with each other for serious purpose.

The importance of peer-group relationships was revealed also in fraternities that were formed less for intellectual relationships than for bringing fellows together. For most of the students college was their first sojourn away from home, and as they bonded with their peers, they formed groups devoted to sports and activities through which they could share experiences. The college presidents tended to look kindly on fraternal associations that imposed a form of order on their members because it allowed the college to devote its energies to areas other than discipline. But the progress of fraternities was not always smooth. Some of the college leaders feared the secret societies because of the control that such groups had over their members at a time when the colleges themselves were expected to be responsible for students' character and moral development. From time to time governing boards passed resolutions forbidding membership in secret societies. For example, in 1849 the faculty at the University of Michigan "announced to the members of two societies that their connection with the University would cease at the opening of the ensuing term unless they renounced their connection with their respective fraternities" (Ten Brook, 1875, p. 196). Misbehavior might be tolerated in the young but only to a point. Organized misbehavior was too much for many college administrations to accept. Where the fraternities developed intercollegiate sports teams, the students might gain a sense of loyalty to the home college, but too often they exercised hostility toward faculty and administrators and aggression toward the other college's team and supporters.

Women entered the colleges, not in great numbers but enough so that their presence made a difference. Oberlin College was the first to enroll women who studied alongside men. Fewer than a half-dozen other colleges became coed before the end of the era. More popular was the separate institution, the first of which was the Georgia Female College, which opened in 1839 (although it was predated by several female "seminaries"). Subsequently, as the state colleges grew they began admitting women; the University of Iowa did so in 1855 and the University of Wisconsin in 1863.

The women students were not welcomed widely, however, and antifemale prejudice was more the norm. Dating from the Colonial Era, women who ventured outside the home were mistrusted. Park (1978) writes, "Women seemed to have a weakness for heresy and were therefore not thought reliable in doctrinal matters . . . education was not considered to be a remedy for these deviationist tendencies" (p. 14). Well into the latter part of the nineteenth century, commentators on higher education were arguing against enrolling women. Ten Brook, who wrote a history of the University of

Michigan shortly after women were admitted in 1870, reacted perhaps typically, saying, "Intelligent and strong-minded women have expended their strength unduly upon formal efforts to prove their equality with men. . . . But the question will arise whether the public ought to bear the expense of the professional education of a class whose services will not be required. . . . Lifelong public occupations will be nearly all in the hands of men, for the marriage of women will always be deemed to disqualify her for such. . . . It may be doubted whether the relative occupations of the sexes will ever be essentially changed. Woman's less physical strength and power of endurance speak the will of the Creator in a language not to be safely disregarded" (1875, pp. 359–362).

Thus the colleges were there but the young people were not clamoring to get in. Student numbers failed to maintain stride with the expanding population. Compulsory schooling beyond the elementary grades and a widespread system of secondary schools were still in the future. The residential pattern established in the Colonial Era persisted, but too many colleges competed for too few students. And too many segments of the population were being systematically excluded.

Faculty

The trend toward faculty professionalization was apparent as the nineteenth century began. Although tutors were still in the majority, a core of full-time professorships had been established at the leading institutions, usually through philanthropic bequests. By 1800, permanent faculty were in place at most of the colleges. The professors had teaching responsibilities, but they were older and more highly educated than the tutors. They taught in an academic specialty and saw the professoriate as a career rather than as a way station while awaiting a better opportunity. By the end of the first quarter of the nineteenth century, professors outnumbered tutors by a three-to-one ratio.

The rise of the professor can be attributed to many influences, especially the introduction of advanced courses in mathematics, natural science, and the arts. Teaching those subjects required a faculty better trained than those who could be drawn from the ranks of recent graduates or from the pool of clergymen who typically taught on an interim or part-time basis. The colleges had expanded their role beyond that of maintaining custody of the young and attempting to instill spiritual and moral values. There were secular tasks to be done: training for careers other than the pulpit; providing general education for an enlightened citizenry; and passing on a shared cultural heritage that centered on American, republican values. Lovett (1993) points out that these goals were "achieved less through changes in the curriculum, which remained largely focused on the Western classics, than through a redefinition of faculty roles and responsibilities" (p. 28).

Other characteristics of the time contributed. One was size, as the institutions grew in number of students and overall faculty. A second was a general acceptance of the idea that a professorship was a worthy occupational goal in its own right, something that a person might aspire to as a lifelong career. Emerson (1838) expressed that view eloquently. A third was that many ministers who in the Colonial Era might have served a parish for a lifetime found that they were being displaced within a few years. Accordingly some clergymen sought the better opportunity afforded by a professorship in the local college, a reversal from the time when the tutors stayed on only until they could find a pulpit. The majority of faculty came to the professorship from nonacademic jobs, primarily the ministry but also law and medicine, and without specialized postbaccalaureate training.

Beginning in the first quarter of the century a number of American college graduates went to Germany for further study and returned with Germanic notions of the professor as an independent researcher responsible for guiding students in a particular subject field and for conducting inquiry in that field according to his own determination of the value of topics to study. An institution might appoint a tutor as a professor and then send him to Europe (at his own expense) to do postgraduate study in a specialized subject. By the 1830s nearly half the Harvard faculty had received such training. In the 1850s several of the faculty at Brown took leaves of absence so that they could study abroad. By the end of the era, half or more of the faculty at Williams and Dartmouth had received graduate training in a specialized area.

Early in the era, few faculty members had sufficient disciplinary commitment to be involved with learned societies or scholarly publications. The professors were publishing, but their works were not in the form of research and scholarship known in a later time; they were more likely to be collections of sermons or orations delivered at public occasions. A sizable number of professors were still involved in occasional preaching, while others were active in community affairs. However, by the mid–nineteenth century, half or more of the faculty at the leading institutions were publishing in their subject field and participating in the activities of professional organizations. Furthermore, the first evidence of the faculty allegiance to an academic discipline being greater than to a single institution appeared at this time, as a senior faculty member might leave one institution for a position at a rival institution. One more indicator of specialized knowledge as an element in the faculty role appeared as the number of faculty involved in itinerant preaching dropped and those who applied their subject-area expertise to local community and state issues grew. In the main these extramural activities centered on public lectures in which the faculty brought their opinions to public view and informed their listeners and readers of their latest discoveries.

Finkelstein (1983) summarizes by pointing out how the academic career began early in the era with traditional professions splitting, so that some practitioners or clinicians maintained their service while others reduced or eliminated clinical functions to become full-time academicians. A class of permanent senior faculty members grew, and the specialized subject-centered professor became prominent toward the end of the era, preceding the emergence of the university in the era that was to begin in 1870. The professorship grew as a career toward which college-trained individuals would aspire, holding greater loyalty to disciplines than to institutions, increasing involvement with disciplinary societies and specialized publications, and entering directly into the profession from graduate training. The lines of the profession were rather clearly drawn before the institutions were ready to provide a permanent home, pay, facilities, and status for the members of the group. In this regard the professionalization of the faculty was a major input to the formation of the university. Even so most of the professors still held outside jobs, many as clergymen, chiefly because salaries were quite low and the honor of serving might be considered recompense enough. Besides, a college could always find a recent graduate to teach classes for little more than room and board. College salaries in this era were "never adequate to support a middle-class lifestyle" (Lovett, 1993, p. 28).

Toward the end of the era, a career-ladder pattern emerged, as a few colleges employed instructors as junior faculty members with the expectation that they might move into the senior professor ranks. Thus the professorship took on one of the characteristics of a profession—the notion of career advancement. It took on another characteristic as well: loyalty to the academic discipline began to erode loyalty to the institution. Still, most of the professors remained leading members of the community, taking part in civic affairs, local literary societies, and clubs.

Curriculum

The trend toward a varied, vocationalized curriculum continued, but the struggle between advocates of classical studies and those who would introduce practical studies for a variety of people and purposes did not abate. Throughout the era, the curriculum was splitting, fragmenting, separating, becoming specialized. Remnants of the integrated studies common in the Colonial Era were present along with new studies in the sciences, social sciences, and fine arts. Curricula especially designed for those who would enter the vocations of engineering, agriculture, mechanics, and manufacturing entered along with all kinds of practical studies. The foundation was being laid for specialized programs and colleges, the elective system, training for every profession and occupation, and numerous avocations. The curriculum offering anything that anyone wanted was being formed.

The organizing principles for this growth in curricular variety can be traced to the separation of philosophy from religion, the rise of the scientific method, and a breakdown in the notion of privilege, hence of a curriculum designed only for a few people who would be civic leaders. One mode of thought was not being superseded by another; all was additive. The philosophers who postulated different ways of accounting for human affairs did not replace the religionists with their appeals to authority. All they did was open the way for social science, which itself organized into subfields of economics, sociology, psychology. Science kept the observations of astronomy and geology but added experimental physics and chemistry. Statistics was introduced as a way of verifying on the one hand and of predicting on the other. Applying scientific methods to human affairs led to studies in morality—no longer a struggle between good and evil but a consequence of convergent forces. A belief in science emerged to rival the belief in religion. Research and experimentation were providing ways of gaining knowledge quite different from the knowledge gained from revelation. Social science promised understanding of human behavior. Humanism, which began as anticlericalism, was transformed into study in the humanities. Freedom of thought was put forth as an antidote to dogma or orthodoxy. Inside the colleges and in the community in general, people were learning to allow religion and different patterns of thought to coexist.

These shifting thought patterns—changes in the way people viewed themselves and their environment—were working themselves out in numerous social organizations. Because the colleges were expanding rapidly, numbering now in the hundreds, there was room within them for all the patterns of scientific thought, philosophy, and humanities to be refined. The colleges were becoming centers of intellectual ferment as well as schools for the molding of young minds. Although the full development of science and curricular election had to await the dawning of the university, the foundations were apparent in the Emergent Nation colleges.

No college was large enough to support scholars to teach specialized courses exclusively. Chemistry, mathematics, natural history, and geology were prominent in most of the institutions, but typically anyone skilled in any branch of science would also teach the other branches. As the social sciences developed, the same instructor would teach all of them. The idea of electives, with professors teaching in their specialties and with students studying what they wanted, was suggested but gained little ground. Similarly, the idea of scholarship or in-depth study in specialized fields was put forward, but it too made little headway. The faculty had begun preparing themselves to specialize, but there was not a sufficient student body to accommodate a full range of curricular specialization; too few students were spread over too many colleges. Science made its most notable inroads in the newly formed technical colleges, especially the United States Military Academy and the Rensselaer Polytechnic Institute (RPI). The curriculum at West Point centered on mathematics, chemistry, and engineering. RPI taught science through laboratories and field work. Graduates of these institutions went on to build the railroads and to open the mining and manufacturing industries that developed rapidly in the second and third quarters of the century.

Curricular expansion was revealed also in the teaching of modern foreign languages, prevalent not so much because of their practicality (although they were useful for foreign travel and for study in Europe) but because they formed a respectable replacement for the Latin and Greek that were falling out of favor. Most of the colleges appointed professors of modern languages; however, few students studied with them unless they were required to do so. The classical languages held on, and Greek and Latin were taught in most institutions throughout the era.

Not surprisingly the expanding curriculum had its adherents and detractors. Students at Yale, for example, typically studied Greek and Latin along with a modified version of the liberal arts, including mathematics, astronomy, grammar, and rhetoric. They also studied chemistry, experimental physics, geology, and French and German. This blend of the old and the new led to a schism in the faculty and administration, with defenders of the traditional clashing with those who would bring the curriculum into a scientific mode. One result was the well-known Yale report of 1828 (reprinted in Goodchild and Wechsler, 1997), in which the president of the college and a committee of professors confronted the issue of studying ancient languages and the liberal arts. The report took the position that young people should be required to study a variety of topics so that all the areas of their mind would be exercised. Each subject assisted the development of a different part of the mind, one leading to the ability to reason, another toward taste, a third to accuracy in expression, and so on. The report provided an example of a statement of educational philosophy that eschewed recourse to religion as the centerpiece of the college. Here was an argument around which defenders of the historic curriculum could gather—one that rationalized it by reference to psychology and views of human thought and behavioral processes.

Across the nation over the next generation, educators frequently referred to the Yale report to justify their own programs. It was quoted and paraphrased repeatedly, and the principles on which it was based became the foundation for curriculum in numerous institutions. The report proved especially useful to small denominational colleges, providing them with a way of justifying a curriculum that straddled the liberal arts and experimental science while holding to Latin and Greek as proper studies for the educated man. When the College of the Western Reserve opened in Ohio, it was to be "the Yale of the west," with a curriculum modeled on that of its predecessor institution (Snow, 1907, p. 145). The faculty of the University of Alabama in 1854 quoted the report in their justification of mandating certain studies as "furnishing the best discipline for the mind, and such as are indispensable to a man of liberal education" (p. 142). The curriculum built strong minds through mental discipline. All subjects had to be studied lest the entire system be upset. A uniform curriculum required for all students held its appeal throughout the era, even as new arrangements were being introduced.

Jefferson's plan for the University of Virginia included curricular differentiation. That institution opened in 1824, just before Jefferson's death, with a faculty subdivided into specialties of languages, mathematics, history, and others, but with no professorship of divinity. The plan was to have each of the various schools organize separately with its own professors, students, and space. Soon after it opened, however, the university abandoned some of the more far-reaching innovations such as separate diplomas awarded by the individual schools and settled back to become a college awarding bachelor's degrees for study in a variety of subjects.

Elsewhere, reforms in curriculum proceeded with greater or lesser success. Electives were being put in along with new types of bachelor's degrees, separate curricular tracks, and courses of study for students who did not intend to complete four-year programs. Yet most of the innovations had to be modified if not abandoned outright as traditionalists resisted the changes. The colleges could not fully reform yet could not hold rigorously to the classical curriculum. They tried to straddle but, as Rudolph (1977) puts it, "It sometimes seemed in the 1820s and 1830s that failure was a certain prospect for any curriculum that held to the past and for any curriculum that dared to move off dead center" (p. 80).

Throughout the era the colleges were fighting for their own survival. Each new institution had to struggle to sustain support. Those blessed with enlightened leadership were sometimes able to install curriculum reforms and make them stick. Union College, for example, had a strong president, one who served for sixty-two years, from 1804 to 1866. Eliphalet Nott's tenure thus straddled almost the entire era, and he was able to introduce and sustain many of the changes necessary to bring his institution to the fore. Union College allowed students to take classes even if they were not headed for degrees and introduced parallel programs for those who did not want to study classical languages. The college had a strong emphasis on science, and one of its programs encouraged students to study mathematics and modern languages in a form that looked much like the distribution requirements that would appear a century later in most American institutions under the guise of general education. The college broke with tradition by awarding bachelor of arts degrees to students who completed either its classical program or its scientific program. President Nott taught the senior-level capstone course in moral philosophy, integrating the various lines of study. The college was successful; its enrollments and graduating classes were among the top five in the nation throughout Nott's tenure.

Despite Union College's success, Harvard, Yale, and Princeton were more influential on the course of higher education. Each supplied leaders for the colleges that were developing across the nation and at which the curriculum resembled the programs in the colleges from which the new presidents came. Uniformity in curriculum was apparent, even though variations in emphasis and sequence were tried. Toward the middle of the century the president of Brown was able to state that the curricula "in all the Northern Colleges are so nearly similar that students, in good standing in one institution, find little difficulty in being admitted to any other" (Snow, 1907, p. 141). The classics, mathematics, science, history, and philosophy—all were represented. Few college leaders dared suggest that any of the traditional subjects be eliminated. The power of tradition was

manifest. Each field of study had its supporters, and little justification could be found for eliminating anything. At most, the time
devoted to studying one or another subject might be reduced.

Those who would model education after changes in thinking
and in student expectations were continually at odds with those
who felt that an anchor with the past was important. Some of the
college leaders contended that if enrollments were to remain high,
programs more suited to what young people wanted were necessary.
A new curriculum was proposed to serve "that large class of young
men, who are not destined to either of the learned professions, and
carry them through a course, which they think better adapted to
their future plans and prospects" (Snow, 1907, p. 155). The faculty
of Amherst College even suggested a department of education in
which teachers might be trained—this in 1827 when teaching had
by no means developed as a profession and when the idea of a separate baccalaureate program to prepare teachers had few adherents.

The spread of different programs points up how curriculum
changes, not by revolution but by accretion. The inauguration of
Josiah Quincy as president of Harvard in 1829 was the occasion for
an address suggesting that a curriculum modeled on the past was not
sufficient for a modern institution. Using terms such as *the spirit of the
age*, he suggested that more students be admitted into special or parallel courses of study so that the "long-established standards of collegiate education" not be upset. He also proposed a set of courses
centering on science that would be useful for a variety of students and
purposes (Snow, 1907, p. 168). But Harvard did not abandon the classics; after much debate it added a separate program in science.

For at least a half-century the parallel curriculum solved the
problem presented by the desire to introduce new courses and
attract more students while maintaining the classical program so
that traditional standards would not be compromised. Separate programs open to students who were not prepared in the classical languages were organized at several institutions. One such program at
Columbia dates from 1830. Termed the "Scientific and Literary

Course," it involved three years of study but led to no degree. Students could be admitted if they knew French grammar, mathematics, and geography. In 1833 Union College established a scientific program but with admission, requirements similar to those for the classical course. Eventually the college opened the scientific program to students who needed no prior preparation greater than English grammar and arithmetic.

Parallel courses leading to separate degrees were formed at many other institutions: Brown and Harvard in 1851; Yale, Dartmouth, and Rochester, in 1852; Michigan in 1853; Columbia in 1864; and at Cornell when it opened in 1869. New degree titles were invented to indicate the difference between these programs and the classical curriculum. The bachelor of science or bachelor in philosophy was often the culminating degree. These parallel courses were not unitary; Cornell, for example, offered nine different programs leading to degrees.

Thus the curriculum remained in flux. A few of the more than five hundred colleges established during the era experimented with modernized curriculum, including sciences and broader applications of mathematics, but most maintained Latin and Greek, moral philosophy, English grammar, and requirements modeled on those that had been established in the Colonial Era. The colleges were not large enough to sustain a varied curriculum, with some students studying science, others humanities, and still others the basics of literacy. Too few students could function as independent scholars—choosing electives and following lines of modern thought. Too many were young and ill prepared. And student complaints about curricular dryness were prevalent. McLachlan (1974) notes, "No single reason why the former curriculum could not have been made interesting to students is immediately apparent" (p. 467).

Where students were present in sufficient numbers to form literary societies, they were able to build what was essentially their own curriculum. These societies engaged student interests through providing reading materials, debating activities, and helping to build an intellectual climate. In some institutions they were elaborately organized and self-governing—colleges within colleges. They enrolled most of the students, awarded diplomas, and operated their own libraries. The most current materials might not be found in the classrooms and the college libraries, but the literary societies typically collected the latest periodicals along with books of history, literature, science, poetry, and public affairs. These societies flourished from the middle of the eighteenth to the middle of the nineteenth century when they were replaced gradually by fraternities. Toward the end of the era the formal curriculum and instructional practices had been modified to accommodate many of the principles on which the literary societies had been founded. The fraternities had a different agenda, which was considerably more reliant on social activities.

The classical curriculum survived not only because of tradition but because it had purpose. It fit with the religious revivalism that swept through sections of the nation periodically and found adherents and a ready audience in the colleges. Some colleges had been founded by revival-oriented ministers, and many presidents found that revival fervor could work to the advantage of the institution by directing youthful emotions and enthusiasms into constructive avenues. The courses in moral philosophy assisted in this channeling. Furthermore, the classical curriculum opened to allow courses in science, fine arts, and social studies. Latin and Greek might form its core in the first two years, but the upper division was much broader. The classical curriculum also retained its utility as training for the professions of law, medicine, and the ministry.

In summation, the curriculum in the Emergent Nation Era was a collectivity of old forms centering on the classics, science splitting and growing, vocational subjects, remedial efforts; in brief, it was a microcosm of the curriculum of the eras to follow. The colleges were gradually absorbing many functions that had previously been performed by other institutions: literary societies, academies of science, seminaries, libraries, and formal apprenticeships. They were tending toward opening programs for an increasing variety of students, not least those who were ill prepared for the higher learning. The conflict between science and religion was not yet a great problem because scientists and moral philosophers alike held the conviction that "by studying the laws of nature scientists confirmed the existence of God, the author of nature, and glorified him in his works" (Sloan, 1971, p. 236). Science was itself in great ferment as new branches continued emerging. Social change was occurring more quickly than the colleges could adjust to it, possibly because they "were not organically knit into the fabric of economic life. . . . Although college training was an advantage, it was not necessary in the early nineteenth century to go to college to become a doctor, lawyer, or even a teacher, much less a successful politician or businessman" (Hofstadter, 1952, p. 21). Higher education tended still to be a luxury.

Francis Wayland (1850), a forward-thinking president of Brown in the second quarter of the century, attacked the curriculum, low admissions standards, the superficiality of teaching, and institutional irrelevance, claiming that although there was a great demand for civil engineers to help build railroads, industry, and the mines, the colleges were doing little to prepare such practitioners. More courses should be organized, including professional curriculum and certificate programs for those who did not want or need to study for a full four years. Abandoning the fixed four-year program of study, introducing a purely elective curriculum, and awarding degrees based on successful completion of examinations could be justified by broadening the base of students served by the institutions. If Latin and Greek could not attract sufficient enrollments, they did not deserve to be offered. President Wayland proposed fifteen courses of instruction: Latin and Greek for those who wanted them and separate programs in English language and rhetoric, teaching, agriculture, chemistry, and modern languages. He mentioned with favor how New York and Massachusetts had considered establishing agricultural colleges. The college leaders did not rush out to introduce the programs that he sketched, but he did summarize the way that curriculum was evolving into separate programs designed for every interest.

Instruction was evolving as well. The reliance on recitation and disputation—hallmarks of the colonial colleges—was giving way to first the lecture method, then the laboratory. As the instructors moved from a tutorial group to a career as professors and specialists, they relegated recitation and disputation to the lower schools, where at least the latter quickly died out. Their lectures were used to supplement texts by conveying information, generating understanding, and stimulating interest; they also transmitted attitudes and values, intentionally or otherwise. Lectures became popular most quickly in the sciences; they were often accompanied by demonstrations of experiments. The combination lecture and demonstration usually started with the enunciation of some specific principle and then moved to a concrete illustration. The professors stimulated the students with their enthusiasm for their specialties and, gradually, as they conducted research of their own, for conveying their latest findings.

The laboratory came in also during this period as a way of teaching the sciences. Here the students would listen to lectures and watch demonstrations and then perform the experiments on their own. Another innovation was the written examination, replacing the public exhibition of recitation or debate with a private demonstration of acquired knowledge. This also led toward uniformity in instruction, as all students reacted to the same set of questions. The beginnings of the university as we know it—and of managing sizable numbers of students—were clear.

Governance

The pattern of college governance with control vested in a nonacademic board of trustees was begun in the Colonial Era. There were not enough scholars to form a self-governing body, but a group of laypeople could organize an institution and employ a president to manage it. The president held office at the pleasure of the board, and as long as the board supported him, he could do what he wanted within the institution; he could employ the tutors and design the curriculum. These characteristics of college governance continued as new colleges were founded in the Emergent Nation Era and marked what would become a lasting pattern of college governance.

The colleges were formed typically under one of three patterns. The first was the civil corporation. Here a group received a charter—essentially a license to do business from a state legislature. When the states began founding public institutions, the legislature typically described the parameters of the college, defining how the trustees would be appointed and often providing a seat on the board for the governor, attorney general, or other state official.

Another form was the private college founded by a religious group. Typically, a church would organize a college, appoint a number of trustees from within or outside the denomination, and apply to the state for a charter or a license to do business. Such charters were readily awarded. It remained then but for the board to find funds, employ a president, and begin offering classes. This form of organization was most responsible for the great number of colleges organized in the Emergent Nation Era because as churches expanded into the western territory they formed colleges in every population center.

A third group of colleges "depended on organized community effort which might, or might not, involve one or several Christian denominations in addition to civic or professional groups" (Herbst, 1980, p. 15). This set included colleges formed under municipal auspices, as well as private, nondenominational institutions.

Regardless of sponsor, the private colleges all shared similar characteristics. If they were closely affiliated with a denomination, the church members would be urged to contribute funds. If nondenominational, they might be supported by people who responded to appeals on the basis of civic pride. In either event the private institutions did not have to beg for funds from legislatures that might from one year to the next have different views of what the colleges ought to be doing. Herbst (1980) points out that partisan rivalries often "prevented legislatures from responding to the demands for additional public colleges," thus allowing private initiative to fill the space. Boosterism was important because "in the United States anyone with enough capital or enthusiasm could become a college founder. As capitalism built towns, canals, and bridges and private business empires, so it also financed and directed higher education" (p. 18).

The president increasingly came to be seen as the representative of the trustees, less as a member of the faculty. Many presidents continued teaching, but more devoted most of their time to fundraising and community relations. The faculty gradually gained a sense of independence and self-worth, especially as professors replaced tutors. The faculty in the specialized institutions, such as medical schools, were earliest to gain some measure of control over curriculum and the internal workings of the colleges. But the faculty role in academic governance was not yet established and, of course, the students had no say in the conduct of institutions.

The pattern of governance was well established before the faculty became a self-conscious professional group. By the time the higher education professoriate developed its own internal hierarchy, tendency toward research and scholarship, and most important, autonomy, it was too late to change the mode of institutional organization and to acquire the prestige accorded to scholars in Europe. The faculty gained responsibility for appointing professors and deciding on curriculum but never the power to appropriate funds, manage the institution, or even to have the final word on students to be admitted. They did not become self-governing in the fashion of the medieval guilds or even as some of the other learned professions in the United States.

Because nearly all the managerial power rested with the president, when additional administrators were needed they became attached to the president's office. In the long run this helped institutions maintain their autonomy, as college officials responsible to state authorities have never been welcome on campus. Trow (1988) concludes, "Strong presidents and their administrative staffs could act in pursuit of self-interests of individual institutions and lay boards could ensure that those institutions would continue to be responsive to the larger society, and to its markets for students and graduates, rather than to the state or professional guilds" (p. 15). However, faculty and administrative interests continued moving in different directions. From the professors' point of view the president was the spokesman and representative of the board of governors, not the leader of the faculty.

Mercantile and professional people made inroads on the boards of trustees as the percentage of clergymen diminished. Alumni and donors also began to influence board membership. Governance was becoming secularized even as most of the colleges retained their nominal status as church-related institutions. One of the major inputs to secularization was the fact that few of the colleges were controlled strictly by a single church group; most were interdenominational or nondenominational, bringing onto the institution's board, faculty, and student body anyone who could assist in keeping the institution afloat.

One of the more prominent characteristics distinguishing public institutions from private was that the former often specifically excluded clergymen from the governing board except to the extent that such individuals were prominent members of the community who might be appointed regardless of their clerical affiliation. In private colleges it was almost axiomatic that the president be a cleric; many institutions had that proviso in their charter. In state universities it was considered important to have a prominent figure who could negotiate for institutional support.

It was not uncommon for a small institution to pay a substantial amount to a prestigious individual, hoping that he might garner institutional prestige and support. Henry Tappan, a graduate of a theological seminary, had been a professor at New York University before taking office as president at the University of Michigan. He had also visited Europe, written several works in philosophy, and published a treatise on university education. In 1852, his first year in office, the total budget of the university was less than $13,000, but he received a salary of $1,500 plus traveling expenses. By his second year, his salary was raised to $2,000 a year, a figure that still approximated 12 percent of the university budget. Paying a large sum to an influential leader was an investment in institutional growth.

In summation, the governance forms established in the colonial colleges were solidified as self-perpetuating or legislatively appointed governing boards maintained control and responsibility. Some of the presidents emerged as prominent leaders taking their colleges into new areas of service. The faculty developed their own codes without gaining voice in institutional management. The stage was set for the boards to be dominated by business leaders, the presidents to become innovators, and the faculty to pursue their own interests.

Finance

The financing of colleges followed the patterns established in the Colonial Era, with funds coming from private donors and the state. The students paid little tuition; instead they were subsidized by the low-paid faculty and by whatever funds the colleges could garner. Money was scarce, and nearly all the institutions survived from year to year, if they survived at all. Private institutions and the newly formed state colleges alike had little money at their disposal.

The colleges depended on private donors for a major portion of their revenue, with most coming in the form of small pledges. Many of the colleges were started when a founding body was able to find enough subscribers to put together a fund sufficient to open the institution's doors. The College of Philadelphia had been formed that way, and most of the later colleges were similarly endowed. Williams College collected $14,000 in small contributions and Amherst $50,000 in order to get started. The existing institutions similarly collected small amounts from as many donors as they could attract. Princeton launched a major fundraising campaign in the 1830s; the top donation received was $5,000. Columbia raised $20,000 from a benefactor.

Fundraising campaigns took various forms. For the most part they rested on individual solicitations conducted by the college president or the faculty members. Any donation was welcome. Cash was preferred, but the colleges were pleased to receive farm produce to keep the staff and students fed or books to augment the library. Frequent sales of homemade artifacts were conducted, along with fairs and lotteries. Some colleges sold perpetual scholarships entitling the owner to free tuition for one person in perpetuity, but these never became popular because the colleges usually priced them too low and were then forced to charge additional fees when the students materialized. Few colleges were fortunate enough to have a president as wealthy as Eliphalet Nott, whose investments yielded more than half a million dollars and made Union College the most highly endowed institution of the era. Overall, little cash was available; as late as 1870, the colleges of the nation were receiving a total of approximately $8 to $9 million per year through private donations.

In cases where the college was closely affiliated with a church, fundraising might be undertaken in tandem. Rudolph (1962) describes the American Education Society, founded in 1815 "to raise funds in the Congregational churches and to help send promising ministerial candidates to the appropriate colleges" (p. 183). Similar organizations were founded by other churches that might sponsor students of their faith or, in some cases, collect cash. Some of the Catholic colleges received funds from European missionary groups. But regardless of denominational affiliation or the lack thereof, nearly all the colleges were impoverished.

The states provided some support to private institutions. Tax exemptions represented a continuing subsidy; some states gave cash. Harvard received a total of $100,000 from the Commonwealth of Massachusetts in the decade following 1814, and Williams and

Bowdoin received around $40,000 each. New York gave over $100,000 to Columbia. The University of Pennsylvania received nearly $300,000 from its home state, and Dickinson College even more. In these cases and in others where states were slow in organizing public institutions, the private colleges were able to tap into the public treasury, a pattern traced in detail by Herbst (1982).

The states had land that they were willing to donate, but generally it was not worth much. Whether the proceeds of land sales went to private institutions or to the newly formed public colleges, it was difficult to turn land into cash. In every state, mismanagement and fraud stained the conversion. Surveys were often found to be inaccurate, and deeds were often litigated because of conflicting claims. Land that was supposed to sell for $20 an acre might go for as little as $2. Millions of acres of land that had been donated by Congress to the states carved out of the Northwest Territories often sold at $1 per acre or less. By 1821 the awarding of great blocks of land to the Western states ran afoul of agitation that the older, Eastern states should receive lands of similar value so that they too could build publicly supported institutions. But it was to be forty years before such a plan was enacted. Congress could afford to be more profligate with land in the West; it held title to more of it. In the Eastern states the public lands were considerably more likely to be owned by the states themselves.

Occasionally, public institutions were able to obtain larger sums. The first sale of land that had been deeded to the newly formed University of Michigan yielded only a few thousand dollars, but by the time Michigan became a state in 1837, land values had increased so that the state was able to sell off property at $20 or $25 per acre. Overall though, throughout the era, public and private institutions alike had to rely on supportive legislators to find ways of keeping the colleges alive. The narrowly sectarian institutions were least successful in obtaining state monies, as the legislatures were careful not to give the appearance of supporting one sect over another.

One indication of the weakness of the college budgets and physical plant can be seen in a report on college library holdings in the middle of the nineteenth century. Only eight colleges, all in the East, had as many as ten thousand volumes, although when the literary society libraries were added in, another ten Eastern institutions crossed that mark. During the decade of the 1840s, only three of the institutions for which data are available had an annual expenditure for books estimated at greater than $1,500. With few exceptions the libraries were open but a couple of hours per week (Hamlin, 1981) (see Table 2.2).

The marginally funded colleges were actually supported by the staff. A few senior professors at the larger institutions earned as much as $1,500 or $2,000, but most less than $1,000 per year—a salary comparable to that of a journeyman mechanic. And even then, the professors were not always paid. Occasionally a college would close for a year to allow the faculty to go out and raise money, or it would defer payment until such time as it had the funds, which as often as not never came. Sometimes a professor was appointed with the understanding that half his salary would be provided by his friends in the form of donations. Or the faculty would agree to have their pay contingent on the receipt of tuition fees. If a professor had an outside source of income, he would be expected to serve with no pay at all, just for the honor of being affiliated with the college.

Exploitation of the faculty was rationalized on the grounds that the colleges were providing a public service, bringing the young to maturity, and acting as a point of pride and honor to the community—all justifications similar to those the churches had been using for centuries. The colleges could not ask the students for much money lest they lose all their enrollment. That too was rationalized on the grounds that the community owed its young an education for as many years as it took for the person to profit from it. Few colleges wanted to be seen as rich men's institutions; they did not want to be accused of turning away poor but worthy students. And the supply of faculty was never in jeopardy. There were always

Table 2.2. American College Libraries in 1849.

| Institution | Estimated Number of Volumes | | | Estimated Average Annual Expenditure for Books 1840–1849 |
	College Library	Society Libraries	Total	
Harvard	56,000	12,000	68,000	$ –
Yale College	20,500	27,200	47,700	1,620
Brown University	23,000	7,200	30,200	2,500
Georgetown College	25,000	1,100	26,100	350
Bowdoin College	11,600	9,900	21,500	200
South Carolina College	17,000	1,400	18,400	2,000
University of Virginia	18,400	–	18,400	550
College of New Jersey	9,000	7,000	16,000	400
Dickinson College	5,100	9,500	14,600	100
Union College	7,800	6,800	14,600	400
Amherst College	5,700	8,000	13,700	300
Columbia College	12,700	–	12,700	200
University of Vermont	7,000	5,300	12,300	60
University of N.C.	3,500	8,800	12,300	–
Wesleyan University	5,600	5,500	11,100	100
Williams College	6,000	4,600	10,600	190

(continued)

Table 2.2. American College Libraries in 1849, continued.

Institution	Estimated Number of Volumes			Estimated Average Annual Expenditure for Books 1840–1849
	College Library	Society Libraries	Total	
Hamilton College, N.Y.	3,500	6,800	10,300	60
Franklin College, Ga.	7,300	3,000	10,300	600
Waterville College, Me.	5,200	3,300	8,500	–
Middlebury College, Vt.	5,000	3,400	8,400	–
Emory and Henry College, Va.	2,600	5,400	8,000	75
Western Reserve College, Ohio	4,600	3,100	7,700	50
Georgetown College, Ky.	6,500	800	7,300	–
University of Alabama	4,500	2,600	7,100	300
Miami University, Ohio	3,500	3,300	6,800	200
Marietta College, Ohio	4,300	2,100	6,400	–
Pennsylvania College	1,800	4,600	6,400	90
Geneva College, N.Y.	2,000	3,700	5,700	–
Maryville College, Tenn.	3,200	500	3,700	–
University of Ohio	1,300	1,500	2,800	–
Emory College, Ga.	1,000	1,700	2,700	–
Bethany College, Va.	1,200	1,100	2,300	–
Norwich University, Vt.	1,000	–	1,000	25

Source: Hamlin, 1981, pp. 230–231. Missing information not available.

junior-level recent graduates who could be found to teach classes for little more than room and board.

Thus from the beginning of the colleges in the Colonial Era and through the Emergent Nation Era, the professors were severely underpaid in terms of the years of education it took before they became qualified. However, they were not the only such group; clergymen were also expected to live in genteel poverty. One of the aspects of the professoriate that retarded its professionalizing itself was this exploitation in the name of a higher calling, with school teachers and professors alike being underpaid well into the middle of the next century. As long as the supply was greater than the demand and as long as there were no contracts to enforce payment of a living wage, the colleges lived on the backs of their staff members.

Outcomes

Higher education's outcomes in the Emergent Nation Era were similar to those yielded by the colleges of the Colonial Era: individual mobility, preparation for careers, assistance in child rearing, and community pride. However, the expanding nation and the growing economy placed additional demands on and expectations of higher education, and so further outcomes can be traced, especially preparation for newly emergent professions and the development of a collegiate style that marked the young people who had been to college with particular ways of acting and their own outlook.

Higher education as an essential component of professional preparation grew during the era. The percentage of lawyers and physicians taking up practice without having been to college dropped steadily, as apprenticeships alone were no longer sufficient for people who wanted to move ahead rapidly in their chosen field. However, as the splintering of denominations and formation of new sects accelerated, the percentage of college-trained ministers actually declined. New church groups sought charismatic leaders who could appeal to a congregation's emotions and effect religious fervor—qualities not typically enhanced in college classrooms. These country preachers were found more in the South and the West than in the New England states, where traditional churches continued to be dominant.

Most of the colleges formed under church auspices attempted to build a faith with teachings directed toward knowledge of the Bible. Connections were formed between populist democracy and religious fundamentalism, merging the notion that the intuitions of the heart of the common man were more to be trusted than the rationalizations of the intellectuals. Religious revivalism reappeared in different sections of the country at various times, leading not only to the splintering of established churches but also retarding shifts in scientific thinking. Eiseley (1970) concludes, "The notion that species were completely immutable seems to have come in with a hardening of the religious temper, particularly in the century between about 1750 and 1859" (p. 70). The church colleges were certainly not going to advance inductive reasoning, therefore an argument might be made that higher education actually delayed the general adoption of science as a way of organizing knowledge.

Higher education as a contributor to social welfare underwent some changes. The number of young people going to college to advance their personal wealth and movement in society grew, and the notion that college was a good personal investment overtook the idea of college as a social investment. Education's contribution to forming an elite group remained prominent, but fewer graduates entered public service. Although five of the first six presidents of this nation were college graduates, only four of the next eleven had been to college. The men who formed the nation had been scientists and classicists, using their knowledge of history and politics to solve problems. But by the time Jackson was elected in 1828, popular democracy had become so ascendant that no politician ever after was able to claim status as an intellectual as a condition for public office. One had to be a man of the people, self-taught, self-made, rooted in the soil, born poor but risen through adversity. The notion that intuitive folk wisdom was superior to an educated intellect grew strong. Common sense as exhibited by ordinary men shouldered its way in as an ideal qualification for public office, just as charisma and emotion became the basic characteristics of successful church leaders.

These trends toward individual mobility and self-educated leaders did not completely supersede the social value of higher education. The colleges still taught moral philosophy—a course that probably did much in shaping the thinking of civic reformers and social activists. The courses covered logic, rhetoric, natural law, politics, and aspects of philosophy. Their aim was to produce a supply of virtuous men who could counter the professional politicians and vulgar businessmen who were becoming increasingly influential in public affairs. The college-affiliated learned societies engaged students in considering social issues such as equality of the sexes, universal suffrage, abolition, temperance, child labor, and reform of social institutions. Many of the most influential writers of the time, including Emerson, Hawthorne, and Thoreau, were college graduates. The old gentry were being diminished with the rise of businessmen and self-trained politicians, but many among them were not relinquishing their concern for social reform. In fact, according to Giele (1995), "Among the major temperance and suffrage leaders, more than half had the equivalent of some college education" (p. 80). The author lists outstanding women reformers, including Elizabeth Cady Stanton and Lillian Wald, and college graduates Lucy Stone (Oberlin), Carrie Chapman Catt (Iowa State), and Jane Addams (Rockford).

The engineers prominent in building the canals, railroads, and public works of the era came from the new colleges established especially to train them. The U.S. Military Academy and Rensselaer Polytechnic Institute prepared a sizable majority of the engineers. The academy at West Point was not offering bachelor's degrees, but it had a rich collection of technical books, and its extensive publications on military subjects made it a national center of scientific study. Rensselaer allowed young people from every background to study engineering using laboratory experimentation and field study.

Trained scientists were coming from many colleges, and even though most of the older institutions clung to the classical curriculum, scientific studies took their place alongside the classics. Toward the end of the era, additional schools, including the Polytechnic Institute of Brooklyn, the Massachusetts Institute of Technology, and Worcester Polytechnic Institute, added to the supply.

A research presence grew in the elite institutions. Joseph Henry, a physicist, developed important work in electromagnetism while he was a professor at Princeton prior to becoming the first director of the Smithsonian Institution. Asa Gray, professor of natural history at Harvard, effectually made that institution the center of botanical study in the United States. The colleges were attracting scientists even as they delayed in developing graduate schools. Wolfle (1972) reports that 1,600 scientists published 9,000 papers in American journals between 1800 and 1860, with the most productive authors affiliated with the science divisions of Yale, Harvard, and the University of Pennsylvania. Overall, though, the colleges were slow to adopt laboratories, departments, and institutes for specialized research, and the German universities remained virtually the only places where a student could be trained in scientific or scholarly research. The contributions of science as fostered within the universities took a back seat to practical inventors in developing commercially useful products and processes.

The colleges changed notions of human development. In earlier eras the transition from childhood to adulthood was direct, as young people left school at age ten or twelve to go to work. As the period of schooling expanded, however, young people's development was suspended. Teenagers living together in colleges developed their own codes and ways of behaving. Indolence, rowdiness, and disrespect for elders became social norms. Delaying entry to adulthood with its attendant responsibilities was now acceptable. Those colleges that acted as surrogate parents fostered the development of a culture of adolescence that has to be marked as an outcome of higher education in the Emergent Nation Era.

3

. . . .

University Transformation as the Nation
Industrializes: 1870–1944

The Civil War—the cataclysmic occurrence in the lengthy history of sectional rivalry—was the most notable event marking the onset of the University Transformation Era. The College Land Grant (Morrill) Act, passed during the war, and the Servicemen's Readjustment Act, passed during a later war, were the two most important pieces of legislation ever enacted by the U.S. Congress in terms of their influence on the course of higher education. The first gave rise to the land-grant colleges, which turned higher education toward broader areas of service. The second—the GI Bill— inaugurated the Mass Higher Education Era by making college possible for millions of veterans.

Societal Context

Table 3.1 shows a statistical picture of the conditions surrounding American higher education in the University Transformation Era.

There had been a trend toward national consolidation since the nation was formed, retarded primarily by the Southern states' insistence on interpreting the Constitution to mean that they could keep their peculiar institution, slavery. The conflict between North and South was only the most immediately calamitous event in a rivalry that had been evident from the time the Constitution was drafted, with its deliberately ambiguous language regarding the

Table 3.1. Statistical Portrait of the University Transformation Era, 1870–1945 (Estimates).

	1870	1945
U.S. population	39,818,449	139,924,000
Number of students enrolled in higher education	63,000	1,677,000
Number of faculty	5,553	150,000
Number of institutions	250	1,768
Number of earned degrees conferred (bachelor's, master's, and doctoral)	9,372	157,349
Current-fund revenue (in thousands of current dollars)	14,000	1,169,394

Source: Snyder, 1993.

relationship between the states and the federal government. Several political compromises regarding admission of new states and various court decisions and legislative acts that inflamed either the North or the South, sometimes both, marked the era leading up to the Civil War and well beyond. The expansion in national territory was effectually completed with the acquisition of Alaska in 1867. The eighty years from the founding of the nation saw its land area spread from the Appalachians to the Bering Sea and its population multiply tenfold. Moreover, the mentality of expansiveness continued through the end of the century, extending now into the Pacific and Caribbean. Population continued increasing, with an incredible growth of 72 percent between 1850 and 1879 alone.

Industrialization was triumphant by the beginning of the University Transformation Era. It affected farming, where newly invented agricultural machinery was enhancing yields, and hence exports. Oil had been found in Pennsylvania and, together with metals in the West, led to great individual fortunes. Railway building alone consolidated wealth. The connivance of the federal government was apparent, as the railroads received a total of 130 million acres of land in return for putting tracks through to the

Pacific. And this was in addition to the 200 million acres that the railway builders had been awarded prior to 1860.

The growth in industry, capital, and population was substantially greater in the North and West than it was in the South. The South had clung to an agrarian tradition, while the North was shifting rapidly toward heavy industry and the growth of cities. The South was so devastated by the Civil War, which stripped it of at least half its wealth, that it could do little to catch up in industry, capital formation, or education. The Civil War had effected a $1.5 billion decrease in the value of its land, and every bank and insurance company in the region was essentially worthless. The loss in bank capital during the war approximated $1 billion, and the emancipation of the slaves represented another $2 billion in lost capital (Adams, 1931). Few Southerners took advantage of the land made available under the Homestead Act, 2.5 million acres of which were taken up mostly by migrants from the North and East in the first two years after the act was passed; 12 million acres were so taken by 1870.

Expansion of wealth and industry in the years following the Civil War was marked by rampant speculation and fortune building that included numerous unsavory characteristics: fraudulent sales and surveys in the West, thrusting aside the indigenous population there by force and deception; scandals and graft reaching into the highest levels of state and federal government; price gouging, monopolistic practices, and disregard for public safety across the industrial sector. The meat packers, railroad owners, oil producers, iron and steel makers, clothing manufacturers, bankers, and business builders of every kind were growing rich and gaining political as well as economic power. Along with increased foreign exports, a domestic market expanding rapidly through population growth of 20 to 30 percent per decade fueled the expansion.

The speculative excesses and profiteering of the Civil War were not the only examples of avarice. Financial panics in 1837 and 1857 were followed by similar panics in 1873 and 1907. All were due to speculation, overextension of credit, failures in the banking system, and causes endemic to unregulated capitalism. Even prior to the Civil War, several factors had led to feverish expansion: the need for housing and land by large numbers of immigrants; the building of railroads; and the exporting of agricultural products to Europe. The expansion led to subsequent, although temporary, financial collapse.

The excesses of the industrialists were so egregious that a counterreaction set in; the giveaway of public lands to railroad builders alone might have triggered some type of regulation. Governmental attempts to check the excesses of the capitalists began to bear fruit toward the end of the century, as in 1887 when the Interstate Commerce Act was passed to protect farmers and manufacturers from the ruinous multiple-pricing practices of the railroads. The Sherman Anti-Trust Act (1890), the Pure Food Act (1906), and the establishment of the Federal Reserve and the Federal Trade Commission (1913) also attempted to put curbs on what the industrialists and bankers were doing. The constitutional amendment establishing an income tax, which was ratified in 1913, enabled the government to restrain some of the immense individual fortune building. Not incidentally, it led to the expansion of philanthropic foundations, which were established to provide a haven for wealth. They later became useful in supporting research and several other areas within higher education.

The moral crusade of the Abolitionists did not stop with emancipation. The so-called Reconstruction Era in which the South was to be punished before being allowed to rejoin the union was only an extension of it. Curiously, the moral crusade hardly extended to indigenous Americans: "The plight of the red man, for example, left Abolitionists cold, though they were willing to pull down the whole fabric of America, if need be, to free the black man" (Adams, 1931, p. 243). Similarly, for all their pleas on behalf of their enslaved brethren, Northerners and not a few Southerners launched periodic campaigns against Catholics and foreigners. The course of moral indignation is never straight.

The emancipation of the slaves took place as a result of the Civil War, but it did not fully liberate the black population. Jim Crow laws in the South kept the former slaves and their descendants legally segregated for another one hundred years, hence at the bottom of the social hierarchy. In the North where they were and had been legally free, economic opportunity was little better. Few had chances to rise higher than the working class at the lowest rungs of the economic ladder. In fact, the blacks who developed large businesses were more likely to do so in Atlanta, Birmingham, or New Orleans than in New York, Boston, or Philadelphia. Well into the Civil War, property-holding and voting restrictions could be found in many Northern states. The American obsession with race was by no means terminated when the slaves were freed and the South was laid prostrate, any more than it was to subside when the Civil Rights Act was passed one hundred years later.

Prior to the Civil War, continued disaffection with narrowly based higher education had retarded the expansion of colleges. The people who moved to the frontier spent their first generation building their communities. Even though they often started colleges as emblems of community pride, higher education was not essential for solving problems of subsistence, nor was it a major contributor to growth. At the beginning of the era there were fewer college students in proportion to the population than there had been when the century began. There were no graduate schools, and the agricultural and mechanical colleges authorized in the Morrill Act had barely begun. Colleges were small; few were teaching religious doctrine, but fewer still appeared to be centers of inquiry.

However, all that changed after 1870. In the three-quarters of a century marked by the University Transformation Era the number of students grew from 63,000 to 1.5 million, the faculty from 5,500 to nearly 150,000. At the beginning of the era, just over 9,000 bachelor's degrees were awarded each year; by its end, more than 135,000 were awarded. Doctoral degrees awarded went from none to 3,300. Higher education's endowment grew from less than

$50 million to $1.75 billion; its revenue and expenditures grew to $900 million per year. This vast expansion was fueled by growth in national population and wealth as well as by notable changes in what higher education meant to the American people. Publicly supported postsecondary study, with research, service, and professional schools added to undergraduate instruction, began defining the enterprise.

The United States emerged from World War I as a wealthy, powerful player on the world stage. Because the nation was not a direct participant until the war had been under way for nearly three years, it was able to profit enormously by exporting agricultural products, manufactured goods, and explosives to the belligerents. Sizable portions of the debt that was owed to European countries as they helped finance the growth of railroads and industry in the latter part of the nineteenth century were repurchased. And even after the United States did become actively involved in the war, it escaped relatively easily. The Civil War had cost the American combatants more than 600,000 deaths in a population approximating 35 million. The United States lost fewer than 120,000 men in World War I, out of a population of 100 million. By the end of the war more than 20,000 new millionaires had been created.

The tension between private capitalism and public welfare was accentuated during the era. Is an economic good tantamount to a moral good? Should the people who earn the money be the sole determinants of how the money should be spent? Do all people, including intellectual workers, owe allegiance to business? How can spiritual values be reconciled with the values of the marketplace? All these questions were to affect the development of higher education and the role it was to play, as the universities transformed the enterprise. One thing was certain: the city on the hill, the light unto the world, the moral beacon that was the dream of a few of the influential colony builders had been thrust totally to the shadow.

Institutions

The seventy-five years of the University Transformation Era saw the greatest shifts in higher education that had occurred up to that time. Most of the change in institutional form occurred in the first forty years, and the largest growth in enrollment in the last thirty-five years. Between 1870 and 1944 the number of colleges quintupled, and enrollments increased by several thousand percent. Much of this expansion would have happened anyway because of population growth, but the main impetus was that both higher education and the secondary schools expanded their offerings, presented new types of programs, and attracted students who in earlier times would not have considered education beyond the lower grades. New types of colleges were formed, including specialized colleges, junior colleges, and colleges for particular student interest, ability, and ethnicity. But the most prominent element in the transformation was the emergence of the university—an institution complete with an undergraduate college, professional schools, graduate departments, and a wide range of service components.

Universities

Pressures for the introduction of universities into higher education had been building for a generation before the institutions came to the fore. The faculty had been transforming themselves into a professional group; and scientific research was spreading. But before the colleges could become universities and before new institutions could be founded with all the characteristics that mark universities, higher education had to modify several concepts to which the colleges had been adhering since early in the Colonial Era. In general it had to do the following: reduce its involvement with religion, especially sectarianism; effect liaisons with incipient professional groups; adopt a service-to-the-community role; encourage or at least allow a professionalized faculty to take form; value research and the advancement of knowledge as ends in themselves; elevate farming, mechanics, and industry to areas worthy of study; exalt science over humanities; move from the perpetuation of tradition and teaching from authority to the position that knowledge was ever-evolving; stretch the educational experience from four years to a greater length of time by organizing graduate schools and awarding advanced degrees; and have access to sizable funds, both from the public treasury and from wealthy donors. All these characteristics fell into place between the 1860s and the end of the century.

The idea of converting colleges to universities can be traced to the men who had been influenced by direct contact with higher education in Germany. George Ticknor was earliest, reporting back to Harvard in 1825 after having visited and studied at the German institutions. Subsequently, Daniel Gilman, Andrew White, Charles Eliot, Theodore Woolsey, and G. Stanley Hall—influential in the forming or transformation of Johns Hopkins, Cornell, Harvard, Yale, and Clark, respectively—stand out. All had been influenced by association with the universities in Germany. Henry Tappan, president of the University of Michigan in the 1850s, had attempted to establish graduate study by bringing in scholars to work on their own research and by accepting advanced students to work with them. Francis Wayland, president of Brown, a decade earlier had tried repeatedly to convert his college to an institution committed to a broader curriculum serving students with a greater variety of interests. Actually, the notion of the university can be traced to Thomas Jefferson, whose plans for the University of Virginia included advanced study and a faculty organized according to academic specialty.

The American university dates from the founding of Cornell in 1869—an institution complete with the characteristics of the comprehensive structures that were to follow. Johns Hopkins, founded in 1876, was dedicated from the outset to research and graduate training, and hence must also be accorded status as a first of its type. Others followed soon thereafter, and many of the older colleges were transforming themselves into universities by adding graduate and professional schools centering on research, scholarship, and public service.

As the universities were formed, graduate enrollment expanded notably. At the outset of the University Transformation Era there were perhaps 200 graduate students in the nation. Twenty years later there were around 2,400, twenty years after that nearly 10,000, and by 1930, nearly 50,000 graduate students were enrolled. As Hofstadter (1952) concludes, "The entire system of graduate teaching and research had developed within the lifetime of one man" (p. 64). As for degrees, in 1876, twenty-five institutions awarded forty-four Ph.D.'s; in 1930, more than two thousand doctorates were granted. The sixteen leading institutions were averaging one hundred Ph.D.'s each per year by 1939.

Higher education's association with occupational groups striving to professionalize themselves expanded notably in the latter years of the nineteenth century. Law, medicine, and theology—the venerable professions—continued to be taught, but taking their place alongside were schools of business, journalism, engineering, architecture, pharmacology, dentistry, agriculture, mining, forestry, librarianship, education, psychology, and sociology. The notion that one had to be specifically trained to enter practice grew rapidly, feeding on three factors: each group's desire to be seen as a profession requiring a lengthy period of training; the expanding knowledge base that was itself transforming practice; and the availability of schools in which the acolytes could be prepared. David S. Jordan (1903), founding president of Stanford, summed the institutions' role with these words: "The value of the college training of today cannot be too strongly emphasized. You cannot save time nor money by omitting it, whatever the profession on which you enter" (p. 36).

An emphasis on research most characteristically marked the beginnings of the universities. The research universities were dedicated to discovering and codifying knowledge as well as to advanced studies, knowledge for practical use, and career preparation. Natural science had obtained a foothold in the science schools founded at Harvard and Yale in the 1840s and 1850s. The Massachusetts Institute of Technology had been organized in 1865 as a separate institution dedicated to scientific study. Natural science, training for practical careers, and research-based graduate education were mutually reinforcing. Rationality was the mark of a modern university. An emphasis on religion, reliance on authority, and study of the classics were in full retreat. The university was more than a college with a group of professional schools clustered around it; its crowning function was original research. The university was the home of scholars and scholarship.

By the time the Association of American Universities (AAU) was formed in 1900, the research universities had themselves become a special group among American institutions. Geiger (1986b) notes that the founders of the association included five state institutions, five formerly colonial colleges, and five that were founded as universities committed to graduate study from the outset. These were the institutions that set the standards for graduate study and research. The universities of California, Illinois, Michigan, Minnesota, and Wisconsin were growing rapidly; they added to the value of their endowments, to their libraries, to the number of doctoral degrees awarded, and to their increasingly prestigious faculties. Yale, Princeton, Harvard, Pennsylvania, and Columbia were the transformed colonial colleges in the group. The institutions founded with a commitment to graduate study included Chicago, Cornell, Johns Hopkins, MIT, and Stanford; Cal Tech was added to the group around ten years after the AAU was formed.

The leading research institutions grew rapidly. In 1876 their libraries averaged under 50,000 volumes. At the turn of the century, they had grown to 171,000 volumes each, led by Harvard's 549,000. Twenty years later they averaged close to three-quarters of a million volumes, and Harvard had over 2 million. Chicago opened in 1892; seven years later it awarded forty-three Ph.D.'s, more than any other university in the nation. Stanford opened in 1891; eight years later its endowment of $18 million was the highest for any institution. By 1930 several of the research universities were numbered among the largest institutions in terms of enrollment; leaders were Columbia with 15,000 regular full-time students, California with 17,000, and Minnesota and Illinois with around 12,500 each.

The universities were able to get off to such a fast start because of the funding they attracted. The coincidence of public funds available through the Morrill Act and private funds coming from the fortunes made during and after the Civil War gave a double boost. The Morrill Act of 1862 permitted every state to select 30,000 acres of federal land times its number of congressmen; nearly 17.5 million acres were thus distributed (Nevins, 1962). Morrill money was used in founding the University of Illinois in 1867, the University of California in 1868, and colleges in a total of thirty states before 1900. Funds from private fortunes went to Johns Hopkins in 1876. Cornell received money from both: $500,000 from Ezra Cornell and New York's share of the Morrill money. The institutions' emphasis on science and research was a natural consequence of the Morrill Act's specifying that the funds be used to endow "at least one college where the leading object shall be, without excluding other scientific and classical studies, and including military tactics, to teach such branches of learning as are related to agriculture and the mechanic arts" (Hofstadter and Smith, 1961, p. 568). And although no such restriction was placed on private contributions, the railroad, steel, oil, and textile barons did not expect that their millions would be used to support the few young people interested in studying philosophy or religion.

Imitation was prominent. What the leading universities did was often adopted by other institutions across the nation. Harvard's elective system became all but universal, as did the academic department as the basic unit of college organization. Graduate and professional schools that were created within the institution but that operated separately from the undergraduate program became the norm. Requirements for the Ph.D. took standard form, especially after the members of the AAU articulated expectations. In fact, within a few years of AAU's establishment it was effectually accrediting other institutions by listing those whose bachelor's degree holders could be deemed ready for graduate study. However, not all the leading institutions' practices were adopted; Harvard's experiment with a three-year undergraduate degree found few takers, and Johns Hopkins's concentration on graduate education never spread to other institutions to the extent that Hopkins pursued it.

Competition with other institutions became a driving force. The universities sought to grow large as a way of effecting prestige. And large size meant more money from students in private universities where tuition accounted for over half the revenue. As the universities raced for status, they began adding specialized facilities: laboratories, football stadiums, students' residence halls, auditoriums, and carillon towers that served as focal points for the campus. Except for Cal Tech, MIT, and a few specialized research institutes, every major research university in the nation at one time had a renowned football team.

Imitation and competition led the universities to become similar. Each claimed to be unique, but they adhered to the same rules about course attendance, time to complete a degree, the nature of the degrees they awarded, and the way students and faculty members conducted themselves. Public relations offices, organized within some of the universities early in the twentieth century, pointed out the institutions' virtues, but in general the students and faculty were relatively homogeneous. They were drawn from among the same social strata; the students were transitory and had no political power; faculty freedom and the ability to move from one institution to another kept them relatively satisfied. The basic characteristics of the university had been established: boards of trustees, now made up of more businessmen than clergymen; a bureaucratically organized administration; a system of faculty ranking; relatively uniform standards for admissions and student progress; and academic departments.

The ostensible mission of the universities—the quest for knowledge and academic excellence—was always subordinate to the institutions' adherence to popular values. They could not stray too far from community mores lest they lose their support. Thus, instead of preparing social revolutionaries, they trained young people to take their place within the established community, furthering the common welfare. Their admissions policies, which discriminated against women and ethnic, racial, and religious minorities, reflected the spirit of the times.

The major contribution of the universities was that they began to produce scientific research of a quality and variety that by the 1940s was preeminent in the world. American physical and natural science overtook the once-leading European institutions, especially after the 1920s. The universities had become involved in research for the war effort in 1917, readily compromising their dedication to intellectual freedom and truth. The Reserve Officers' Training Corps (ROTC) was formed in 1916 and the Students' Army Training Corps (SATC) in 1918, both of which allowed male students to enlist, stay on campus, and receive military training. Research in explosives and industrial processes that would further the war effort was supported by governmental funds, eagerly accepted by the institutions. Both research and military training foreshadowed a lengthy list of war-related relations that marked higher education during World War II and well beyond.

Other Institutions

Not all the colleges shared the growth in size, prestige, and programs and services exhibited by the universities. Many remained too small to offer much breadth in curriculum, let alone to construct modern laboratories or libraries. The colleges had to make vertical moves, extending themselves to graduate study if they were to attract the funding and faculty that would in turn lead to enrollment growth. Clark (1995) points out that a college might well add science to the undergraduate curriculum but "advanced research could hardly be put alongside tutoring in Greek and Latin" (p. 120). Some commentators at the turn of the century recommended that the smaller colleges close if they could not transform themselves into institutions with greater breadth. Thwing (1910) comments that "the presence of the poor college is a weakness to the whole college system" (p. 146). Chicago's President Harper suggested that the weaker institutions drop the upper division and become junior colleges that prepared students for entry into the universities; by 1940, 15 percent of the institutions with 150 or fewer students in 1900 had become junior colleges, and an additional 40 percent had closed their doors or merged with other institutions. However, enough small liberal arts colleges survived so that the institution remained part of the American educational scene.

Other institutions showed high growth as they expanded their offerings, not necessarily in research and graduate education but in professional studies, a broader undergraduate curriculum, and involvement with public service. Many, especially those in urban areas, emphasized part-time and summer-session enrollment, so much so that by 1930, when Columbia, New York University, and City College of New York had the largest total enrollment in the nation, considerably fewer than half their students were full-timers (Geiger, 1986b, p. 112). Several other urban institutions, including Hunter (New York), Northwestern (Chicago), Southern California (Los Angeles), Northeastern (Boston), and Western Reserve (Cleveland) also had total enrollments in which regular, full-time students were in the minority.

Because the universities could not or would not matriculate everyone who sought upward mobility through higher education, several other institutional forms developed. Colleges for Negroes were a notable example. Prior to the Civil War, scarcely two dozen African Americans had graduated from colleges in the United States, despite the fact that freedmen numbered close to one-quarter of a million in 1825 and nearly half a million by the time the Civil War started. Few colleges in the North or South would consider enrolling them. Lincoln University in Pennsylvania and Wilberforce in Ohio, formed in the 1850s, and Howard, a creation of the U.S. Congress in 1867, were organized especially to admit Negro students. Soon after the Civil War several churches and philanthropic foundations funded the creation of private colleges especially for the children of recently freed slave families. Over fifty historically black, private, four-year colleges were set up. A few, such as Tuskegee and Fisk, became prominent, but several others remained unaccredited well into the middle of the twentieth century. Publicly supported colleges for African Americans received a major boost in 1890 when a second Morrill Act was passed stipulating that "no appropriations would go to states that denied admission to the colleges on the basis of race unless they also set up separate but equal facilities. Seventeen states were so moved" (Rudolph, 1962, p. 254).

Women's colleges began during the same period, some growing out of all-female seminaries, others started through benefactions. Not until Vassar, Smith, and Wellesley opened in the 1860s and 1870s did the group of colleges take its eventual form. Women had begun entering higher education in greater numbers as liberal arts colleges and state universities, especially in the Midwest, opened to them. But apparently many educators and students' families felt that young women would be better served in institutions of their own. The women's colleges adopted the male collegiate tradition of professional faculty, four-year curriculum, and dormitory living but modified it somewhat with a greater emphasis on the arts, languages, and humanities. By the end of the century Harvard, Brown, Columbia, and a few other old-line institutions that were not yet ready to admit women on equal status had organized Radcliffe, Pembroke, and Barnard as annexes where women took equivalent classes and exams.

The junior colleges were successful innovations. Defined as institutions offering two years of collegiate instruction, they began originally with the support of a few university leaders who insisted that the universities would not become true research and professional development centers as long as they retained their freshman and sophomore classes. The foremost impetus for their growth was the pressure for further education occasioned by the rising number of high school graduates. By 1922, 207 junior colleges, 137 of which were privately supported, were operating in thirty-seven states. Most were quite small; total enrollment for all institutions was around 20,000. By 1930, 450 junior colleges could be found in all but five states; total enrollment was around 70,000. By the end of the University Transformation Era, more than 600 junior colleges were functioning, most still small, averaging around 400 students. California was an early leader in forming public junior colleges, with a large number founded also in Illinois, Texas, and Missouri. Many private junior colleges in the East and Midwest served as finishing schools for young women who would not go on to university studies. Many others were designed to allow students to take the first two years of college in their home town and eventually to transfer to a baccalaureate-degree-granting institution. In the 1930s and 1940s, the junior colleges began providing courses in numerous occupational areas and hence took on a hybrid form as institutions preparing people either for further collegiate studies or for immediate employment.

State colleges—sometimes characterized as comprehensive universities, another successful institutional form—grew notably as various professional and quasi-professional groups began encouraging aspirants to obtain specialized preparation that required less than a doctoral degree. Approximately one hundred public normal schools were opened in the last third of the nineteenth century. Most were transformed into state colleges offering bachelor's degrees and eventually the master's to young people who would become school teachers. These comprehensive institutions expanded into other professional areas, including nursing, accounting, business, and various trades and technologies. They also developed programs in home economics and several specialties within agriculture such as farm management, animal husbandry, and crop production.

Overall, the college population expanded so that any area of esoteric studies could find students to enroll in it, just as experimental
or deviant colleges could survive by matriculating students who valued the institution's eccentricity. But not many such institutions
were built as freestanding entities; more common was the university with an experimental college, a cluster of colleges, or a separate
college within it. Here a few students and professors could indulge
in a wide range of studies, a modified curriculum, and different
instructional forms without disturbing the broader institutional setting. The University of Wisconsin's Experimental College, centering on the few students and instructors who wanted to interact
without concerning themselves with fixed curriculum or instructional forms, opened in 1927 and lasted for five years, thus fore-
shadowing both in duration and intent many experimental colleges
of the 1960s. The more successful General College of the University of Minnesota opened in 1932 and acted as a junior college. It
tested and sorted students, provided orientation to postsecondary
study, and passed students through to the upper division or provided
them with what was called at the time a terminal general education. St. John's College also reorganized in the 1930s around a particular theme: the Great Books. Its hallmarks were seminars, a
faculty made up of tutors without specialization, and a fully prescribed curriculum. Entire colleges were built around the idea that
young people should be creative. Bennington, Sarah Lawrence,
Bard, Rollins, and Black Mountain, among others, all shared enthusiasm for artistic expression.

By the early years of the century an enduring pattern of higher
education had been established. All took place within the forty-year
tenure of Charles Eliot, the president of Harvard, who in 1869 had
articulated many of the principles on which the system was based.
With greater or lesser emphasis on the various functions, universities both public and private exhibited several characteristics that
they had inherited from earlier models. Their treatment of undergraduates followed the British form of residential college. Graduate

study and research was adopted from the German universities. Service to the community and preparation of students for a wide number of occupations had developed indigenously. As Kerr describes it, "The resulting combination does not seem plausible but it has given America a remarkably effective educational institution" (1963, p. 18).

Students

At the beginning of the University Transformation Era, fewer than 2 percent of the nation's eighteen-year-olds were entering college. Of the 63,000 students enrolled, one in five was female. The numbers increased steadily along with the nation's population; by 1900, 250,000 students were enrolled. The ratio of women had gone up to two in five and was to reach nearly half the undergraduates by 1920; it fell back to one-third by the end of the era. Overall, the percentage of eighteen-year-olds matriculating increased steadily, reaching 3 percent in 1890, 4 percent in 1900, 5 percent in 1910, 8 percent in 1920, and 16 percent in 1940.

Enrollment growth was greatest during the 1920s. Most of the expansion took place in existing institutions, but the newly formed junior colleges and the transformation of teacher education into baccalaureate study contributed heavily. The number of high school graduates, up by 150 percent between 1920 and 1930, contributed as well. Institutions and programs expanded at different rates. Engineering, law, and medicine declined as a percentage of the whole, while nonprofessional graduate education increased. Also contributing to the overall enrollment figures was the increase in length of time required to complete a program; law increased to three years, medicine and teacher education to four years. Contributing to the massive enrollment gains were more institutions, a longer time to complete programs, more high school graduates, and an increased demand for professional training as more occupational groups began expecting some college education for their new initiates.

The belief that education could serve as a means of ascending from lower to middle class and from middle to upper class was growing steadily. Bledstein (1976) comments, "In a nation without an effective apprenticeship system and without a significant gentry, the school diploma more and more served as the license with which an individual sought entry into the respectability and rewards of a profession. By 1870, there were more institutions in America awarding bachelor's degrees, more medical schools, and more law schools than in all of Europe" (p. 33).

Admissions

College admissions requirements broadened during the early years of the era. Academic merit was always at the top of the list, although a parent who was an alumnus of the institution or who had a deep pocket might well cause the admission officers to look kindly upon an otherwise-less-than-qualified applicant. An acquaintance with at least a dozen subjects was expected; however, not all subjects at all institutions, nor all to the same level, were standard. In the first years of the University Transformation Era, physical geography, English composition, physical science, English literature, and modern languages were added to the subjects that had been introduced earlier. Most of the innovations were led by Harvard, with Princeton and Michigan taking the lead in a few subjects.

Admission to the bachelor of arts program at the leading colleges centered on some combination of subjects. Although the roster was similar across the institutions, the amount or depth of preparation differed. Harvard demanded the most mathematics, Michigan the least Greek. English had not been a requirement before the beginning of the era, probably because an interest in English literature was secondary to classical literature read in the original. Furthermore, because English was the vernacular language, the college leaders anticipated that students would come adequately prepared, especially as public school systems expanded. English composition found its way into admissions requirements at Princeton in 1870, Harvard in 1874, Michigan in 1878, and Columbia and Cornell in 1882. This requirement usually took the form of applicants' being required to write a short English composition—a requirement that survives in the essay that applicants have been expected to write ever since. The physical and natural sciences came into admissions; physical geography, which was introduced at Harvard and Michigan in 1870, was the leader. Cornell began requiring a knowledge of physiology in 1877, and botany and natural philosophy were part of Michigan's requirements in 1890. By the end of the century, physics was becoming a general requirement for admission to a bachelor's program.

The expansion in types of programs led to different requirements. The Lawrence Scientific School, founded at Harvard in 1847, required physics and chemistry for admission, but curiously the schools of science at Yale and Princeton were slow to expect their applicants to have prior knowledge of science. As late as 1888, Princeton's John C. Green School of Science required five books of Caesar and four orations of Cicero, and not until 1895 was botany introduced as an admissions requirement to the Sheffield Scientific School at Yale. The latter institutions clung to the notion that drill in the classics and mathematics was a well-disciplined preparation for studying science. Furthermore, not much science instruction was available in the secondary schools of the time.

As the University Transformation Era evolved, more changes in the amount or quality of study expected of entering students were taking place than were changes in the subjects themselves. The leading institutions, pushing toward advanced study and research, increased their expectations for students applying for admission as freshmen. They also effected a downward pressure on the secondary schools to prepare students in various subjects. As for foreign languages, the actual use of the language and the ability to read literature in the original supplanted drill in grammar.

Toward the end of the nineteenth century the United States Bureau of Education collected data on admissions requirements from 475 institutions and found that of the 432 institutions offering bachelor of arts degrees, 93 percent were requiring Latin and 73 percent Greek (see Table 3.2). This scaled down in the other programs; few institutions offering bachelor of letters or bachelor of science degrees required Greek, but more than 38 percent of them expected a modern language (Broome, 1903, p. 82).

As the pressure for college entrance increased in the 1920s, issues of access plagued the universities. Facilities and resources simply could not accommodate all who sought entry. Wealth and family position were contrary to the myth of egalitarianism and the idea that higher education enables individuals to move between social classes on the basis of their intelligence and demonstrated academic qualifications. The institutions looked for defensible criteria on which to discriminate. College presidents, especially in the private Eastern institutions, posted finite numbers to which they would limit the size of their freshman class. In some of the colleges the limitations were undertaken in an attempt to limit the number of Jewish students entering—students who exhibited the qualities of intellect and drive for achievement that the presidents otherwise lauded. Here the multiplicity of university roles came to the fore. Were the colleges places for individuals to study, learn, and move on to higher pursuits? Were they places for people to make contacts, gain personality characteristics, attain access to an old boy's network? Were they to prepare students to feed the graduate schools?

Table 3.2. Admissions Requirements for Four Degree Programs, 1897.

Degree Program	Number of Institutions	Percent of Institutions Requiring		
		Latin	Greek	A Modern Language
Bachelor of Arts	432	93.0	73.6	14.0
Bachelor of Philosophy	123	81.3	5.6	41.6
Bachelor of Letters	98	68.3	2.0	38.7
Bachelor of Science	318	55.3	2.0	38.6

Source: Broome, 1903, p. 248.

All came into play along with anti-Semitism and discrimination against blacks and the children of southern Europeans. The colleges in the other sections of the country, especially the state universities in the Midwest, continued admitting sizeable numbers of students with minimal restrictions; for many, high school graduation was sufficient.

Examining the changes in requirements for entering students reveals the evolution in expectations, but it begs the question of why colleges select students on the basis of academic merit. All colleges have limited resources and hence must restrict enrollment. However, academic capabilities, defined as prior school achievement or scores on entrance tests, have been by far the most widely employed criteria, for the following reasons:

- *Institutional reputation.* The more academically able are likely to go on to more successful careers, hence to make the college appear to have taught well.

- *Ease of instruction.* The bright students better fit the faculty ideal and keep faculty morale high.

- *Higher return on investment.* Greater learning occurs even with less effort in teaching.

- *Individual motivation.* The most conforming young people are rewarded for doing what they were supposed to do in the lower schools.

- *Societal value.* Bright young people are stimulated by researchers and encouraged to make their own contributions to advancing knowledge.

- *Maintaining a community of common discourse.* The business of college is conducted through dialogue, rational language, and the interplay of ideas better suited to the academically able.

During the 1920s and 1930s the elite Eastern institutions adopted several forms of admissions criteria that depended on more than academic merit. Columbia required its applicants to provide letters of reference, personal data, aspirations, and so on, with the understanding that the admissions office could accept or reject on the basis of subjective criteria. Its percentage of Jewish students dropped in half. Harvard's president Lowell tried to establish a Jewish quota and, after the Harvard faculty rejected the idea, built subjective criteria into the admissions process. Geiger (1986b) concludes, "Harvard's experience made it clear to other schools that overt quotas could not be publicly admitted; and Harvard seems to have learned from others that discrimination required a cloak of ambiguity" (p. 135). Princeton blatantly gave priority to social over intellectual qualifications, and only secondarily used examination scores for selection. The private institutions also gave preference to graduates of exclusive secondary schools and to children of alumni.

Selective admissions based on a variety of criteria—never the same from one decade to the next or one institution to another—have been less of a problem in American higher education than in other countries because of the number of colleges in the nation. There is always some institution someplace that will take any student. Furthermore, the United States has never had a national examination, with all of its accompanying problems. However, the shifting basis for admissions frequently reflects the biases in institutions, especially those where the alumni play a significant role or where an intracollegiate belief system is relatively homogeneous. It also means that the order of prestige among institutions is to an extent dependent on the selection criteria they employ. The basis on which students are selected reflects the relative status of American social groups and the changes in social mores over time.

As selective admissions became more prominent in the 1920s, various standardized tests such as the Scholastic Aptitude Test were developed. In the 1930s the College Education Examination Board began developing examinations for use by elite institutions, and during that decade the Graduate Record Examination was also installed. All these tests were used most frequently in the elite Eastern institutions, especially as those institutions tried to broaden their student base. During the 1930s the private secondary school source of students for the Eastern institutions shrank, and the colleges tried to become more national than regional. In 1934 Harvard began a program of scholarships awarded to bright prospective students from the Midwest, and Yale and Princeton similarly sought students from across the nation. Academic merit was supposed to be the main criterion, and standardized tests were considered the best measure. Along with formalized courses of study, these types of admissions screens helped college educators convince the public that objective principles determined competence.

In summation, race, religion, gender, ethnicity, family wealth, or social standing—all have been used as admissions screens. Because these characteristics seem discriminatory on the basis of criteria that are inherent in the individual, not the result of effort or accomplishment, they have been rejected as unfair or anti-egalitarian. Prior school attainment or scores on an achievement test seemed more acceptable as the University Transformation Era came to an end.

The Collegiate Way

The idea of going to college as a way of life came into full bloom during the University Transformation Era. The residential experience and association with peers took center stage as aids to cultivating the maturing young person and helping individuals generate associations that would last a lifetime. Just as the part-time, commuter students were growing as a percentage of the whole by virtue of their attendance at junior and municipal colleges and universities that made special provision for them, the students at the older, residential institutions were increasing their claim to exclusivity by effecting a semblance of collegiate life that the commuters and part-timers could never duplicate.

The value of the four-year collegiate experience became an American myth. This echo of the English undergraduate residential college, imported to the United States along with other English social institutions, refused to be quieted in the face of expanding graduate and research enterprises. A college had to provide tutorials, housing, and extracurricular activities if it were to remain true to its principles; it had to be sustained, even within the broader university. As the institutions expanded, the proportion of students that could be accommodated in college-sponsored housing diminished, but many institutions took the expedient of limiting their enrollment if they could not find residences for the students. When students lived in the surrounding community, the colleges attempted to enforce rules on their behavior and conduct. In general the notion that the college was responsible for the lives of its undergraduates remained strong, even as the institutions grew larger.

The myth of the four-year residential experience so influenced the belief in what a true college was about that it led to generations of research on the effect of the collegiate experience in which the paradigm was a residential setting complete with extracurricular activities. This environment became synonymous with what college was supposed to be. The effect of college on part-timers or commuters by comparison was studied hardly at all. By the 1930s a student personnel point of view had been codified, that is, the belief that a college was responsible for all aspects of a young person's life, including emotional and psychological characteristics as well as learning and cognitive development.

The peculiarity of the four-year residential college had been present from the beginnings of higher education in America. As the colleges expanded they constructed new residential facilities in order to sustain this special experience. The insularity exhibited in the curriculum, divorced as it was from most of secular life, extended to the extracurriculum as well. Campus activities including sports, dramatics clubs, debating societies, fraternities, and religious observances expanded. The extracurriculum became a form of surrogate involvement—a substitute for attendance at comparable activities in the outside world. College activities that reached beyond the walls associated the students with their counterparts elsewhere. This was the era in which organized sports and organized debating clubs grew into intercollegiate activities. Even religion followed, with the creation of the intercollegiate YMCA in the late nineteenth century.

The University Transformation Era saw intercollegiate athletics blossom into major endeavors. Athletics departments had their own budgets; massive stadiums were erected; sporting events filled the pages of the newspapers and were broadcast nationally as radio became widespread. Athletics were part of the collegiate experience in English and German universities as well, but they were different in the United States because of commercialization. Once intercollegiate sports began in the latter part of the nineteenth century, they grew rapidly, as though they were "rushing in to fill an emotional vacuum" (Hofstadter, 1952, p. 113). Athletics certainly displaced much of the rowdiness common among students in colleges of an earlier era and joined the alumni to the institution, sustaining their loyalty and, not incidentally, their donations.

As the collegiate way became codified, student rebellions against the staff became less common. Occasional rebellions against the colleges' surrogate-parent status were seen, but even these confrontations were less acrimonious, relatively free of the violence and mayhem characteristic of student riots during the mid–nineteenth century. Part of the difference might be attributed to the fact that students in the latter part of the century faced greater economic opportunity—more professions from which to choose. "Students in the 1890s, especially those at prestigious colleges and universities, could confidently view college education as a pleasant interlude on a well-marked path" (Kett, 1977, p. 175). Gradually, as older students populated the campuses, the modes of control that had been installed to manage young adolescents were modified.

Throughout the history of higher education, students have expected college to contribute to their social mobility. The students in the University Transformation Era were no different. As the curriculum broadened and the social milieu shifted, the students found a mix of peers through which they could develop associations lasting a lifetime. Each of the colleges was a community apart, imprinting its own values on the developing youth and anticipating lifelong loyalty. Within these isolated enclaves the students developed their own codes of behavior, which were so powerful that by the 1920s the term *college man* had a ready reference: someone with an intense loyalty to his institution; a special mode of dress; the expectation that he drank socially, if not to excess; a devil-may-care attitude regarding young women; and a marginal association with the life of the mind—the latter being exemplified by the "gentlemen's C."

The colleges continually put forth ideals of equality and egalitarianism, emphasizing that anyone with academic qualifications could attend. In Eliot's inaugural address as president of Harvard in 1869, he mentioned how the institution would never turn away any student who had the capacity and character for college work. However, he also pointed out that women were not yet welcome, not because of any limiting notions about their innate capacities but because of the difficulty of establishing segregated housing facilities. Despite the leaders' rhetoric, the colleges more reflected than led their contemporary society.

Not all of student life was athletics and socializing. Student involvement in social issues grew. Women students and faculty members were involved with the suffrage movement; fifteen colleges formed the National College Women's Equal Suffrage League in 1908. During the 1930s, antiwar activities included student protests against required participation in ROTC. Students also took part in strikes at coal mines and clothing manufacturers. Some joined clubs aligned with communist movements. The end of Prohibition took away the thrill of illegal drinking, and the Depression sobered students in other ways as they came to realize that full-time, well-paying jobs were not going to be readily available. A popular song of the era featured a young man lamenting his working his way through college in order to acquire knowledge he would most likely never use after graduation. The U.S. entry into World War II effected an even greater change in student life, as most of the young men were called into the armed services and as the campuses became centers of training for the vast numbers of military officers who were needed to pursue the war effort. But the way of college life had been codified.

Faculty

At the beginning of the University Transformation Era few of the 250 or so colleges in the nation employed as many as two dozen instructors. Probably half the faculty had professorial status but differentiation into academic ranks, the formation of disciplinary departments and associations, academic freedom, and faculty autonomy were as yet but dimly seen. Along with other characteristics of the modern faculty, these were put in place less than a half-century after the blossoming of the university. In fact the universities and the faculty as a professional group grew in tandem in the late nineteenth and early twentieth centuries.

Efforts to define the concept of professionalism have had a long history. The problem of definition remains because occupational roles vary depending on the setting in which they are performed. Professions continually evolve, and different segments of society may view professions as having more or less status. By most definitions the professional works full-time and has a lifetime commitment to a career. A professional gains a specialized body of knowledge during a long period of formal education. Ministry to a client population, autonomy of judgment, adherence to ethical standards, licensure or formal entry requirements, and associations that monitor all the above characterize the group.

As the University Transformation Era began, the faculty had evolved from the status of tutors, expecting that they would spend only a short time teaching a variety of subjects, to that of professors, knowledgeable in a particular academic discipline with a commitment to long-term, full-time employment. The profession had been slow to form because of the tutors' low pay, low status, and lack of secure employment. State governments were unconcerned with the instructors; nowhere did they enjoy status as civil servants, and their pay and working conditions were rarely the concerns of a governing body outside the institution. College presidents could hire and fire, paying only as much as necessary to attract a staff they considered qualified.

All that changed after 1870. One indication of the rise of faculty status is provided by William Rainey Harper's behavior as soon as he was appointed president of the fledgling University of Chicago. The university had been organized with sizable donations from John D. Rockefeller and several Chicago business leaders. Therefore, Harper had money to work with, and one of his first actions was to go around the country seeking the best professors. He recruited professors from Yale and employed several former college presidents, including the president of the University of Wisconsin. His raid on Clark University was notable. Shamelessly, without the president's knowledge, he met with the majority of the Clark faculty, offering to double their salaries. When the Clark president objected, Harper invited him also to join the Chicago faculty. When all settled, he had engaged fifteen of Clark's professors, thus stripping the institution of most of its staff. And Clark had been open only three years at the time (Hofstadter and Smith, 1961, pp. 759–761).

Although universities differed in size and emphasis, most included an undergraduate college, a graduate division, and several professional schools. The rise of the faculty depended on the latter two characteristics; the faculty would not have become professionalized nearly as rapidly if they had been involved solely with undergraduate teaching. From the beginning, the number of hours that a faculty member was expected to spend in the classroom differed between research universities and liberal arts colleges. Although it is difficult to estimate actual teaching hours, there was no question that expectations in the university were lower. As graduate schools developed in the older colleges and as the new universities such as Cornell, Johns Hopkins, Clark, Chicago, and Stanford were formed with graduate and professional schools from the outset, the expectations continued shifting so that professors at the leading institutions were spending less time in the classroom.

Still, the professors continually sought reduced teaching hours. The faculty at less-prestigious institutions pointed to their counterparts at the leading universities; those at the leading institutions pointed to the teaching hours expected of the professors in Europe. However, even though the number of hours devoted to teaching and research varied between types of institutions, among departments in the same institution, and among faculty ranks, in few cases were individuals expected to devote all their time to one or the other endeavor. The notion that professors were supposed to be engaged at least some of the time in teaching and some in research became part of the ethos of the American university. All were supposed to be, at the same time, teachers and scholars.

Other characteristics of the profession appeared at various times. Sabbatical leaves began at Harvard around 1880. The practice spread so that by the turn of the century several other research universities were doing the same thing: offering professors every seventh year off, with some proportion of their pay sustained. Set in place originally so that professors would have time to engage in further study and remain current in their field, the sabbatical became a fringe benefit and bargaining chip as professors were recruited. In the first two decades of the twentieth century, the practice of offering sabbaticals and intra-institutional funds for research spread. An example of the latter appeared at the University of California in 1915 when a provision for faculty expenses related to research was included in the budget. However, salaries did not increase commensurately. At the time of World War I, the assembly line workers at the Ford Motor Company were earning as much as associate professors at the University of Michigan (Kreger, 1998).

The professionalization of the faculty meant that increasing numbers of learned people, especially scientists, took faculty positions. In an earlier era the most prominent scholars might have been freelancers, but the rise of the university drew them into the faculty ranks. One study conducted in 1906 showed that of the one .thousand "Leading American Men of Science," more than four hundred were employed at fifteen leading research universities and nearly two hundred more at other colleges (Geiger, 1986b, p. 39). All this had happened in but one generation after Eliot's inaugural address when he said, "The university does not hold a single fund primarily intended to secure to men of learning the leisure and means to prosecute original researches" (Hofstadter and Smith, 1961, p. 617).

Despite the shifting emphasis, research could be conducted only after teaching responsibilities were fulfilled. In the first decade of the century, the professors at research universities averaged eight to ten hours of teaching per week, which was considerably less than the fifteen to eighteen hours spent in the classroom by their colleagues at most colleges. By 1920, the hours spent on teaching and research were becoming further differentiated, with the prestigious, wealthy, and graduate-oriented institutions requiring progressively fewer teaching hours of their faculty. However, because the higher education system was being differentiated, with junior colleges and teachers colleges growing rapidly, the overall student-teacher ratio of ten to one did not change throughout the era. This average figure obviously masked a continual decline in the number of students per teacher at research institutions and the increasing enrollments and class size in undergraduate colleges.

Research was clearly the endeavor that marked the rise of the professoriate. The conduct of research led the professors to become more and more specialized as they pursued their studies into narrower channels. By the 1890s the special interests of the faculty had led them to form departments organized along academic disciplinary lines. These specialized units resulted from the German influence, the prevailing assumptions about the nature of knowledge, and the ambitions of young scholars looking for new fields in which to make a name for themselves. Furthermore, as the universities grew larger, the unitary supervision of curriculum, teaching responsibilities, and student progress toward degrees had become inadequate. The rise in institutional administration led also to the formation of academic departments, as the professors sought organizational units that would provide them with a power base from which they might counter untoward demands on their time and activities.

The rise of the academic department coincided with expectations of academic freedom. The German tradition of freedom for students to choose their own studies and freedom for professors to study and teach what they would was well received by the incipient faculty professionals. Administrators and governing boards were considerably less enamored of academic freedom, especially when the faculty conceived of it as the right to advance unpopular ideas. The struggle derived not from educational theory but from institutional relationships. Faculty proponents of academic freedom modified the original concept of freedom to study and to teach to include protection for professors who would comment on the affairs of government, business, and other trends and events away from the campus. Many presidents took a different view, contending that freedom to take positions was limited to the classroom.

A few celebrated cases of professors being dismissed for espousing unpopular views led to the forming of the American Association of University Professors (AAUP) in 1915. Much of the energy of this nationwide, cross-institutional association in its early years was devoted to addressing grievances of members who had been dismissed or who felt they were being treated unfairly by their institution's administration. Toward the end of the era, in 1940, the AAUP published a Statement of Principle, holding that faculty tenure was a right that could not be abrogated by an institution's governors merely because a professor expressed unpopular views. At that time also, the AAUP was recommending that the faculty have a role in institutional governance, particularly in the selection of administrators and in the formation of educational policy. Competition among universities, each wishing to attract the most notable scholars in a field, and the relationships among scholars who interacted with their counterparts in the same discipline in other institutions gradually mitigated restrictions on what they could publish or pronounce.

Part of the faculty's difficulty in advancing ideas of tenure and job rights was that power would shift as people formerly regarded as employees took command of the essential aspects of the workplace. A more subtle retardant was that standards for judging competence changed as reliance on religion and authority were replaced with ideals of rationality. The Enlightenment dream was that debates on justice and equity would take place in a public arena, that an ever-evolving quest for truth would replace tradition. Research, experimentation, and rational inquiry in the universities fit the dream. The faculty code of pursuing truth became a cornerstone of the profession, and within that code the faculty claimed the right of maintaining their own views and speaking out on matters of public policy. But by deliberately ignoring the personal convictions or beliefs of the faculty, as MacIntyre (1988) postulates, "Universities became institutions committed to upholding a fictitious objectivity" (p. 399). When objectivity is the ideal, not only are professors appointed and advanced on the basis of scholarly competence and independently of their opinions and prejudices but anything becomes admissible as scholarship and all scholarship is deemed of equal merit. This posture, elevated to the status of a golden rule, eventually affected not only the rights of faculty but also the evolution of curriculum.

The faculty as a professional group differed from most other professions in that they did not appeal to the states to impose restrictions governing admission to practice. University instructors did not have the equivalent of a board of medical examiners, a bar examination, or state licensure requirements. They imposed their own standards within the context of their own institutions, hence the standards varied depending on institutional emphasis. Other professions depended on public recognition; the faculty practiced within an academy and as such were more dependent on its accepting them as professionals. Even so, the faculty soon adopted a practice of migrating between schools if they felt they could better their positions.

Faculty professionalization was furthered by the academic disciplines as inquiry became more and more specialized. Separate associations were formed to bring together members of the different disciplines who could then discuss scholarship in their own sectors, review each other's work, and advance knowledge along accepted lines of inquiry. Nearly all the interinstitutional disciplinary associations date from the early years of the University Transformation Era, from the American Philological Association, founded in 1869, through the Modern Language Association, American Historical Association, and American Economic Association, formed in the 1880s, the American Chemical Society, and American Psychological Association, organized in the 1890s, and the American Philosophical Association, American Anthropological Association, American Political Science Association, and American Sociological Society—all dating from the first five years of the twentieth century. Eventually, associations concerned more with issues of teaching than with research were formed, with the National Council of Teachers of English as an example. The faculty now had colleagues in institutions other than their own—reference groups who judged their work according to national standards.

For much of the University Transformation Era the faculty at the leading research institutions were appointed from among those who had earned their doctoral degrees at the same institution. Geiger (1986b) reports that in 1930, between one-half and three-quarters of the faculty at Chicago, Illinois, Minnesota, Cornell, and Wisconsin Universities and at MIT had received all or part of their graduate training at the university where they were employed

(p. 224). Several factors came into play. Graduate students were being employed as teaching assistants and, because most appointments of junior faculty members were made on the recommendation of the academic department, the person known to the staff had the inside track when a faculty position opened. The expansion in employment opportunities that was occasioned by increased enrollments early in the century led to numerous faculty positions, and the academic departments were often reluctant to take a chance on an outsider. By 1940 a majority of the faculty at many leading institutions had received all or part of their graduate education at the same institution. Most of these professors had begun at the institution as graduate assistants, then became instructors working their way up the academic ladder. Because the leading universities had begun demanding the Ph.D. early in the century and because the same institutions were producing most of the doctorates, the departments merely retained their graduates. Concerns about this type of inbreeding developed only later, after the pool of candidates had broadened considerably.

The practice of ranking faculty from instructor through assistant professor, associate professor, and professor dates from the latter years of the nineteenth century. The University of Chicago began with an elaborate system of academic ranking, and other universities fell quickly into line. Instructors might be employed and kept at the lower ranks indefinitely. Only gradually did the idea take hold that professors had to be promoted or dismissed within a certain number of years. Not until the AAUP's 1940 Statement of Principle did the tendency of allowing junior professors only a finite time at one institution become widespread. The AAUP policy was that after a probationary period lasting not more than seven years, a junior faculty member had to be advanced to tenure or dismissed. Most institutions adopted some version of that policy, writing it into their codes, regulations, and faculty manuals.

As the faculty became more professionalized, they added public service to their responsibilities. The academic social scientists, especially, tended to seek a voice in affairs in the broader society, and public service was on the agenda when the leading social science disciplinary associations were formed. Independent social science departments had been present in universities beginning with Cornell's founding and had gained stature at Johns Hopkins and with the establishment of a School of Political Science at Columbia. These early social scientists taught classic principles of social and political organization in a historical perspective, attempting to extend those principles to contemporary times and depending on their students to carry their message to the public. With the growth of professional associations, efforts to educate the public became more prominent. This was a time when great strides in explaining natural and physical science were perceived as leading to man's control of the world. If the scientists could do that for the natural and physical world, the social scientists should be able to do that for the world of human affairs. In actuality, of course, they proved considerably less successful in verifying their findings and influencing public policy. Even so, they began working with all types of governmental agencies and eventually became quite visible as members of President Franklin Roosevelt's Brain Trust. The progression of faculty members to federal service in the 1930s only followed the appointments that many had held in state governments in the 1920s.

The professionalization of the faculty proceeded rapidly at the universities, less so at the liberal arts colleges and specialized institutions. But even at the leading institutions the faculty did not police their ranks as vigorously as they might have. A fully professionalized faculty would take measures to weed out the incompetents—the professors who should not have been appointed or who, with the passage of years, lost the ability to contribute either in teaching or in research. However, although the faculty exercised the right of initial appointment and promotion, they never developed a tendency to dismiss any but the most blatant miscreants, and even then relied on the administration and board to take action. As a group, the faculty acted more like a protective or welfare association for their members, relying on early socialization and amorphous codes of ethics to control individual functioning throughout a lifetime.

Early in the era the faculty in many institutions took over the responsibility for admitting undergraduates. In 1884 the academic senate of the University of California developed entrance exams for undergraduates and criteria for accrediting high schools, similar to measures at other state universities, especially in the Midwest. However, the faculty lost those prerogatives. They first lost the accreditation standards, which were taken over by interinstitutional accrediting agencies on which university faculty might be represented but were far from a majority; then they lost the power to control admissions. As the institutions grew large and administrative positions proliferated, deans of students, registrars, and other administrative functionaries began enforcing criteria for admissions, which soon became intertwined with public relations and finances—areas outside the faculty's main purview.

By the end of the era enrollments had grown so that, on average, more than eighty-five instructors were employed in each institution. An occupational group well on its way toward a high level of professionalization had arisen. It had specialized, formed disciplinary associations, gained power through academic departments, differentiated itself into academic ranks, employed and promoted its own members, and enjoyed much freedom of functioning. Except in the higher ranks of the professoriate and in a minority of institutions, the faculty were still underpaid relative to their length of training, but that too was changing along with the public's view of the profession.

Curriculum

What is the curriculum? It is any set of courses—a summation of the syllabi and activities of students and faculty members functioning in isolated units. It is a set of intended learnings. It is all those experiences designed for the students and under college control, everything from libraries to residence halls. It is the courses required for a particular degree or certificate. Add the identification of curriculum in undergraduate, technical, and professional schools, among others—the wonder is that there can be any discussion of curriculum at all. The term is as variable as any in higher education.

As the number of students increased, the curriculum trend toward vocations and variety accelerated. To state it most basically, the curriculum simply exploded. Most attempts to bring students to general learnings disappeared as one specialization after another was introduced. Allowing the faculty to teach what they wanted and the students to take what they wanted became exalted as a measure of freedom. Actually, it was a tacit admission that the colleges' unifying theme was based not on teaching common knowledge or values but on adding enrollments, preparing young people for various careers, providing a home for organized research in all areas, and gaining prestige. A unified curriculum was feasible when all the nation's colleges enrolled a total of a few thousand students. It takes a great stretch of imagination to visualize a million young people studying philosophy and the classics of their own volition.

Breadth

Under the impetus of various forces the curriculum broadened in several directions. One of the forces came from the organizers of new institutions. Cornell prided itself on converting knowledge from abstract subject matter into education that students could use for practical interests. Not only did it propel students toward professional careers, it expanded the definition of professions to include such occupational groups as farming, social service, and teaching. But it sustained the study of history and philosophy with the argument that learning in those areas would be valuable for students entering political or social service. In college after college the retention of favored subjects was similarly justified on practical grounds. Johns Hopkins opened with a commitment to research, scholarship, and advanced learning. The curriculum in its graduate school was as specialized as its scholars wanted it to be. In its undergraduate school it pioneered the academic major and minor, as students were channeled toward graduate specializations. Hopkins also broadened professional studies by furthering the idea that a doctoral degree was a necessary credential for university teaching.

The older institutions also were transforming their curriculum. Liberal education at Yale included science, literature, and other modern studies as well as the classics. Its Sheffield Scientific School modified curriculum by developing preprofessional studies, especially a new premedical option. Harvard opened the elective system full-blown, rationalizing it as that which allowed young people to follow their own interests and learn whatever they felt would be useful. It also enabled its professors to teach in their own areas of interest. The elective system made such rapid headway in other institutions that by the turn of the century more than half the course enrollments across the nation were in optional classes.

Vocationalism represented another force, as bachelor's programs in every conceivable occupation were organized. Departments of education were formed as teacher training became part of the university curriculum. Journalism and business joined the list early in the twentieth century, taking their place along with various subsets of engineering, forestry, and agriculture. Social work and public administration became popular as career opportunities in those areas emerged. Some of the occupational groupings such as radio repair, automotive mechanics, commercial art, and practical nursing were so ill-formed or so lacking in prestige that few universities were willing to mount baccalaureate programs around them, but they found a home in the junior colleges.

The faculty exerted a force on curriculum transformation. The new professors were coming from ever more specialized graduate programs in which they learned principles within academic disciplines that had not been available to earlier schoolmasters and tutors. The political power that they gained by organizing themselves into academic departments provided a base from which they could take the curriculum into narrower channels. By the 1890s the academic departments at the leading institutions were controlling professorial appointments. The system thus fed on itself; the graduate schools produced narrowly trained scholars, who were selected for employment by the members of specialized academic departments, where they taught courses in their area of narrow expertise. The schools exalted the academic disciplines—intellectual domains with their own concepts, theories, and methods for gathering data and validating knowledge.

All areas of study were transformed. Experimentation was the hallmark of academic science. Professors in the social sciences elevated inductive inquiry in reaction against appeals to authority or moral judgment and in imitation of the physical sciences. Once the notion that the study of fine arts was suitable only for women dissipated, departments of art, music, dance, and subsequently creative writing, film, drama, and art history and appreciation flourished. With church doctrine segregated to a specialized area of inquiry, philosophy and literature could emerge, along with numerous subspecializations within each. The extent to which the curriculum formerly had been balanced and unified is debatable, but it is certain that during the University Transformation Era it spread in every conceivable direction.

This splintering of the curriculum made it impossible to sustain the moral philosophy course—the senior-year experience that attempted to tie together all threads of knowledge. Too many forces were against it. All but a few presidents stopped teaching, and the faculty became so specialized that few had the ability to organize a unifying course. Which academic department could lay claim to moral philosophy? The sciences had taken completely different directions; chemistry, physics, and biology were held together only by their adherence to inductive inquiry; none alone could explain the world. The social sciences were becoming so fractionated that no department could create a course that brought economics, political science, sociology, and history together to explain how society functioned. Humanistic studies tended toward criticism, particularity, and subspecialties organized by author, artist, or era.

Recognition came early that the specialties and electives had made a shambles of bachelor's degree requirements. But only in the smallest colleges could the staff specify degree requirements centering on the unification of knowledge. Most accommodated the broadening curriculum not by changing degree requirements but by adding new programs, degree titles, and paths to the old degrees. Even before the Civil War, the bachelor of philosophy, bachelor of science, and bachelor of literature had been introduced in the older, Eastern institutions. In the West, bachelor's degrees in music, home economics, and agriculture were introduced, along with special bachelor's degrees for teachers and engineers. The University Transformation Era saw these variant degrees proliferate until a bachelor's degree in practically any specialized area of study was available.

Preparatory Programs

As degree titles and requirements expanded, requirements for admission to college shifted as well. In 1900, prior study in Latin was still required for admission to degree programs in philosophy, letters, and science in a majority of institutions, but French and German were gradually replacing it. Charges were raised early on that students who entered programs leading to the variant degrees were less well prepared than those who sought a classical curriculum. The leading institutions were giving more nonclassical degrees than they were awarding bachelor's of arts degrees anyway, but contentions of inadequate student preparation were widespread. As the different degrees with their different sets of learning requirements took over, admissions requirements shifted as well. When Stanford opened in 1891, it required only English for admission, along with any ten subjects from a list of twenty-five others. As early as 1870 Harvard's President Eliot had commented that students with superior training in mathematics might use that as a substitute for deficiencies in the study of the classics. And few institutions required admissions tests; most accepted prior years of study in a subject as tantamount to ability in that area.

Attention turned to the public high schools, which year by year were graduating more students and sending many on to the universities. According to Rudolph (1977), by 1895, 41 percent of the students admitted to college came from public high schools, 40 percent from the preparatory departments of the colleges themselves, and 17 percent from private preparatory schools. As public high schools took over the preparatory work, senior institutions began abandoning it, but a dilemma was quickly observed: the public high schools were teaching increasing numbers of students who would not go to college, hence their curriculum had to be designed for broader purposes. They taught modern languages, applied science, agriculture, homemaking, manual training—not the areas that the colleges pretended to. If the founding of higher education institutions had followed instead of preceded the secondary schools, the colleges might have developed their curriculum as the natural outgrowth of that which the schools taught the younger students. But by the turn of the century the lack of articulation between the late-blooming secondary school system and the college course of study, which had expanded into innumerable areas, was so evident that the college leaders determined to rectify the situation. What they could not control in their own house, they would impose on the institutions sending people to it.

Under the auspices of the National Education Association the Committee of Ten was formed in 1892. Made up of college presidents along with the U.S. Commissioner of Education, a college professor, two private school headmasters, and a public high school principal, the committee issued a report proposing a model high school curriculum, including recommended courses for each of the four secondary school years. Students were to take four years each of Latin, history, English literature and composition, and German or French; three years of Greek and algebra and geometry; and a year each of physics, chemistry, botany, geography, astronomy and meteorology, and anatomy and physiology.

The committee's recommendations came at an inconvenient time. Compulsory attendance through age sixteen was spreading in tandem with laws restricting child labor. Whereas in 1890, only twenty-seven states had compulsory attendance laws that reached into the secondary school years, by 1918 all the states had such mandates. But a minority of high school students were graduating, with fewer still going to college. Only a rare high school principal could demand a strict college preparatory curriculum for all students. The colleges may have preferred that high schools serve as preparatory institutions, but high school diplomas were being awarded for a variety of activities at far reach from the undergraduate curriculum. The schools were considerably larger and more widespread than the colleges. The public high schools alone graduated more than 61,000 students in 1900, of whom perhaps 30 percent followed a college preparatory curriculum.

The colleges' attempts to dictate curriculum in the high schools were criticized repeatedly. A major contention was that schools with requirements pointing toward subsequent levels of schooling did a disservice to the majority of students who would progress no further in the graded-education system. Flexner (1908) was particularly negative, saying that the high schools should remain free to innovate, that forcing students to study subjects (Latin, for example) that they would not pursue in college was wasteful, that prescribed entrance exams encouraged cramming and memorization, and that the list of required courses was not an educational program but a politically inspired compromise among contending groups within the universities. Furthermore, the rigid requirements were not preparing students for the colleges' own elective systems.

Still, the colleges continued attempting to impose their expectations on the secondary schools. Many universities set themselves up as secondary school accreditation bodies; the state universities in Michigan, Indiana, Wisconsin, and California were leaders in this activity. The Board of Regents of the University of California in 1884 noted that upon the request of the principal of any public school in the state, a committee of the faculty would visit the school and report on the quality of instruction there. By the end of the century, nearly two hundred colleges were certifying high schools—a pattern that broke down only after the accreditation associations were formed.

As high school enrollments continued growing, the schools developed parallel tracks—one leading to college, the other leading to employment or to a person's place in the community as homemaker or good citizen. Thus a pattern of sorting young people at an early age was established. Prior sorting had been made on the basis of who went to school and who did not; now, with a majority of young people in school until age sixteen, the sorting took place within institutions. As for the colleges, dissatisfaction with the adequacy of preparation displayed even by students coming from the college preparatory programs led to other devices, especially admissions tests. The first entrance examinations administered by the colleges were idiosyncratic, reflecting the preferences or specialties of the few professors who devised them. Quickly though, the colleges moved toward developing examining boards that set standards across institutions. Formed early in the century, the College Entrance Examination Board held great promise because of its practice of applying tests uniformly across institutions and in various cities across the country. However, it was several decades before more than a small percentage of college applicants sat for those exams. Most colleges still administered their own.

The colleges' relations with the secondary schools were confounded further by the types of teachers that the schools employed. Teacher training had come into higher education as a separate area of study early in the nineteenth century, but at the outset of the University Transformation Era there were only a dozen or so normal schools. Even though the number grew rapidly, by the end of the century, only around 20 percent of the school teachers had been college trained. The early normal schools had a curriculum of two or three years that was presented to students entering after perhaps two years of high school. Accordingly, students graduated from normal schools with considerably less than a full college education. Even in 1940 only 18 percent of the nation's current graduates of teachers colleges and normal schools had had four-year programs. The universities, then, were attempting to dictate curriculum to a set of institutions in which the majority of teachers had not studied the subjects themselves.

As the percentage of young people in secondary school expanded and as the number of college students grew, the paths to college diverged. The curriculum endorsed by the Committee of Ten, picked up by only a minority of the secondary schools, actually declined further after the early years of the century. By the 1940s, only around 20 percent of the high school enrollment was in college preparatory courses. For example, just under half of the public high school students took Latin in 1910, and by the end of World War II, fewer than 10 percent enrolled in Latin classes. Less precipitous declines were seen in enrollments in modern foreign languages, mathematics, and science.

Because the colleges could not rely on the public secondary schools to supply sufficient numbers of what they considered to be adequately prepared students, they shifted their sights. Most had reduced their reliance on their own preparatory departments as the high schools expanded, but they reinstated these activities under the guise of remedial or developmental education. Many, especially the Eastern institutions, reconciled the problem by selecting their students from private preparatory schools that adhered to a collegiate-type curriculum. Many others took the expedient of lowering admissions standards so that they could enroll freshmen who were not as well prepared as they might have liked. That way they could at least maintain their enrollments. And many, especially the public colleges in the Midwest, began admitting as many students as possible regardless of prior academic preparation, with the intention of dismissing half the freshmen before the end of their first year.

The Centrifugal Curriculum

It is rather indicative of the insularity of many college leaders that they thought they could impose a curriculum on the schools even as they themselves were embracing the elective system. Electives and subsequent major and minor requirements may have been necessary to effect the conversion of colleges into universities and to elevate research and the graduate schools to the prominent positions that they quickly attained, but they drove the undergraduate curriculum toward chaos. The main argument against the elective system was that the bachelor's degree referred to no patterned learning experience. Two people could go through the same college at the same time without ever having taken a course in common. The degree signified nothing except that a person had accumulated 120 or so college credits, not necessarily even from the same institution. Why this should be a problem has never been quite clear, except that the expectations for the learning attained by a bachelor's degree holder became totally vague. The elective idea further gave the faculty a license to dissociate themselves from the growth of the undergraduates, to prepare courses in narrow areas of interests. The concepts of freedom to study and freedom to learn established the rationale for an environment in which everyone could do much as they pleased. The uniform college experience disappeared, along with the idea that the faculty in particular or the curriculum in general was in any way responsible for what became of the students.

The notion of curriculum as a set of disparate courses became the dominant definition. A major institution might offer five hundred different courses, suggesting that knowledge could be splintered into minuscule pieces. Vocational courses took their place alongside the remnants of classical languages; preprofessional students sat next to those without a clear career orientation. And as the curriculum expanded, little was abandoned. There was no need to deny any course that a professor wished to teach and for which a few students could be found. All that had to be done was to make the degree requirements labile. Then, an individual professor's popularity or a course that students perceived as being useful could become the dominant influence. The organization of curriculum into structural units, each signifying a number of hours of study and all to be aggregated into the requisite number for graduation, completely overcame any intention of equipping students with common understandings.

The idea that students should be allowed to pursue any course of study that fit their interests and aspirations was widely accepted. It was easy to justify. What could be more democratic than providing courses and activities of enough variety that any student might follow a desirable path? But the elective system was also a philosophical statement saying, in the main, that the college had no authority to prescribe a curriculum, that any study was as useful as any other, that no area of knowledge was of greater worth, that knowledge was ever-evolving. The system accommodated several powerful forces: ever-increasing numbers of students attending for vocational training; departments centered on academic disciplines with professors desirous of protecting enrollments—hence budgets—in their areas; and a paucity of institutional leaders willing to take the position that some areas of knowledge were more valuable than others, that students should leave their colleges with certain areas of learning in common, and that their institutions contributed to the maintenance of a society unified around certain values and understandings.

Reaction against the fractionated curriculum coalesced in the general education idea that was especially prominent in the 1920s and 1930s. General education has been variously defined, but one of the more lasting definitions is that all students should gain a common body of knowledge so that they can take their place as members of a community with shared understandings. The problem that it tried to solve was how to sustain a set of common values in an era of fragmented and specialized knowledge. In 1919 Columbia declared that there was a certain minimum intellectual and spiritual tradition that people must understand if they were to be called educated; the school built an integrated course in Western civilization. Courses that combined threads of knowledge that had been split out into specialized areas became prevalent at other institutions. Integrated courses in the social sciences, with titles such as "The Individual in Society," were most prominent, with interdisciplinary humanities courses such as "Modern Culture and the Arts" in second place. The physical and life sciences had the most difficulty unifying strands of knowledge.

General education in the form of interdisciplinary courses actually reflected the moral philosophy courses that had all but disappeared as the professors tended toward specialized study. It made headway in institutions where academic or administrative leaders were willing to pursue it against the specialized interests that acted as centrifugal forces on the curriculum. Entire institutions such as Sarah Lawrence and Bennington were organized around integrated general education, and schools within schools were formed at several leading universities, notably Wayne State University and the University of Minnesota, for the same purpose. However, in most institutions the specialized faculty within and the specialized professions without continually subverted the notion of the unity of knowledge. Curriculum planners could not impose curriculum standards any more than the faculty could divorce themselves from the specialized areas of learning that they had come to enjoy.

As the era drew to a close, general education in most applications had been redefined as a set of distribution requirements. This provided the curriculum with a rationale: students should take classes in the humanities, science, social science, mathematics, and fine arts so that they would have a breadth of knowledge. It satisfied the academic departments as well; they could list several classes and allow students to choose from the menu. This form of curriculum distribution, that is, one or two classes from each of a set loosely organized under broad titles, went into effect in most institutions and remained the dominant model. Actually, the old classical curriculum provided more of a general education than the distribution requirements did. At least it had purpose and order. Majors and minors, fields of concentration, and various permutations among them gave the appearance of rationality but were in effect a compromise with the bureaucratic organization of the institutions. General education could not penetrate the power base that the faculty had built within their departments.

A related curriculum controversy emerged as a struggle between the humanists—successors to the classicists—and the vocationalists, for whom the highest calling of college was to prepare people for specific occupations. The former coalesced around the idea of liberal education—one that leads to reflection and self-knowledge—and the latter around the purpose of education as preparing people to earn their way in the world of work. Curriculum centering on study of the classics, rationalized from the Yale Report of 1828 to the Great Books of the 1930s, sustained a small place in the overall fabric of higher education, mostly in such private institutions as St. John's College and some of the smaller Catholic colleges. Liberal or humanistic studies remained as the centerpiece of curriculum in institutions large enough to maintain them as separate programs and in those that had neither the resources nor the desire to build graduate schools or to see themselves as vocational training centers. Vocational education became the hallmark of the junior colleges and of the professional schools that prepared people for specific callings. All coexisted, some in the same institution, others in specialized colleges.

The Collegiate Experience

The colleges claimed continually that they offered more than courses; they determined lives. The liberal arts colleges especially rationalized that they provided culture, that they were places where small groups of young people would gain lifelong associations with peers of similar social standing. They put themselves forward as protectors of a tradition and molders of character. Concepts of loyalty to the alma mater, the class reunion, the successive generations that matriculated in the same institution—all testified to a college experience that went far beyond the classroom. Social affairs, school colors, fight songs, and intramural activities all contributed.

Whether freestanding or under the umbrella of the university the professional schools also built sets of experiences that reached beyond teaching the skills of the trade. They added coloration, ways of thinking and behaving, and loyalty to the fraternity of professional practitioners. Less concerned with building school ties, they were forging connections with groups of like-minded colleagues across the landscape of professional practice. They developed ceremonies and rituals and examinations that tested not only knowledge but also the candidate's ability to perform under stress. The internships they arranged, the professional association meetings they sponsored, the journals they edited, the placement services they provided for their graduates—all served ceremonial functions. The acolyte was being indoctrinated into a select society. The importance of where one went to school had more than symbolic meaning.

The other specialized institutions that developed at the time similarly built curriculum designed in the broadest sense to develop in young people particular ways of acting. The colleges for black students imitated the liberal arts colleges, offering comparable courses along with a complete roster of fraternities, sports, and rituals designed to duplicate the collegiate experience. However, because so many of the students coming to them were academically ill-prepared, they were forced to develop intense programs in basic skills. And because expectations for the careers that their graduates could enter were so limited, they were obliged to sustain programs in manual training and industrial technology well after most of the four-year colleges had abandoned them.

The early colleges for women developed curriculum considered appropriate for their charges. On the one hand, they followed the men's colleges in providing instruction in humanities, science, and social science. On the other, they elevated to the status of collegiate studies and professions areas that were considered traditionally peculiar to women. Home economics and social work became prominent, along with music and art, child care, and teaching in elementary school. The programs offered a fit with the careers and activities that the nation expected of its women: librarians, social workers, nurses, and school teachers—areas in which women constituted 90 percent or more of the practitioners. And just as the professional schools populated largely by men taught ways of behaving, the women learned as much in professional mannerisms as they did in the exercise of skills.

Instruction

The University Transformation Era saw a broadening in instructional forms as well as in curriculum. Libraries remained open for longer hours as collections grew and as instruction centering on students' finding and reporting on sources became prevalent. Discussion groups became a favored form; they imitated the German university seminars, and they suggested that the students were thinkers, not inmates of a reformatory. Laboratory work became required in the scientific fields. Correspondence courses opened up and field trips, especially in the occupationally oriented institutions, were started. Written examinations became prevalent, with the same exams given to all the members of a class, as differentiated from the previous individual recitations. Honors programs were introduced as the larger institutions tried to accommodate an increasingly diverse student body. Beginning in the 1920s, courses by radio were tried, justified by innovators who claimed they were the wave of the future and would eventually replace the classroom.

The growth in student enrollment led to the necessity of managing large numbers of students economically. Class size grew. "As early as 1901 thirty-nine Harvard courses enrolled over 100 students, fourteen over 200" (Rudolph, 1977, p. 233). Princeton, along with a few other institutions, clung to a tutorial system, with preceptors or young instructors responsible for small groups of students. Elsewhere large classes, often with attendant small discussion sections, were brought forward to display the best lecturers.

Other ways of managing the growing numbers of students were introduced. One that had been put forth in earlier eras and that had never died was the idea that the time to the baccalaureate should be reduced to three years or even two. An idea that had somewhat greater success was the year-round calendar. Orientation programs became prevalent by the 1920s as a way of introducing masses of students to college, providing an introduction to the methodology of learning, helping the students to sort themselves into programs consonant with their abilities and aspirations, and assisting them in making psychological adjustments to college. Counselors and guidance personnel took over these responsibilities from the task masters of an earlier time.

The era saw also efforts to standardize examinations. The principle that examinations be conducted by outsiders rather than by professors was mentioned repeatedly but was just as often resisted with the argument, Who but the instructor knows what the students should know? The professors may have been certain of the uniqueness of their courses, but the curriculum and instructional forms provided by various institutions made courses of comparable size and emphasis seem almost interchangeable. Students could and did transfer from one to the other, carrying course credits as readily as their clothing. Faculty trained in one institution carried academic styles to the others. Textbooks marketed nationally lent uniformity to courses. No governmental control was needed to effect similarity in institutional functioning; imitation did the job.

Grade marks that purported to indicate the depth of student learning in particular areas were introduced. Whereas written statements of a student's progress were commonly provided in earlier eras, the large numbers that had to be handled precluded this form of assessment. Furthermore, written statements were obviously subjective, whereas single letters or numbers suggested objectivity. A written commentary on a student's progress might encompass deportment and attitude along with cognitive learning; the grade mark collapsed all into a code usable by professors who might not recognize their students on campus but who could mark written examinations and reduce the results to letters or numbers. The computing of grade averages across courses and of class rank spread. Letters from A to F were used along with numbers on 4-, 10-, or 100-point scales. No grading system was universally satisfying because too many purposes were subsumed within it: stimulating students, satisfying professors, encouraging scholarship, and, above all, providing a reference point for institutions and programs to which the student might subsequently apply—in other words, creating a credential. Students' grade point averages appeared on their transcripts along with the concentration of courses (the major) that they had followed. The other part of the credential was the standardized course unit or credit earned. Academic credits were tied to hours spent in a class and, along with the grades earned, became academic tender. Students involved with such a system could transfer between institutions, satisfy the requirements of more than one program so that they could switch academic majors, or drop out and return to college while maintaining the credits toward a degree that they had banked. Higher education was on its way toward regimentation in handling students, taking on an industrial character even as curriculum and instruction were becoming more varied.

The move toward uniform systems of accounting for the college experience was accelerated by the national institutional associations, regional accrediting bodies, and philanthropic foundations that became increasingly influential after the turn of the century. The Carnegie Foundation for the Advancement of Teaching, the Carnegie Corporation, and the Rockefeller Foundation restricted their grant-making activities to institutions that met minimum standards in faculty salaries or library holdings. The Carnegie Foundation also listed a minimum number of units of high school credit that applicants must present for admission, a certain number of full-time professors, department heads with doctorates, a four-year program leading to the bachelor's degree, and a minimum funded endowment as its criteria for a college that was worthy of receiving funds. The Association of American Universities published minimum requirements for libraries and laboratories. By 1919 the American Council on Education had spelled out the expectations for a college: an institution that required for admission the completion of an accredited four-year secondary program, required at least 120 semester hours for graduation with a baccalaureate, had at least one hundred students and eight department heads, had professors who taught no more than sixteen hours per week in classes averaging no more than thirty students, had an annual operating income of at least $50,000 and a library of at least eight thousand volumes. Nowhere in these criteria was there any comment about what or how much the students were supposed to be learning. Order was coming to the system of higher education, not to the curriculum but to the display of quantifiable data regarding students, faculty, physical plant, and funding.

The spread of variant instructional forms and of different ways of managing the numbers of students was manifest in still other ways. Several institutions, especially those in urban areas, developed extension courses and courses offered in the evening so that older, working students could attend. The University of Chicago pursued the idea of separating portions of its lower division into a junior college and, on the other end, establishing strong graduate schools not only in traditional scientific and professional areas but also in the fine arts and education. It pioneered the associate degree, which was awarded to students who completed a general education program in their freshman and sophomore years. However, in institutions across the nation, growth rate, funding, and size remained the major determinants of curriculum and instructional forms, far outstripping governing-board philosophy. Furthermore, the failure of institutions to connect degree awards to academic examinations evidenced the widespread belief that the experience of attending was evidence enough that the graduate's knowledge and attitudes had been shaped.

Governance

The governance of higher education during the University Transformation Era displayed an increasing trend toward secularism. Enrollments in state colleges grew at a far greater rate than those in the private sector. Within the private institutions, church influence declined, especially in colleges that were converting themselves into universities. The presidency and the ranks of the faculty, which had been dominated by clergymen in prior years, were being filled by laymen. The idea that college was a business grew rapidly, along with institutional size and budgets.

Governance structures shifted notably in the direction of administrative hierarchies and bureaucratic management systems. Accrediting and professional associations acted as quasi-governmental entities to the extent that they could influence faculty-student ratio, laboratory size, and staff qualifications in specific programs. The faculty gained power in terms of hiring, curriculum, and degree requirements; the trustees became corporate directors responsible for institutional maintenance; and the administrators became business managers. The larger the institution the more it developed conglomerations of component parts, each with a supervisor and a certain amount of responsibility for its own budgets and staffing.

The composition of governing boards shifted as businessmen were appointed in greater numbers. People were selected for any of several reasons, including having built successful businesses on their own, having social or political connections or access to wealthy donors, or being popular community figures. A few were scholars or clergymen, and some appreciated the opportunity to engage in public service. The trustees in public institutions were often appointed by the state governor, sometimes with confirmation by the senate.

In the private institutions most were elected by a church body or, as growing numbers of private colleges reduced their dependence on a church group, were self-perpetuating lay boards. When term limits were specified the norm was three to six years. In both public and private colleges, the alumni might be represented; the University of California designated an alumni seat on its board beginning in 1915.

The governing boards maintained oversight in matters relating to the institution and represented the school to the public. In public institutions the trustees often helped preserve institutional independence by acting as a buffer between university and legislature, serving as advocates even when the legislature, swayed by the politics of the moment, might have preferred different policies. They solicited donations, pointed directions for construction, and approved institutional budgets. Most important, they employed the president.

Presidents

The exercise of presidential power varied among institutions. Some presidents behaved nearly autocratically, demanding that they have a part in all decisions. Others developed hierarchical management systems. Few maintained more than the semblance of a democracy. Their role was to guide the institutions in new directions while managing complex organizations. All could not sustain this dual effort with equal facility, but many built both strong academic programs and powerful administrative empires. Most were appointed more for their managerial skills than for their allegiance to any particular academic program. They tended to be pragmatists, empire builders, fundraisers, and experts at public relations. Although on ceremonial occasions they espoused individualism, academic freedom, and noble virtues, they were more likely to value those policies that brought prestige and, above all, income to the institution.

The leading presidents were key figures, standing astride the institutions, gaining power as budgets and enrollments grew. They were builders, converting the college form into that of the university complete with graduate and professional schools, a professionalized faculty, and a position of eminence it had not previously enjoyed. The era saw a number of influential presidents. In any list of the ten most prominent presidents in the history of higher education, eight would be from the University Transformation Era. They were not universally loved but they were effective.

Although clergymen had been far in the majority of college presidents, by the end of the era not more than 10 percent had backgrounds in theology. Charles Eliot was the first nonclerical president in Harvard's 233-year history. Yale's first nonclergyman was appointed in 1899, Princeton's in 1902. The new presidents were cosmopolitan; they were students of the history of higher education, and above all, observers of European practices. To a man they determined to build great universities that would serve the business, professional, and industrial interests of the nation. The classical curriculum might be tolerated for a time, but it certainly would not be allowed to stand in the way of the more practical emphases in which the trustees were interested. Daniel Coit Gilman opened Johns Hopkins as a graduate school, enrolling undergraduates but with the majority of students and funds directed toward the graduate program. James Angell built Michigan's research and graduate emphasis in a way that his predecessor, Henry Tappan, had dreamed of but was unable to effect. Andrew White at Cornell and Frederick Barnard at Columbia led their institutions toward graduate education and also emphasized public service with programs for working professionals. William Folwell did the same for the University of Minnesota. David Starr Jordan and William Rainey Harper, founding presidents at Stanford and Chicago, respectively, manipulated the sizable funding at their disposal to create institutions that from their inception were leaders in research and graduate education, typifying what the major institutions were becoming. And the era of the strong president continued into the twentieth century, as Nicholas Murray Butler at Columbia, A. Lawrence Lowell at

Harvard, Lotus Coffman at Minnesota, Benjamin Wheeler at California, and Robert Hutchins at Chicago followed their illustrious predecessors by taking their institutions into even broader areas of service.

Several characteristics linked these outstanding presidents. For one, they tended to be both autocrats and compromisers. They knew how to accommodate the desires of the board and to negotiate with the faculty, although their tendencies toward strong leadership often brought them into conflict with a faculty becoming aware of its own power. Butler's role in censuring the faculty at Columbia and Jordan's stance in a similar conflict at Stanford were major inputs to the faculty's forming the American Association of University Professors. The strong presidents were innovators who converted small colleges into great universities by building new types of programs. Many of them had a vision of what they wanted their institutions to be and were able to remain in office long enough to see their ideas become reality. Eliot served forty years at Harvard. Even when their vision differed from that of their predecessor, as when Eliot's successor, Lowell, wanted to emphasize undergraduate education at Harvard, they were able to merge their ideas without jeopardizing institutional status. But part of that is a result of what the universities had become—institutions with "a unique capacity for riding off in all directions and still staying in the same place," absorbing new ideas into what had become massive corporate bodies (Kerr, 1963, p. 17).

Administration

The era saw the rise of administrative bureaucracies. Just as large business enterprises were emphasizing functional organization and efficiency, the universities were incorporating such practices. Authority was centered in the office of the president, deans were appointed to preside over schools, the academic departments had chairmen responsible for interpreting institutional policies, practices of faculty rank came to the fore, and an administrative bureaucracy filled with registrars, administrative officers, physical plant managers, alumni relations directors, and the like was spawned. In all but the smallest colleges the vision of faculty and students meeting with the president to discuss academic affairs fell into the realm of nostalgia.

Student affairs developed as a separate category. The position of dean of women dates from the founding of the University of Chicago in 1892; by 1903 an association of deans of women had been formed. Most institutions began adding deans of men in the first quarter of the twentieth century; in 1919 that group met to form an association. In 1934 the Council of Guidance and Personnel Associations was on the scene, and later in the decade a book, *The Student Personnel Point of View*, was published (American Council on Education, 1937). Harvard's dean of students, appointed in 1890, and the subsequent deans of women and men now saw their work codified so that battalions of counselors, guidance personnel, admissions officers, alumni relations officials, and student-management personnel became part of the bureaucracy.

The faculty resisted becoming quite so bureaucratized; even so, the academic department was established as the locus of power. Early in the history of the research university the autocratic department head, modeled on the German system, was seen in some institutions, but that type of governance was short-lived. Academic departments became more democratic, with rotating chairs, equal voting rights, and equal voices for the members. Early in the century the departments gained control of appointments so that except in the smallest institutions, although the trustees retained the final say, new instructors were employed on the recommendation of the department. The departments developed their own curriculum and examinations and controlled the academic requirements for students who would gain a degree in their specialty. But organized faculty control did not become influential in the general pattern of university development. The faculty tended to stay within their own departments, and the departments were so competitive with each other for a share of institutional resources that general institutional direction continued to be set by the president and the trustees.

With the establishment of academic senates, the faculty did gain some measure of influence over university management. Several of the state universities provided for the formation of an academic senate when they were established. But these senates never took power to the extent that the administration developed. Most important decisions continued to be made by governing boards which, in the early years, may have micromanaged to the extent of revising curriculum. The formal agreements between faculty organizations and the trustees typically limited senate powers to determining conditions for awarding certificates and degrees, adding or deleting courses, and appointing professors. In all other areas, the faculty senate had at most an advisory role, which effectually circumscribed its influence on educational policy and budget issues.

Influences

It is difficult to divorce governance from influences. Governance usually refers to the formal structure by means of which policies are developed and decisions made. But influence may come from many less-formal sources. Private grants made to an institution for specific projects or programs have an effect on institutional emphases. For example, a donor who provides funds to construct a laboratory for scientific research has a different effect on an institution from one who endows a theater or symphony hall. States can provide funds in greater or lesser amounts for different programs or different categories of students. State funds based on enrollment can lead to colleges' recruiting as many students as they can handle without increasing costs.

A major influence on institutional conduct came as accrediting associations began establishing standards for library holdings, classroom and laboratory size, programs, degrees, and numerous facets of institutional functioning. Regional associations made up of representatives from the colleges in an area were formed; the Northeast Association of Colleges and Secondary Schools dates from 1885. By 1909 the North Central Association had adopted explicit standards for the institutions in its region, and by 1924 associations were functioning in the other regions. Institutional accrediting spread largely because the plethora of academic degrees was confusing institutions to which students might transfer to do graduate work. What was a bachelor of philosophy? Did a bachelor of arts from one college suggest preparation similar to a bachelor of arts from a different institution? Institutional accreditation dated from the turn of the century, formed especially so that other institutions or outside agencies could estimate the value of a degree. The North Central Association published a list of accredited institutions in 1913, the Southern Association in 1921. The Association of American Universities maintained a list. The U.S. Bureau of Education attempted to produce its own list of accredited institutions but withdrew from the process in 1911 because of reaction against what the institutions perceived as government interference.

Other types of accreditation were conducted by the specialized cadres that grew out of academic disciplinary associations and professional groups. They worked continually to establish standards for curriculum and for entrance and graduation requirements, as well as to persuade states that graduation from an accredited program should be a prerequisite for licensure in an occupation. The entire process is an example of how higher education attempted to regulate itself at a time of immense growth before an outside governmental force could be introduced—the type of regulation that most institutional leaders feared.

The students in American institutions never developed the type of political power enjoyed by their counterparts in Europe and Latin America. Most institutions developed some form of student government, but only rarely did it grow past the stage of responsibility for extracurricular activities. Students gained another type of power through the elective system, as they could choose which programs to enter and which faculty members' courses to enroll in, and thus have an effect on curricular directions and staff appointments.

The nature of institutions allowed for entrepreneurship. Program heads, whether faculty members or administrators, might see opportunity for new types of service. If they were resourceful, willing to work hard on their own time, able to enlist allies within or outside their college, and successful in finding funding, they could influence institutional functioning. No program developed on its own. External mandates were few. The changes in areas of service typically came as a result of staff members whose vision drove them to modify practices.

A less direct influence on institutional functioning was exercised by the associations formed by faculty members, notably the AAUP, and by the various types of administrators who developed interinstitutional groups, from associations of university presidents to affiliations of registrars, business officers, and numerous others. By sharing ideas across institutions the members brought home ways of organizing their affairs. Standards for curriculum and graduation were promulgated by the members of academic associations. All these affected institutional development as though sets of national norms had been legislated.

Overall, though, the states fostered institutional development, some vigorously, others laggingly. They were influential in the development of publicly supported junior colleges, as legislatures controlled public school districts' spending funds on post-high school programs. State boards of education that set requirements for teacher certification effectually managed the teachers colleges. State funds built the campuses and supported the programs. The major influence of the federal government was yet to come.

Out of all these direct and indirect forces grew a system of higher education held together considerably more by voluntary agreements, imitation, internal competition, and generalized rules of conduct than by legislation. A superficial view of the system perceives competition, waste, inefficiency, duplication, misdirection, a lack of economy. But the system's power lay in its variety of institutions and the way they competed with each other to serve the public. Its fluidity of form allowed for experimentation with different types of curriculum, academic calendars, and management in all areas of institutional functioning.

Finance

Who was supposed to pay the bills? During the Emergent Nation Era, Brown's President Wayland commented that since the colleges were not self-supporting they had two choices: either they could give people a product that they needed and were willing to pay for, or they could throw themselves on the mercy of the broader society and beg for funds like any charitable organization. His either-or argument was hyperbole, so stated because of his desire to see the colleges build curriculum suited to a broader population. As higher education developed it did broaden its curriculum, but it never had to choose between tuition and charitable fundraising; it drew from both sources and from public funds as well.

Philanthropy

Philanthropy was essential in the formation or conversion of private universities. Each president solicited donations continually. Here, higher education's roots in the church paid off, as institutional fundraisers contended that the colleges elevated society, contributed to the development of high culture, and were noble enterprises. They said also that worthy students from less-wealthy families should not be barred and that students from wealthy families should attend because the country benefited when poor and rich people alike became enlightened. They argued both for unrestricted funds and for funds for special purposes such as buildings, scholarships, and book collections.

Private donations, always an important source of revenue, accelerated rapidly, so that by the 1890s some single institutions were receiving $1 million or more. After the turn of the twentieth century, even before the tax laws changed, many of the large private donors organized philanthropic foundations as conduits for their funds. As income and inheritance taxes grew, foundations became even more prominent.

The donors' interests and the needs of the institution had to be carefully balanced. A few of the institutions that had access to sizable funds were in the fortunate position of being able to support all types of activities. Ezra Cornell's $500,000 donation was huge in 1869, but it was soon eclipsed by Vanderbilt's $1 million, Johns Hopkins's $3.5 million, the Stanford estate's $20 million, and Rockefeller's $30 million to the University of Chicago. Duke, Clark, Carnegie, and Mellon, either personally or through testaments or foundations, also contributed substantially to the institutions that bear their names. But at most of the colleges, funds came in smaller increments, and donations might be made for distinct purposes such as scholarships for students, certain extracurricular activities, and books or funds for the library. Money for a gymnasium or classroom building with the donor's name prominently displayed at the entrance was usually welcomed; few colleges in the nation did not have such a building on campus.

At first the support was solicited solely through personal contacts made by the president or a member of the board of trustees, but after the turn of the century fundraising became organized. The more prominent universities set up the most sophisticated solicitation systems, seeking funds from businessmen and industrialists and developing networks of alumni to whom they directed regular appeals. As the numbers of alumni grew larger, the funds they contributed grew as well. These organized campaigns rapidly replaced the occasional, individual appeals, but a wealthy potential benefactor could still be assured of a personal visit from the president.

The systematic fundraising efforts proved salutary as institutions became less dependent on single fortunes and as philanthropic foundations became prominent. The universities were spreading out their sources of funds; they were particularly vigorous in soliciting money from agencies that had been formed for the purpose of distributing tax-sheltered fortunes. The foundations often concentrated their giving for special purposes such as the education of black students or research in the health fields. But whether the money came from a private donor or a foundation, the college's development organizations had continually to convince donors to support the university's general fund. Costs were increasing as professional schools sought their own buildings, faculty petitioned for salary increases, students needed scholarships, and library and laboratory construction was necessary. Donations earmarked for particular purposes have always been a problem for institutions because they force adherence to special requests, thus exerting a measure of control outside regular governance channels. Institutional expansion was so rapid that some institutions went into debt to expand their facilities and thus had to seek additional donations continually merely to maintain the debt service.

A few of the philanthropic foundations sought to raise institutional functioning across the board. Instead of, or usually in addition to, earmarking contributions for particular purposes, they promised to give money to institutions that met certain standards. Operating with Rockefeller money, the General Education Board was especially generous to colleges for Negroes and offered funds for permanent endowment on a matching basis to institutions deemed fiscally and educationally sound. By way of strengthening an entire sector, The Carnegie Foundation funded a nationwide review of medical education that culminated in the famous Flexner Report (1910), a document that revolutionized the training of physicians. However, for the smaller colleges, fundraising remained local, with institutions more likely to find money from among their alumni and charitable people in their own communities.

The prosperous decade of the 1920s enhanced the gifts from foundations and private donors. The total of $65 million donated in 1920 more than doubled to $148 million by 1930. Three-fourths of the 1920 funds were given for institutional endowment, but this ratio dropped to less than half by the end of the decade as more money went into buildings. The General Education Board had stimulated giving for endowment as it publicized a desirable standard of around $250 per student. However, even though the board offered matching money to all of higher education, few institutions could meet the $250 standard. The rich got richer as Chicago, Columbia, Harvard, and Yale gained the lion's share of the funds.

Endowments and Appropriations

The spread in income between the prominent institutions and the rank and file of colleges grew wider around the turn of the century. Not only did Stanford and Chicago start with more money than most of the colleges had ever dreamed of, the older institutions that had successfully converted themselves into universities grew wealthy as well. Harvard, Columbia, Yale, and Princeton had access to well-developed networks of alumni and were skilled at obtaining funds from them. They also built research entities that attracted funds from the foundations. The national wealth was growing at a rapid rate, hence the research universities could ride an expanding economy and grow just as other industries grew, receiving a disproportionate share of the funds. Their physical plants and the size of their libraries expanded, far exceeding the growth of the student body. As for the rest of the nation's colleges, most remained "still fairly small, even marginal operations, with annual incomes of less than $50,000" (Geiger, 1986b, p. 40).

The leading public universities developed in parallel fashion. State legislatures began committing funds on a regular basis and, because the country was prosperous and the tax base was expanding, were able to support the rapidly growing enrollments. A building boom, especially of laboratories and libraries, took place at most state universities early in the century. The states also helped support academic research, even if indirectly, as they funded buildings that although not specifically earmarked could be used for research, and also the salaries of faculty members who included research among their responsibilities. Overall, in most states the notion that universities were permanent responsibilities was prevalent, and funds were appropriated in a fashion similar to the way other state agencies were supported. West of the Mississippi, where public institutions dominated, the states provided nearly half of all higher education funds from the 1920s to 1940s.

Income per student varied widely across types of institutions. The private research universities received more than the liberal arts colleges; the state universities, some becoming major flagship institutions, received more than the lesser-known public colleges. Funding varied among states, which was often a reflection of their relative wealth. Accordingly, it is difficult to draw interinstitutional comparisons except among similar types. For the major private research universities, income at the turn of the century was around $150 to $300 per student; for the major state universities, $70 to $200 per student. The ratio changed somewhat toward the end of the era when the gap between the lower end of the public and private universities was reduced and that at the higher end widened. In 1937 the major state research universities were receiving $350 to $450 per student and the private institutions $500 to $1,400 (Geiger, 1986b, pp. 273–275).

The major private institutions were able to build sizable endowments as their professionally directed fundraising campaigns brought income greater than their annual expenditures. Harvard's endowment reached $20 million by the end of Eliot's presidency in 1909. A few fortunate institutions, such as Johns Hopkins and Stanford, that had been endowed with sizable funds from the outset were receiving more than 70 percent of their current expenditure funds from endowments. Several of the others had expenditures totaling about half from endowment income and half from tuition. The discrepancy between per-student charges at public and private universities was not as great early in the century as it would become later. The private institutions "charged from $100 to $160 per year, while state universities typically charged $30 to $40" (Geiger, 1986b, p. 41). The ratio of state funds added to tuition in the public institutions and endowment income added to tuition in the private institutions was approximately equal.

The proportion of receipts for endowment declined primarily because funds earmarked for physical capital and current expenditures increased. The 1920s saw a building boom across the landscape of higher education, both public and private. Fundraising and the extracurriculum went hand in hand, as laypeople and alumni alike took pride in their institutions. Success on the athletic field brought sizable sums. Whether built through donations or funded through deficit financing, the giant football stadiums still in use at California, Illinois, Michigan, Minnesota, Wisconsin, and Yale were built in the 1920s. Some of the donations spilled over into buildings with other uses. Auditoriums, art museums, student union buildings, and residence halls dotted the campuses. Overall, though, and in spite of the largesse of the foundations, the institutions depended most on their alumni. Wealthy graduates gave sizable sums, the rank and file smaller gifts, but all were courted, especially those who would donate funds with no strings attached that could be used for general institutional purposes.

Financing suffered during the Great Depression. State appropriations were considerably lower in the early 1930s than they had been in the 1920s. Foundation grants declined from $52 million in 1930 to $40 million in 1940. Capital spending almost disappeared entirely and across-the-board cuts became the norm. Faculty salaries declined by around 15 percent from 1931 to 1933. Between 1930 and 1940, instructional costs per full-time equivalent faculty member declined by more than 10 percent at public institutions. Alumni giving declined and endowment income fell at the private universities, as dividend cuts and lower interest rates affected the amount that they could garner from their endowments. However, higher education overall suffered less in the 1930s than did many other social institutions because the facilities it had built when funds were readily available in the 1920s were still in place, and its labor-intensive character meant that teaching assistants and post-doctoral fellows could be employed for very little money to replace higher-cost professors. Some colleges tried to force the retirement of older professors, whereas others declined to promote instructors and lecturers to professorial positions and were thus able to accommodate increased enrollments with only slight increases in instructional costs.

The federal government, by now an important contributor of funds, took up some of the slack in institutional income. The Smith-Lever Act of 1914, which authorized funding for agriculture and home economics programs, and the Smith-Hughes Act of 1917, designed to provide money to higher education to train vocational education teachers, continued to be sources of income. In the 1930s, the Public Works Administration helped to construct residence halls, and the National Youth Administration funded part-time jobs for students. Funds authorized under the Morrill Act of 1890 were used to support land-grant institutions. Various federal agencies supported scientific research. Overall, the growth rate of federal funding between 1930 and 1940 was 6.6 percent—lower than it had been in prior decades but still greater than that of any other source of institutional income. When World War II began in the 1940s, federal funding of university-based scientific research accelerated dramatically. Questions of federal interference with institutional autonomy and of the extent to which geographic considerations should play a part in federal appropriations were set aside, as research and personnel training for the war effort dominated the scene.

In summation, college patterns of finding funds from multiple sources continued. Private philanthropy accelerated as wealth concentrated and foundations were formed. The institutions that had benefited from industrialists' largesse early in the era remained most successful in their fundraising efforts and expanded their endowments. State support varied depending on the economy. Federal funding expanded beyond the Morrill Act donations to include support for particular purposes. Higher education's leaders were learning to be ever more nimble and creative in their pursuit of an essential commodity.

Outcomes

Higher education's outcomes were varied. Some were continuations of effects that could be discerned in earlier eras; some were new, as the institutions expanded more deeply into different areas.

Community pride represented a continuing effect. Towns vied with each other to become the site of a new institution. Land developers donated property to colleges that would build in the center of their tracts, assuming that the worth of the surrounding property would increase. Colleges served as secure enclaves. Their campuses were well maintained, their buildings attractive beacons. They offered lectures, concerts, recitals, and sporting events to which the public was invited. Few people living in a community that included a college felt they were in a backwater.

Contributions to a war effort were a new outcome. Many institutions served as military training centers in both world wars. They maintained officer training programs both for recruits and for servicemen upgrading from enlisted to officer ranks. Under government contract, they developed weaponry and processes enhancing the nation's military capabilities. The role of the universities in the two world wars can be contrasted with that of higher education during the Civil War, when a college would have been the last place a military procurement official would have looked for training soldiers or for weapons.

Research in the natural sciences grew rapidly. The difference in support between it and research in the humanities and social sciences was evident early on. Donations for the humanities typically came in the form of individual support for libraries and perhaps an endowed professorship or campus-based museum, whereas the natural sciences had more ready access to foundation funds. Much university-based research in the sciences was led by the medical schools, which were converting to scientific research institutes in their own right as the old form of medical education through apprenticeship fell into disrepute. Scientific research led also to patentable industrial processes.

Research in agriculture took longer to develop. The early agricultural and mechanical colleges were slow to organize their research effort. Many of them assigned the teaching of agriculture or science to professors of divinity or classical languages, whose own fields were dying out but for whom work had to be found. That generation had to pass through before research in agriculture could gain a firm footing. The institutions were not surfeited with students of agriculture either, as farmers were slow to understand that colleges had anything useful to teach their sons. Engineering students outnumbered students of agriculture in the agricultural and mechanical (A&M) institutions until the second decade of the twentieth century. Congress noted the slow development of agricultural research and passed the Hatch Act in 1887, funding federal experiment stations to assist the agricultural colleges in establishing agricultural research. Further federal intervention through the Smith-Lever Act in 1914 established an agricultural extension system—something that the colleges should have been doing earlier. Those two additions to the land-grant colleges came one-quarter century and one-half century after the institutions were authorized. Gradually, their assistance in increasing crop yields and in understanding animal husbandry proved notable in enhancing agricultural productivity.

Preparing individuals for service in the professions and adding to the professionalization of numerous occupational groups accelerated. The older professions of law, medicine, and theology, and the profession of engineering that had come into the institutions in the first quarter of the nineteenth century, all continued to develop with the help of higher education. Many other learned professions were newly professionalized, in part by requiring more years of schooling for people aspiring to their ranks and in gaining prestige in the eyes of the public by having graduate schools especially designed to prepare their practitioners. The national associations that the professions formed all had connections with the schools that were training their people. The professional schools were attentive to state licensure boards, and the licensing process itself often tied the award to graduation from the school. By the end of the nineteenth century one-third of the states were requiring degrees from accredited medical schools before a physician would be allowed to practice. And entrance to various medical subspecialties was coming through the colleges as pharmacists, nurses, laboratory technicians and, eventually, medical secretaries all became specialties within higher education.

Higher education was prominent also in assisting other professions to gain status. Bledstein (1976) has traced the culture of professionalism, showing how the various groups began insisting that their practitioners receive theoretical training that included a degree from a recognized institution. Economists, librarians, dentists, psychologists, and at least one hundred other groups all began insisting that before entering practice or apprenticeships, people aspiring to the field gain scholarly knowledge of it. Even public administration became professionalized, as college graduates began entering the service sector. Higher education became a social necessity for upwardly striving individuals, and the bridge between college and the professions grew at the same time that the new occupational groupings were taking on professional garb.

The training of professionals and the concomitant professionalization of numerous groups was undoubtedly a major outcome. The universities seized eagerly on this function. Here was the avenue to claiming service to society because the nation needed people trained to staff its clinics, pulpits, classrooms, and laboratories. The training of professionals also accorded with institutional drive toward scientific specialization because the preparation of practitioners rested on their learning the scientific principles under-girding their specialties. It helped higher education break away from the churches, thus contributing to the system's secularization. It assisted in sustaining the ties of loyal alumni because practitioners could be enlisted as clinical professors. Earlier assumptions that lib-erally educated people could acquire professional skill on the job weakened as separate curricula were developed for various profes-sional subdivisions, technologists, and support staff. Higher educa-tion became essential for professional practice, and the professions depended on it.

The college role in assisting students to enter society acceler-ated during the University Transformation Era. As greater percent-ages of young people began attending college the institutions channeled them into specific occupations, allocating them to posi-tions that they would not otherwise have gained. At the same time it held numbers of young people off the labor market, thus support-ing the child labor laws that were becoming increasingly stringent. The degrees came to carry special meaning: the bachelor's in engi-neering included channels for civil, mechanical, electrical, chemi-cal, metallurgical, and so on through the range of specialties within the profession. Toward the end of the era the junior colleges were preparing young people for specialized trades and for positions as support staff for the professions. The system was serving the nation through preparing a trained workforce. It was also contributing indi-rectly to cultural change that venerated the individual above the group.

The old liberal arts emphasis was not abandoned; the profes-sional and occupational curricula grew alongside it. Just as the colleges certified competence in the practice of a profession, they conferred status on the graduates of their liberal arts programs. Schooling was tantamount with education. As they always had, the colleges taught manners, cultural awareness, humanitarian impulses. The students gained literacy, awareness of societal con-cerns, the stamp of having attended. Young people learned the art of maintaining a household—skills taught formerly by parents or grandparents. The specialized programs in graduate and professional schools taught the skills and rituals associated with specific callings. Mental and moral discipline remained high on the list of outcomes. Artistic and literary standards were fostered along with the shaping of character. The well-rounded person able to function in various social settings, that is, the individual who could tolerate ambiguity and remain flexible, was identified in studies conducted by educators, psychologists, and sociologists from the 1920s onward. The liberal arts and general education programs did not abandon their mission.

College as an economic generator in its own right came to the fore. As enrollments and budgets increased and philanthropy and state appropriations grew, each institution became a fiscal engine. Funds coming into the colleges from state capitals and from distant donors were spent in local communities. The staff paid rent or bought homes; the college bought materials and services. Although such effects can be traced to the presence of any institution that attracts funds from outside the community, the colleges were distinctive because they brought not only money but also people who might command higher wages.

Critiques and Commentaries

Higher education attracted some pointed criticism during the era. The earlier colleges had been narrowly based, touching the lives of only a minuscule portion of the population, but as institutions became more prominent they came in for their share of disapprobation. The criticisms ran from the way the colleges were organized and functioning to the goals they held and their role in what was termed corporate America. The colleges were accused of having lost their soul because they provided too many curricular options. Businessmen on the boards of trustees were distant from the institutions' missions. Trustees and administrators were managing instead of the faculty. There was too much emphasis on occupations, too little on the liberal arts. Masses of young people were enrolled, but only a few were fit for the higher learning. The colleges had shifted from pure research to applied research. Through their developing weaponry they were parties to mass destruction. Instead of assisting in building an equitable society, they enhanced the reproduction of the preexisting social structure. Colleges were unwilling to take risks; accreditation standards made them all alike. The faculty were so concerned with their own professional growth that they lost touch with the young, turning them over instead to student personnel workers. The list of accusations was long and some of the diatribes were vicious. Higher education must have been important to attract as much attention as it did.

Thorstein Veblen ([1918] 1957), an especially vituperative critic, contended that scholarship should be primary, that the teaching function belonged in the university only to the extent it facilitated inquiry by professors and equipped students for the process of inquiry. Learning was a matter of personal contact between teacher and student. Technical and professional schools should not be associated with universities because the interests of the university professors and those in the trade schools did not sufficiently overlap. A university should not have an undergraduate school either but should concentrate on research for its own sake. Boards of trustees were unneeded; the faculty should be in charge. As long as business principles guided the management of higher learning, the future of science and scholarship was threatened. Vocational training was anathema; it grew out of the elective system and open admissions, allowing all students to come in and giving them a voice in shaping the curriculum, whereupon they began to select courses that would train them for personal success. All types of business principles and training for commerce tended to defeat the primary purpose of a university: the independent pursuit of knowledge. And, in particular, businessmen should not be allowed a voice in institutional management.

Veblen's concerns were followed a few years later by Upton Sinclair's scathing critique (1923). Sinclair's contention was that the
universities were not furthering the welfare of mankind but merely
were keeping the capitalistic system with all its evils at the forefront
of national thinking. Universities had boards of trustees made up of
corporation lawyers, bankers, real estate owners, and merchants who
were also directors of large-scale corporations. University presidents
were in the business of cultivating the rich and the powerful, running back and forth between business and learning, moderating the
clash between greed and service. Presidents and trustees alike were
inimical to a free faculty and a student body engaged in learning.
The students were homogeneous not only in terms of ideas but also
in religious and ethnic composition. The prejudice against Jews and
Negroes was symptomatic of the snobbery of college life. The
alumni were more concerned with the success of the athletic teams
than with the academic programs. Philanthropic foundations were
part of the conspiracy, demanding institutional conformity before
they would release funds. Nothing would do except that the faculty
would unionize and the students would work for change in their
institutions and in society. Freedom for both was tied up with the
rise of the working class.

Robert Hutchins, president of the University of Chicago, in
1936 published an argument in favor of a return to the first principles on which higher education was founded. Job preparation and
vocationalism as well as professional schools and business interests
should be sloughed off. Rather than contributing to the academic
life of the institution, the professional schools enhanced disintegration of the enterprise. Young people should be kept out of the
university, at least until they had concluded their sophomore year
at another type of college, obtaining a liberal education when they
were aged sixteen to twenty. That education should cultivate the
intellectual virtues, useful for any of life's endeavors, from contem-
plation to action. Applied research should be conducted in insti-

tutes that might be attached to the universities but not part of them. Similarly, the professions should center in technical institutes. Students should not be admitted to either without having completed an education in the classics of Western civilization and the liberal arts including grammar, rhetoric, logic, and arithmetic. Only then would they be qualified to enter upon university studies that themselves centered on metaphysics, the social sciences, and the natural sciences. Such studies would be undertaken with no specific vocation in mind.

Other critics took completely contrary views. Ortega y Gasset (1944) pointed out that scientific inquiries should not be confounded with training for the professions because the conduct of inquiry is separate from professional practice. The institution's prime concern should be the training of future professionals by emphasizing first principles and the transmission of the higher culture. Flexner, whose 1910 report on the status of medical education in the United States had exposed conditions that stimulated reforms revolutionizing the preparation of physicians, commented twenty years later on American universities, contrasting them with those in Europe. His position (Flexner, 1930) was that regardless of locale, higher education should be concerned with the conservation and interpretation of knowledge and ideas and with the search for truth and the training of students to think as scholars and scientists. The universities were only one of many educational structures; accordingly, they should not try to do everything but should allow other agencies to do what they could do well.

The criticisms are instructive because they reflect the magnitude of change in higher education and the speed with which it occurred. But the critics had little effect. At most they caused a stir among a few students, faculty, and administrators; board members were probably less likely cognizant of their ideas. Overall, the critics seemed unable to accept what higher education was becoming. They could not find a place for research universities, agricultural schools, junior colleges, professional schools, and the numerous other permutations, sometimes all under the umbrella of a single institution. The explosion in enrollments, purposes, professional training, and involvements with the broader society was more than they could reconcile. It was much easier to postulate an institution with singular motive, concentrating only on pure research, the transmission of the culture, professional training, the application of knowledge to social problems—*any* of these, but certainly not all of them together.

4

Mass Higher Education in the Era of American Hegemony: 1945–1975

The thirty years of the Mass Higher Education Era were higher education's golden age. Enrollments, finances, institutions— all aspects of the system expanded. The earlier eras had set the stage for this growth; now it happened as new campuses were opened, new types of students began attending, and new curricula were introduced. The trends in all the areas accelerated.

Societal Context

Table 4.1 shows a statistical picture of the conditions surrounding American higher education in the Mass Higher Education Era.

The context for this expansion was a country that had come out of World War II as the most powerful nation on earth. Its population continued expanding, and its economy, released from the depressing grip of the 1930s, enjoyed a rate of growth that had been seen previously only during occasional periods of prosperity. Although 400,000 American servicemen were killed during the war and more than $300 billion was spent prosecuting it, the United States' suffering was light compared with that of a devastated Europe.

Several trends pervaded the era. One was the search for security in a world made unstable by collapsing colonial regimes; the rise of the Soviet Union as a military power; the increase in nationalist

Table 4.1. Statistical Portrait of the Mass Higher Education Era, 1945–1975.

	1945	1975
United States population	139,924,000	215,465,000
Number of students enrolled in higher education	1,677,000	11,185,000
Number of faculty	150,000	628,000
Number of institutions (excluding branch campuses)	1,768	2,747
Number of earned degrees conferred (bachelor's, master's, and doctoral; also associate for 1975)	157,349	1,665,553
Current-fund revenue (in thousands of current dollars)	1,169,394	39,703,166

Source: National Center for Education Statistics, 1996b; Snyder, 1993.

expectations among ethnic and linguistic groups in Europe, Africa, and the Pacific; and the fearsome new military capabilities, headed by atomic weaponry. A Cold War resulted, with the United States attempting to contain communism wherever in the world it seemed likely to appear.

In the first few years after the war, the United States was sufficiently influential so that the United Nations functioned essentially as its arm. At the insistence of the United States, the General Assembly of the United Nations approved an international force to be sent to defend South Korea when it was invaded by North Korea. By keeping the idea of admitting the People's Republic of China (PRC) to the United Nations off the agenda, the United States was able to delay the PRC's admission until 1971, by which time the original fifty-one member nations had tripled in number. In 1947 President Truman convinced Congress that the United States should assist Greece and Turkey in opposing communism, and by 1950 the United States had sent more than $600 million to those two countries. The Marshall Plan, also developed in 1947, distributed $12 billion in aid to Western European nations. The North Atlantic Treaty Organization, the Organization of American States, and the Southeast Asia Treaty Organization evidenced the American attempt to resist Soviet expansion.

The armaments race that accompanied this policy of containment not only yielded a massive buildup in war material but also spawned research on new weaponry, with a sizable proportion of the funds going to the universities. Old questions about whether the universities should engage in basic, disinterested research or whether they should apply their research capabilities to specific problems went by the board. The universities had started working on war-related research during World War I and by the time of World War II were deeply engaged. Scientists in the academy might have thought it would be a wonderful idea if the federal government granted money to universities for unrestricted research, but that was not the way most of the funds were dispersed. Department of Defense priorities did not extend to general science. The National Defense Research Committee had spent $1.5 billion on radar, much of it at MIT, and the Army Corps of Engineers had spent $2 billion on the atomic bomb, with university-based scientists involved. The Office of Strategic Research and Development coordinated other contracts. The idea that universities could take federal funds to work on special projects had been proved successful.

A postwar population surge contributed to major social changes. In the thirty years after the war, the American population increased by 60 percent, with the highest increases in the earlier years. Restrictive immigration laws reduced the size of the foreign-born population, but American families were larger through the 1950s. This was an era of optimism. Economic conditions were considerably better than they had been in the 1930s. The federal government was subsidizing interest rates for housing through loans guaranteed by the Veterans Administration and the Federal Housing Administration. Housing expanded into the suburbs as more Americans were owning homes than renting them. In 1950,

3.5 million babies were born—an increase of 1 million over the number born just ten years earlier. This baby boom created a rising demand for dishwashers, freezers, clothes dryers, and garbage disposals—appliances that were luxuries in an earlier era but now available on easy credit. Business boomed as taxes were cut and wartime price controls were removed. Inflation grew but was partially contained by productivity that expanded at an average rate of 2.8 percent per year throughout the era. Economic expansion led to disposable income and to a delay in the time when young people had to enter the workforce, both contributing to the massive increases in college enrollments.

The nature of work and the relationship of workers to the broader American society shifted. Heavy industry declined as a percentage of the whole. For example, in 1947, 85 percent of the nation's products contained some form of steel made in the United States, and 40 percent of the labor force depended either directly or indirectly on the steel industry. Steel production grew by around 40 percent during the era, but this was nothing in comparison to overall worldwide production, which expanded by 400 percent. Other heavy industries such as automobile production declined also, as foreign nations built more efficient industries resting at least initially on a lower-paid labor force. American corporations began moving plants overseas in search of cheap labor. By the mid-1970s only about 33 percent of the American labor force was producing goods—down from more than 40 percent in the prewar era. The service sector had increased from less than 60 percent to more than 67 percent. The fastest-growing occupations were professional and technical workers, increasing from about 30 percent of the labor force in 1940 to 50 percent by the end of the era.

The shift in industrial production and in labor force competition took place gradually. For the first generation after the war, the pent-up demand for goods was so high that American industry was able to coast on its previous strengths. Much of the manufacturing capability had been built prior to World War I, based on technologies that were already established. The inventions and industrial processes of the late nineteenth century spawned steel, automobile, and agricultural production capabilities. In agriculture alone, mechanization was so effective that whereas at the turn of the century half the labor force was working on the land, the number had dropped to fewer than one-third by 1945, and by the 1960s to fewer than one-tenth. But although these shifts seem rapid in retrospect, at the time the nation was undergoing them they were disruptive. The heavy industries enjoyed a sizable domestic market, hence were slow to adopt new technologies, means of production, or relationships with their labor force. Workers who were pushed out of agriculture were able to make the transition to assembly-line jobs, but as these shrank in favor of professional and technical positions, many tended to be left behind for lack of skills.

The pattern of labor relations in the postwar era reflects some of these changes. The labor unions, whose power centered in the heavy industries, tried to hold on to the gains they had made during the prior half-century. By nature conservative, they were slow to adapt to the changing conditions of work. A backlash against the unions took form in 1947 with the passage of the Taft-Hartley Act. The act legalized so-called right-to-work laws passed by states in which requiring union membership as a condition of employment could be prohibited. Labor's response was to merge the American Federation of Labor with the Congress of Industrial Organizations as a way of consolidating the former craft-based and industrial-based groups. By the late 1950s, nearly 40 percent of the private sector workforce was covered by union contracts.

The unions changed direction in other ways as well. They became more politically sensitive, attempting to influence elections at every level. They also began organizing white-collar workers and government employees. The American Federation of Teachers and the American Federation of State, County, and Municipal Employees made great gains in membership and political power, as in one state after another legislation was passed allowing public employees to form bargaining units. Sanitation workers, firefighters, prison guards, public school teachers, and eventually postsecondary faculty all took advantage of the opportunity.

Concern about the environment grew steadily. In the decade from 1965 to 1975, "Congress enacted some twenty new major regulatory laws, governing clean air, clean water, toxic waste, occupational safety and health, highway safety, consumer-product safety . . . and creating an elaborate new regime for assessing environmental impacts" (Kuttner, 1997, p. 232). The Occupational Safety and Health Administration was formed in 1970. The Motor Vehicle Safety Act in 1966 and the 1975 Energy Policy Conservation Act affected automobile safety and fuel efficiency. The Clean Air Act of 1970 required the Environmental Protection Agency to reduce pollution. Taking a broad view, all of these were an extension of the federal government's concern with the quality of life—concern that extended back to the Pure Food Act of 1906 but now reached into many more areas of life, from mandating warning labels on cigarette packages to providing massive sums for medical research.

Periodically, the United States goes through eras of witch hunting, superpatriotism, and repression of free speech. Such times are similar to religious revivalism; they occur when the nation is undergoing rapid change or when people perceive threats to mainstream ideas—most typically when they do not understand what is happening, when their formerly secure foundations seem shaken. The early 1950s were such a time. The United States had emerged from World War II as the dominant power, but it was challenged almost immediately by the Soviet Union. The Soviets exploded their atomic bomb in 1949, thus demonstrating that the United States did not have an exclusive right to that fearsome weapon. In 1950 North Korea's invasion of South Korea was perceived to be a communist move toward world domination. Coupled with communist-led rebellions in Eastern and southern Europe and threats of governmental destabilization in Latin America and Southeast Asia, it seemed as though the United States was under attack. Threats of a worldwide trend toward establishing communist governments under the leadership of the Soviets were voiced repeatedly.

This unease both arose from and fed the xenophobia that had arisen from time to time since the late eighteenth century, when the freedom-of-speech-limiting Alien and Sedition Acts were passed. Examples were the nativism of the mid–nineteenth century, which attempted to keep immigrants out of public office; the periodic, localized strength of the Ku Klux Klan from the 1860s onward; and the subversive-chasing activities of the justice department in the Harding administration. These tendencies coalesced with full force in the early 1950s, as Wisconsin's Senator Joseph McCarthy led a campaign to rid the nation of communists. The Communist Party in the United States was never very influential, but it served as a symbol of disloyalty at a time when the super patriots wanted everyone to swear allegiance to the flag. People were measured by the extent to which they proclaimed their patriotism. Candidates for minor public offices tried to show how they were more loyal than their opponents.

Even before Senator McCarthy became the figurehead for the anticommunist crusade, the Congress and state department had laid the groundwork for loyalty investigations. In 1947 President Truman ordered an investigation of all federal employees to determine if they had been associated with any of the ninety organizations considered disloyal. Within four years more than three million records had been examined and around three thousand civil servants had resigned. The House Un-American Activities Committee held hearings considering the political associations of people in any area that they considered influential in affecting the course of American thought. The Hollywood investigations led to the studio heads' forming a blacklist of people who refused to testify and were thereby deprived of their right to work in the film industry. Congress also passed the McCarran Internal Security Act over the president's veto in 1950 and two years later passed the McCarran-Walter Immigration Act, again over the president's veto. Under the first act, individuals could be arrested if there was any suspicion that they might be considering an act of espionage or sabotage; under the second, subversives were to be screened out from among potential immigrants and deported, even after becoming naturalized citizens. President Truman characterized the measures as dangerous to the Bill of Rights, but Congress was reflecting the mood of the nation; most people favored making it a crime to join the Communist Party. Capitalizing on this national mood, Senator McCarthy continued making accusations, even implicating America's heroes Generals Marshall and Eisenhower in a plot to destroy the nation by furthering the cause of world communism. By 1954 the Senate had had enough and censured him for conduct unbecoming a member.

A different type of federal intervention gave rise to a major change in the way Americans viewed college, hence an eventual shift in the proportion of people attending. The Servicemen's Readjustment Act of 1944 ushered in the Mass Higher Education Era. The GI Bill, as it was called, was passed by a Congress fearful of mass unemployment when millions of servicemen were demobilized. The bill provided several veterans' benefits: a year of unemployment insurance; medical care; counseling services; and tuition, books, and living expenses while attending any educational program. Each veteran was entitled to one year of schooling as a full-time student plus an additional month for each month served in the armed forces. A veteran with two years of active duty could complete a four-year college program at governmental expense because the three years of credit translated into four nine-month academic years. Nearly half of the fifteen million veterans participated; 29 percent went to college, the others to precollegiate and on-the-job programs (Committee on Veterans Affairs, 1973). Higher education enrollment doubled its prewar level, as over two million veterans attended in the six years following the war. Because the Veterans Administration paid the out-of-state tuition rate, the state universities received a sizable windfall. Most important, the belief that everyone could go to college became firmly established in the minds of the American people; college was no longer reserved for an elite few.

Equal Opportunity

A social change of similarly long-lasting effect accelerated in the early 1950s. In the 1890s, various Supreme Court rulings had held either that the federal government had no jurisdiction over state laws regarding racial segregation or that equal rights were obtained if separate facilities were equal. During the 1930s and 1940s the National Association for the Advancement of Colored People (NAACP) had been pressing legislators and bringing suits in an attempt to gain equal employment and educational opportunities for black people. Some progress toward desegregation had been made in other areas. For example, President Truman in 1948 issued an executive order calling for racial equality in the armed services, and under his leadership various committees called for equality in other areas. Some gains had been made also in postsecondary education with two Supreme Court rulings in 1950. *Sweatt* v. *Painter* held that separate law schools in Texas were not truly equal because the associations that students make during their school years have an effect on their success. And in *McLaurin* v. *Oklahoma State Regents for Higher Education*, the University of Oklahoma was directed to accord a black doctoral student the same privileges and treatment as all its students. But segregation was still entrenched across the American landscape—de jure in the South, de facto in many institutions in the North.

The breakthrough challenge to the concept of separate but equal came in *Brown* v. *Board of Education* in 1954, when the Supreme Court ruled that separating children solely because of their race generates a feeling of inferiority, therefore separate educational facilities are inherently unequal; the Court extended the ruling to higher education in *Florida ex rel. Hawkins* v. *Board of Control* (1956). Based on the equal protection clause of the Fourteenth Amendment, the rulings overturned the legalities on which segregation had rested, but the problem would not disappear. The Supreme Court did not specify when the schools should be desegregated; it left that issue to the local courts. Desegregation took place rapidly in the border states but most of the old Confederacy resisted. First came overt defiance, as in Little Rock in 1957 when the Arkansas governor blocked black children entering high school by calling out the National Guard. The governor of Virginia ordered the closing of racially integrated schools. When local courts ordered the University of Mississippi and the University of Alabama to admit black students, the governors of those states similarly defied the orders.

In the 1950s, moves were made against segregation in other areas. Civil rights acts were passed, with the intent to guarantee that no one would be barred from voting or from employment because of race. But segregation continued as states, municipalities, and private businesses used various stratagems to sustain the practices they had followed for the century that had passed since emancipation of the slaves. The groups favoring integration and equal opportunity kept up the pressure by staging sit-ins at segregated facilities, boycotting transportation facilities that segregated the races, and returning to the courts frequently. The segregationists countered with open defiance; they realigned school and voting districts and petitioned repeatedly for more time before they had to modify their conduct. The Civil Rights Act of 1964, passed during the first year of President Johnson's administration, brought together the strands of desegregation effort by authorizing federal power to be brought to bear on the right of all people to vote, use public facilities, and gain jobs according to their ability. It also supported colleges and schools in providing in-service training designed to assist staff in dealing with problems caused by school desegregation. Some progress toward equal opportunity was made, but the problem persisted, varying in degree from community to community and region to region.

One of the most notable effects of the drive toward equal opportunity was the federal bureaucracy set in place to enforce it. Hundreds of thousands of jobs were created to administer antipoverty programs, the Voting Rights Act, and the numerous antidiscrimination efforts. President Johnson's Executive Order 11375 specified that beginning in 1968, every federal contract had to state that potential employees would not be discriminated against because of their race, moreover that if contractors seemed to be lagging in employing minority group members, they were to develop plans to rectify the situation. This led to an expansion in the Office of Civil Rights, which began issuing directives and investigating complaints. In turn this affected the colleges, because every institution that did not have a proportionate number of minorities on its staff was considered guilty of noncompliance. All the universities that had been staffing up rapidly to meet the surge in enrollments were guilty of having an oversupply of white employees. Title IX of the Education Amendments of 1972, which prohibited sex bias in any educational program or activity, added women to the group that had to be proportionately represented. The federal government now seemed to be the champion of social justice and the universities to be lagging in their civic responsibilities. As in the efforts to integrate that were being made in other walks of life, one set of observers saw resistance and inadequate progress toward parity, and another saw untoward pressure toward goals that were impossible to attain. Regardless of specific outcome, the categories of gender and ethnicity became firmly entrenched and remained prominent throughout the era and beyond.

The successes won by the NAACP in the courts and legislatures led other self-aware groups to press for similar measures. People with disabilities gained a national voice and legislation demanding equal access to public buildings, along with special facilities in the schools. Women's groups founded the National Organization for Women in 1966, seeking in particular equal pay for equal work and equality in employment and education. Congress passed an equal rights amendment to the Constitution that simply specified, "equality of rights under the law shall not be denied or abridged by any state on account of sex." However, the amendment fell short of ratification by three states of the thirty-eight needed; hence, it did not become law. Title VII of the Civil Rights Act, which banned discrimination in employment, and Title IX of the Education Amendments of 1972, which prohibited sex bias in college admissions, remained the key provisions by which women gained equal protection.

In 1970 a Texas district court ruled that Mexican Americans should be treated as an identifiable minority group, a first step in attaining equality under the law. Groups representing prisoners, mental patients, and homosexuals sought such status but were less successful in attaining it. Even so, there was a shift in social relations as these groups, along with those representing the ethnic, racial, and gender subdivisions, continued petitioning for redress of what they perceived as unequal treatment in employment, educational opportunity, and enforcement of the laws.

A shift in the direction of equal opportunity cases came toward the end of the Mass Higher Education Era. In 1972 the Supreme Court ruled in the case of *Griggs* v. *Duke Power* that requiring a person to complete a certain level of schooling before being considered for employment was unconstitutional if the school level was not relevant to the performance of the job and if the imposition of that requirement effectually discriminated against members of a protected group. Even when there was no discrimination on the basis of race, if it could be shown that whatever requirement was, set up had the effect of tilting the composition of the workforce away from proportional representation, that requirement could be struck down. This ruling, and others that flowed from it, was to have implications for school admissions as well as for employment opportunities. The envelope labeled "disparate impact" had been opened.

Institutions

The drive toward larger public institutions accelerated. The states that had not developed an extensive public sector—those in New England for example—hastened to catch up. In the West and Midwest, where public institutions were already strong, the institutions expanded by building branch campuses, converting specialized colleges to all-purpose institutions, and opening community colleges. More than 600 public institutions were added, 500 of them two-year colleges. In the private sector, 650 new institutions were opened, but half as many closed, for a net gain of 325. The move toward comprehensiveness continued; the conversion of normal schools to state colleges offering a full range of programs and usually the master's degree was completed; and few freestanding teacher education institutions remained by the end of the era. A major shift took place as well in single-sex institutions. The era started with more than 25 percent of the colleges enrolling only men or only women. By 1970 this had dropped to 14 percent as many closed or became coeducational.

The turning point in the ratio of enrollments in public and private higher education came soon after World War II. At the beginning of the 1930s, enrollments had been about equal in both sectors and remained at that level for more than a decade. The early years of the Depression were difficult for the state universities, but by the end of the 1930s the drop in interest rates and in voluntary donations had affected the private institutions more. During the war, inflation continued squeezing the private institutions, but as the war ended, the state colleges had sizable funds at their disposal. By the first decade after the war, expenditures for campus expansion in the public sector were running at least 50 percent higher than at the private institutions. The tuition paid by veterans attending under the GI Bill helped, but as their numbers declined in the early 1950s the private institutions had to increase tuition notably, thereby helping to divert most of the increased enrollment to the public sector.

The trend toward secularization was steady throughout the era. The ratio of public to private institutions changed from 35 to 44 percent of the total; that of enrollments went from 49 to 79 percent. This growth in the public sector was reflected also in degrees awarded. By 1975 the public institutions were awarding 88 percent of the associate degrees, 69 percent of the bachelor's degrees, 66 percent of the master's degrees, 65 percent of the doctorates, and 42 percent of the first professional degrees. They conferred the majority of bachelor's degrees in every field except philosophy and religion. The private sector held on to its lead in the number of master's degrees awarded in business, law, and psychology.

Institutional Types

Research and comprehensive universities expanded along with proprietary and community colleges. Most of the push for higher status as measured by graduate program enrollments, research funds gained, and more selective undergraduate admissions was made in the public sector, where aspiring universities could raise admissions requirements because they were able to divert less-qualified students to community colleges. The availability of state funds made it possible for them to expand their graduate programs, and federal money helped construct laboratories and research facilities. The University of Texas built on substantial revenues from oil lands. The University of Washington expanded its research and graduate effort. The University of California, especially the Berkeley campus, was shaken by a loyalty-oath controversy in the late 1940s, but it was so strong in academic research that it maintained a preeminent position. State appropriations to the University of California increased by 24 percent per year for the first five years after the war, and the university also enrolled the largest number of veterans; hence, it was the foremost beneficiary of tuition payments coming from the GI Bill. Its new campuses made it into a statewide university with nine branches by the 1960s. UCLA increased its stature as Los Angeles grew to become the second-largest metropolitan area in the nation. But for it to become a world-class research university, it had to relinquish many of the vocational programs that it had established when it started and also to stop awarding the associate degree.

Some of the stronger institutions in the private sector did well also, as the gap between the haves and the have-nots grew wider.

Stanford had been noted as a research university early on when it opened with a large endowment. But its funding was on a narrow base; it had few active benefactors and suffered more from the Depression than most other institutions of its stature. When the Office of Naval Research and the Department of Defense began funding research on electronics in the late 1940s, Stanford rose quickly. Its distinguished faculty members in electronics studies and its close ties with private industry put it in position to grow along with the electronics industry.

The expansion in number of institutions aspiring to be seen as major research enterprises leveled off by the end of the era. Many institutions that had tried to develop strong graduate programs and major support for research efforts found that the fiscal climate was too difficult. Federal support for basic research had flattened out, the research effort itself had become too expensive, and the tone of higher education in general was in the direction of egalitarianism, access, social commitment, and community relations. The leading state institutions in Florida and Arizona continued to advance because the expanding economy in those states made funds available to build extensive community college systems and to elevate the major universities. However, many of the private, Northeastern institutions that had once aspired to become major research enterprises withdrew from the race.

Comprehensive Institutions

The tier of state institutions known as comprehensive colleges or regional universities grew notably. They had begun as post–high school academies, normal schools, state-supported liberal arts colleges, schools of agriculture, institutions providing instruction in industrial arts and home economics, and as schools emphasizing engineering and business administration. Around 8 percent of them had begun as junior colleges, 25 percent as normal schools, and a few as four-year institutions sponsored by municipalities. Around 30 percent of the group were founded in the Mass Higher Education

Era; three hundred were in place by 1970. Whether they developed into multicollege systems or continued as freestanding universities, in most states they educated a majority of the teachers and technicians. By 1975 they enrolled 25 percent of all students in higher education and granted 33 percent of the bachelor's, 30 percent of the master's, 30 percent of the first professional, and 5 percent of the doctoral degrees.

The California experience offers an example of that group's evolution. The state's six normal schools became teachers colleges in 1921; in 1935 they dropped the word *teachers* from their titles and became state colleges. In the 1960s they were authorized to add the word *university* to their title as an indication of the comprehensive programs that they were offering. By 1975 the then eighteen campuses had been organized into a statewide group known as the California State College and University System, and many of them changed their name to reflect the new status. For example, Long Beach State College became California State University at Long Beach. San Diego State was on its way to becoming a regional university; the 1960 master plan that allocated functions among the state's public institutions, precluded it from offering the doctorate, but it still secured sizeable funding for research. Sonoma State was like a rural liberal arts college; Stanislaus State continued emphasizing agriculture. The group overall was preparing most of the state's school teachers.

Several specialized institutions remained within the comprehensive-school designation: military colleges such as The Citadel, technical and trade schools such as New Jersey Institute of Technology, municipal colleges such as the University of Akron, and many of the traditionally black institutions. The designation thus covered a great spread in type, emphasis, and size; more than half the state colleges had fewer than six thousand students, some of the others more than thirty thousand. And the variety of programs spanned the field. Although they were most prominent in teacher education and agriculture, they were offering a sizable proportion of the degrees in business, engineering, nursing, and all the trades and technologies. The institutions spanned a broad middle ground; 40 percent of them provided less-than-baccalaureate-level technical and occupational programs, whereas 15 percent offered the doctorate.

The state colleges and universities were distinguished also by their patterns of funding and governance. Tuition, which covered around one-third of instructional expenditures, was lower than the student charges in the publicly supported research universities but higher than in the community colleges. They were deriving half their current-fund revenues from state and local sources. The American Association of State Colleges and Universities, their major national organization, was formed in 1961 in order to give a voice to this rapidly expanding sector. In size, variety, and comprehensiveness they resembled the community colleges except that they were even more aggressive in establishing programs because they covered a wider range of degrees and service areas.

Liberal Arts Colleges

The liberal arts colleges took a different direction. Most of them had been founded before the Civil War. During the twentieth century, in order to survive, many of them began offering graduate or professional programs, thereby diluting their traditional undergraduate emphasis. But twice as many closed or became comprehensive in the five years from 1971 to 1975 as had opened in the prior twenty-five years. They could not compete with the lower-cost, publicly supported state colleges and community colleges.

In many instances the lines between comprehensive institutions and liberal arts colleges became increasingly blurred. The Carnegie Commission (1973a, pp. 3–4) broadly defined a liberal arts college as an institution with a strong liberal arts tradition that also offered modest occupational programs, including engineering and teacher training. Additionally, any public institutions with enrollments under 1,000 and private institutions with enrollments under 1,500 were automatically considered liberal arts colleges, regardless of their course offerings. Using these criteria the commission classified 719 public and private institutions as liberal arts colleges. In contrast, some researchers, such as Breneman (1994), considered liberal arts colleges to be only those private, small (enrollments under 2,500), primarily residential colleges that limited majors to fields in the humanities, languages, social sciences, physical sciences, and the arts. Less than one-half of the Carnegie Commission's liberal arts colleges conformed to this more restrictive definition.

Regardless of the definition employed, the decrease in the number of liberal arts colleges toward the end of the era was apparent; the 719 liberal arts colleges of 1970 had been reduced to 583 by 1976 (Carnegie Foundation, 1994, p. xii). Many students sought an education that would point them toward immediate employment and had little patience with the arts and humanities. No matter how much the liberal arts colleges attempted to convince prospective students that the degree they earned would fit them for employment in a number of fields, most were unconvinced. Furthermore, public colleges costing several thousand dollars less per year had become widely accessible, and it was difficult to assure students and their families that attending a liberal arts college was worth the difference.

Decreases in the proportion of students attending these institutions matched the decline in the number of liberal arts colleges. At the turn of the century these colleges enrolled around two-thirds of all students in higher education. In the 1950s this ratio dropped to around 25 percent and by the end of the Mass Higher Education Era to under 8 percent. They tried to keep their enrollments up by pointing to the benefits of small classes, single-purpose curriculums, and residential life. Each sought to be considered unique and excellent so that it could attract full-paying students, but most had to engage in price cutting, discounts, and other sorts of financial incentives. Few had sizable endowments to fall back on, and although half of them still had some affiliation with an organized religious group, they could not expect much help from that quarter. Many that were unable to support more than a few students from college funds began restricting admissions to students who could pay full tuition through a combination of their own funds and grants and loans derived from state and federal sources. By the end of the era the colleges were accepting around 40 percent of their applicants, but this figure masks many differences within the group; some colleges were enrolling one in six applicants; others, one in two. Each college tried to maintain a certain size and usually did so by being more or less selective in its acceptance of applicants. The greatest competition for students was within the private sector, because once a family had decided that their young one should attend a liberal arts college, the decision of which one to attend might have been made on the basis of an aid package that the college was able to put together. A student bound for Kalamazoo College might be diverted to Albion, but Western Michigan University would not usually be a contender.

Other Institutions

The private junior colleges did not fare well in the Mass Higher Education Era. In 1922, 137 of the 207 junior colleges were private. In 1947 half the 650 two-year colleges were private, including 180 church-related, 108 independent nonprofit, and 34 proprietary colleges. By 1975 the total number of community and junior colleges had reached 1,200, but the private institutions among them had dropped to 222; one-third of those closed in the next twenty years. The median for private colleges was fewer than five hundred students, whereas the median public college enrolled nearly three thousand. Like the liberal arts colleges, they depended almost entirely on tuition revenue and had difficulty competing.

The community college sector, dominated by public institutions, showed many differences within it. Transfer rates were quite variable, depending in large measure on the proximity of a community college to a four-year college or university and on the strictures that the senior institutions placed on freshman enrollment. The relative vocational emphasis varied between states and between colleges in the same state. Where the colleges had grown out of technical institutes and vocational training centers, as in Indiana and North Carolina, occupational programs and enrollments were high. Where the colleges were responsible for adult basic education, as in San Francisco and San Diego, literacy programs swelled enrollments. In some states the colleges under the aegis of the university system, as in Kentucky and Hawaii, provided both transfer and occupational studies. Pennsylvania State University and the Universities of South Carolina and Wisconsin built two-year branch campuses that emphasized prebaccalaureate studies, but those states organized separate comprehensive or technical college systems as well.

The spread of institutional types brought significant investments in colleges without walls. New York formed Empire State in 1971 to accommodate students whose life situations precluded residence status and who lived in areas too remote for commuting to a campus. Further expansion of adult education took place in programs sponsored by museums, libraries, corporations, extension divisions of the universities, and noncredit programs provided by community colleges. Figures are imprecise, but a reasonable estimate is that these types of educational situations outnumbered the formal institutions by at least five to one and involved three or four times as many students.

The proprietary schools are the sector most difficult to describe. These for-profit postsecondary structures gained enormously in the late 1940s as the GI Bill funded veterans who attended vocational colleges and technical institutions—schools teaching all types of trades. More than five thousand proprietary schools were organized in the first five years after the war, but their enrollment figures were usually omitted from the data on higher education. Only when Guaranteed Student Loans were made available did the proprietary schools become an area of concern in studies of postsecondary education. That was because those students were attracting more than 25 percent of the loan money and defaulting at a considerably higher rate than students in other sectors. Other types of institutions at the periphery of the traditional degree-granting, higher education sector included worker colleges and cooperative or community universities. Together with the proprietary trade schools, perhaps ten thousand such institutions were operating, again with little public attention until they began tapping funds that might otherwise have run to students in the traditional sector.

In summation, several institutional shifts occurred. The public sector eclipsed the private in terms of enrollment. Propelled by funds for research, a number of public and private universities grew large and prestigious. The comprehensive state universities grew by expanding their business and technical programs, while the liberal arts colleges shrank due to a dearth of students willing to pay the cost of the special experience they provided. The public community colleges showed the most phenomenal growth, reaching five million students in 1975—as many as had been enrolled in *all* of higher education a dozen years earlier. The private junior colleges all but disappeared, along with the normal schools whose function had been assumed by the comprehensive institutions. And single-sex colleges shrank as styles in education changed. Overall, the institutions grew large as the average college enrolled four thousand students at the end of the era compared with twelve hundred at its start.

As higher education grew in enrollment, it grew in power. By its admissions policies it decided who would benefit, and through its programs and associations with professional groups, it allocated its matriculants to various positions within society. It steadily increased its ability to control access to opportunity and, through its in-service and adult education programs, to advancement. Even matriculating more of the adolescent population was a form of power; institutions kept the young among their peers and steered the course of their development as adults. And the public had granted these powers to education because everyone had a stake in its accomplishments.

Students

The Mass Higher Education Era was marked by student access and activism. Enrollments increased phenomenally—in the thirty years between 1945 and 1975 by more than 500 percent, from around two million to eleven million students. The public sector gained most; enrollment in public institutions was approximately equal to private at the start of the era but more than four times greater by its end. The public community colleges gained an increasing share, reaching nearly half of the total of first-time freshman enrollments. High school graduates enrolled in the year following graduation reached 49 percent in 1962 and hovered around the 50 percent mark for the next twenty years. The percentage of male and female students shifted. In 1940, 60 percent of the student body was male; in 1950, temporarily inflated by returning veterans, it was 70 percent. But male and female undergraduate enrollments almost reached parity by the end of the era. Students aged twenty-five or older accounted for one-third of the total. The University Transformation Era had set the framework; now higher education and, by extension, the entire nation was reaping the benefits.

By any measure the growth was incredible. People who in an earlier era would not have thought of attending matriculated as colleges were opened in their hometowns. Those who could not afford the tuition took advantage of financial aid that was made available, first through the GI Bill, then through various state and federal grant and loan programs. The public community colleges charged little tuition, and in most cases their students were able to live at home and commute. The doors swung wide and the population surged, so much so that the managers of higher education institutions took the position that growth was salutary and stasis or decline in enrollment meant that people were being denied access. Anyone who did not want to attend college was considered misguided and in need of special encouragement.

Access

One of the longest-standing questions in education has been, If a potential student chooses not to attend college, whose fault is it? One-third of the high school graduates aged sixteen to twenty-four and not enrolled in college reported, "no desire to go," in a poll taken in the fall of 1959 (Harris, 1972, p. 49). What could be done to bring them in? Which came first, societal changes encouraging women to enter the workforce in greater numbers and thus to attend college where they can be trained for better-paying jobs, or a reduction in barriers to college attendance by women? If members of a particular social stratum defined by economics or ethnicity attend college in greater numbers than those of another stratum, how can higher education avoid the charge of discrimination against the latter group? People who were not attending college found that their employment options had shrunk and their wages had fallen in relation to those who had graduated. What could the institutions do to convince them to attend?

The colleges continuously tried to attract students, to break down all academic, attitudinal, and economic barriers. For the low-ability students, they expanded their remedial programs. Most colleges had always had some provision for poorly qualified students, but with decline in ability displayed by students graduating from high school beginning in the mid-1960s, remedial programs grew so that by the mid-1970s all but the most selective colleges were providing them. Students with the highest ability tended to enroll in the leading research universities and the most prestigious liberal arts colleges. Institutions that prided themselves on the abilities of their entering freshmen competed for the students with the highest scores. Most other colleges organized honors programs and scholarships for high-ability students so that they too might obtain their share of well-qualified individuals.

Family income had a high correlation with attendance patterns. The lower the income, the less likely a student was to matriculate. In 1967, 11 percent of American families with dependents had incomes under $3,000; their children accounted for fewer than 5 percent of the freshmen. At the other extreme, 12 percent of the families had incomes greater than $15,000; more than 22 percent of the freshman class was made up of their children. Clearly this was an area in which changes might be made if funding were available; state and federal grant and loan programs were established and expanded throughout the era. Using constant 1994 dollars, federal aid increased from just over $1 billion in 1963–64 to nearly $16.5 billion in 1973–74, state grants increased from $262 million to $1.1 billion, and institutional and other grants went from $1.3 billion to $3.1 billion (Gladieux and Hauptman, 1995, pp. 10–11). (See Table 4.2 for an early example of federal loans to students.)

Major steps were taken to encourage the enrollment of, first, black students and then Hispanic and Native American students. These moves were made primarily through the courts, as state legislatures and the U.S. Congress were slow in developing antidiscrimination measures. Low-income students benefited also from

Table 4.2. Student War Loan Program Disbursements, 1943 (in Current Dollars).

Field	Number of Loans	Dollar Amount	% of Total
Medicine	3,867	1,150,072	39.5
Engineering	4,066	933,208	32.1
Dentistry	1,217	343,225	11.8
Chemistry	835	205,444	7.1
Pharmacy	438	114,104	3.9
Veterinary	394	106,821	3.7
Physics	264	57,633	1.9
Total	11,081	2,910,507	100.0

Source: U.S. Office of Education, 1945, p. 12.

these decisions because of the overrepresentation of ethnic minorities in that group. In fact most of the financial aid appropriated by
state legislatures and the U.S. Congress was rationalized on the
grounds that it assisted ethnic minority groups who, not incidentally, were represented by organizations much more prominent than
those speaking on behalf of low-income people in general.

Access for women accelerated during the era, as shown by the
enrollment figures. Much was due to changes in social relations; by
the time specific legislation and court decisions on behalf of gender
equity appeared, the enrollment of women had almost reached parity. The issue of women then turned less on admission to college
than it did on admission to certain programs. Under interpretations
of Title IX, women were not to be barred from matriculating in traditionally male fields such as engineering, construction trades, auto
mechanics, and certain of the sciences. Most of the law schools and
medical schools did not have to be prodded by threats of legal
action; they had opened to women already. However, the number
of degrees conferred in those fields did jump in the few years after
1972, when Title IX was passed. In that year women received
830 degrees in medicine—9 percent of the total awarded. Three
years later that number had doubled to 1,629, representing 13 percent of the awards. The parallel figures for law show women receiving 1,498 degrees (7 percent of the total) in 1972 and 4,415
(15 percent of the total) in 1975. Women entered the field of dentistry at a slower pace. In 1972, 43 dentistry doctorates were
awarded to women (1 percent of the total), and in 1975, 146 were
awarded (3 percent of the total).

People with disabilities also began attending colleges at a higher
rate. Section 504 of the Rehabilitation Act of 1973 prohibited dis-
ability-based discrimination in federally funded programs, including admission to institutions of higher education. A disabled student
who otherwise met academic and technical standards requisite to
admission might not be refused. The section also required that the
institutions make reasonable accommodation to allow disabled

students to participate in college programs. The language "otherwise qualified" and "reasonable accommodation" led to subsequent cases circumscribing what had to be done to make facilities and programs amenable to the progress of handicapped students. One basic problem was that the many different types of disabilities—visual, auditory, psychological, and ambulatory—demanded different forms of institutional accommodation.

The relationship between access and socioeconomic status (SES) was traced, showing a high correlation between college entrance and graduation and family SES. One study reported in 1961 showed that 67 percent of the high school graduates whose father was professional or semiprofessional entered college compared with 25 percent of those whose father was a farmer, craftsman, or unskilled worker (Harris, 1972, p. 61). Another study showed a relationship between SES and type of college attended, with the high-SES students going to private universities or four-year colleges and the lower group attending public two-year or four-year colleges (Harris, 1972, p. 57). Higher education's response was to increase the scholarships and fellowships awarded. A total of around $172 million granted by all institutions in 1960 increased to $1.45 billion by 1975, and that did not include Pell Grant awards.

The drive to stimulate access also extended to high-ability students regardless of their status as members of any other special group. Concerns were raised that the nation was losing brainpower to the extent that some of its most talented young people did not go to college. Several studies conducted in the 1950s found that as many as one-half the students graduating in the top 20 percent of their high school class did not continue their schooling (Wolfle, 1954). Ability was related not only to whether students entered college but also to whether they graduated. All came together in correlations demonstrating that high ability and high family income related positively to student entrance to college, the types of colleges they entered, and to whether or not they graduated. The push was on to get more of the high-ability students into college, especially those from low-SES families. The National Merit Scholarship Program took a lead in enabling such students to matriculate. In 1957, more than 96 percent of the nearly fifteen thousand Merit Scholars, finalists, and semifinalists went on to college (Harris, 1972, p. 50).

Most colleges that had selective admissions used some combination of high school rank and test score to determine student ability. The highest correlation with achievement in college came when that performance was compared with performance in high school; the best way of predicting what people will do tomorrow is to view what they did yesterday. But the use of ability tests grew; by 1964 more than one million prospective students each year took the SAT. The standardized tests were applauded as objective measures of a person's ability to succeed in college. The highest predictions of success in the freshman class could be gained by combining high school grade point average with the score made on the SAT. But what were the tests measuring? Soon after the introduction of IQ tests in the late teens and early 1920s, they were criticized for reflecting the taker's social and economic background. By the 1940s, defenders of the tests insisted that they were measuring "the one essential human ability," whereas detractors proclaimed that they were only reflecting the "existing class structure, in which the better-off economic and ethnic groups are found to be more intelligent and the worse-off are found to be less so" (Lemann, 1995, p. 84).

The controversy was only of academic interest until 1951, when a new draft began to provide troops for the Korean War. College students might obtain deferments from service on the ground that the nation needed scientific personnel and people with special skills. The tests thus indirectly helped to determine who would go to war. Questions of test fairness were extended, as the difference in scores made by members of various ethnic groups was brought up repeatedly to show cultural bias. Nonetheless, testing became entrenched as a way of selecting students for college, and its use continued growing. The American College Testing Program, founded in 1959, began offering a test similar to the Educational Testing Service's SAT. Both ETS and ACT expanded their repertoire and developed specialized tests that professional and graduate schools might use in screening applicants.

The campus scene shifted markedly during the era. Whereas the prevalent view had seen the undergraduate of the 1920s as a carousing, delayed adolescent, by the late 1940s and, with the bulging enrollments of veterans of World War II, this had shifted to a vision of mature, serious students eager to graduate and get on with their lives. Some one-half to three-quarters of the male students at the larger universities were veterans. Many were married, and a sizable proportion of them had children; they had little patience for fraternity hazing and other pranks that had gone along with college life in an earlier time. In the 1950s, after most of the veterans had passed through, the students were known as the silent generation because they seemed disinterested in social and political affairs. Accordingly they were criticized as conformists, lacking in independent thought.

Activism

By the 1960s the baby-boom group was more determined to question social values and to take part in attempts to rectify perceived injustices. Many were involved with the civil rights movement, which was led by the churches. Many of the demonstrations on behalf of desegregation and voting rights saw college students arm in arm with ministers and other concerned citizens. Students at the traditionally black institutions in the South were especially involved, and many white students from Northern and Southern colleges participated along with them.

Student activism of a different form took the institutions by surprise. In the fall of 1964 a decision made by the University of California at Berkeley administration to prohibit the solicitation of funds for off-campus political groups sparked a student demonstration that resulted in numerous arrests. The movement spread to other colleges and included protests against parietal rules, college grading systems that seemed better suited to managing children, faculty who expected students to remain as passive learners, curricular irrelevance, civil rights for ethnic minorities, and eventually, the draft and the Vietnam War. The targets shifted but the patterns were similar: raucous parades, sit-ins at campus buildings, outrageous demands. Failure to moderate the so-called Free Speech Movement at its outset may be attributable to missteps by the Berkeley administration and also to the nature of the community where there was a large, sympathetic nonstudent population adjacent to the campus. However, other types of activism appeared on hundreds of campuses in the United States and in universities as far away as Paris, Mexico City, and Tokyo. Around the world, students in the late 1960s were rebelling for a variety of reasons: an unpopular war, civil rights, access to college, curricular and instructional forms, environmental issues, and what they perceived as the evils of a corporate world.

The most virulent upheavals in the United States occurred where there was a resident student population and a strong student subculture that centered on the students' feeling apart from the rules and traditions governing the institution. Graduate students were less involved than undergraduates, commuter students less than resident, older students less than younger, part-timers less than full-timers, students in the sciences less than those in the humanities and social sciences. The hardcore, self-styled revolutionaries such as those who signed the Port Huron Statement drafted by the Students for a Democratic Society, probably never amounted to more than 1 or 2 percent of the student body. However, as many as ten times that number took part in the demonstrations on some campuses. And not all of the activism was pointed at perceived injustices in the broader society or outmoded campus rules; membership in conservative groups such as the Young Americans for Freedom grew as well. The campuses were polarized at the extreme fringes, even as the majority of students recognized that college was but a way station toward a better life and career.

Overall, the universities proved vulnerable. Dedicated as they were to freedom of speech and opinion, they had little defense against students who wanted to turn the campus into a platform for social action. It was a difficult time for university administrators. More used to referring all types of demands to committees, the administrators were rarely able to effect any meaningful change with sufficient rapidity to satisfy the student demonstrators. In the manner of youth, the students were demanding immediate action, refusing to be set aside with promises that committees would investigate the concerns that they raised. Furthermore, student demands ranged from the trivial through the reasonable to the unattainable, from permission to set up a table and distribute literature, to demands that they be allowed to vote on faculty tenure, to insistence that the Vietnam War be ended. As one dean said to a group of students camped in his office, "OK, I agree that the United States should pull out of Vietnam. Where do I sign?" But the students who saw the university as complicitous with transcendent evil were not to be mollified. When university administrators, presiding over what were supposedly consensual communities with broadly diffused authority, overreacted and called in local police forces, the protests took a new form as charges of brutality brought sympathy for the small numbers of students actually involved. The faculty also were divided, with some supporting the protesters, others deploring their activities but not knowing what to do, a few meeting with the students in attempts to defuse the situations, and others putting their heads in the sand.

Why did it happen? No satisfactory answer is apparent. If the activism had been confined to the United States, it might have been accurately perceived as a reaction to an unpopular war. But the French, Mexican, and Japanese students were not threatened with a draft; their countries' troops were not in Vietnam. They wanted less-rigid institutional forms, and subgroups often reacted vehemently against the protesters. In the United States, student activism shifted back and forth, from national to local concerns, from protests against the war to activism on behalf of civil rights. Students at many colleges protested against ROTC and campus recruiting stations for the military. At Columbia they protested campus expansion into the surrounding neighborhood. However, regardless of the numerous causes for which the students demonstrated, revulsion against the war proved the longest-lasting. A sizable percentage of the draft-eligible young men were in college, and rumors about whether or not they would continue to enjoy deferments kept them on edge. The assassination of Martin Luther King Jr. in 1968 and the American military incursion into Cambodia in 1970 kept the protests going. The dissensions were also fueled by the popular media eager to publish lurid displays of every confrontation.

By one line of reasoning the protests took place on the campuses because that's where the young people were and because institutional controls on their behavior had weakened. The universities had apparently relinquished their scholarly standing to one of immediate utility and thus lost their claim to a higher moral position. Riots had taken place in prisons and mutinies in armies, but short of a major revolution such as that in Russia in 1917, not with such widespread fervor and, most notably, with so little punishment for the rebels. Hardly a student was expelled from college as a result of outrageous behavior; hardly a faculty member was censured by his colleagues for condoning that behavior; only a few chief administrators were dismissed by governing boards unwilling to tolerate the deviancy. The major individual casualties were several martyred students, slain tragically when events escalated at Kent State and Jackson State, and armed authorities overreacted.

The student protests subsided with the end of the military draft in 1973. Whether or not they had succeeded in shortening the war itself is uncertain. The progression toward enhanced civil liberties and an open society continued, but any link between student demonstrations and congressional actions and Supreme Court decisions in the mid-1970s is questionable at best. As for relaxation of parental-type regulations on student life, these had been eroding for decades; the student rebellion merely hastened them along. After the early 1970s it became difficult to find a campus where strict rules limited the tendency of students to socialize in any way they chose. Many colleges opened residence halls where unmarried men and women students lived together—arrangements that would have sent the deans of students of an earlier generation into catatonic shock. The broader rules of the general community came into play on the campuses and, except for sexual harassment, overt drunkenness, and disobedience of the prevailing civil code, few regulations remained to be enforced. One marked but temporary effect might have been the relations between universities and the Department of Defense; Pentagon support for academic research declined "from a high of $279 million in 1969 to a low of $184 million just five years later" (Geiger, 1993, p. 241). Whether or not there was a direct relationship between the student activism and these reductions, they did evidence one point of the protests—the universities' complicity with the military.

Faculty

The professionalization of the faculty accelerated. Salaries increased steadily, so that by the end of the era they reached what might be called a living wage. The faculty took greater control by establishing collective bargaining units and by gaining a say in institutional governance. Their job rights were codified through legislation and court decisions. Academic freedom was no longer merely a concept that appeared in statements of principle; it became a privilege upheld by the courts.

Even so, toward the end of the era several developments made it seem as though further gains toward professionalization would be more difficult to attain. The percentage of part-time instructors was growing, but those instructors were not serving as assistants to the full-time faculty members in the manner that a profession might demand; instead, they were independent instructors with fewer responsibilities and lower pay. The move to unionize, which rose rapidly in the 1970s, may have weakened the public's view of the faculty as a professional group. The tenure system, long sought by the faculty as a way of protecting their members from capricious dismissal, began to be seen as a way the group retained members who were no longer productive. Faculty complicity in student activism raised further questions about professionalism. And the sheer growth in numbers removed the distinction of rarity and weakened the special status and aura of mystery that surrounds the most prestigious professions.

Demography and Salary

The growth was impressive. From fewer than 150,000 faculty members in 1940, overall head count rose to 565,000 by 1975. The percentage growth in student enrollment had been greater, however, and the ratio of students to faculty grew from its historic pattern of ten to one to seventeen to one. The average number of faculty per institution, which had been less than forty in 1910, reached eighty-six by 1940 and was two hundred by 1975. Much of the change in faculty relations with their peers, students, and institutions stemmed from this shift in institutional size. The relationships among people are one thing when there is face-to-face contact among most members of the community, quite another when a bureaucracy develops to manage massive structures.

The demographics of the faculty shifted somewhat. Women, especially, grew as a percentage of the total, from 20 percent early in the century to around 33 percent by 1975. Toward the latter part of the era the number of faculty members from minority groups grew as well, reaching around 8 percent. These percentages differed according to type of institution. Women were most highly represented in community colleges and in the humanities and social sciences in universities. The minority group instructors were also severely underrepresented in the sciences and tended to cluster in the social sciences in public institutions. When the colleges were staffing up to meet the surging enrollments, the percentage of young instructors increased, and the median age declined notably. After the 1960s, when relatively fewer new appointments were made, the median age gradually increased.

A spread in the religious background of the faculty was also noted. In the 1970s, 66 percent of the faculty were Protestant, 18 percent Catholic, and 9 percent Jewish; 4 percent reported "other" and 3 percent "none" (Ladd and Lipset, 1975). Here again the distribution across institutions was uneven. Nearly 20 percent of the combined faculties of the most highly ranked universities represented themselves as Jewish, with the percentages highest in law (36 percent), sociology (34 percent), economics (28 percent), and physics (26 percent). The Jewish instructors had benefited from a decline in publicly espoused anti-Semitism after World War II, just when academic jobs were opening up in great numbers. The argument for opening faculty ranks turned not on the issue that the curriculum needed a Jewish perspective or that the students needed particular role models but simply on the point that when prevailing professional standards were applied and an expanding academy needed talent, it became more difficult to justify excluding anyone. Women also benefited from a decline in prejudice and from their greatly increased attendance at all levels of higher education. For the minorities the road was bumpier and slower; increases in their ranks had to await legislation, court rulings, and targeted expansion in their educational preparation.

Sources of faculty remained the same, with one major exception. Faculty beginning employment at the community colleges tended to come from secondary school teaching positions, many with extensive teaching experience. Most of the recruits held master's degrees. In the middle 1970s, around one in eight junior or community college instructors held the doctorate, and many of those had obtained it while they were teaching at the colleges. For them the doctorate was not the beginning of a research career but served primarily to elevate them on the salary schedule at the institution where they were already working. At the universities the graduate schools continued as the major source of staff, with the number of master's and doctoral degrees awarded increasing tenfold during the era. Not until the early 1970s did the number of Ph.D.'s awarded exceed the number of new, junior-level faculty appointments at the universities. By the late 1970s the employment of doctorates in government and industry outpaced the growth of employment within higher education, as increasing numbers of degree holders found jobs outside academe.

Affirmative action with regard to faculty employment and promotion reveals just how gradually but steadily the turn toward ethnic diversity occurred. In 1972, Title VII of the Civil Rights Act of 1964 was expanded to forbid discrimination in employment on the basis of race, color, religion, sex, or national origin in public and private educational institutions unless it could be proved that the operation of the institution depended on people with particular characteristics. Claims of discrimination based on Title VII came in two forms: disparate treatment and disparate impact. In a claim of disparate treatment, individuals must show that they were discriminated against in hiring, firing, promotions, or condition of employment, based on one of the forbidden criteria. In the case of disparate impact, plaintiffs must show that they belong to a protected group, that they were qualified for the job for which they applied, that despite qualifications they were rejected, and that after rejection the position remained open and the employer continued to seek applicants from people who had comparable qualifications.

The federal Office of Civil Rights began requiring that every institution draw up an affirmative action plan, set goals, and establish specific procedures by which faculty would be recruited and the goals met. Initially the pool of women and minority candidates was too small to satisfy the affirmative action goals. Furthermore, there were questions whether the goals should be institutionwide or enforced at the departmental level, and whether they should be applied to women and members of various ethnic groups separately or in total. University response to the affirmative action mandates took several forms. Where the faculty in a particular academic area said, rightfully in many cases, that there were no qualified candidates from among the groups sought, the university might make additional slots available contingent on the department's finding women or minorities to fill them. New positions were also created to which people could be appointed without holding doctoral degrees or specific qualifications in particular areas of inquiry. Nationwide searches were organized, letters written to the heads of all the academic departments from which students in particular fields were obtaining degrees, and advertisements placed in journals and newspapers. The number of position listings in the *Chronicle of Higher Education* made it appear as though that periodical were founded in the 1960s especially to provide a vehicle for these searches. But despite the laborious processes set in place, results were slow in coming; the target that kept shifting among various minority groups and women, and from institution to department to rank, did not make the tallying of gains any easier.

A more significant change in the composition of the faculty was the increase in numbers of part-timers. In 1960 the part-time faculty made up about one-third of the total—many of them employed even if they did not possess graduate degrees. Ten years later, when the number of people receiving master's degrees annually had jumped from fewer than 75,000 to more than 200,000 and the number receiving the doctorate from fewer than 10,000 to nearly 30,000, the number of part-timers on staff declined to 22 percent. The prior decade had seen qualified people coming onstream, and the institutions were willing to grant them full-time status. By 1975 the ratio of part-timers climbed back up to 30 percent of the total faculty, occasioned now not by a shortage of qualified candidates but by the desire of administrators to save money at a time of rapidly increasing expenditures. The growth of community colleges where the use of part-time instructors has always been higher than the ratio for all of higher education also contributed to this increase. Their percentage of part-time to full-time instructors had been at around 40 percent in 1970, but by 1975 it climbed to more than 50 percent.

Salaries for the full-time faculty continued increasing but at a slower rate. The median doubled from $6,015 in 1957–58 to $12,710 in 1970–71. It then increased to $15,622 in 1974–75, a rise of 23 percent in four years. But when viewed in constant dollars the gains in the early 1970s actually represented a decline of 6 percent. Salary increments were harder to attain, especially as the faculty were accused of complicity in the student activism of the time and as other public employees, who were better organized to present demands to the legislature, took more of the states' budgets. The faculty found they could not receive pay increments sufficient to keep up with inflation.

The faculty meanwhile had been advancing their professionalization through solidifying control over many aspects of their work. In the universities, they were able to spend time on teaching, research, and public service, often shifting from one to the other as they chose. This flexibility proved a plus in attracting people to the profession. Few faculty members took university positions because they wanted to tutor youth exclusively; more likely, they sought an environment where they might follow a variety of pursuits. Research and scholarship did not come into direct conflict with teaching because the rapidly expanding institutions could accommodate scholars while they also developed additional cadres of counselors, ombudsmen, advisers, registration officials, and the like to take care of the students' general concerns. The downside for the faculty was that these student management specialists took money that might otherwise have been used to increase salaries. As for the faculty in community colleges and in four-year institutions where expectation for hours spent in the classroom remained high, those who had obtained positions immediately after graduate school did not expect to spend time on research, and for those who had entered from secondary school positions, research had never been part of their professional life.

Working conditions shifted somewhat toward the end of the era. Bowen and Schuster (1986) list four changes. First, in anticipation of declining student enrollments, many institutions cut back on support staff and reduced funds available for professional travel. Second, the increased number of inadequately prepared students forced the faculty to teach remedial classes, which few enjoyed. A third change was in student preference for fields that were strongly professional or practical: agriculture, business, health, trades, and technologies. This produced a poor distribution of professors, as those who had expected to teach in their fields of specialization, especially in the humanities or social sciences, found themselves teaching in areas only marginally related to the fields in which they had obtained their degrees. The fourth concern was that faculty participation in academic decision making was becoming less direct as the larger-sized institutions and the newly formed statewide coordinating boards contributed to a decline in collegiality.

One more factor might be noted. The faculty were aware that their purchasing power had been eroded and were inclined to blame legislators and trustees for their inability to obtain sufficient salary, especially as they saw other public employees gaining. The faculty might also have been demoralized by the variations in pay received by instructors in the different disciplines. Competition from the nonacademic sector drove faculty salaries up in such fields as business, engineering, and computer science, as those in the liberal arts fell behind.

Academic Freedom

The concept of academic freedom that had been gaining acceptance for the prior half-century was wracked by a loyalty oath controversy in the late 1940s, when several universities and state legislatures ruled that every employee had to sign a disclaimer stating that they were not communists nor members or supporters of any group that advocated overthrowing the United States government. The mass hysteria known as McCarthyism had spread to what were supposed to be bastions of intellectual freedom. The AAUP's position was that nothing in the nature of the teaching profession required the automatic exclusion of communists, and college teachers should not be subjected to civic limitations not imposed on other citizens. The major private universities typically did not impose such require- ments, but state legislators pressured public institutions' governing boards, and thirty-one University of California professors were dis- missed for refusing to sign the oath. The board of regents rescinded the requirement in 1951, and in 1952 the California Supreme Court ruled that the nonsigners be reinstated. It seemed in retrospect that the controversy had been less about finding communists than about whether the center of power regarding the faculty should be in the governing board, administration, or academic senate.

By this time the universities had become closely associated with the broader community, as revealed in a statement by the Associa- tion of American Universities in 1953. Written by a committee chaired by the president of Yale and endorsed by thirty-seven lead- ing institutions, "The Rights and Responsibilities of Universities and Their Faculties" described the university as comprising schol- ars loyal to the nation and to its form of government. The docu- ment declared further that anyone belonging to the Communist Party had no right to remain on staff. Granted that the statement might have been issued as a sop for posturing politicians, it does sug- gest that the presidents of several models of free inquiry did not think of themselves as sufficiently independent to say, "We under- stand that the nation is involved in a Cold War. Be assured that we have no intention of aiding the enemy. At the same time we will continue to respect the freedom of thought exhibited by the peo- ple around whom our institutions are built." Since the time their institutions' budgets passed the million-dollar mark, few presidents had the courage to make such statements, although Chicago's Hutchins, Harvard's Conant, and Boston University's Marsh did go on record as deploring witch hunts. By the end of the decade, the furor over party membership had subsided, but fifteen states still had statutes requiring that employees refrain from membership in subversive groups.

When the student uprisings began in the mid-1960s, a number of instructors were sympathetic to the antiwar, anticorporate structure, anticapitalist, and eventually antiracist charges that were raised. Some even pandered to the most untoward aspects of the young people in their charge, accepting their mode of dress, their opinions, and their tendency toward institutional disruption. But the profession as a whole did not attempt to sanction them. The venerable concept of academic freedom protected the professors, even those who blatantly incited their students to rebel against the academy.

Even though many universities had become effectually extensions of the surrounding community, the faculty tended to behave as though the campuses were still sequestered enclaves. They abhorred the idea of police coming on campus to quiet the students who were threatening to burn buildings, smash laboratories, and destroy other university property. Such abhorrence stemmed from the ancient pretext that the campus was a sacred environment, different from the surrounding community, deserving to be self-governing and to mete out its own sanctions. The notion that an institution with forty thousand students and staff members and billions of dollars in buildings and equipment was quite different from the small band of students and scholars from which the university sprang seemed to have eluded not only some faculty but also those administrators who would promise anything to students as long as they would go away without breaking the windows of the administration building. This is an example of the way parts of an institution evolve while other parts remain frozen; the professional schools, research laboratories, and mass enrollment of undergraduates put the university squarely in the middle of American society, but when it suited their purpose, the liberal arts faculty acted as though they were the true scholars of antiquity, sitting in dingy rooms, reading classics with small groups of young people, and with Do Not Disturb signs on the doors.

Academic freedom is a subtle concept, and it is not easy to draw the line between liberty and license. The faculty had been seeking rules forbidding that they be sanctioned for speaking out on controversial issues. Beginning in the 1950s the Supreme Court developed a constitutional framework for this right, granted mainly under the freedom of speech and association guarantee of the First Amendment but also in the due process clause of the Fourteenth Amendment and the protection against self-incrimination of the Fifth Amendment. In 1957 the Supreme Court, in *Sweezy v. New Hampshire*, overturned a contempt conviction when a professor had refused to answer questions about a lecture he had delivered. In *Shelton v. Tucker*, in 1960, the Supreme Court rejected as unconstitutional a state law requiring faculty at public institutions to provide information on their membership in or financial support of any organizations. Seven years later, in *Keyishian v. Board of Regents*, the Court ruled that state laws requiring faculty members to sign a certificate stating they were not and never had been communists were unconstitutionally vague and overly broad; therefore, faculty members who had lost their jobs for refusing to sign had been improperly terminated. This case overturned a 1951 case that had upheld a New York State law excluding from employment teachers who were members of specified subversive groups.

In the late 1960s the Court began extending its application of the constitutional principles of academic freedom from protection against state interference to issues of protecting the faculty from their home institution. In 1968, in *Pickering v. Board of Education*, the Court ruled on a case in which a teacher was terminated for writing a letter criticizing the school board's financial operating strategy. As Kaplin and Lee (1995) summarize the situation, the Court upheld the teacher because there was no working relationship between him and those he criticized; the letter was of public concern and had no detrimental impact; the teacher's performance was not affected; he wrote as a citizen; and the school board's interest in efficient operation of its schools was outweighed by the plaintiff's free speech interest.

Tenure and the right to continuing contracts also came under Court review. In cases adjudicated in 1972, the Supreme Court decided that faculty members at public institutions are entitled to a fair hearing under the due process clause of the Fourteenth Amendment when their contracts are not renewed if they have been deprived of property or liberty interests. In *Board of Regents* v. *Roth*, where a professor was given no hearing when his initial one-year contract at the University of Wisconsin was not renewed, the Court found no violation of due process, holding that he had not been deprived of a liberty interest because the university had made no charge against him nor was there any potential damage to his reputation. His one-year contract, made in accordance with state law, did not give him a reasonable expectation of continued employment, therefore he had no property interest in his position, and the institution did not have to grant him a notice of dismissal or a hearing. However, in *Perry* v. *Sindermann*, a professor who had been employed by the Texas college and university system for ten years on a series of one-year contracts was determined to have a reasonable expectation of continued employment. The institution had no formal tenure system, but its faculty guide did suggest certain assurances of continued employment. Thus Professor Perry had been deprived of a property interest and was entitled to a hearing as to why he was not being retained. The property interest was also applied in 1978 in the case of *McLendon* v. *Morton*; a faculty member at Petersburg Community College had fulfilled the institution's published criteria for tenure (six years as a full-time instructor and achievement of the rank of assistant professor) but was denied on the grounds of incompetence, without a hearing. The Court ruled that by satisfying the objective criteria the teacher had gained a property interest in continued employment and was entitled to due process consisting of notice of grounds for discontinuation, a hearing before a neutral fact finder, and an opportunity to refute the charges brought against her.

In summation, in the 1970s the faculty were found to have rights to continuing contracts and the award of tenure if the institution had given reasonable expectation of continued employment or if the professor had followed the guidelines as stated in the institution's list of regulations. These decisions were rendered on the basis of a property interest created when the policies of the institution or the mutually explicit understandings between it and the faculty member supported the claim of entitlement to continuation. The Court ruled also that a liberty interest was created in a case when the institution, in the process of failing to renew a contract or denying tenure, charged a faculty member with conduct that "could seriously damage his or her reputation, standing, or associations in the community" (Kaplin and Lee, 1995, p. 283). A liberty interest was created also where nonrenewal was so damaging that the faculty member was precluded from obtaining employment elsewhere.

Collective Bargaining

Tenure, working conditions, and salaries were all connected with the rise of faculty unions in higher education in the latter years of the Mass Higher Education Era. The laws governing the right of faculty to organize and be recognized as collective bargaining units depended on whether an institution was public or private. In general, public institutions were subject to state law, whereas private institutions were under the jurisdiction of federal law, specifically the National Labor Relations Act. The act, passed in 1935, "was amended in 1947 to exclude supervisors from the category of employees entitled to a protected right to organize and bargain" (Garbarino, 1977, p. 106). At the same time it was amended to point out that professional employees could organize; professionals were defined as those employees engaged in predominantly intellectual work involving the consistent exercise of discretion and judgment—the work should be of such a character that its results are not standardized in relation to a given time period and it tends to require advanced knowledge resting on prolonged, specialized study in an institution of higher learning (Garbarino, 1977, p. 107). Thus the amendment actually spelled out several of the characteristics of a profession and noted that professional workers were covered. However, not until 1971 did the National Labor Relations Board grant full-time college faculty at private institutions the right to organize into unions by classifying them as employees.

During this same period federal and state employees were gaining the right to organize. An executive order issued in 1962 stipulated that federal employees could form bargaining units, and by 1970 more than half of the 2.7 million working for the federal government belonged to a union or employee association. Wisconsin was the first state to pass legislation enabling public employees to bargain collectively. By 1970, half the states had mandated collective bargaining for some sector of public employees, whereas another fifteen permitted negotiations; only two states specifically prohibited recognition of public employee organizations. Overall, in 1970, around one-third of all public employees in the United States were represented by bargaining organizations—a ratio slightly higher than the percentage of private, nonagricultural workers who were organized into unions.

Faculty unions followed closely on the laws governing public employee organizations. Milwaukee Technical Institute, a two-year college, was the first postsecondary institution to be organized—this in 1963, whereas the first four-year institution was the United States Merchant Marine Academy, a federal institution where the bargaining unit was recognized in 1966. Faculty unions were recognized in the university sector beginning in 1968 in state institutions in Michigan and Massachusetts and in the City University of New York system.

From these beginnings the unionization movement spread rapidly. In 1966 a total of twenty-three institutions—only one of which was a four-year college—had bargaining units, covering a total of 5,200 faculty. By 1974, 331 institutions (132 of them four-year colleges or universities) had organized units representing 92,300 faculty. These numbers included around one-eighth of all higher education institutions, with the two-year colleges overrepresented: 25 percent of that group had faculty unions, whereas around 6 percent of the four-year institutions were so represented. All the growth had taken place in less than a decade (Garbarino, 1975, p. 56).

The rapid moves toward unionization drew much commentary and figurative hand-wringing. The faculty were professionals; what did they want? They had gained in public esteem, prospered financially, attracted capable and ambitious individuals to their ranks. They were making recruiting and hiring decisions and shaping academic content—functions that in earlier eras had been under the aegis of the president. The 1966 "Statement on Government of Colleges and Universities," issued by the American Association of University Professors, American Council on Education, and Association of Governing Boards of Universities and Colleges, said that the faculty had primary responsibility for curriculum, instruction, and research and that the governing board or the president had the power of review or final decision, but that was to be "exercised adversely only in exceptional circumstances" (The Carnegie Foundation, 1982, p. 18). The sponsoring organizations of that statement included the leading faculty, administrative, and trustee associations. No objections to it were raised. The statement further suggested that the faculty should participate in college governance whenever issues related to their primary responsibility might be discussed. The rush to unionize in the early 1970s struck many observers as untoward. What happened to collegiality?

Numerous reasons for unionization were put forward. The faculty were young; in 1969 one-third of them were less than thirty-five years old, a reflection of the intense hiring of the late 1950s and early 1960s. Two-thirds of the faculty were in public institutions, most in large ones; in 1970, 209 colleges had more than ten thousand students each and 40 had more than thirty thousand. The number of multi-institutional systems had grown, as branch campuses were set up to accommodate the increased enrollments. A shift in level of control had occurred: in 1959, seventeen states had no coordinating agency for higher education; ten years later only two states had no coordinating group. Unionization had spread first in the public schools and was most prominent in the community colleges in the postsecondary sector. Flush with victory and with treasuries bulging with contributions from new members in the two-year colleges, the unions campaigned to organize the faculty in the senior institutions.

Presumably, the younger faculty were more militant, unused to deliberations and the slow pace of decision making that was traditional in higher education. The faculty in large public institutions, especially those with multiple campuses, had become isolated and felt apart from institutional decision making; they wanted a voice. The state-level coordinating agencies had shifted the locus of control from individual campuses to larger units with greater responsibility; the faculty sought countervailing power. Bowen and Schuster (1986) comment that collective bargaining would not be needed in institutions where faculty members were treated with respect, played an important role in decision making, received reasonable compensation, and were part of a genuine academic community. They ascribed much to the deteriorating working conditions and the loss of real earnings but still expressed the conventional belief that collective bargaining was not appropriate in an environment in which collegiality and community were essential.

Surveys were conducted to gauge faculty attitudes. A report by Ladd and Lipset (1975) analyzes data from the national faculty survey conducted by the Carnegie Commission in 1969. In that year 59 percent of all faculty were found to support unionism. And when the item "Collective bargaining by faculty members has no place in a college or university" (agree or disagree) appeared in a 1972 study, the percentage disagreeing had risen to 66 percent (Garbarino, 1975, p. 52). Attitudes had obviously shifted as membership in faculty organizations had grown. By 1974 the American Federation of Teachers (AFT) boasted of 30,000 members in more than 200 higher education units. Although it had been active since 1916, the AFT formed a colleges and universities department only in 1967 and became aggressive in recruiting members and establishing chapters in colleges across the country. The American Association of University Professors (AAUP), which had begun in 1915 as a professional organization devoted to review and discussion of matters pertaining to faculty, now had 75,000 members. The National Education Association (NEA) also joined the ranks of agencies seeking recognition as bargaining agents. Most of its members were in the public schools, but by 1970 it had 28,000 members on 234 college campuses and by 1974 had reached parity with the higher education membership of the AFT. NEA had started as a professional organization in 1870, but like its higher education counterpart, the AAUP, it was developing strong subunits seeking recognition at the colleges.

The AFT, AAUP, and NEA competed for the allegiance of professors, with each promising to negotiate benefits, especially pay raises, if the faculty members would join and vote them in as a unit to be recognized by the governing boards of the institutions. Their success was measured by the number of bargaining units they established, first in the strong labor states of Michigan and Wisconsin, then in the multi-institutional systems in New York, Florida, and Hawaii and in states where nonacademic state employees had organized, including Pennsylvania, New Jersey, Nebraska, and Minnesota. Traditional observers of the faculty might be horrified to see them marching down the same path as office clerks and prison guards, but so they did. Collective bargaining and traditional forms of academic governance were coexisting. The faculty associations and academic senates, dependent on the institution for funding and support, continued discussing economic and academic issues and consulting with the administration as appropriate. The newer organizations were supported by membership dues and were recognized by law as official organizations empowered to conduct formal negotiations and enter into written contracts covering everything from salaries to grievance procedures. Garbarino (1975) concludes that "any attempt to limit the scope of bargaining in order to provide separate compartments for academic government . . . is essentially unworkable" (p. 80).

In summation, the faculty moved toward professionalization by gaining control over many areas of practice that had been formerly held by administrators and trustees. In all but the community colleges they were solidly in control of decisions pertaining to curriculum and instruction and had begun participating in institutional governance to the point of being represented on boards of trustees in a few institutions; Cornell for example had appointed four faculty members as voting trustees in 1956. Threats to tenure had been countered both in the courts, which tended to protect it on grounds of due process and freedom of speech, and in practice when a contract achieved through collective bargaining spelled out rules for tenure in great detail. But by the end of the era the faculty reached a plateau in their trend toward professionalization. Faculty lobbying in state capitals and negotiating collectively on the campuses made them appear as just another labor organization. Mass higher education had removed the mystique from college-going. The increase in the number of part-time instructors certainly weakened any image of a higher calling. But at least the faculty were no longer poverty-stricken scholars, as Harvard's President Eliot had characterized them one hundred years earlier.

Curriculum

Patterns of curriculum that had been developed in earlier eras persisted. The curriculum was divided into courses, with each course carrying a specified number of credits that were usually tied to a measure of hours spent with an instructor in a classroom. A specified number of units led to a degree. Typically, the requirements included 60 units, or around twenty courses for an associate's degree, and 120 units, forty courses, for a bachelor's. In addition to the specialized classes required for students in certain programs, most students took a few courses in the liberal arts, divided among science, social science, humanities, mathematics, and English usage. Whether a student was attending a community college, liberal arts college, university, technical institute, or vocational school, the pattern was similar. The faculty controlled the curriculum. Student voices were muted; they took what the faculty prescribed in order to complete their degree programs and were often glad for the opportunity of adding a few elective courses when their prescribed major left openings. The units were usually transferable between institutions, and they kept their value even as more students began attending sporadically, dropping out for awhile and returning to complete a degree program at the same or a different institution.

Within that framework certain curricular emphases rose while others fell. During the University Transformation Era the curriculum had swung in the direction of human capital formation—courses that had content directly applicable to the performance of jobs and the practice of professions. By the opening of the Mass Higher Education Era the enrollment of more types of students and the splintering of academic disciplines into numerous subfields resulted in a greater variety of courses: more courses in the arts and sciences, subdisciplinary courses for nonmajors in a field, highly specialized courses centering on esoteric snippets of knowledge.

Knowledge—one of the university's main products—became a basis for economic and social growth. But knowledge takes many forms. The scientific idealism so prized in universities has never been accepted across the span of American higher education. Science as the application of intellect based on rationality has battled religion, intuition, and emotion. The long-standing dispute between science and humanism was overshadowed by other events of the

1960s but remained prominent within the academy, especially as funding for vocational training and scientific research increasingly put pressure on the liberal arts tradition. Many of the humanists had been content to bask in the prestige that science and the professional schools had brought to the universities and willingly accepted the pay increments that followed. But others grumbled, even as the National Defense Education Act in 1958 provided funds for foreign language training and the National Foundation of the Arts and Humanities, created in 1965, effected a channel for federal grants. Their pleasant little campuses and meditative studies had been compromised beyond hope of redress.

Should higher education serve society or should it center on some ideal vision of truth? Should it prepare people for the marketplace or create citizens who can make objective judgments based on evidence? How much should people's individualism and competitiveness be engendered as contrasted to their commitment to assisting each other? Except in the few institutions dedicated almost exclusively to science on the one hand or to the liberal arts tradition on the other, these questions were not answered. The vast majority of the institutions were attempting to do everything: to be social servants and knowledge seekers, to assist individuals and groups, to espouse freedom of inquiry along with development of the creative impulse. Still, the questions remained, affecting student and staff positions on every issue from admissions to program funding, public relations to staff appointments, presidential searches to campus expansion.

One of the fascinating aspects of the era is the reversal in the political dimensions of science and humanism. Early in the century science was considered elitist because it attracted the brightest students and sent people on to high-paying careers. Now humanism was being called elitist because its programs centered on criticism, the apprehension of texts, and traditions of literacy. The older America had seemed secure in its village society and industrial capitalism. Now it had to confront modernism in religion, literature, and art, along with relativity in morals. Might democracy be better served by assaulting a meritocratic tradition?

Every curriculum change has been justified as being practical, timely, and necessary for the different groups of students attending and for the purposes toward which higher education was directed. Personality and character formation took their place along with career and vocational skills as essential curricular elements. The humanities were practical because all citizens needed frames of reference on which to make judgments in the polity. Reading and writing were practical, else how could one function in society? Computational skills were practical because business demanded them. Women's studies and ethnic studies were practical because students could gain understanding of different cultures and function better in a global society. All changes were practical; all were relevant.

Claims of practicality were not sufficient to hold certain curricular emphases. The cultural heritage of Western civilization, formerly prominent, had declined steadily, but its shadow could still be seen in the required courses in the humanities. Home economics dropped out as women entered the workforce and as automated appliances and packaged foods liberated them from their kitchens. Farm management declined as family farms gave way to giant agricultural businesses. Journalism was folded into communications. Degrees earned at any level in philosophy, religion, or theology shrank to such a small proportion of the overall awards that the National Center for Education Statistics began listing them along with home economics, ethnic studies, parks and recreation, and a few additional categories in a column called "Other."

By 1960, more than 2,400 differently named degrees had been awarded since Harvard introduced the bachelor of science in 1851, and 1,600 of them were still being awarded, from the associate through the doctoral level; 43 percent were various kinds of bachelor's degrees. The student as consumer and the faculty as specialist were in full control. Few colleges were able to maintain requirements beyond lists of courses in various broad areas from which students might choose. Whatever the students wanted to study became, for them, the collegiate experience. Whatever the faculty wanted to teach gained a place in the curriculum.

The number of different courses offered reached into the thousands (see Table 4.3). By the 1970s the fifty leading universities (as measured by federal support of academic science) averaged more than 4,500 different courses each—nearly 2,400 at the undergraduate level and more than 2,100 graduate courses. Other universities averaged from 1,000 to 4,000 courses, and many liberal arts colleges and community colleges had 500 listed in their catalogues (Clark, 1995, p. 148).

This mass of courses spread steadily so that specialization and electives ruled the day. Between 1967 and 1974 the number of institutions requiring at least one course in English for students receiving bachelor's degrees declined from 90 to 72 percent; those requiring a foreign language declined from 72 to 53 percent; and those requiring a course in mathematics from 33 to 20 percent (The Carnegie Foundation, 1977, p. 271). Nearly 60 percent of the students were majoring in professional or preprofessional areas, with

Table 4.3. Undergraduate and Graduate Courses in American Institutions, by Type of University and College, 1977.

| Type of University | Average Number of Courses per Institution | | | |
	Total	Undergraduate	Graduate	% Graduate
Research universities	4,278	2,335	1,943	45.4
Doctoral-degree-granting universities	2,781	1,801	980	35.2
Comprehensive universities and colleges	1,253	1,050	203	16.2
Liberal arts colleges	548	540	8	1.4
Two-year colleges	463	463	0	0.0

Source: Clark, 1995, p. 148.

the others divided into social sciences (11 percent), biological sciences (7 percent), arts (6 percent), humanities (5 percent), and physical sciences (4 percent). All other fields totaled around 8 percent. In general the students were dividing their time almost equally between their major field, electives, and the breadth or distribution requirements that the institutions imposed. The holistic, humanistic tradition had been completely submerged.

Forces on Curriculum

Student ability joined faculty interests as a force affecting curriculum. As the proportion of students entering college expanded, the literacy level of the average entrant declined. Among students taking the SAT in 1952, the math score averaged 494. It increased to 502 in 1963, then declined to 480 in 1975. The verbal scores showed a similar pattern: 476 in 1952, 478 in 1963, 440 in 1975. The decline that began in the mid-1960s was attributed to many causes: the coming of age of the first generation of students reared on a diet of television; the youth counterculture, which glorified drugs and disrespect for authority; and the rise in the number of single-parent households. All were named as contributors. The public schools too were blamed as they reduced the length of the school year, began teaching driver education and other nonacademic subjects, expanded their pattern of passing through students who were marginally literate, reduced the number of academic requirements for high school graduation, and deemphasized reading and writing. The percentage of high school students enrolled in English courses dropped from 95 to 71 percent between 1960 and 1972 and proportionately in social studies, science, and mathematics. The high school graduates of 1960 had averaged four years of English, their 1972 counterparts only three years. As these students entered college the proportion diverted to remedial reading, writing, and arithmetic courses increased in all types of institutions, with the largest increase coming in the open-access community colleges. By the 1970s, around three in eight English classes and nearly one in three mathematics classes at the community colleges were being presented at below college level, and remedial classes accounted for 13 percent of the enrollments in chemistry (Cohen and Brawer, 1996, p. 258).

Remedial studies were forced on the colleges by the matriculation of underprepared students, but career and vocational studies expanded for different reasons. Students have always gone to college as a way of gaining skills and certification enabling them to enter the workplace at a higher level, but the number of occupations requiring more years of schooling expanded so that more of the curriculum was taken up by specialized vocational classes. In the early colleges, prospective doctors, lawyers, and clergymen had studied the liberal arts. Specialized programs and schools for engineers and professional schools for physicians, attorneys, architects, and others followed soon thereafter. However, not until the Mass Higher Education Era did the expectations of employers and the modifications in college curriculum follow each other with such rapidity. More people stayed in school longer; therefore the different occupational groups could demand more years of schooling. As apprenticeships and on-the-job training declined, the schools expanded the number of different skills they taught. Specialized groups sought the prestige of college degrees. For example, nursing education moved from the hospitals, and police education moved from the academies into the bachelor's-degree-granting institutions. The community colleges took on much of this vocational effort. In 1963, 26 percent of their enrollments were in occupational programs from which students expected to enter the job market, not to proceed toward the baccalaureate; the figure reached 35 percent by 1975. The curriculum was vocational because students were seen as consumers, education was considered a commodity, institutions were competing for enrollment, the public was accepting the idea of human capital formation through education, and colleges were attempting to enhance a local economy by providing skilled workers.

The curriculum moved simultaneously toward remediation, vocationalism, and academic subspecialties in a centrifugal pattern. No sector was immune; the community colleges took the brunt of remediation and occupational studies; the liberal arts colleges added business and preprofessional studies; the research universities expanded academic majors and graduate school specialties; and the state colleges and universities attempted everything. In all institutions the curriculum reflected political influence, opportunism, the power and ambition of small groups of faculty, the abilities and desires of students, and the pressure exerted by legislators, benefactors, and chambers of commerce. The faculty remained the dominant force, slicing everything into distribution requirements, fiercely maintaining their prerogatives, defending their favorite courses. The influence exerted by students paled in comparison; after all, a student attended for a few years at most, while the staff were there for a lifetime.

Even so, the idea of college as a place where values, judgment, and the examined life were exalted would not die. A vocal minority within higher education continued calling for an integrated curriculum, one that would assist students in developing a framework on which to place knowledge stemming from various sources and teach them to think critically, develop values, understand traditions, respect diverse opinions. The term *general education*, coined early in the century, was continually brought forward as the descriptor for this form of holistic education. It was difficult to argue for a set of coherent learnings; there were too many areas of knowledge, each with an equivalent claim on the curriculum, and most educators had given up on the concept. However, some of the faculty in the humanities and social sciences and a few administrators who believed in a tradition of rationalism spoke out repeatedly. The Mass Higher Education Era began and ended with the publication of two vigorous statements on behalf of integrated studies: *General Education in a Free Society* (Committee on the Objectives . . . , 1945) and *Missions of the College Curriculum* (The Carnegie Foundation, 1977).

But most institutions did little to guarantee their students an inte-grated learning experience; essentially, all they did was trot out the old distribution lists periodically and make new sets of courses from which students might choose in order to fulfill their general educa-tion requirements. The Carnegie Foundation report described what had happened to the curriculum, deplored the excessive specializa-tion, and argued in favor of a common experience for the students, but acknowledged that general education was moribund.

The calls for interdisciplinary studies that would unify patterns of learning began to sound like echoes of the Yale report of 1828, in which classical studies were justified for the discipline they imposed on developing minds. A latter-day liberal education would show students how to recognize commonalities among recurrent problems and to apply creative solutions, help them to tolerate ambiguity, and teach them to organize their thoughts logically and to write and speak coherently. This would be done through inde-pendent study, honors programs, integrative seminars, work-study and study abroad, collaborative learning, and community or service learning. The colleges would regain their central purpose—one that had been lost in the rush to provide something tailored for each matriculant. These ideas were to little avail; the curriculum had taken a Humpty-Dumpty fall and would not be reintegrated.

At least a portion of the activism of the late 1960s was directed against a curriculum that students saw as unresponsive. They wanted courses that were relevant to their desires and aspirations, nestled in an institution that cared for them as sentient human beings, not as units to be processed. A few institutions reacted to what the students were calling a dehumanized undergraduate expe-rience by developing smaller units, experimental colleges, colleges within colleges, and other configurations designed to bring students and faculty closer together. Some of the students and some of the instructors were given an opportunity to recreate the personal rela-tionship, the shared quest for common understanding that they believed had characterized the institutions before higher education became bureaucratic, impersonal, and highly specialized. However, most of the settings in which students and instructors came together to design their own curriculum lasted but a short time. Desks replaced with pillows, faculty on call twenty-four hours a day, unstructured curriculum, students with a minimum of guidance and a maximum of permissiveness—all reflected the fervor of righteousness but few could be sustained. Most students wanted to get on with their degrees and most faculty with their research and quest for promotion within the academic ranks. Several of the colleges named in Grant and Riesman's *The Perpetual Dream* (1978) and in MacDonald's *Five Experimental Colleges* (1973) sank without a trace or were so transformed that they hardly resembled the intentions of their founders.

Effects on the curriculum were negligible. Reactions against the elective system pursued with such vigor earlier in the century had led toward interdisciplinary courses. The later modifications brought forward in the name of satisfying student demands for a relevant curriculum led once again toward the interdisciplinary, forming and re-forming continually. But the lists of courses from which students might choose in order to fulfill degree requirements grew ever longer. The curriculum had no more direction, rigor, or overall coherence than it did before the students' cries for guidance and values on which they could construct their lives. When an institution has no basis for judging the relative worth among forms of learning, how can it deny any area of study?

The curriculum fractionated even further. A sizable number of the faculty and increasing numbers of students became more vocal in espousing their views on the shortcomings of the broader community, especially those having to do with the rights and progress of women and minorities. By the 1970s it had become common for institutions to take positions on societal issues and especially to make proclamations against racism, sexism, and other social ills. After student activism had brought these issues to the fore, the institutions could no longer afford accusations that they were unresponsive to social change or that they retained intellectual positions that opposed the dominant themes in the broader community. The multiversity, so named by Clark Kerr in the early 1960s, had been characterized as objective, neutral, and dedicated to the advancement of knowledge and service to the community. By the end of that decade and on into the 1970s, increasing numbers of students and faculty members identified areas where they said higher education was not objective, where its practices of exclusion in admitting students and employing faculty from particular groups, along with its Western-centered curriculum, revealed its values in ways that its claims to neutrality could not counter.

Controversies over the curricular canon accelerated. The faculty had attempted to remain apart from and morally superior to the surrounding communities. In large measure that was why they had entered the university in the first place; the notion of the ivory tower was not born in the 1970s. Now they were being called on to use their exalted position to remedy social ills. Each time a change in the canon was made, some faculty and other commentators argued that it meant the end of the search for truth. When the classics were abandoned early in the University Transformation Era, the heritage of Western civilization was debased. Toward the end of the Mass Higher Education Era when black studies, women's studies, and studies of other cultures were proposed, the same controversies were brought forward. But the institutions' leaders had learned to compromise, and it was not difficult for them to encourage the development of new, specialized curriculum in ethnic and women's studies. After all, what was the addition of another few courses to a catalogue that listed a thousand or more already? Besides, let the faculty and students wrangle over the curriculum; the administrators and trustees had buildings and budgets to occupy them.

Still, the controversies remained heated. When the classics had been diminished, only a few scholars objected. When vocationalism squeezed the humanities, most objections came from the instructors in those disciplines. Now the students, empowered by moral righteousness and using tactics learned in the activist period, kept the pressure on. And their sympathizers among the faculty smoothed the path. Courses in area and ethnic studies, esoteric foreign languages, and women's studies did not engage more than a minuscule proportion of the students or staff, but they represented symbolic victories. Their introduction also pointed up how egalitarianism had crept in to occupy a center position in the ethos of academe. The courses were to show young people that every subgroup was as worthy as any other, but as the era ended, the campuses and of course the broader society, were as fractionated as they had been when it began.

Instruction

The Mass Higher Education Era encompassed a full slate of innovations in instruction. Some were new; more were variations on earlier practices. The lecture and the laboratory remained dominant, but they were surrounded by an array of pedagogical innovations. Some instruction was designed for students to proceed at their own pace, but most was conducted with groups in classes. The power of the faculty was absolute; each instructor was free to design a method of teaching following the procedures judged suitable for the subject area under consideration and the students in the class. As had been true since the beginnings of schools, some instructors were creative, skilled at tailoring instruction to the situation, inspiring. Others were dull, lethargic, inflexible. One characteristic of the institution covered them all: peer evaluation was pro forma, and administrative evaluation was practically nonexistent. Only the students, voting with their feet, maintaining an informal network of commentary about which instructor's classes were useful, and especially beginning in the 1960s, publishing critiques that were based on classroom evaluations, attempted to influence the pedagogy. And even that right was hard-won, as the professors in many institutions expressed abhorrence at the idea of being evaluated by their charges. Nonetheless, student evaluations were accepted eventually, and in many institutions the completed forms became part of each professor's dossier.

Innovations in instruction became pervasive. The College Level Examination Program, established by the College Board in 1967, spread so that students might earn credits without participating in the courses. Awarding "Pass Only" grades and allowing students to withdraw from courses without penalty up until the last weeks of the term were introduced as ways of reducing grade inflation, avoiding penalties on students for not keeping up in the class, encouraging students to take courses in subjects outside their main interests, and leveling outcomes in required courses.

The Keller Plan was introduced in 1966 as a form of self-paced instruction. Learning laboratories in which students might proceed through self-instructional materials became popular. Computerized tutorials, autoinstructional workbooks, and a host of other technological aids to instruction were tried on the grounds that different students had different learning styles. In addition the chimera of reduced instructional costs lured college administrators to fund new technology. Publishers brought to market programmed workbooks, audio-tutorial instructional systems, and various mechanized ways of presenting material. A few instructors adopted the innovative programs, changing their own teaching methods to accommodate the self-paced characteristic of the materials. Many instructors acknowledged that the materials might be useful and urged the libraries or learning laboratories to purchase them so that students could use them as supplements. Most went on teaching as they had before the words *automated instruction* had been coined.

The various forms of instruction that were tried provided a splendid view of an institution attempting to accommodate numerous forces: a variety of students differing in abilities, aspirations, and interests; academic disciplines that were splitting and re-forming continually; the need to keep costs under control; and professors who effectually modified the curriculum every time they organized a course. Curriculum committees tried to control course proliferation but could do nothing about instructional innovation; in fact, in most institutions new forms of instruction were encouraged and money set aside so that professors could develop new courses and purchase different types of instructional materials. Colleges that did not introduce new programs or ways of instruction were deemed stodgy; the professor teaching from yellowed lecture notes was a caricature; the catalogue that each year did not list numerous cutting-edge courses was archaic. The modifications continued in a never-ending kaleidoscope.

The effect of all the innovation was to give the appearance that higher education was responsive to changing social conditions, new types of students, and advances in knowledge. Did students learn more? No method was shown to be consistently superior to any other. The conditions of instruction were so fluid and the students and professors so varied that claims for greater learning outcomes proved impossible to verify. McKeachie (1963) summed much of the research on teaching by pointing out how it could say little more than in college A, on day B, instructor C used method D to teach subject E to students F. Modify any of the variables and the results would differ. Instructors continued trying different techniques and insisting that they were effecting student learning, even as they resisted deliberate attempts to measure it reliably.

Neither instructional innovation nor course proliferation could be brought under control. In most institutions if a course was not presented over a period of a few years, it was removed from the catalogue. But for each one removed, more were added, with the presumption that if professors wanted to teach them, if students would take them, and if they did not substantially duplicate others, they must be worthy. Any form of instruction that did not increase the per-student cost showed that the college was not afraid to experiment. This atomistic approach to curriculum and instructional reformation was not without its critics: the students needed more nurturing as they made their way into adulthood, hence the college should function more as a therapeutic center, said Rogers (1969); society was oppressive, and students should be taught how to combat the evils of the economic and social system, said Freire (1970). All were given hearings and then thoroughly compromised by the magnitude of the system.

Too much structure or too little, too many choices or too few, too much or too little adherence to the heritage of Western civilization, an excessive concern with liberal arts or with careers or with scientific research—all criticisms were as marshmallows tossed at a juggernaut. The curriculum encompassed every bit of esoterica, every view of truth, every skill that anyone might need to have. The instructional forms sustained the debates, recitals, lectures, examinations, and independent study variations prominent throughout history. Added to them were all of the technologies that could be purchased and introduced. Yet overall, the system remained the same. Students came to college and attended classes; professors interacted with them; books were available in the library. For everyone concerned, the campuses were nice places to be associated with the life of the mind.

Governance

The expansion of public institutions and more state-level coordination reveal how higher education was viewed as a public good. No state wanted to be left behind in the race to provide it for as many of its citizens as possible. Plans were developed and efforts were made to put a college within commuting distance of every resident—tendencies revealed in the reports emanating from commissions organized to review higher education at the state level and for the nation as a whole. Revealing the attitude of the era, these reports both reflected and influenced legislation.

A review of a few of these commissions illustrates the point. The President's Commission on Higher Education, 1947–48, recommended that at least half the high school graduates could benefit from going to college to extend their general education and to learn occupational skills. Two years later the Commission on Financing Higher Education reiterated the view that half the college-age students could benefit from enrollment and foresaw an accentuation of the separate tracks between collegiate and vocational studies. During the Johnson administration the White House Conference on Education acknowledged that education was a primary instrument for solving societal problems. The Task Force for Reform in Higher Education released a report in 1970 suggesting that education should be the goal, and research and direct public service should be deemphasized. It too argued that higher education should be expanded to accommodate more people. In the same year, the Assembly on University Goals and Governance recommended expanding general education while reducing attempts to serve the public directly. The Educational Policies Commission of the National Education Association called for expansion and egalitarianism. And so it went through the era, as various conferences and commissions urged each state to expand its higher education effort so that none would be left behind.

The most prolific group was the Carnegie Commission on Higher Education, which published more than fifty books in the late 1960s and early 1970s. Its general tone was that higher education should be expanded to include more of the population and that the system should sustain a proper balance between public and private and undergraduate and graduate education. The commission's books considered institutional growth, admissions policies, budgets, mission, and accounting practices, all of which they said should be under state-level coordination. The states should be judged on the extent to which they offered access and equality in educational opportunity. They should encourage educational diversity, preserving college autonomy even while insisting on public accountability. The states should prepare people for the workforce and provide incentives for institutional innovation. Statewide coordinating agencies should take precedence over boards of control. The commission's other recommendations covered the field:

- More people should be prepared for the health professions because that area was expanding, and fewer people should be prepared as teachers because public school enrollments would be declining in the 1970s.

- The proportion of higher education income derived from federal sources should increase so that parity among the states could be approached.

- Enrollments should increase and tuition should be kept low so that universal access would become the norm across the nation.

- Faculty salaries should increase to bring the wages of professors closer to those of comparably trained professionals in other fields.

- More curricular options should be explored, including remedial education for students who failed to learn the basics in the lower schools.

- Intellectual competence should be nurtured and seen as the proper way of differentiating among people; all other types of discrimination were to be shunned.

The commission acknowledged that most state master plans made few provisions for the private sector and foresaw major difficulty in sustaining institutional diversity and a variety of possible educational experiences. Its reports came toward the end of an era in which public funding had already accelerated manifold. The states had built extensive college systems, and federal appropriations were going into research, facilities, professional study, financial aid for students at all levels, libraries, and the improvement of instruction. By accepting these funds, higher education became responsible

for following state and federal mandates—characteristics of governance that were to become more pronounced as the years went by.

The reports also followed developments in several states where
plans for expanding and coordinating higher education were under
way. Notable among these was the 1960 Master Plan for Higher
Education in California, a voluntary compact (Clark Kerr, its principal author, called it a treaty) that divided responsibilities among
the state's community colleges, comprehensive colleges, and university. The University of California was to admit students from the
top one-eighth of the high school graduating classes and be the sole
public-institution provider of doctoral studies. The state colleges
would take students from the upper one-third of the high school
graduates and provide programs through the master's level. Anyone
aged eighteen or older would be eligible to attend the community
colleges, which would provide general education through grade
fourteen, along with occupational certificate programs. In short, the
various public institutions would divide the territory. Each had
developed separately—the university as a land-grant institution
named in the state constitution, the comprehensive colleges as normal schools or occupational training centers, the community colleges as extensions of the lower-school districts. Instead of
competing, they would cooperate in providing education for every
purpose. By 1970 they were enrolling as many students as were the
public institutions of New York, Illinois, and Texas combined.

The federal government stepped up its involvement with and
influence on higher education. Year after year, beginning with the
GI Bill in 1944, more laws, more funds, and more regulation evidenced this concern. A mere rundown of some of the acts passed
points up this development. In 1950 the Housing Act authorized
loans to construct college residence halls. The 1958 National
Defense Education Act authorized loans and fellowships for college
students and funds to provide for foreign language study. In 1963 several acts expanded the involvement, including the Health Professions Educational Assistance Act, the Vocational Education Act,
and the Higher Education Facilities Act. The Higher Education

Act of 1965 provided grants for several types of college services, including libraries and undergraduate programs; it authorized guaranteed student loans. During the same year a Medical Library Assistance Act added funds for libraries, and a National Vocational Student Loan Insurance Act expanded loan insurance programs. The Adult Education Act of 1966 and the Education Professions Development Act in 1967 expanded teacher training. The Vocational Education Act and the Higher Education Act both were amended in 1968 to expand their original scope and funding. In 1971 the Comprehensive Health Manpower Training Act and the Nurse Training Act expanded provisions in those areas. The Education Amendments of 1972 established the education division in the Department of Health, Education, and Welfare and authorized a Bureau of Occupational and Adult Education. The Education Amendments of 1974 established the National Center for Education Statistics.

This review of legislative action displays much of what the federal government was doing to increase access and to turn higher education ever more in the direction of professional and vocational training. And the list does not include the numerous programs that although not directly pointed toward higher education, enhanced the funding available for applied research. Higher education had always been regarded as an agent of social change, first through its providing for individual mobility, then through its research on social issues and its role in economic development. But in the Mass Higher Education Era, its role expanded as it conformed with rulings regarding discrimination, student aid, affirmative action, focused research, and institutions and programs for especially designated groups. The association between campus and state, which grew steadily after the beginning of the University Transformation Era, accelerated.

State Coordination

Federal legislation reached into all areas. The Higher Education Act of 1965 was an omnibus bill, with sections covering financial aid to students, construction of facilities, aid to institutions that wanted to work on societal issues, and not least, the directive that each state establish a coordinating agency for higher education. This latter provision led to a powerful and long-lasting influence. It forced coordination of all sectors, as state-level coordinating boards or boards of governors were erected or strengthened so that more decisions reaching deeper into institutional affairs were negotiated in state capitals, thus accelerating a trend toward consolidation that had been in place since the era began.

The states were quick to create boards or commissions to comply with Section 1202 of the Higher Education Act; within ten years all but four had established a new commission or converted an existing agency into a commission in the form recommended. These groups were composed of members from all the sectors identified as part of higher education in each state: the public four-year institutions, public community colleges, public vocational or technical institutes, and private colleges, augmented by representatives of the general public. Each 1202 commission had between eight and twenty-nine delegates, with the median at around fifteen.

The 1202 commissions accelerated trends toward state-level coordination that had been developing in most of the states and prodded the others to create coordinating groups. They had several effects initially. They coordinated data collection, wrote position papers, and provided a forum for debate among representatives of the various sectors. Gradually they began defining categories of higher education and recommending that one or another sector expand certain types of programs. The differences between universities, community colleges, and vocational-technical institutes were brought forward and attempts made at integration for planning purposes. In some states they were able to effect better coordination of higher education resources, but in most they found it difficult to gain cooperation among the various agencies responsible for one or another area of education. In particular they were not often able to present a unified voice to the state legislature, as each sector and many of the interest groups within it maintained their own offices in the capital, sending representatives to the commissions but making their own demands and appeals to the legislature.

One of the effects of the move toward coordinating commissions was that most states developed comprehensive plans or studies of education and financial needs for higher education. The California master plan had been developed under the Coordinating Council for Higher Education, and when that group was converted to the California Postsecondary Education Commission, restudies and ways of ironing out wrinkles in the master plan were pursued. The 1202 commissions were not legislative bodies. They could study and recommend, but any change in funding or control still had to work its way through traditional channels in the legislatures or in the institutions' governing boards. Coordination implied continuing autonomy for each institution, that is, the prerogative of the campuses to develop their own programs and areas of service. The trend toward state coordination was intact, but it had not yet reached a point at which major decisions affecting programs on individual campuses were being decided. Actually, increased state-level activity often improved the quality of campus decision making by setting it in a broader framework. The tradition of individual campus autonomy, stemming from the earliest colleges, still dominated.

While the 1202 commissions were studying cooperative relations, planning mechanisms, financial needs, and relationships among the sectors, a parallel trend toward state-level governance had been developing. In several states the universities were linked with a governing board managing all of them. The idea was that centralized governing boards would streamline the system, present a unified voice to the legislature, and reduce program duplication. Centralized management and budgeting would reduce waste. Operational guidelines would ensure that funds were allocated properly. Public relations statements promised greater efficiency as governing boards took command.

The experience of higher education's move toward state-level governance turned out somewhat differently. Merely because a multicampus system evolved from a set of individual institutions did not guarantee change in the essential characteristics of the system. One area of contention came over the question of whether a particular campus should offer a graduate degree in a certain field. The tradition of individual campus autonomy was so strong that issues of curriculum and program modification were usually debated in the abstract, with campus representatives participating in discussions but with intramural groups, often allied with local supporters, making the final determination. For example, the University of California opened four new medical schools in addition to the one it already had, three of them in the 1960s alone. The systemwide governing board questioned program duplication, but local politics and campus ambitions won the day.

The governing boards found the rhetoric easier than the reality in other areas as well. The central administrations were supposed to be accountable to the state for expenditures across campuses, but individual units demanded and usually retained the flexibility of shifting funds among programs. The campuses clung also to requirements for student admissions and graduation and to most issues related to curriculum. As an example of the latter, getting a statewide, uniform course-numbering system in place usually proved to be a lengthy process and in many states did not reach fruition. However, the multi-institution governing boards did achieve program coordination in some areas, especially in occupational programs, probably because those were the ones most nearly associated with employer demand and employment rates that could be calculated for the state as a whole. And in many multi-institution systems, staff salary schedules were set uniformly so that everyone at a certain level would earn the same regardless of the institution in which they were employed.

A general effect of the statewide boards was that the institutions within a system became more equal. The major research universities—Illinois at Urbana, Texas at Austin, Michigan at Ann Arbor—saw resources being spread more widely across their states' higher education system. Part of this was inevitable as rising student populations in the second-tier institutions demanded more resources. But where state budgets were limited, this diffusion seemed to penalize the flagship institutions that previously had been at the head of the line in obtaining state funds. The leading universities' share of state appropriations declined, and support for sister institutions and state colleges rose significantly. Another effect was that the universities' budgetary requests became negotiable, along with demands of other public agencies. In some states higher education budgets grew much more slowly than did those for welfare and health services. The question of the extent to which this would have happened in the absence of state governing boards is not answerable; perhaps higher education would have suffered more if each college still had to make a separate budgetary plea.

The era also saw the public gaining influence over the conduct of institutions, which was not surprising. As higher education increased its expenditures as a proportion of gross domestic product, the public became more concerned. One effect was to open the governing boards to people whose major concerns might be more as watchdogs than as institutional spokespeople or fundraisers. More state-level boards meant that more officials were appointed by governors; in some cases the superintendent of public instruction, lieutenant governor, or governor became a member of the board automatically. The traditional idea of a governing board as an independent agency serving as a buffer between the campus on the one hand and the public and legislature on the other was compromised.

State-level governance did little to reduce competition among institutions or among groups within them. As the systems and each unit in the systems grew larger, the likelihood that the college reflected a community of people with shared interests and values grew more remote. Most institutions seemed more like business corporations, governmental bureaus, or agencies in which contending parties vied for a greater share of power. This view of the university as a center of conflict or political contentiousness received much attention in the early 1970s when student activism, faculty unionization, and program expansion were prominent. Competition among institutions was matched by competition within, as each department and each group—faculty, students, teaching assistants, deans, business officers, and other officials—sought more resources. Many of the groups formed statewide associations and presented their own requests to the governing board or directly to the legislature. Perhaps the idea of the college as a community had been unrealistic; certainly the student rebellions of the nineteenth century suggested that a generational split was the norm. But until the Mass Higher Education Era the various subgroups within each campus had not been sufficiently large or well enough organized to take their case to the next level.

Management

Greater size led to complexity in management, as each institution added administrators in greater proportion than it did students and faculty. Complying with state and federal regulations, managing financial aid and affirmative action, and providing assurances that the institution was accountable in everything from student admissions to pollution control demanded that additional offices be opened. Tasks that were once performed by the president and the faculty, along with many that were previously unknown, were assigned to middle management. Allocating economic resources and reforming educational programs necessarily brought administrators into conflict with faculty, students, and alumni groups. These tensions began occupying much of the time that the parties might otherwise have spent on education—the essence of the enterprise—and additional offices were created to resolve issues among them.

Most institutions divided their administrative structure into three general functions: academic affairs, student affairs, and business affairs. Under academic affairs were the deans of the various schools, director of the library, registrar, and financial aid officers. Student affairs typically were in charge of housing and food services, counseling, placement, student organizations, and student health. The business affairs office was concerned with financial operations, personnel, buildings and grounds, security, purchasing, mail, and administrative computing. These divisions varied somewhat. In one institution the director of admissions might be under academic affairs, in another under student affairs, but one axiom held: the larger the institution, the more the administration was subdivided into smaller units.

In systems managed at the state level, these administrative units were usually duplicated in statewide offices mirroring the campus offices and providing a coordinating function among them. To a board of regents and president were added vice presidents for academic affairs, administration, health, and finance. Each of them supervised officials responsible for affirmative action, personnel policy, academic planning, liaison with the faculty, admissions, library, and five or ten other functions. The vice president for finance managed offices for alumni relations, budget analysis, long-range development plans, capital improvement, construction, gifts and endowments, governmental relations, and everything from space utilization to resource administration. The vice president for administration would oversee business operations, collective bargaining services, contracts and grants, accounting, faculty housing, patents, and several other services. Attempts to enhance efficiency in institutional management were usually negated by the demands for interoffice review, data, and assurance of compliance with systemwide regulations. The larger independent institutions were spared much of that type of reporting and oversight but had as many administrative offices within them. The smaller private colleges added administrators to ensure compliance with federal and state regulations regarding affirmative action, health services, and financial aid packages. No level or sector of higher education was exempt from administrative expansion.

The role of the president shifted notably from leader of the educational program to manager of the bureaucracy. The president who could stamp the institution with a specific academic style could no longer prevail against all the countervailing forces. The academic senates had become increasingly well organized and powerful. They had almost total responsibility for what happened within the departments and had gained various universitywide responsibilities as well. A growing number of public institutions had faculty representation on the governing board. And within public and private universities alike, the faculty typically had responsibility for determining what research and public service projects should be undertaken. They also determined the admissions and graduation requirements in the various schools; the appointment, promotion, and dismissal of professors; the purchase of books and journals by the library; and the allocation of clerical and research support. In the larger institutions, the senates had their own committees, councils, and task forces to facilitate communication among the departments and between the faculty and the administration. Together with the various administrator groups, the faculty senates ensured that the president's role was limited to macromanaging, fundraising, and representing the institution to the governing board.

Student government changed. In the early American colleges the students had no voice in institutional management, curricular affairs, or any other aspect of student life. Subsequently, colleges developed honor codes, making students responsible for their conduct. By the turn of the twentieth century, student governments had been formed to include honor systems, advisory councils to the faculty, committees with power of discipline, oversight of residence halls, and management of extracurricular activities. It was easy to justify student involvement in governance; it was supposed to train for citizenship, give experience in policy making, provide for student expression, develop leaders, and in general enhance the morale of the college community. By the end of the University Transformation Era most institutions had a student government made up of an executive council, a lawmaking body with elected representatives, and a student court to adjudicate violations of regulations.

Subsequently, the scope of student participation in institutional governance expanded. One of the goals of the student activism of the 1960s had been to gain a greater voice in academic management. Accordingly, students gained seats on institutional governing boards and on college committees where they could discuss admissions policies and faculty and administrative appointments. They might have been invited to sit on faculty and administrative committees, but there they found not centers of power where sweeping decisions were made but tedious, lengthy, boring discussions of the most mundane details without conclusions ever being reached—the real world of academic decision making. The students who developed statewide associations and public interest research groups found that influence could be exerted more effectively. The goal of campus-level community government with students, faculty, and administrators meeting, conferring, and deciding remained elusive, as student associations began acting as one more pressure group among many.

Accreditation

The influence of accreditation grew. Six regional associations took responsibility for institutional accreditation, that is, the process whereby a college was recognized as having met certain predetermined standards. The GI Bill specified that veterans were entitled to educational benefits if they attended institutions approved by state educational agencies, thus solidifying accreditation as an essential feature in higher education. Its successor, the Veterans Readjustment Act of 1952, directed the U.S. commissioner of education to publish a list of approved accrediting associations; from then on, access to federal funds was limited to institutions that had been accredited by one of the agencies recognized by the U.S. Office of Education.

The process of institutional accreditation took many forms, but in general the accrediting group established standards, and each applicant institution performed a self-study comparing itself to those standards. A team selected by the accrediting agency visited the institution or program to determine if the standards were being met; if the agency was satisfied, the institution was officially accredited. Accreditation might be for a period of a year or two or as much as ten years. Programs that did not meet standards typically were put on probation and, after a time, visited again to see if they had come into compliance. All was designed to stimulate institutional self-improvement.

The accrediting of professional programs and special types of colleges proceeded along with the accrediting of generic institutions. The American Medical Association, the first of the specialized accrediting groups, was organized in 1847. It challenged schools to improve their curriculum and to enforce stricter entrance and graduation requirements. The American Association of Teachers Colleges began accrediting teacher education nationwide in 1923. By 1948 it had become the American Association of Colleges for Teacher Education and had accredited fewer than 250 of the 1,200 institutions then involved in preparing instructors. The National Council for Accreditation of Teacher Education took over in 1954 and was recognized as the sole accrediting agency for that field by the National Commission on Accrediting in 1956. Other fields became involved with accreditation so that the National League for Nursing, the American Dental Association, and at least fifty other groups were functioning. Some of them had persuaded the states that graduation from an accredited program was necessary for licensure in that occupation, thus demonstrating considerable power in the management of higher education.

From the standpoint of institutional governance the accreditation process segmented responsibility. It has been criticized for emphasizing the interests of certain programs; for reinforcing the status quo by limiting deviation from conventional practice;

for effectually requiring governing boards to spend funds for buildings, equipment, and staff when it specified faculty-student ratios and minimum square footage for program operation; and for having standards that tend to be quantitative rather than qualitative. However, the accreditation process has been higher education's way of managing itself in the absence of the national ministry of education found in most other nations. And in peculiarly American fashion the federal agency most responsible for education accredited the accrediting groups; thus far and no further.

In summation, governance in the Mass Higher Education Era moved steadily toward larger units. In the public sector, statewide coordinating or governing boards spread along with linkages among what had previously been independent college and universities. Expansion in campus-level administration occurred in both public and private institutions, as offices were created to manage the complexities of larger units and to satisfy demands for compliance with state and federal regulations. Accrediting associations gained quasi-official status when the federal government stipulated that they be approved by the U.S. Office of Education if the programs and institutions they accredited were to be eligible for federal funds. The connections among higher education's thousands of units took the form of a gigantic spider web or a skein of yarn tossed by a kitten. All were interconnected yet at the same time independently functioning.

Finance

Recounting finances over time is a multifaceted exercise. The gross numbers tell one story, the numbers adjusted for inflation quite another. The data can be displayed for all of higher education, subdivided by sector or level, or compared with funding for some other public institution. Revenue can be considered by source and expenditures by category, and broken out again on a per-student basis. The figures can be displayed for any span of years. Accordingly, it is possible to show that during the Mass Higher Education Era finances for higher education increased, decreased, or remained the same. As the truism has it, torture the data enough and they will confess to anything. However, a realistic conclusion is that the colleges and universities did quite well.

Sources

The raw numbers are certainly impressive. In 1945 higher education received around $1 billion from all sources; by 1975 this figure had increased to $35 billion. Adjusting for inflation and using 1967 dollars as a base, the 1945 total would be $1.7 billion, and the 1975 figure would be $14.4 billion—a substantial increase. Using those same constant-dollar figures and dividing by the number of students enrolled yields an expenditure of around $850 per student in 1945 and $1,270 per student in 1975—much more modest but still a sizable gain.

The value of higher education property increased from $5 billion in 1945 to $75 billion in 1975. The total physical plant, land, buildings, and equipment equaled $3 billion in the earlier year, $62 billion in the latter, or $7,800 per full-time equivalent student. The balance was made up by the value of endowment: $2 billion in 1945, $15 billion in 1975. Higher education was adding around $4.7 billion per year to its total capital base at the end of the era (National Center for Education Statistics, 1992, tables 338 and 339).

Patterns of financing most directly differentiate the public and private sectors. Tuition is one example. Private universities at the beginning of the era were deriving around one-third of their current-fund income from tuition, whereas the figure for public institutions was 12 percent. By 1974 the proportion of income derived from tuition had dropped to 27 percent in the private institutions but had remained steady at 12 percent in the public sector. For higher education as a whole, tuition was contributing around 20 percent at the end of the era (National Center for Education Statistics, 1992, table 315).

The other sources of income show differences as well (see Table 4.4). Early in the era government as a whole was contributing

Table 4.4. Distribution of Current-Fund Revenue of Private and Public Universities, by Source, Selected Academic Years 1949–50 to 1975–76 (Percentage of Total Income).

Source	1949–50		1965–66		1975–76	
	Private Institutions	Public Institutions	Private Institutions	Public Institutions	Private Institutions	Public Institutions
Governments, total	16	69	32	77	29	79
Federal	12	13	30	23	25	18
State and local	4	56	2	54	4	61
Tuition and fees	57	25	43	14	48	16
Gifts and endowment earnings	23	3	18	3	19	3
Other educational and general revenue	5	3	6	5	4	2

Note: Figures do not include revenue from auxiliary enterprises or from sales and services. Student aid is included under tuition.

Source: McPherson and Schapiro, 1991, p. 21.

about 16 percent of the income in the private institutions and
69 percent in the public. At its end the private institutions were
gaining 29 percent from government, whereas the public percentage had increased to 79 percent. Gifts and endowment earnings had
made up 23 percent of the income in the private sector, dropping
to 19 percent by the end of the era. Never a major source of funding for the public sector, gifts and endowment earnings began the
era at 3 percent and ended at 3 percent.

Within each sector different types of institutions showed different dependencies on the various sources and different rates of
change in each of them. The annual growth rate in gross tuition
charged, which was 13 percent between 1940 and 1950, dropped to
5 percent between 1950 and 1960 and increased again to 14 percent
between 1960 and 1968 when governmental grants and loans began
enabling the private institutions to increase tuition substantially.
State appropriations went from $150 million in 1940, to $500 million in 1950, to $1.4 billion in 1960, to $5.8 billion in 1970, and to
$12.2 billion in 1975. In the latter years the share going to univer-
sities declined, and that for community colleges rose as the states
increased funds in the sector that was accounting for more of the
rise in enrollment. In addition, half the states, led by New York and
Pennsylvania, provided some institutional support to the private
colleges. Federal expenditures for higher education (exclusive of student aid) rose from less than $40 million in 1940 to $500 million in
1950, $1 billion in 1960, $3.1 billion in 1970, and $5.5 billion in
1975. The percentage of overall current-fund revenue provided by
the states was 21 percent in 1950 and 31 percent in 1975. The federal government provided 22 percent in 1950 and 16 percent in
1975, as its contributions swung from support for research and facilities construction toward aid to students (Snyder, 1993).

Efficiency

Efficiency is an index of how well an institution uses its funds in
relation to the outcomes it achieves. However, because every institution desires educational excellence and prestige, there is no limit

to the amount of money it could spend to improve what it does. Accordingly, each raises all the money it can and spends all it raises. This distorts concepts of efficiency because specific outcomes are rarely attributable to additional funds.

Efficiency is associated with gains in productivity. It has always been more difficult for higher education to enhance productivity than it has been for most other industries. Some service industries became more productive by adopting technology; banks, insurance companies, and brokerage firms that automated their processes were leaders. But the creative and performing arts, churches, and higher education have not been able to benefit from technology to nearly as great a degree. This may have been because the tradition of professions as ministering to clients meant that they touched sensitive aspects of people's lives, and best practice usually required personal contact. Just as health services required the presence of physicians and nurses, instruction depended on teachers. Few technological adoptions affected productivity in the Mass Higher Education Era. The colleges continually sought more funds to pay their staff, and when these were not forthcoming, saw wages fall behind those in industries where technology had spawned productivity gains.

Comparatively large increases in revenue per student came to an end in the early 1970s, and the institutions began reducing the rate of staff salary increases, deferring maintenance, and looking for other places to save money. They increased class size, employed more part-time instructors, added distance learning possibilities through television, built audio-tutorial laboratories and computer-assisted instructional programs, awarded credit for independent study and for experience, and tried to enhance the use of buildings by offering courses for longer periods of the day and on weekends. Funds for libraries that had been running at about 4 percent of total institutional expenditures began a steady decline. There were no data to show how much maintenance was deferred, but it seems likely that most institutions retrenched there; the paint may have been flaking off a building's walls but at least it was not pounding the table and demanding an increase in salary. Arguments were continually raised to the effect that further cost cutting would sacrifice program quality, but the budget makers had little choice. And overriding all the contentions about where to make cuts was the great unknown: the relationship between expenditures and outcomes. The cost of education per student was lower in some institutions than in others, but it was certainly not clear that cost-per-student or expenditures in any area were associated with effects.

Comprehensive reviews of costs and benefits were made by Bowen (1980), who subdivided colleges by type, level, control, size, and so forth and found wide variation in the allocation of funds. No matter how calculated—whether or not doctoral students, upper-division students, and lower-division students were weighted differently—the range among institutions of the same type was greater than the median differences among types of institutions. This variance was mirrored in the way institutions spent their funds on different functions. The spread of charges showed private liberal arts colleges allocating 38 percent of their expenditures to teaching and research universities putting 59 percent in that category. However, in the latter case, departmental research was calculated as part of instructional cost. The private liberal arts colleges spent more than other institutions on institutional support, scholarships and fellowships, and student services—no surprise because they prided themselves on what they provided to enhance student life.

Bowen found few differences in percentage allocations among the richest and the poorest institutions in the same category. Apparently, as the institutions gained access to more funds, they spread them around so that almost all functions got a share. Every department, every section could always use additional money; whenever new funds came in, they all reached for them. The effect was that the historical pattern of allocations within institutions tended to be perpetuated. The richer institutions spent more for everything; the less well endowed institutions made do with less across the board. The one exception was that the more affluent institutions seemed to "apply their incremental expenditures to successively less important purposes" (Bowen, 1980, pp. 150–151). They were more likely to have more administrators and clerks, office equipment and supplies, and budgets for travel. Bowen felt that one useful way of analyzing institutions might be to focus on the ratio of nonacademic staff to students instead of on the ratio of faculty to students. But he concluded, "The dispersion of costs is astonishingly great—so great that one may reasonably question the rationality or equity in the allocation of resources among higher educational institutions" (pp. 120–121).

Seeking the optimum institutional size proved elusive. Every college had to have some faculty and administrators, some buildings and books. The cost per student in each of these areas decreased as the number of students increased, hence up to a point growth seemed to suggest efficiency. However, as institutions grew they often found certain costs going up, in particular the increased cost of internal coordination, the overlapping managerial functions, and the necessity of expanding the market area in order to recruit greater numbers of students. Accordingly, costs per student seemed to decline sharply as an institution grew until a certain point of enrollment was reached and they leveled off. The larger institutions were spending more for administration and student services, less for plant operation and maintenance. Scholarships and academic support showed little relationship to size. The increase in funds spent for coordination resulted from the growth in interdepartmental committees, personnel officers, formal newsletters, and other means of communication. Large institutions were able to save money though because they could use their buildings more efficiently. In summation, institutional size had considerable impact on certain unit costs, but overall costs per student differed little. There seemed no way to calculate the most efficient size for an institution.

In the quest for efficiency, efforts to manage college allocations were made continually by legislators, coordinating boards, and other types of governance structures. The extramural agencies often tried to micromanage expenditures, using the argument that because colleges were not run as businesses and because educators continually sought more money, governing agencies must show them how to spend their funds. They often set up detailed financial controls and prepared impressive-looking reports but did not capture the essence of the colleges because the categories had elastic boundaries and it was relatively easy for an institution to shift costs around within them. Bowen (1980) contended that public agencies wanting to control costs might do only two things: "First, to establish in broad general terms the basic scope and mission of the institutions for which they are responsible, and second, to set the total amount of money to be available to each institution each year" (p. 24). When this was done the individual colleges could allocate resources according to their best determination. But in most states systemwide management had advanced too far for that type of budgeting autonomy to be sustained.

Staff Salaries

In 1975, American colleges and universities were employing almost 1.6 million people, including faculty, support staff, maintenance workers, and administrators. Fringe benefits accounted for nearly 19 percent in addition to salaries. The payroll totaled over 57 percent of current-fund expenditures. Salaries charged to instruction came to 34 percent—practically the same as at the beginning of the era. Even though the faculty had gained in compensation during the 1950s and 1960s, the costs of everything else that the colleges purchased had increased at a greater rate and accounted for more of the increase in per-student expenditures.

The higher education labor market is different from many others. Faculty members may migrate from one college to another readily, but they rarely move out of higher education at large. They have invested much in their training, and the decision to become a professor is often tantamount to a lifetime commitment, not affected by temporary increases or decreases in compensation. Once in, the individual usually stays. This gives colleges some latitude when deciding whether or not to raise salaries. Within reasonable limits a qualified staff can always be employed. Concerns that not enough professors could be found to staff the colleges when enrollments increased rapidly in the 1960s proved unfounded. The feared shortage never materialized.

For several decades, trends in faculty pay shifted only slightly in constant-dollar terms. The slow advance after the turn of the century turned into a decline during World War I. A rapid advance in the early 1920s slowed in the latter part of the decade but increased again in the early 1930s. A moderate decline during the latter 1930s turned into a sharp decline during World War II as inflation eroded faculty pay. The decline slowed in the late 1940s, and then in the 1950s and 1960s a marked, steady advance occurred. Early in the 1970s the trend turned down again. Because faculty salaries had started at such a low baseline—around $5,000 in constant 1967 dollars at the turn of the century—not until 1950 did they begin a rise toward what might be called a living wage.

Faculty pay rates have little to do with the supply of or demand for qualified instructors, and they are not closely associated with rates of inflation or deflation in the general economy. They relate more to public attitudes and the political power of the faculty. Because the faculty did not exhibit any significant bargaining ability prior to the late 1960s, the wage gains of the preceding decade cannot be attributed to such efforts. Similarly, if market forces were operating properly, faculty compensation would decline along with student enrollments and with a growing supply of potential instructors. But the rise and fall in faculty salaries relative to salaries paid to other professional groups showed little relationship to any of those forces.

Faculty compensation includes more than salaries and fringe benefits. In many private institutions a faculty member's family may receive tuition remission. In most institutions access to campus events and sports facilities, long vacations, sabbatical leaves, tenure, flexibility in responsibilities and schedules, and in some cases subsidized housing add to the pay package. Furthermore, most instructors have the opportunity of earning outside income. Some estimates in the 1970s were that three-fourths of the faculty on academic-year appointments were earning outside income that added about 20 percent on average to their base salary. Accordingly, when all the supplemental compensation was totaled, faculty earnings were comparable to their counterparts in government service.

Of course the amount that faculty earn from second jobs is never calculated as a cost of higher education because it does not show up in expenditures. However, administrators and other salaried employees do not receive outside income to a degree nearly comparable; thus, when total faculty income is compared with administrators' income, the difference between the two is not really as great. The recognition that faculty can and should earn money from other pursuits arose when the faculty were considerably underpaid; pay for administrators was set when they shifted from faculty ranks and were given additional stipends for administrative service. Although top administrators are sometimes paid to consult and to serve on corporation boards, compared with the compensation that managers in other industries receive, the higher education administrators overall are probably more underpaid than are the faculty.

Federal Government Support

The main federal support for higher education shifted eventually from research to aid to students, but for two decades expenditures for research grew even while enrollments were soaring. At the conclusion of World War II, the universities' contribution was evidenced by the pool of qualified researchers on staff and the number of scientific and technical laboratories that had been built. Not wanting to waste this accumulated wealth of talent and capability by retreating to prewar levels, the universities sought continuing support from the federal government. On the government side, the conviction that the university was a proper setting for research was reiterated continually: in a report to President Roosevelt by Vannevar Bush, director of the Office of Scientific Research and Development during the war; in the formation of the National Science Foundation during the Truman Administration that omitted support for constructing governmental laboratories; in a Bureau of the Budget report to President Eisenhower maintaining that research and development that could be procured from the private sector ought not to be undertaken by federal agencies; and in a task force report to President Kennedy concluding that the government should continue relying on the private sector for its scientific and technical work. Accordingly, the government continually shifted its R&D work from its own laboratories to external contracts, and the bulk of those contracts went to the universities.

The push for an enhanced research presence was most notable between 1950 and 1970. In 1950 the National Science Foundation (NSF) was established, with the universities well represented on its board of directors. Its appropriation in 1952 was only $3.5 million, but it grew steadily and by 1958 had distributed more than $75 million in research grants and graduate and postgraduate fellowships. The National Aeronautics and Space Administration (NASA), authorized in 1958, began channeling additional funds for academic science. Overall, federal funds for academic research reached over $1.25 billion by 1964. Most of the money went for basic research; nearly 60 percent of the federal support came from NSF and NIH (National Institutes of Health)—agencies that typically did not direct programs but that funded institutions and allowed them to develop their own programs. However, by the latter 1960s, applied research was added to the mission of NSF, as the fervor of federal spending for undifferentiated purposes in higher education subsided and research solutions to specific problems were sought.

Other agencies that would bring federal assistance into various areas of research were formed in 1946: the National Institute of Mental Health, the Office of Naval Research, and the Atomic Energy Commission. By 1950 the Atomic Energy Commission was spending nearly $100 million for research. The universities were sending in proposals also to other agencies concerned with pursuing the Cold War; the Air Force had contracts with fifty institutions. Altogether, in 1950 federal support for research totaled around $140 billion, most of it for projects related to the nation's war-making capacity, a sizable proportion going to the universities, and much to faculty members soliciting support for their own studies.

The Cold War continued throughout the era, and the support for university research granted by federal agencies grew every year except for a downturn toward the end of the 1960s. The United States was committed to developing new types of weaponry, and entrepreneurial professors became the conduits through which vast sums of federal money flowed into the universities. The Cold War effort never turned on maintaining a large standing army or on stockpiling traditional weaponry; it was fought with inventions and new technologies, better ways of targeting missiles, more powerful atomic bombs, new types of submarines and airplanes, and weapons that could find their own targets. Technological innovation was dependent on scientific expertise and large capital investment in laboratories, with the universities in the position of being in a seller's market.

The National Institutes of Health, a primary channel for federal funding of scientific research, led the shift toward problem-related studies. Whereas NSF represented natural science in general, NIH was concerned primarily with biomedical studies. Funds continued pouring into NIH on the hope that the studies it sponsored would eventually cure various problems of health. In 1954, NIH appropriations were over $70 million. They increased to $98 million in 1956, and according to Geiger (1993), "for the next five years the average annual *increase* in the NIH budget was $96 million, and for the next six years the average rise was $156 million" (p. 181). By 1960, NIH had surpassed the Department of Defense in its support of academic research, and by 1965, it was three times larger than

NSF. NIH funds were used for numerous purposes in medical and biological science: as matching funds for capital costs for health-research facilities; for supporting graduate and postdoctoral students in the health fields; and for research grants—the latter accounting for half the NIH appropriations in 1967. Medical education in general benefited; practically every medical school in the nation was receiving at least a million dollars a year from NIH.

Geiger's (1986b and 1993) books—landmarks in examining the field of academic research—showed how federal funds were transforming the landscape not only in the health fields but in all other areas of inquiry. The National Institute of Mental Health, which separated from NIH in 1967, provided more than 40 percent of the federal support for studies in psychology and sociology. The National Defense Education Act supported research in languages and area studies. The Atomic Energy Commission, Department of Defense, and National Aeronautics and Space Administration emphasized development but still supported academic research. The latter agency funded more than $100 million in academic science in 1964. Many of the subagencies of the Department of Defense funded academic research, but when the Vietnam War protesters and some members of Congress demanded that DOD-supported activities be abolished from the campuses, that agency's support for basic research declined precipitously. DOD had accounted for one-third of the total federal support for academic research in 1960, but by 1975 it was down to just 8 percent. Overall, federal support for science was highest between 1958 and 1968 and support for students highest from 1963 to 1972. Geiger (1993) concludes, "The five years in the middle of the 1960s when both these revolutions overlapped appear in retrospect to have been the golden age for research universities" (p. 195).

Federal funding for research in science and social science had several effects. In 1968, thirty-six large, separately organized university research centers employed more than twelve thousand professionals and graduate students and spent over half a billion dollars.

Even education was represented with a set of research centers, laboratories, and ERIC, the Educational Resources Information Center. By 1970 the universities and their associated research centers collectively were responsible for 60 percent of the basic research and 10 to 15 percent of the applied research conducted in the United States (Wolfle, 1972, p. 120). Science was able to attract the best students because they received fellowship support; science faculty often earned more than faculty in other areas.

Wealth continued concentrating in the universities that received research grants and charged the highest indirect cost rate. The top twenty institutions, beginning with Cal Tech, MIT, and the Universities of California and Chicago, received 61 percent of the federal dollars in 1958, up from 32 percent ten years earlier (Orlans, 1962, p. 140). But as other universities, especially in the public sector, gained research capacity, the funds were spread more widely. By 1968, forty universities were receiving at least $10 million each—half the annual total of federal research funds. This tended to reduce the disparity but by no means to eliminate it; Cal Tech, Johns Hopkins, MIT, Chicago, and Stanford still received over one-fourth of the money. Centers of excellence in research were developed from the ground up; federal funds alone could not create them. The science Ph.D.'s they trained tended to seek positions in research-oriented institutions, thus reducing the talent available to small colleges. Although the proportion of students and faculty in the sciences did not increase, the support for their work set them apart. "The most unfortunate consequence of federal science programs has been the cleavage they have engendered between the status and rewards of faculty in the sciences and humanities" (Orlans, 1962, p. 134). Questions were raised also about what would happen if federal funding decreased. Was academic science becoming too dependent on one source?

Put into perspective with other higher education expenditures, organized research commanded a constant 8 percent of total current-fund expenditures between 1945 and 1975. Other current-fund

Table 4.5. Educational and General Expenditures of Institutions of Higher Education as a Percentage of Current-Fund Expenditures, 1945–46 and 1975–76.

Purpose of Educational and General Expenditures	% in 1945–46	% in 1975–76
Administration and general expense	10	13
Instruction and departmental research	· 34	34
Organized research	8	8
Libraries	2	3
Plant operation and maintenance	10	8
Organized activities related to instructional departments	6	3
Extension and public service	5	3
Scholarships and fellowships	—	4
Other general expenditures	—	1
Auxiliary enterprises	22	12
Independent operations	—	3
Hospitals	—	7
Other current expenditures	2	—

Source: National Center for Education Statistics, 1996b, pp. 344–345.

expenditures are shown in Table 4.5. Even though the federal government was providing the lion's share of funds for research, the universities were gathering money from other sources, including their own endowment funds, state and local governments, industry, and foundations.

Other federal programs were proposed but not enacted. A national foundation for higher education was debated in the early 1970s, but the prestigious research institutions were opposed to it because it would have spread funds for research and for graduate education across the spectrum of universities. This was only one example of how higher education found it difficult to speak with a unified voice. Its different interests kept colliding with each other. The elite universities wanted federal funds for research; the community colleges wanted aid to low-income students; the state colleges wanted funds deployed across a wider array of institutions. Even the National Institute of Education, formed to sponsor and fund research in issues of teaching, learning, student access, and student aid, died within a few years because of inept leadership and lack of support from the higher education community, although it was succeeded by the Office of Educational Research and Improvement. Defenses of institutional autonomy were raised continually, as mistrust of the federal government, coupled with the desire of the elite private institutions to maintain their eminence, perpetuated the disunity. Senator Daniel Moynihan (1975) concludes that "initiatives concerning higher education arose primarily from the political interests and objectives of successive Presidents and their Administrations. Rarely did higher education *act*; it was acted upon" (p. 139).

Relations between the higher education institutions collectively and the federal government resembled a couple of behemoths circling each other warily. Each kept doing things to verify the suspicions of the other. The federal government placed a requirement for a loyalty oath in the NDEA legislation, something that many of the campuses opposed. Student demands that ROTC and military recruiters be banned from the campuses antagonized legislators. Even so, the federal government and higher education maintained mutual dependencies. Student aid became a lasting feature in federal appropriations, and funds for research continued to run to the universities through numerous channels. Most of the federal measures broadened access by providing funds to low-income and other underrepresented students and allowed the institutions to increase tuition. It is amazing that all this happened without a concentrated political effort by institutions of higher education. In one respect higher education rode on the coattails of the well-organized elementary and secondary school associations. In another, Congress and the presidential administrations of the era were responding to a broad public will that the benefits of higher education be available to everyone.

By the end of the era the Carnegie Commission on Higher Education was recommending federal support across the board, saying that because of the rapidly increasing costs in higher education, additional federal funding was essential. The commission argued for many types of support, including direct payments to institutions, construction funds to accommodate increased enrollments, more money for research, and a national student loan bank that would make it possible for all students to go to college and repay their loans at low rates of interest over extended periods of time. The commission recommended increasing Basic Education Opportunity Grants that had been authorized in 1972, making a plea for fully funding that program along with the college work-study program. Vocational studies, libraries, graduate student fellowships, all should receive augmented federal funding. The commission acknowledged that federal funds in all those areas had increased but argued that the rate of inflation was accelerating even more rapidly, thus diminishing the actual support received from the federal government. However, the commission did not maintain a presence in Washington, and the influence of its scores of books and press releases was indirect at best. Even so, federal support for graduate student fellowships dropped by 60 percent in the decade following 1967, and aid to undergraduates rose rapidly. The shift toward enhancing access was on.

Philanthropy

Voluntary support increased tenfold during the era. Alumni and other individuals, corporations, foundations, and religious organizations all stepped up their donations. Giving by high-income individuals was stimulated by income tax rates, which for a time were such that a $100 gift might cost the giver as little as $30. Led by the larger private institutions, the universities made notable appeals for this money. Harvard organized an $82-million drive in 1957, and shortly thereafter Stanford opened a $100-million campaign.

Corporate giving was particularly sought. A change in the federal tax code in 1935 allowing corporations to deduct up to 5 percent of their pretax net income for charitable gifts stimulated increased donations. However, only in 1945 did corporate contributions exceed 1 percent of their pretax income. One of the problems was a lingering question over whether corporate gifts were subject to shareholder approval. That question reached the New Jersey Supreme Court in a case brought by the shareholders of the A.P. Smith Company, which had contributed $1,500 to Princeton University in 1951. The court approved the donation, allowing the company to make it without prior approval of the shareholders. Other corporations began various forms of support; Ford Motor Company announced a scholarship program for children of employees, and in 1955, General Electric began a matching gift program whereby employees might have their donations matched by the company. In 1975 around one out of every six donated dollars was coming from corporations.

Eleemosynary foundations continued supporting higher education. The federal excess profits tax that had been imposed during World War II and put into effect again during the Korean War stimulated corporations to form foundations as a way of sheltering income. Five times as many such foundations were formed during those years as had been established in all previous years, and some of the larger foundations were quite generous to higher education. The Ford Foundation after 1950 eclipsed the Rockefeller Foundation and The Carnegie Foundation, both of which had been prominent in the earlier part of the century. In 1953, Ford's donations equaled more than one-third of foundation giving, and three years later it made grants totaling over $200 million to the entire population of private colleges and universities. These funds were to be used for faculty salary increases, and they proved quite welcome, especially at the smaller private institutions where faculty salaries were lagging. Ford also made funds available through challenge grants, whereby the private institutions could put up matching funds to strengthen areas they wished to pursue.

The philanthropic foundations were generous toward medical research and university research in general, and in support of the social and behavioral sciences that were being left behind by the federal government's programmatic efforts. Carnegie assisted the Russian Research Center at Harvard and other types of work on international studies elsewhere. Rockefeller helped establish a Russian Institute at Columbia, designed to train specialists for governmental work. Ford money went toward social concerns; its assistance to the Center for Advanced Study in the Behavioral Sciences at Stanford effected a major achievement in that area. The University of Chicago also received funds to support study in the social sciences.

Overall, as shown in Table 4.6, the proportion of voluntary support received from each source between 1949–50 and 1975–76 remained steady, with the exception that corporation giving increased from 12 to 16 percent. However, because the public sector had grown large, the proportion of total support for higher education accounted for by private gifts declined from around 9 percent of institutional revenue at the start of the era to 6 percent at the

Table 4.6. Voluntary Support for Institutions of Higher Education, by Source and Purpose of Support (in Millions of Current Dollars).

Source and Purpose of Support	1949–50	1975–76
Total voluntary support	$240	$2,410
Sources		
Alumni	60	588
Nonalumni individuals	60	569
Corporations	28	379
Foundations	60	549
Religious organizations	16	130
Other	16	195
Purpose		
Current operations	101	1,480
Capital purposes	139	930
Voluntary support as % of total expenditures	9.0	5.5

Source: National Center for Education Statistics, 1996b, p. 350.

end. The percentage of revenue accounted for by endowment income and by sales and services, auxiliary enterprises, and hospitals declined as well; state and local government support increased to more than one-third of the total.

Expenditures

Expenditures rose along with enrollments and revenue. The increases were not uniform; different time periods and expenditures for different purposes showed varying rates of acceleration. For example, during the 1960s, faculty salaries increased at more than double the rate of inflation, as the institutions sought to play catch-up for a professional group whose wages lagged behind those of other groups with comparable training. Administrative costs increased as additional staff were added to manage the growing number of programs and responsibilities that in earlier times were unknown. The cost of utilities and supplies increased, and there were few ways to find new income to purchase them. The price of a new building might be obtained from a generous benefactor or governmental agency, but the building had to be heated, lighted, cleaned, and repaired forever thereafter. The colleges had to find more scholarship money to advance to students who would help them reach their diversification goals. Tuition discounts became widespread in the private sector, as gross tuition charges began pricing all but the richer students out of the institutions. Campus infrastructure demanded funds as computers and communication equipment became vital. The shortfall between revenues and expenditures could not be rationalized away as a temporary phenomenon; costs in all areas were rising more rapidly than income and, for at least part of the era, more rapidly than the rate of inflation. Between 1954 and 1967, educational costs per student credit hour went up at an annual average of 3.5 percent, whereas the consumer price index was increasing by only half that much.

All these cost increases take on a different cast when placed in a longer time perspective. Between 1930 and 1976, total expenditures for all purposes, including capital improvements, increased from $632 million to $43.6 billion, an average annual rate of increase of 9.6 percent. But much of that was due to increased enrollments and to a decline in the value of the dollar. During the forty-six-year span, full-time-equivalent enrollment increased from 890,000 to nearly 8.5 million while the purchasing power of the dollar declined by 70 percent. Putting those two figures together, the per-student cost grew on the average by only around 1.4 percent per year. As a percentage of gross national product, total higher education expenditures increased from 0.7 percent to 2.7 percent over those same years, primarily because of the nearly tenfold growth in enrollment. Bowen (1980) concludes, "The data hardly support the notion that higher educational costs rise steadily and inevitably over time . . . . When expressed in constant dollars, they have held steady or declined over long periods, for example, during the period 1929–30 to 1949–1950, and also during the 1970s. Only in the golden years of the 1950s and 1960s did unit costs increase" (pp. 36–37). From 1930 to 1950 expenditures per student declined slowly as measured in constant dollars, whereas from 1950 to 1970 they increased tremendously and after 1970 again began a slow decline (see Table 4.7). The surge of expenditures in the 1950s and 1960s "was a unique event that lifted costs per student in constant dollars to a new and unprecedented plateau from which the higher educational system is now slowly receding" (pp. 43–45).

Several socially imposed costs rendered the institutions powerless to control certain expenditures. Security costs went up along with insurance and unemployment compensation for workers. The cost of due process rulings, environmental protection, nondiscrimination clauses, sunshine laws, and associated demands that information be made public brought additional costs. These were not merely the arbitrary decisions of government but they reflected basic changes that were occurring in society, new directions effected by pressure groups that led to governmental action, or shifts that

Table 4.7. Prices or Expenditures per Unit of Service in 1976, Higher Education and Selected Other Commodities and Services (Base Price or Expenditure in 1950 = 100).

	1976
Higher education institutions	
Expenditures for education per full-time equivalent student	429
Public elementary and secondary schools	
Expenditures per pupil in average daily attendance	656
Medical and related services	
All medical care items	345
Physicians' fees	341
Prescriptions	142
Semiprivate hospital room rates	886
All hospitals: total expense per patient day	1,750
Churches: contribution per member	254
Government	
Purchases of goods and services per capita: federal, state, and local	939
U.S. Congress: expenditures per U.S. resident	924
Postal rate: one-ounce first-class letter	433
Hotels and motels: room rates	274
Publications: average retail prices	
Hard-cover books	426
Periodicals	557
Consumer Price Index (1959 = 100)	
All items	236
Food (at home)	231
Apparel	180
Home ownership costs	256
Rent for housing	205
New automobiles	163
Television sets	66

Source: Bowen, 1980, p. 44.

brought direct response on the part of the institutions without governmental intervention.

The demands came with increasing frequency. During the 1930s the Social Security Act and the Wagner Labor Relations Act had caused some increase in the costs of staff. But these were modest in comparison with the legislation of the 1960s and 1970s: Title VII of the Civil Rights Act of 1964, as amended by the Equal Employment Opportunity Act of 1972; Affirmative Action Executive Order of 1965; Occupational Safety and Health Act of 1970; Title IX of the Educational Amendments of 1972; Employment Retirement Income Security Act of 1974. These various acts prohibited discrimination either in admissions or employment on the basis of sex, age, or race; they controlled pension plans and workplace safety. Local or state actions affected building codes and workers' compensation, both of which imposed additional costs. Some of the expenses appeared significant but were one-time costs such as making buildings accessible to handicapped people. These costs were not very great when amortized over the life of a building. Other changes cost little initially but over the years turned out to be expensive—women's athletic programs, for example. The costs of compliance in supplying certain data seemed high initially, as the institutions had to adopt new procedures to compile the data but became lower as the provision of data became routine. Bowen (1980) estimates all these mandates effected additional expenditures of around $2 billion to $2.5 billion annually.

A few observers deplored the socially imposed costs as an assault on academic freedom, but most contended that higher education was just being brought more in line with societal changes from which it might have preferred to remain aloof. At any rate the institutions had little choice in the matter and could not pass along much of the increased cost to their consumers as profit-making corporations often do. In the case of public institutions, tuition might be regulated by a state legislature, hence not easy to change merely because costs had gone up. And except for the few most prestigious among them, the private institutions could raise tuition only so much lest they price themselves out of the market. In both sectors, financial aid, tutorial programs, and other costs associated with lower-ability students added to the burden. And those students had to be admitted; in the case of the public institutions because legislatures often demanded it; in the private sector because the alumni, trustees, staff, and extramural pressure groups insisted on it.

An overview of expenditures in higher education for 1975 shows that around 33 percent of the total went for instruction and departmental research, 25 percent to student services, scholarships, and fellowships, and around 40 percent to organized research, public service, and auxiliary enterprises, including hospitals. Those figures conceal much variation among sectors. They are also subject to various interpretations because the categories are not distinct. Higher education was funded well though, spreading its sources of revenue, controlling its expenditures in spite of inflation and socially imposed costs, and paying essentially a living wage to its staff. Issues of government's compromising institutional autonomy continued to be raised, but they were anachronistic. Higher education was embedded in American society and had become thoroughly dependent on diversified funds.

Outcomes

Higher education's effects can be tabulated in many ways. The most common indexes are based on student flow-through: the number of degrees awarded relative to the number of students matriculating and the employment found and salaries earned by graduates. A second set of measures associates students' learning with their change in attitude while in college. A third relates to the benefits that educated people bring to society. The contributions of research present a fourth measure: To what extent did research conducted within higher education institutions contribute to the nation's knowledge base? How much did the institutions contribute to industrial and economic development?

Degrees and Wages

The 500 percent enrollment increase between 1945 and 1975 naturally affected the number of degrees awarded. Associate degrees increased in number from 50,000 to 350,000, bachelor's and first professional degrees from 135,000 to nearly 1 million, master's degrees from 20,000 to nearly 300,000, and doctoral degrees from 2,000 to 34,000. The fields in which degrees were awarded shifted, especially toward the end of the era. Between 1970 and 1975, bachelor's degrees awarded in business increased by 30 percent, in life sciences by 50 percent, and in the health professions and in communications by more than 100 percent. At the same time, bachelor's degrees in mathematics declined by 33 percent, in social sciences and history by 18 percent, and in education by 12 percent. At the master's level, numbers of degrees in education increased by 40 percent and in business by 65 percent, as requirements for entry into those fields ratcheted up. Library science showed a similar effect, as bachelor's awards declined by 17 percent but master's degrees rose by 15 percent. Some progress toward gender equity was made as well: bachelor's degrees were being awarded to twice the number of men as women when the era began, but by 1975 the difference had shrunk to 55 percent to men and 45 percent to women.

Production of doctoral degrees pointed to the push for additional years of schooling as well as to higher education's contribution to the professional workforce. A major impetus to the tenfold growth in doctorates was the impending increase in the eighteen-year-old population and the greater percentage who would be attending college. More professors would be needed, and as long as the colleges held to the idea that they had to have people with doctoral degrees to staff the classrooms, a crisis was perceived: where would all these doctoral degree holders come from? In 1953 around 30 percent of new faculty members held the doctorate, a ratio that could not continue as enrollments swelled rapidly in the later 1950s and 1960s. A few analysts observed that a substantial number of new faculty members completed their doctorates after entering the profession and that nondoctoral holders exited the profession much more quickly than did those who held doctorates; thus the anticipated shortfall in doctoral degree production would be much less than had been feared. Nevertheless, the shortage of doctorate-holding college teachers served the universities well. Those seeking the greater prestige accompanying doctoral programs used the anticipated shortfall as a rationale for seeking more highly qualified faculty, expanding research, and appealing for more state funds. The number of doctoral-degree-granting institutions increased, from around one hundred in 1949 to twice that number by 1970.

Other measures for ameliorating the presumed crisis in doctoral degree production were brought forward. The doctor of arts in teaching degree was introduced, never to gain ground beyond a scant few institutions. Several philanthropic foundations put additional funds into graduate study, and the federal government supported predoctoral students through the NDEA (National Defense Education Act), NSF, and NASA. By the 1960s a sizable majority of full-time doctoral students were receiving fellowship assistance. Programs were also introduced that were supposed to increase the number of doctorates by shortening the time to degree, the idea being that if students could be put through doctoral programs more rapidly, the production of doctorates would increase and space made available for more students. Students in the sciences took much less time gaining the doctorate than did those in the humanities and social sciences. However, the students entering academic careers in the sciences typically engaged in extensive postdoctoral work so that the actual time from the beginning of the program until the end of training approached that for students in other fields.

The time-to-degree issue provided another excuse for the graduate institutions to plead for more funds. Surely the time could be reduced if more students had fellowships and did not have to take time away from their studies to work on paying jobs. But this proved not to be the case; students who took assistantships and similar jobs on campus often worked diligently and received their degrees at an equal rate with their fellows who were being supported on scholarship funds. Furthermore, the faculty in the humanities and social sciences were not concerned about the length of time it took their students to complete their programs. In Geiger's (1993) felicitous phrase, "In more ruminative subjects, like literature or philosophy, faculty thought it desirable that there be ample time for, well, rumination" (p. 228). Eventually the crisis subsided, not because substantially greater numbers of doctoral holders were being produced but because it was supplanted by expectations that the lower number of eighteen-year-olds in the 1980s would result in a reduced demand for faculty members and because of the notable expansion in undergraduate education in the community colleges, where possession of a master's degree was considered sufficient training for an instructor.

Numerous studies related income to schooling. In their compendium of research on students, Pascarella and Terenzini (1991) show that when intelligence, socioeconomic status, and work experience are held constant, having a bachelor's degree provides a 25 to 30 percent advantage in earnings over students who leave the educational system after high school. The influence of different levels of education on earnings is not uniformly linear; the bachelor's degree is the major turning point, more important than the difference between people with or without high school diplomas or with some college or no college. Pascarella and Terenzini conclude that "attainment of the bachelor's degree may be the single most important educational step in the occupational and economic attainment process" (p. 501).

However, the difference in earnings attained by students leaving school at various levels is subject to caveat. Much depends on the time in a person's life when earnings are calculated, for example, within a year or two after leaving school or five, ten, or twenty years later. And it has always been difficult to correlate earnings with capability in the many well-paying occupations for which possession of a degree is required before a person may be considered for employment—a phenomenon known as the sheepskin effect. There is no way of knowing how much people without degrees might have earned if they had been allowed to enter those fields. It is also difficult to parcel out the effect of innate capabilities. As nearly all the bright young people enter college, it is impossible to determine their life chances if they had not attended.

Personal and Social Benefits

The effects of college on personal and social relations have been studied extensively. Pace (1979) reviewed ten major studies that had been conducted from the 1930s to the 1970s and found positive links between college attendance and job satisfaction, participation in political activities (voting, campaigning), pursuit of cultural interests (attending concerts, reading, visiting museums), interpersonal relations, and development of personal values, goals, and philosophy. He reported also that the median family income of college graduates was twice that of the U.S. median and that between 70 and 90 percent of the bachelor's degree holders were in professional or managerial positions, the difference depending on the number of years they had been out of college. He concluded that college graduates have good jobs and incomes, like their jobs and think their education was relevant to them, participate in civic affairs, and agree that the college experience was beneficial in many ways. The studies covered many decades, therefore, "If consistency is cause for confidence, we can be confident in what we know about college graduates" (p. 106).

Feldman and Newcomb (1969) synthesized the findings of studies conducted from the mid-1920s to 1967 and concluded that the impact of college on student development has several consistencies:

- Freshman-to-senior changes in several characteristics occur with considerable uniformity.

- Within the same college, experiences associated with different majors typically have effects above and beyond those that can be accounted for by initial selection into those fields.

- Although individual instructors often are influential, college faculties do not appear to be responsible for campuswide impact except in settings where the influence of student peers and faculty complement and reinforce one another.

- Attitudes held by students on leaving college tend to persist, possibly as a result of living in post-college environments that support those attitudes.

- Whatever the characteristics of individuals that selectively propel them toward particular types of colleges, those same characteristics are apt to be reinforced and extended by the experience incurred; in short, selection and impact are interdependent.

Higher education's effects spilled over into society. Graduates who participated in civic affairs eventually changed social institutions. The faculty were more likely to be engaged in public service than were members of most other professional groups. These contributions to the polity related to institutional goals. The Carnegie Commission (1973b) translated the traditional purposes of higher education—teaching, research, and service—into five sets of goals: (1) providing opportunities for the intellectual, aesthetic, ethical, and skill development of individual students; (2) advancing human capability in society at large; (3) enlarging educational justice; (4) transmitting and advancing learning; and (5) critically evaluating society for the sake of society's self-renewal. Bowen's (1977) list of goals for individual students includes verbal and quantitative skills, substantive knowledge, rationality, intellectual tolerance, personal self-discovery, human understanding, and refinement of taste.

His list of practical competencies includes leadership, adaptability, and the need for achievement along with citizenship and economic productivity. And for society he saw higher education's goals as advancing knowledge, preserving the cultural heritage, discovering new knowledge, and encouraging talent.

It has always been easier to describe such lists than it has been feasible to find the data showing the extent to which higher education produces the desired impact. Even so, Bowen (1977) reviewed a number of studies supporting his conclusions that higher education led to several changes: openness to change itself, the realization that the prevailing conditions of society can be improved; involvement in public affairs and a resultant increase in the level of accountability on the part of government and social institutions; social responsibility such as concern for environment and tolerance for differences among people; enhanced efficiency in the economy because of the knowledge that graduates bring to business and government; improved international relations, including assisting in dissemination of technology and information; and a generally healthier lifestyle, including less violent behavior, more involvement in volunteer work, and better appreciation of the arts. He also recounted four societal benefits of higher education's research efforts: scholarship that preserves the heritage of the culture; scientific research that yields vaccines, medical techniques, electronics, computers, and agricultural products; social science research on the effects of public policy plus societal criticism that assists the nation in maintaining its values; and public service in the form of on-site activities with governmental agencies.

The Carnegie Commission (1973b) reported on higher education's role in effecting a more just society by reducing barriers to individual advancement and helping individuals move between social strata. This tended to assist in creating a more just society because when individuals have equal opportunities to gain access to various avenues of employment and to participate more fully in the polity, the background from which they sprang becomes a weaker influence. Although there was inequity in college attendance as lower-income people were less likely to matriculate, the system was more open by far than that of any other nation. Extending the idea of the common school to the post-compulsory sector did more to equalize opportunity than any other social institution.

Enhancing human capital was being done in more complex ways than merely training and shifting people into various avenues of employment. Developing individuals' skills and maintaining the proper levels of manpower for society were seen as dual, overlapping purposes of higher education. The system was developing talent, allocating people toward the areas of greatest economic and social need, enhancing individual mobility (both occupational and geographic), and adding to the ability of people to continue developing throughout their lifetime. The economy was being served by producing highly trained workers and assisting them in entering the fields most appropriate for their skills.

The Carnegie Commission straddled the fence on the proper role and effects of higher education in criticizing society. The group saw a role for social criticism and evaluation by individual students or faculty members but not for the system as a whole. Too much criticism would lead to ideological positions and backlash from the institutions' main supporters. The commission advised against taking direct action, favoring instead the development of rules to guide evaluation and analysis; rather than specifying changes, the institutions should be enhancing society's capacity for self-renewal; to the extent that higher education contributed to heightened concern over social ills, it was performing its role and did even better when it recommended ways of assessing social inequities. However, higher education has never been effective in taking direct action on social ills; if it had been, the Vietnam War would have ended five years earlier than it did.

Differing Effects

Attempts to demonstrate the peculiar effects of different colleges, programs, instructors, or instructional methods usually were unconvincing. Variations in achievement between individual students completing the same program or institution typically were greater than the average achievement for all students completing. Effects of different institutions were difficult to discern because of differences in the entering classes, especially those affected by different criteria of selectivity. Even after controlling for all quantifiable variables, including the students' gender, ethnicity, entering test scores, prior achievement, and socioeconomic status, and for less reliable measures such as student attitude and aspirations, the researchers were left with several key unknowns. Why did certain students select certain institutions? What types of experiences did they have while they were there? What happened in their lives while they were enrolled that was not institutionally related? After controlling for many of the students' preexisting differences, Astin (1977) reports that the experience of attending full-time and residing on campus had the most marked effects.

Undoubtedly, students graduating from various institutions differed widely in terms of academic achievement, religious interests, and aesthetic sensibility. However, the differences among graduates from one institution or another, substantial as they were, could be explained largely by the differences among the same students when they entered the freshman class. The overlap among colleges in what they did and how they did it was so great that finding large differences in outcomes would be highly unlikely. Even though the more affluent institutions appeared to generate greater outcomes, they could probably perform as well with less money, and many more institutions could probably achieve greater results with no additional funds. Some of the expenditures in high-cost institutions were "almost surely designed more largely for the students' satisfaction than for their educational growth" (Bowen, 1980, p. 167). Some of the difference, then, in the effects of affluent institutions might be that the students reporting on their college experience felt they derived greater benefit—a finding that may have resulted from the extra money spent on student affairs and extracurriculars.

Does the public get its money's worth? Any consideration of the proportion of a state's resources that should be devoted to higher education brings an implicit comparison of the social benefits that might be derived if those funds were allocated to other agencies. And even within higher education it has been impossible to demonstrate that a dollar spent at a research university is more or less socially beneficial than one spent at a community college; the two types of institutions serve different clients and provide different services.

Some analysts have contended that the greater support for research universities and graduate programs effected unequal benefits. In the public sector the expenditures per FTE student in 1975–76 totaled less than $1,800 at community colleges and around $4,000 at the high-selectivity universities. At the same time, the median income of parents of freshmen was $13,579 for the community college students and nearly $22,000 in the high-selectivity universities. (See Table 4.8.)

In their study, Hansen and Weisbrod (1969) reported that because family income was related to the type of institution that students enrolled in and because the state paid more to the universities that the higher-income students attended, the wealthier families were receiving subsidies. Furthermore, the longer students remained in college, the higher the subsidy, because each year of attendance meant that the student was receiving an additional benefit, and students at the university tended to stay in school longer. Their "rather startling conclusion" was that while 9 percent of the high school graduates received subsidies exceeding $5,000, "more than half of California's young people receive under $750 . . . and a substantial fraction—41 percent—receive no subsidy at all" (p. 181).

Higher education's outcomes could not reasonably be validated in the long term. What students learned while they were in college and in the jobs that they entered immediately upon graduation were amenable to measurement. But the colleges could not be held responsible for the jobs available to their graduates or for the par-

Table 4.8. Institutional Expenditures and Students' Economic Background by Type of Institution, 1975–76.

Type of Institution	Educational and General Expenditures per Full-Time Equivalent Student	Median Income of Parents of Entering Freshmen
Public institutions		
Two-year colleges	$1,778	$13,579
Four-year colleges		
Low selectivity	1,741	13,895
Medium selectivity	2,071	16,593
High selectivity	3,888	17,802
Universities		
Low selectivity	2,678	17,813
Medium selectivity	3,086	18,618
High selectivity	4,153	21,946
Private institutions		
Four-year nonsectarian colleges		
Low selectivity	2,627	13,978
Medium selectivity	2,485	17,977
High selectivity	2,835	20,150
Very high selectivity	4,275	26,117
Universities		
Low selectivity	2,142	20,977
Medium selectivity	3,514	27,986
High selectivity	5,954	23,573

Source: Bowen, 1980, p. 243.

ticular jobs they took; students going through one type of preparation program might well enter a different field. As the supply of college graduates grew, different types of businesses and newly emergent professions employed more of them. The more that corporations began requiring college degrees as prerequisite for employment, the more higher education became "the personnel office for white-collar America" (Lemann, 1995, p. 97). The framers of the National Defense Education Act had rationalized that if the better students were recruited by top colleges, they would become scientists working on projects to enhance the nation's security. Instead, most of them went into law, medicine, finance, and teaching in areas other than science. The dream of manpower development in socially useful areas had been "substantially realized in the intake, but not in the outflow" (p. 97).

Research

From the beginning of the University Transformation Era the institutions contended that research was good for industry, and they gained support from industrialists. In the Mass Higher Education Era they contended that research was essential for national defense, and they gained funding from governmental agencies. Funds from the states were acquired by pointing out that the universities would assist economic development. In large measure such rationalizations were based on true outcomes. Many industrial processes were pioneered in university research laboratories, and entire industries such as electronics were based on such efforts. The universities operated atomic research laboratories and conducted basic research that supported the development of weapons systems. Most state universities could point both to research in agriculture that led to better crop yields and land use, and to local industries that grew because of the state's trained workforce.

The research emphasis changed higher education. By combining undergraduate instruction, research, and professional training in the same institution, the universities gained strength and independence even while the contradictions among the three purposes effected internal tensions. Additional tensions emerged as separately organized research centers within universities began acting as independent organizations, sometimes competing with academic departments by providing research support to faculty members and, in effect, enabling them to buy their way out of their teaching responsibilities. The research effort had been so stimulated and so successful that it became tantamount to the academic ethos; faculty in research universities became the normative group to which faculty in other institutions aspired. Because scientific research had become the sine qua non of a major university and because it was so expensive, the institutions leading in the research effort and those aspiring to move into the top ranks of research universities had to find increasing amounts of money. They had to pay for faculty who were teaching fewer students and for the laboratories and equipment that research demanded.

One result of this effort was a symbiotic relationship between the research universities and the industries that both supported them and benefited from their work. The electronics industry was one of the first to grow along with university-based work in electrical engineering. Varian Associates and Hewlett-Packard were among the industrial firms that had close ties with Stanford. "What clearly had emerged by 1950 was a triangular nexus between electrical engineering at Stanford, the Department of Defense, and the electronics industry" (Geiger, 1993, p. 121). Different types of university organizations and different relationships with governmental agencies and industries developed. Separate research centers, institutes, and laboratories that were organized within universities coordinated research, individual budgets, and the work of faculty members.

Some of these centers, institutes, and laboratories became dominant in their area of study. The Michigan Institute for Social Research and the Columbia Bureau of Applied Social Research, both dating from the 1940s, developed the methodologies and set the standards for sociological studies. The National Opinion Research Center at the University of Chicago similarly gained respect for the validity of its work. The Jet Propulsion Laboratory at the California Institute of Technology and the Lawrence Livermore Laboratory at the University of California took the lead in space exploration and nuclear physics development, respectively. The Massachusetts Institute of Technology had several organized research units with military connections: its Research Laboratory of Electronics, Center for International Studies, and Instrumentation Laboratory were funded by and worked closely with military units, including the Air Force, CIA, and Office of Naval Research. In some of the research universities early in the era, budgets for funded research were larger than academic budgets.

The faculty who were interested in research thrived on the system. They maintained intellectual sovereignty in their fields and sought grants for projects that fit their expertise. The universities earned overhead money based on the awards that faculty members brought in and were able often to support lesser-funded areas with the money provided. The faculty gained autonomy because, as they brought in their own funds, they controlled allocations; the universities gained prestige, which was useful in attracting donations, as well as the ability to sustain less-popular programs; students gained support for their graduate studies; the federal government and many large business corporations gained the products of research without having to build their own research enterprises. The outcomes were manifold, complex, and interrelated.

Critiques and Commentaries

In 1974 the editors of *Daedalus*, the journal of the American Academy of Arts and Sciences, invited more than one hundred people to write essays reflecting on the previous ten years of higher education and considering where higher education might be headed in the years ahead. Around eighty university professors and presidents, psychologists, theologians, and other authors responded. They were sobered by the upheavals that higher education had experienced in the prior decade. Little boosterism appeared; more prominent were comments on the problems facing higher education and the need for and likelihood of reform. Most of the authors perceived the dawning of an era of consolidation, variously called no-growth, or steady-state, and of demands for institutional accountability, often seen as a turn away from the freedoms that institutions had enjoyed.

Scanning the articles is like reviewing all the concerns about higher education that had been expressed in the preceding century and that would continue to be articulated in the ensuing decades: How much education should be general, how much specialized? How can education for an elite be reconciled with American democratic traditions? Why do the institutions insist on the doctorate as preparation for their faculty when so few professors pursue a research agenda? Why does higher education devote most of its resources to educating young people when lifelong learning should be its goal?

Few of the authors called for equity in racial and ethnic representation or for a multicultural curriculum. Although some noted that the rising tide of expectations would eventually engulf the colleges, forcing them to revise their positions on egalitarianism, they used the term *diversity* to indicate a variety of types of programs and institutions. The idea of equity was still distant; many of the authors commented on it disparagingly, mentioning how attempts to rectify unequal treatment would exhaust the moral and intellectual energies of the enterprise. "What we are witnessing is the routinization or bureaucratization of the radical egalitarianism which was the essence of the student demands of the sixties" (Bloom, 1974, p. 66). Some authors acknowledged that student activism had been influential in enhancing civil rights both within higher education and the broader community, but few predicted that this trend of speaking out on behalf of social justice would continue. Several noted that the ethnic studies courses that had been introduced as a result of student demands were already subsiding. According to Notre Dame's President Hesburgh (1974), "Most of the black studies programs introduced during the student revolution are either dead or moribund" (p. 69).

The authors acknowledged that the years of activism had resulted in students' gaining representation on university councils but said that made little difference to institutional governance. Relaxing the rules governing student behavior was viewed as a mixed event. On the one hand it sent the message that students were adults and responsible for their own actions; on the other, it suggested that the institution did not care what the young people in its charge did. Hesburgh summed the activist era by saying, "The worst results of the happenings of the sixties were the crisis of confidence and loss of nerve they produced in the universities, coupled with a growing disdain and even contempt for the universities on the part of those who had loved them most: parents, alumni, benefactors, legislators, students, too" (p. 70). But neither he nor other authors translated this disdain into reduced support. They sensed that the university had lost some of its isolation and mystique but that its framework had survived. Its governance structures, faculty roles, and curriculum had been attacked and shaken, but with minor adjustments they continued as before.

The authors did not foresee that the loss of confidence would lead to a time when the institutions had to struggle to maintain their support. They did not anticipate the rapid rise of tuition such that its proportion of overall revenues would double. Even Kerr, who noted that the public had clearly lost some confidence in higher education as evidenced by public bond issues failing to pass, did not foresee the difficult fiscal times ahead. Some of the authors did point out that institutional costs would continue to rise more rapidly than income because of pressure for salary increases and other inflationary factors that would not be accompanied by increased productivity. But overall, the shock of the student activism of the sixties evidently was the most marked influence on the writings.

The Carnegie Commission on Higher Education brought out a series of books between 1968 and 1973, followed by another set published by its successor, the Carnegie Council on Policy Studies in Higher Education. Together the reports totaled 118 volumes, enough to have individual essays on what colleges ought to be; separate examinations of every type of institution; speculation on the proper role of students, faculty, and administrators; and statistical compendia verifying everything that happened in higher education in the prior few decades. The resultant recommendations were rather straightforward: higher education deserved support as a valuable resource for the nation; the students should pay a higher percentage of the cost because they are the ones who benefit most directly from attending college; a wide array of institutions from community colleges to liberal arts colleges and universities, public and private, should be sustained.

Viewing the Carnegie series along with the essays in *Daedalus* yields the impression that the authors, often characterized as an intellectual elite, presented few alternatives to the existing structure of higher education. Many of them deplored certain aspects of how the system operated, but their commentaries usually concluded with pleas to support the status quo, or at least their favorite program, institution, or practice within it. Affirmative action was but dimly seen. Community service was defined as opening access to all who wished to attend, thus enabling people to take their place as better-functioning, higher-paid members of the workforce, and as responsible citizens. Other forms of direct social action were considered much beyond the scope of higher education. The colleges were not to be social service agencies.

Many authors noted the impending reduction in the number of eighteen-year-olds in the American population and, matching that with the leveling in the rate of college-going exhibited by recent high school graduates, predicted enrollment declines for the 1980s. Many deplored the tendency of higher education institutions to be managed like business corporations, with administrators making decisions based on economic principles and on satisfying a broad constituency within and outside. The differences between faculty who wanted the freedom to pursue their interests and governing boards or state officials who wanted to rationalize institutional costs and outcomes seemed irreconcilable. Several analysts insisted that a college should not be measured in terms of outcomes, impacts, or benefits; the nature of learning and the human experience could not so readily be captured.

The move toward secularization, community service, and activities on behalf of governmental agencies and industry came in for its share of opprobrium. One commentator's view of the trend led him to conclude that it "means that the college or university as an institution is becoming less distinguishable from other institutions in this society such as business, government, deliberative bodies, or the Pentagon" (Tollett, 1975, p. 293). Unionization and cost-benefit analysis made higher education like a business; programs designed for community uplift or social welfare made it like government; a preoccupation with consensus building on campus, parliamentary procedure, and constituency formation made it like a deliberative body; and "proliferating bureaucracies and mindlessly escalating budgets are reminiscent of the Pentagon" (p. 293).

Nonetheless, the system had become so complex and so successful that it ignored criticism the way that a supertanker traveling at high speed shrugs off an errant wave. It was a huge economic engine devouring billions of dollars per year. It had mitigated the problem of access for everyone who wanted to attend by erecting a thousand community colleges, even while preserving every type of college that had ever been founded: residential and commuter; liberal arts and occupational; single-sex and coed; religious and secular. Its faculty had gained salary increments that were bringing them into the category of adequately paid professionals. Its programs were so diverse that the logo "Any person, Any study," coined at Cornell one hundred years earlier had been surpassed; the three thousand institutions and branch campuses had converted it to "Any person, Any study, Any place," as higher education was now available to people living in every corner of the nation, regardless of their economic or social status. It was engaged in basic and applied research, general education, high school make-up studies, professional development, job-entry skills, career upgrading, and personal interest studies. It had sustained its definition of productivity as passing more students through to graduation and its definition of prestige as high selectivity in student admissions, faculty publications and awards, and a sizeable dollar amount in extramural grant funding. It had weathered attacks from within and outside. It was a marvel, if not the envy of the world.

5

Maintaining the Diverse System in the
Contemporary Era: 1976–1998

The period since the mid-1970s has been marked by a continuation of several trends in American society and some events that could be considered turning points. The trends have included an aging population, increased participation in education at all levels, a higher ratio of women in the workforce, and more children being reared in single-parent homes. The events have been the end of the Cold War, the demise of the Soviet Union, and, on the domestic scene, revisions in the tax codes that have led to an increased gap between the higher-income and lower-income sectors. Some of the trends during the prior thirty years reversed: organized labor's influence diminished; the ratio of part-time to full-time jobs increased; the percentage of citizens participating in civic affairs decreased; immigration accelerated but with Central and South America and Eastern Asia, not Europe, as the source of most of the new arrivals.

Societal Context

Table 5.1 shows a statistical picture of the conditions surrounding higher education in the Contemporary Era.

The 1980s marked a shift in America's relations with the rest of the world. U.S. troops had left Vietnam at the start of the era, but the communist threat was perceived as continuing. In 1983

Table 5.1. Statistical Portrait of the Contemporary Era, 1975–1995.

	1975	1995
U.S. population	215,465,000	262,755,000
Number of students enrolled in higher education	11,185,000	14,262,000
Number of faculty	628,000	915,000
Number of institutions (including branch campuses)	3,026	3,706
Number of earned degrees conferred (associate, bachelor's, master's, first professional, and doctoral)	1,665,553	2,246,300
Current-fund revenue (in thousands of current dollars)	39,703,166	189,120,570

Source: National Center for Education Statistics, 1997e, 1997g; Snyder, 1993.

President Reagan declared the Soviet Union to be an evil empire bent on world conquest—one that must be stopped by the United States as leader of the forces of freedom, light, and progress. Interventions were made in El Salvador, Nicaragua, and Grenada on the grounds that communist influence there had to be rooted out. Within Eastern Europe the Poles, Hungarians, and several other national groups began holding free elections and sending the Soviet troops away. The Berlin Wall came down in 1989 after twenty-nine years of dividing the city, and by the end of the following year, East and West Germany were united.

Within the nation the federal debt continued climbing, fueled in part by tax reductions enacted during the 1980s. The Reagan and Bush administrations had attempted to reduce domestic spending for welfare, health, and various other social programs, but because of continued increases in military spending and interest payments on the debt, and the growing cost of Social Security and Medicare occasioned by the aging population, the federal budget continued expanding. Annual growth in productivity slowed to 1 percent, and the growth in gross domestic product that had averaged 3.9 percent between 1950 and the mid-1990s dropped to 2.6 percent ("Making America Rich," 1998). In the 1990s the annual deficit reached record levels, but low inflation, interest, and unemployment rates, along with an expanding economy, moved the federal budget into the black at the end of 1997.

Deregulation became an article of faith in the 1980s. Led by a president who promised to reduce governmental involvement, legislators restricted antipollution laws and laws governing health and safety in the workplace. Organized labor was set back when the air controllers went on strike in 1981 and were replaced by nonunion workers. Labor began to recover only in 1997 when the United Parcel Service strike was settled on terms favorable to the Teamsters Union. But by then only 10 percent of the private sector employees were working under union contracts.

The weakened unions proved unable to protect full-time positions. A high proportion of the new jobs created in the 1980s paid less than poverty wages; between 1981 and 1987 the number of people working for minimum wage grew from just over five million to nearly eight million. The number of women working outside the home continued climbing, passing the 70 percent mark in 1990—a year when well over half of all mothers with children under the age of six were in the labor force. Many people were laid off because of so-called restructuring, which typically meant the dismissal of full-time employees in favor of part-timers who could be paid at a lower wage, denied fringe benefits and retirement packages, and dismissed whenever conditions warranted.

This change in the configuration of the workforce led to an increased disparity between the incomes of the wealthy and the poor. By 1989 there were around 1.5 million millionaires and at least 50 billionaires in the United States. "The share of national income going to the wealthiest 1 percent rose from 8.1 percent in 1981 to 14.7 percent in 1986. . . . The bottom fifth of income distribution suffered a 1 percent decline . . . from 1973 to 1979, but a

10 percent decline from 1979 to 1987" (Jordan and Litwack, 1994, pp. 481–482). Wealth reached its point of greatest concentration since the 1920s. The gap between the upper and lower 20 percent of the population grew greater than in any other major industrial nation. In 1995, 87,000 federal tax returns indicated income of more than $1 million, up from 66,500 returns in 1993 and 32,000 in 1983 (Wessel, 1998). Most of the gains to economic equality of the postwar boom were lost, even though by the late 1990s the unemployment rate had dropped to a level lower than it had been for thirty years.

The health care sector changed notably as well. By the middle 1990s, the United States was spending 14 percent of its gross domestic product on medical care, compared with around 6 to 7 percent in Japan and less than 6 percent in Britain. Attempts to bring health care costs under control led to managed care through health maintenance organizations and other arrangements whereby costs and types of treatment were being decided less by the physician and patient and more by the insurance company. By 1995, 39 percent of the physicians were salaried employees of HMOs, whereas only a decade earlier 90 percent had been self-employed.

The change in the health care industry was accompanied also by changes in public health activities. Smoking was banned on airplanes and in restaurants and public buildings in many states. Dietary labeling on food packages spread. But the United States still suffered the world's largest murder rate; drug use expanded despite continuing campaigns to educate people against its evils and to interdict importation; and AIDS, unknown before the early 1980s, assumed epidemic proportions. The questions surrounding abortion continued to be debated. In 1973 the Supreme Court ruled that abortion could not be considered a crime. In 1989 the Court recanted somewhat and ruled that states could impose certain restrictions on abortion. Many of these health-related issues were confounded by broader social concerns that affected attitudes about them: drugs were self-inflicted; AIDS was originally a disease

associated with homosexual behavior; abortion violated fundamental religious teachings.

Racism persisted. Whether it was benign or pernicious, rationalized or unreasoned, displayed by whites or blacks, or people in
or out of power, by any measure it continued. Laws were passed forbidding it in one context; it appeared in another. Practically every
public action—tax law changes, welfare reform, the choice of school
sites, student aid, the content of school textbooks, representation
on governmental bodies, individual behavior, jobs gained, and promotions granted—was viewed with an eye to which of the several
ethnic or racial groups appeared to gain or lose benefits. The United
States, for most of its history an outpost of Europe, escaped the
worst of the religious prejudice and class warfare that wracked its
parent nations for centuries. Instead, it developed its own form of
tribalism.

Many people seemed to believe that virtually all public sector
activity was more harmful than beneficial. This antagonism toward,
or at least suspicion of, government was displayed in legislation limiting terms of office, as well as by candidates for public office who
promised to reduce the size of governmental programs and by several tax-limitation initiatives. Fewer qualified voters went to the
polls: in national elections in 1960, 63 percent voted compared
with 50 percent in 1988. Expenditures on private security, including residential and commercial guards and security systems, grew so
that they were higher than the allocations to the police force. By
the late 1990s more people were employed as private security guards
than as public police officers, and the state prisons under construction far outnumbered the new college campuses.

Disaffection with governmental processes has been an undercurrent arising periodically; people forget that the nation's economy
has always combined elements of both laissez-faire and governmental stimulation and regulation. In the nineteenth century both
federal and state governments promoted the development of
railroads and canals and in the twentieth century promoted the

development of radio, civil aviation, and the electronics industry. Governmental support of basic research has led to enhanced processes in everything from farming to pharmaceuticals to the government-university-private capital nexus to gigantic industrial corporations. Still, the United States was in one of its cyclical phases in which a belief in a free-market economy, along with puritanical control of personal behavior, dominated.

Thus the context for higher education shifted during the first twenty years of the Contemporary Era. The access that had been opened to an earlier generation by the GI Bill was extended to include people from groups who had either been systematically excluded or had chosen not to attend. College-going became ever more a necessity for entry into lucrative occupations. The rate of college-going that had leveled from 1965 to the 1980s turned up again and by the mid-1990s reached a peak never before attained. In the mid-1970s the federal government defined racial categories and thus solidified the differentiation of groups to whom special treatment should be accorded; the Rehabilitation Act of 1973 and the Americans with Disabilities Act of 1990 extended the categories. Collective bargaining for faculty slowed, and calls for faculty to spend more time teaching and to pay more attention to students accelerated. The use of reproducible media, especially computers, expanded; by the 1990s the Internet had opened access to information to a degree that was growing exponentially. Private higher education, which had been predicted to disappear, held its own as governmental programs supplementing tuition payments for students from all socioeconomic groups were extended.

Equal Opportunity

The Contemporary Era has seen an acceleration of forces striving for proportional representation and differential treatment—all in the name of equality. Each group, whether based on commonality of race, ethnicity, gender, age, economic status, disability, or some combination of those, has organized to lobby against the discrimination it feels has limited its progress. The goal of a color-blind society in which individuals would be judged on their own qualifications, not as members of a group, in which everyone would be accorded equal treatment under the laws, evolved into a quest for equality. Wherever unequal results were perceived and wherever one group was not proportionately represented, laws, court rulings, and differential treatment were sought to rectify the apparent imbalances.

Equality has always been an elusive goal. For most of the nation's history Americans tended to accept inequality, even as they believed in what they called equal opportunity and endorsed the general principle of fair competition. Certainly some people were wealthy and others poor, but most felt that the system was open so that individuals could rise within it. Wealth was the major measure of success. There was much economic mobility from one generation to another, and even among people who started life in essentially identical circumstances, lifetime income was not equal; a view of the different incomes among siblings demonstrated that. Some people became richer than others but not solely because of differences in their cognitive skills; luck, on-the-job competence, perseverance, motivation, personal connections, and a host of intangibles seemed to make the difference. As for education, scores on standardized tests were only modestly related to economic success, and as Jencks (1972) points out, "Equalizing everyone's reading scores would not appreciably reduce the number of economic failures" (p. 8).

Paradoxically, the open system brings attendant problems. Education is valued for its ability to assist everyone from whatever social class to sustain the hope of moving higher. If social norms were locking individuals into the strata into which they were born, then their failure to achieve would be society's fault. But if anyone can take advantage of the schools and the laws that protect equal opportunity, then the people who fail to achieve must accept responsibility. Eiseley (1970) anticipated the spirit of the times running toward an abandonment of individual responsibility, and people saying: "I cannot help myself. What I did was forced on me by things that happened because of what other people did." And he made a plea for personal responsibility: "The group may abstractly desire an ethic, theologians may preach an ethic, but no group ethic ever could, or should, replace the personal ethic of individual responsible men" (p. 147). Henry (1994) comments that "self-proclaimed victims of society have lost sight of the proportion of their faith that reflects free will" (p. 138). Thiederman (1996) concludes, "Equal opportunity is about individual fairness, achievement, ability and the elimination of individual victimization" (p. B9).

The Civil Rights Act of 1964 and the Voting Rights Act of 1965 were attempts to abolish discrimination against African Americans. The black-white distinctions that had been made since the earliest years of the nation and used to defend slavery and segregation were to be set aside. Gradually, beginning in the 1960s, the attempts to redress the evils of segregation were transformed into sets of remedies for past discrimination, and a racial preference system was developed. However, the air became murky as other racial or ethnic groups were added to the list of those who might be accorded preferential treatment. The President's Commission on Equal Employment Opportunity identified government employees as American Indians, Asian Americans, and Hispanic Americans— groups that in the 1960 census had been listed as "other." Subsequently, court cases appeared routinely, mandating integrated schools for blacks and Hispanics, and seeking equal employment opportunity for all the groups.

The subdivision of the population into five permanently distinct categories was given official status by the Federal Interagency Committee on Education, which codified the groups in 1973. Chinese, Indians, and Filipinos were identified as Asian Americans along with Japanese, Vietnamese, Indonesians, Hawaiians, and numerous other nationalities and population groupings reaching over nearly half the globe. Whites, blacks, and American Indians were the other races. Mexicans, Cubans, people whose forebears came from Spain or South America, black people who spoke Spanish, people with Spanish surnames who didn't speak Spanish, those whose families had lived in the United States for generations or those who themselves immigrated—all became ethnically Hispanic Americans. The arbitrariness of the categories was revealed frequently, as courts, councils, and legislatures were forced to determine the group to which petitioners belonged. For example, depending on who was counting and for what purpose, Spanish-speaking black immigrants from the Caribbean might have been labeled Hispanics or African Americans. In 1997, after deliberating and holding hearings for four years, a thirty-agency administration task force directed the U.S. Bureau of the Census to modify the wording of several classifications, and instead of adding a "multiracial" listing, it was to instruct respondents that they could check more than one category. How various agencies would use the data was not made clear; one agency might count each box checked as a full person of the designated group, but another might credit each check as one-half or one-third of a person, depending on the number of categories marked by a single respondent. Ridiculous premises necessarily produce absurd dilemmas.

Affirmative Action

Affirmative action, an instrumental policy dating from the mid-1960s, was promulgated originally to remedy the underrepresentation of certain groups in contracts awarded and employment within and outside the academy. Four designated racial groups, along with women, were the original target, and legislative acts and court decisions subsequently broadened it to include people with disabilities. By the 1990s, various other subsets of the population were added in specific applications: immigrant Portuguese in Massachusetts; Acadians in Louisiana; Hassidim in New York; and lesbians and gays in a few universities. However, these latter specialized situations only point up how other groups have attempted to crawl under the tent of policies that promise to provide certain benefits. Affirmative action grew out of the civil rights struggles that had been spearheaded by the African American community. The addition of other ethnic or racial groups, women, and various other population subdivisions both extended and diluted its original intent.

Affirmative action in higher education has been marked by changes in many areas. The largest gains have been by made by women whose representation on the faculty grew from 23 percent in 1970 to 40 percent in 1995. The faculty ranks have also seen African American, American Indian, Asian American, and Hispanic representation increase from 40,000 in 1980 to more than 65,000. The percentage of minorities enrolled in college and gains in degree attainment were made for all categories—the largest for the Asian Americans. Hispanics, rapidly becoming the most numerous officially designated minority, have benefited least.

Affirmative action in the 1960s and 1970s was based on the belief that talented people were being excluded from academe because of racial and sexual prejudice. The history of higher education gave credence to that argument; such barriers, overt and covert alike, could be identified across the system. Most of the barriers have been struck down, but equal opportunity and colorblind selection policies have not been achieved. In fact, in an inversion of logic, many proponents of affirmative action have claimed that admissions policies in which race is *not* considered are discriminatory. Moreover, the closer higher education got to equal access, the more difficult it became to explain unequal outcomes. Because all groups were not participating and achieving at the same rate, numerous researchers in higher education continually sought evidence of injustice—overt or covert, mystical or psychological. Discrimination existed. It had to. Otherwise, all groups would have been proportionately represented in all student bodies, faculties, programs, and graduation exercises. The tail of an impossible goal was wagging the entire enterprise.

Institutions

Higher education continued expanding, albeit at a slower rate. By the late 1990s some 3,700 accredited colleges and universities were awarding associate or bachelor's degrees. In addition more than

6,000 institutions variously called proprietary, noncollegiate, or postsecondary were providing everything from short-term, occupationally related education to graduate degrees. The number of degrees awarded by the traditional sector expanded so that nearly 540,000 associate degrees, 1.4 million bachelor's and first professional degrees, 400,000 master's degrees, and 45,000 doctorates were conferred each year. Tuition, room, and board for undergraduate residential students reached nearly $8,000 per year on average— $5,700 in the public sector and $15,500 in private institutions. Forty-four percent of the students were receiving some type of financial aid. Of the 181 million adults in the United States, 32 percent were participating in some form of adult education annually.

College building came almost to a halt after the frenzied pace of the 1960s, when new institutions sprang up in every state. In 1976 there were 1,898 four-year public and private nonprofit institutions; in 1995 there were 2,115. During that same interval 50 public, two-year institutions were opened, bringing the total to 1082. The 28 percent enrollment growth over that span of years was accommodated by increasing enrollments at preexisting campuses and by building 500 branch campuses. Furthermore, because 43 percent of the students were attending part-time, up from 39 percent in the earlier year, the institutions' capacity was not as taxed as it might have been.

Private Institutions

The status of the private sector is a notable characteristic of the era. During the middle 1970s, several commentators were pessimistic about the survival of private, nonprofit colleges. They looked at inflation and the financial difficulties plaguing the institutions and concluded, "By the 1990s private universities as they are now known could well have disappeared, been absorbed in state systems, or divested themselves of all but their few profitable operations. . . . Some predict Harvard will survive" (Moynihan, 1975, pp. 143, 146). It is not difficult to understand why many predicted the demise of private higher education. From the beginnings of colleges in the nation, the private sector had been dominant. Even after the Morrill Act and the rise of strong public universities, the private institutions' share of enrollment did not decline below half the total. But enrollments reached parity between the sectors in 1951, and by 1975 the private group's share had declined to 26 percent, leading one writer to lament, "There is no end in sight" (Lyman, 1975, p. 156).

The defenders of the private sector fell back continually on the argument that pluralism, a diversity of institutions, and autonomous institutions free of external control should be sustained. They deplored the term *postsecondary education*, saying that it described a place "in which proprietary schools of hairdressing or massage techniques rubbed elbows with Yale" (Lyman, 1975, p. 157). In commentary continuing well into the 1990s the private sector enthusiasts deplored coordinating boards, oversight commissions, and any other forces that would homogenize higher education. Secularization and cost-benefit analysis were making higher education like a business; programs designed for community uplift or social welfare were reminiscent of government; the rapidly escalating budgets could lead only to institutional downfall.

However, the privately controlled institutions proved resilient, cutting costs where they could and finding sufficient funds to sustain operations. The share of enrollment in the private, four-year colleges held steady at not much lower than the 1975 level. Unionization of their faculty practically halted after the Yeshiva case. Pell Grants and various student loan programs made it possible for them to continue increasing tuition, a rising stock market helped to triple their endowment income, and gifts and grants tripled as well. By 1994, private sector revenue accounted for 37 percent of all the funds coming into higher education.

As had been the case for a century, the private sector was dominated by research universities, nonsectarian colleges, and religiously affiliated institutions. The top five institutions in terms of current-fund revenue received from the federal government were private universities, with between one-half and two-thirds of their students enrolled at the graduate level. The sectarian colleges of the Colonial Era had become elite and secularized; the contemporary sectarian colleges remained small and selective; the liberal arts colleges survived, with many adding programs in business and the professions. Institutional diversity—prized as an ideological pillar of American higher education—was intact.

Even though nearly all private institutions expanded the types of programs they offered, thus decreasing the difference between themselves and other institutions, each had programs in which it excelled. In 1973 the Carnegie Commission on Higher Education published a classification of institutions (1973a), separating them into eighteen categories from specialized schools to research universities; private institutions were represented in all of them. In the early 1980s the National Center for Education Statistics developed a similar classification system with seventeen categories, and private institutions again appeared in all of them. The private sector institutions dominated bachelor's degree awards in philosophy, religion, and theological studies and, at the graduate level, in business and psychology. They awarded bachelor's degrees to 54 percent of their full-timers within six years, compared with 43 percent of the full-time students who completed degrees in public institutions. They enrolled one in five undergraduates but produced one in three of the baccalaureates. Their tuition charges doubled in the 1980s, but their students, most attending on a combination of extramurally funded loans, institutional scholarships and discounts, work-study or other self-generated income, and family support, were not driven away by the increased costs.

Liberal Arts Colleges

The liberal arts colleges, at least those conforming to Breneman's purist definition (1994), are one of the most distinctive components of private higher education. Whereas the private research universities look and act much like their counterparts in the public sector, the liberal arts colleges have few duplicates. Their enrollments range from a few hundred to less than three thousand; their student-faculty ratio is rarely higher than fifteen to one, hence their average class size tends to be small; they are single-purpose institutions, educating undergraduate students in the main; their faculty reward structure centers on teaching; and they exercise selective admissions and on-campus residence. They appeal to young people who prefer to avoid the tumult associated with large, public institutions.

Most of the liberal arts colleges were able to maintain their uniqueness. More important from the standpoint of recruiting students, they were able to offer discounts from the posted tuition price. Each attempted to differentiate itself "from its peers by some combination of location, history, religious affiliation, single-sex or racial orientation, curricular emphasis, and perceived quality (or prestige)" (Breneman, 1994, p. 43). They competed with each other on the basis of these qualities and also on the extent to which they were able to fashion a combination of financial aid that brought their net cost to the student down to an acceptable level.

Even as the number of eighteen-year-olds in the American population declined in the 1980s, the liberal arts colleges enjoyed a substantial increase in student applications. They became more selective, admitting only 53 percent of their applicants in 1989, compared with 63 percent in 1977. After factoring in the percentage of accepted students who enrolled, their overall intake was thirty students for every one hundred applicants in 1977 and twenty-one per hundred in 1991. Because the colleges continually strived to maintain what they considered an optimum size, student-faculty ratio, and balance among all their financial characteristics, their number of students remained stable. As an example, the annual new-student enrollment at seventeen women's colleges totaled 4,866 in 1977 and 4,231 in 1991—an average of 249 students per college in the latter year. Over the same period new-student enrollments at nineteen Presbyterian colleges increased from 5,335 to 5,671; they decreased from 6,009 to 5,181 at seventeen Methodist colleges and from 2,706 to 2,259 at nine Catholic colleges. At all three types of schools the average intake hovered at just under 300 students per year (Breneman, 1994, pp. 56–57).

Elasticity in tuition and financial aid allowed high-prestige liberal arts colleges to maintain their selectivity, primarily because they were more handsomely endowed and also because their allure enabled them to attract a greater number of full-pay students. At the other end of the continuum the low-prestige institutions attracted students because they kept their tuition low and relied more heavily on extramurally funded student aid. The share of funds that the private colleges derived from all sources remained steady for thirty years prior to 1989, as the proportion gained from endowment income, gifts, and tuition declined slightly and governmental support grew. Expenditures shifted somewhat more significantly, with the percentage of funds devoted to instruction declining from 50 to 38 percent and funds going to physical plant operation and maintenance from 16 to 12 percent. Increases showed up in general administration, as administrative demands grew more complex, as well as in college development, recruitment, and student services. Breneman's analysis (1994) of the liberal arts colleges concludes that they were financially sound, as their key revenue sources grew more rapidly than their expenditures. In 1992, when state funding for public sector institutions was under attack, concerns about whether the community colleges and state universities would be able to offer the courses that the students wanted became prominent. The private-college recruiters were able to argue convincingly that by limiting enrollment, their institutions would be able to maintain small classes and the courses basic to a core curriculum.

Even so, the liberal arts colleges and other institutions in the private sector tended to have excess capacity in the mid-1990s, and calls were being made to increase the state grants that could be used to defray tuition. In California, for example, in 1976 a $2,650 maximum grant equaled about 75 percent of private-college tuition, whereas by 1991, although the maximum had doubled, tuition had gone up so that the grant would cover only about 40 percent. The result was that the independent colleges, which at one time were receiving half of all the students who were getting state aid, were matriculating only about one-fourth of them. Increasing the state funds going to students in the private sector would accordingly cost the state less than if it had to expand capacity in the public institutions.

The few liberal arts colleges in the public sector developed primarily in the 1960s as alternatives to the large-size institutions. Built within existing state higher education systems, they managed to maintain their appeal much as did the private liberal arts colleges: residential settings, small classes, prescribed curriculum. Some of the more successful institutions were the University of California at Santa Cruz, Evergreen State in Washington, the University of North Carolina at Asheville, and Ramapo College of New Jersey, which, along with others of the type, sustained the traditional liberal arts while adding international, multicultural, and interdisciplinary studies.

The faculty in liberal arts colleges typically spent their time differently. They taught for more hours and were paid less, but there was no shortage of applicants because people who had gone through those types of colleges often wanted to return to teach in them. Clark (1997) reports that the faculty in the best undergraduate-centered liberal arts colleges were able to combine an interest in research with their concern for students. Astin and Chang (1995) examined a few colleges that emphasized both research and teaching and found several characteristics common among them. For one, they were all private, residential colleges spending twice as much per student on instruction and 50 percent more for student services than the norm. They sported frequent interactions among students and faculty, had a strong humanities orientation, including interdisciplinary, history, and foreign language courses, and emphasized student writing and student involvement in the professors' research. The faculty were both interested in students and in writing articles for publication in academic or professional journals. Their list included Bard, Bryn Mawr, Carleton, Occidental, Williams, and a half-dozen others. But such institutions were rare. Most of the staff in the liberal arts colleges were strongly interested in student progress, and research was much less a consideration.

Graduate and Professional Education

Graduate and research universities reached a peak in influence as the Contemporary Era opened. Their academic departments had overpowered the undergraduate curriculum, helping to segment it and reducing its capacity for holistic studies. Their master's and doctoral degrees were requisite for entry to an increasing number of occupations. The institutions were thoroughly involved with service to government and to the economy. Their scientific and technical roles so dominated that humanistic studies were occupying an ever-smaller portion of the curriculum. Their greater size had led to more administration, and their extramural support base had continually to be cultivated. If ever there had been a golden era when graduate school professors could contemplate their next area of inquiry and share it with a few humble acolytes, it was tarnished beyond recognition. The university was a busy place indeed.

The numbers are instructive. By the late 1980s the doctorate-granting universities were enrolling more than one-fourth of all students in the United States, and the institutions awarding the master's as their highest degree enrolled almost as many. By 1994, master's degrees were being conferred in 1,342 institutions, two-thirds of them private, and doctorates in 472, half private. Concentration was such that 70 leading institutions were awarding 65 percent of the doctorates and 40 percent of the master's degrees. Practitioner-oriented fields dominated: master's degrees in business, education, health professions, and psychology were being awarded in 500 or more institutions; doctorates in biological and life sciences, education, physical sciences, and psychology in at least 200.

Of the two thousand different master's degree programs, seven in eight were practitioner-oriented. Five hundred different doctoral programs led to fifty degrees in addition to the Ph.D. The public institutions conferred nearly twice as many doctorates and held nearly a three-to-two edge in master's degree awards.

The forces affecting undergraduate education, such as expanded access and redefinition of the curriculum, had considerably less effect on graduate and professional schools. Undergraduate studies were being pulled increasingly by politically aware social groupings on and off campus, but fewer calls for redefining the role of the institution were directed at the graduate levels. There, program content and research topics might be shaped by external constituencies, but in the main, the programs were still based on cognitive rationality and direct service to the professions. The research role had maintained its stability in the face of student protests of the 1960s and 1970s and continued in spite of efforts to reform curriculum to accommodate various subgroups and purposes.

Clark (1996) discusses the effect of academic growth on the universities, especially the splitting and re-forming of academic disciplines. He contends that "disciplinary differentiation is many times greater than institutional differentiation" (p. 419). It is an independent force, operating internationally apart from the nature of systems or the sectors within them. When research within academe became a primary activity, the practitioners began producing scholarly reports in increasing volume and, as the various disciplines led to specialized departments and research institutes, further expansion of scholarship within particular fields occurred.

The splitting and re-formation of disciplines is a frequent occurrence, as formerly excluded fields are added and as existing fields extend their coverage. New departments are created along with new scholarly journals and new professional associations. By the 1990s there were more than one thousand journals in mathematics. Psychology had split into forty-five major specialties; one of them— social psychology—had seventeen subfields. This disciplinary fragmentation adds to system complexity. University administrators and state agency officials usually give high priority to coping with student expansion, but growth in the disciplines "leads to more esoteric academic specialties that organizationally become elite enclaves" (Clark, 1996, p. 424). Research universities and other institutions in the same system may grow further apart as one group enhances its research capacity and emphasizes faculty research while another group in the same system focuses primarily on access for greater numbers and different types of students.

During the late 1970s the number of degrees awarded in professional schools and the number of schools awarding them continued the increase that had swelled in the Mass Higher Education Era but then flattened out. Between 1983 and 1994 the total number of first professional degrees conferred showed little growth. Some fields actually declined—dentistry and theology most notably. Degrees in pharmacy showed the greatest increase. And nursing education continued its steady march toward requiring higher degrees for entry into practice.

The law schools were moving toward an increased emphasis on clinical education, training for public policy, and a concern for relevant social activities. The number of institutions conferring the L.L.B. or the J.D. increased slightly, from 166 in 1976 to 185 in 1994; degrees awarded, most in three-year programs, went up by 24 percent. Although the demand for legal services increased and large law firms were employing greater numbers of the graduates, the market for newly minted attorneys was fragmented. In some cases the legal profession faced competition from accountants, as tax attorneys found their practice overlapping with graduates of accounting programs. Many attorneys also had to learn to concern themselves with the laws of other nations as their practice involved them with international trade. But in general, although schools and areas of practice were stratified among functions, the profession was still protected by state regulations regarding entry and the various specializations were able to accommodate each other within the schools.

The number of institutions awarding the doctor of medicine degree increased from 107 to 121 in the first twenty years of the Contemporary Era, and the number of degrees awarded went up by 14 percent. However, this was in step with the increased population, and although some specialties seemed overpopulated, there was certainly no glut of general practitioners. Most of the private schools were either receiving public funds or obtaining grants and contracts for research, training, and patient-care activities. Some were freestanding; most were affiliated with universities, but all had some association with a teaching hospital. "Many medical schools own their own hospitals and/or are affiliated with hospitals that give them complete control over the medical management of the hospital" (Rothstein, 1992, p. 1166). Many of the basic medical science courses were taught by specialists in biological sciences, not necessarily physicians, but the clinical faculty members were usually members of the medical profession. Practically all the internships were taken in the hospitals associated with the schools so that the faculty were directly involved. Medical research was so much a part of physician training that the joint M.D.-Ph.D. became well established. One of the continuing concerns in medical education has been the relative emphasis that the programs were placing on research and patient care, with a concomitant issue being specialization versus holistic studies. The growing dominance of health maintenance organizations in the delivery of medical care in the United States had yet to have a marked influence on the conduct of the medical schools.

The bachelor's degree in nursing had become the preferred degree for nurse practitioners, relegating the associate degree in nursing, conferred by the community colleges predominantly, for nurses' aides and other subspecialties. Even so, the associate degree in nursing was awarded to 54,000 students in 1993 and the bachelor's in nursing to 39,000. The master of science degree was being awarded to clinical specialists and the doctorate in nursing for those conducting research in that field. As with all the professions, the conversion of degree requirements was taking many decades to be realized. The one certainty was that nearly all nursing education had come under the oversight of degree-granting institutions of higher education, with the clinical-practice component, but not the control, remaining in the teaching hospitals.

Theological studies—the original centerpiece of the colleges— were barely holding their place within the universities. In no other field was the historical secularization of higher education shown as graphically. In the first twenty years of the Contemporary Era, their proportion of bachelor's degrees awarded shrank from .6 percent to .5 percent; however, their master's and doctoral degrees awarded showed a slight increase, with the master's degrees going up to just over 1 percent and the doctorates to over 3 percent. Because there were no rules governing the ordination of ministers, any group could begin a school and award degrees in divinity. Therefore, most theological training was taking place outside the formal higher education establishment in numerous seminaries that were specialized according to religious bodies and according to doctrinal differentiations within them. Religiously affiliated institutions constituted nearly half the private institutions of higher education in 1994—a slight increase from the proportion seen at the start of the era, but few specialized in training theologians.

Teacher education had moved from normal schools to four-year colleges and universities prior to the start of the Contemporary Era. Few freestanding schools of education remained. By 1994 the number of bachelor's degrees awarded in education was equaled by the master's degrees and doctorates in that field. Similarly, the 1,146 institutions awarding bachelor's degrees in education were matched by 1,036 awarding the master's degree and/or the doctorate. Teacher education was being provided in every type of college, public and private. And even though the major research universities had deemphasized teacher education, most of them retained schools of education that conducted research and awarded graduate degrees. In many states public school teachers were required to have undergraduate majors in one of the subjects they would teach, but a fifth year of coursework or a master's degree in education had become prevalent. And because practically all school systems granted salary increases to teachers who obtained higher degrees, the universities that maintained graduate programs in education continued enrolling numerous practitioners who attended part-time, even as they were working in the school.

Accordingly, graduate and professional education remained prominent in the Contemporary Era as schools broadened their base of support and avoided most of the controversies afflicting the undergraduate schools. The professional schools enjoyed the luxury of sustaining selective admissions policies as the number of students seeking access increased relative to the number of places. Because graduate and professional education depended heavily on internships, apprenticeships, and clinical studies, it was more difficult to expand than was undergraduate education, much of which could be opened to greater numbers of students merely by adding chairs to a classroom. Even though the charge was raised that graduate and professional schools were not sensitive to the employment market, more master's and doctoral recipients were able to find employment in the fields for which they were trained than was the case for graduates at other levels. The self-regulation of students seeking training, the places that were available for them, the amount of programmatic funding, and the marketplace all served to maintain equilibrium.

Community Colleges

The community colleges—the preferred appellation for public institutions awarding the associate as their highest degree—reflected the consolidation that marked the beginning of the Contemporary Era. The number of colleges, the ratio of full- to part-time students, and the types of degrees awarded showed little change between the mid-1970s and the mid-1990s. The percentage of associate degrees conferred in occupational areas that had reached 58 percent in the mid-1970s was at just over 60 percent in the mid-1990s (Cohen and Brawer, 1996). The number of public colleges had nearly tripled in the twenty years prior to 1975, going from 336 to 981, but in the ensuing twenty years, only 10 percent more were added. The colleges accommodated the 33 percent increase in enrollment by adding buildings, extending instructional hours, providing classes in rented space off campus, opening branch centers, and employing additional part-time faculty. In 1975 the community colleges were enrolling 35 percent of all students in higher education; by 1994 this had risen to 39 percent. The percentage of part-time students that had reached 63 percent in 1980 remained steady. At the beginning of the era half the faculty were part-time instructors—a group that climbed to over 60 percent of the staff in 1995, twice the ratio employed in the senior institutions. The part-time students were being met by teachers who shared at least one of their characteristics.

This pattern reveals a mature system of institutions—a system that has taken its place as a permanent component of higher education. The colleges enroll around 45 percent of all first-time freshmen, and more than 20 percent of those who complete at least four courses transfer to in-state, public universities within four years of matriculation. The existence of open-admissions community colleges enables the public university systems in nearly every state to maintain their selective admissions policies; without an institution available to receive nearly half the higher education seekers—80 percent in some states—the pressure for freshman admissions would be too great for the universities to resist.

The community colleges continued to be attractive to older students, especially those needing to return to college to learn skills that would enable them to enter a new career or to upgrade their skills and their standing in a job they already had. Over 15 percent of the students were aged forty or older. Tuition charges at community colleges held steady at around 44 percent of the cost of attending an in-state, public, four-year institution. These lower fees meant that community college students received less financial aid; the colleges enrolled 43 percent of all undergraduates attending public institutions, but their students were receiving 30 percent of the Pell Grant funds.

By the late 1990s the community colleges were solidifying their position even more. The welfare-to-work initiatives included a job-training component that the colleges were in a unique position to provide. The 1998 tuition tax credit plan stepped up the incentives for low-income students to attend. As low-cost, well-located institutions, the colleges were in good position to accommodate a majority of the rising population of college seekers.

Other Institutions

The higher education system is usually considered to include the 3,700 degree-granting public and private accredited community colleges, four-year colleges, and universities that the U.S. Department of Education recognizes as "higher education." However, a parallel system of accredited proprietary schools has grown, fueled especially by the availability of federal financial aid for its students. That sector has a long history, dating to the business schools established in the early nineteenth century; by World War I they were enrolling a quarter of a million students. Subsequently, various other trade schools were opened and sought recognition for their contributions. An Association of Independent Colleges and Schools, representing primarily business schools, was founded in 1912; the National Accrediting Commission of Cosmetology Arts and Sciences began in 1924; and the National Association of Trade and Technical Schools was founded in 1965.

The proprietary schools grew notably after the GI Bill allowed their students to be eligible for financial aid. Over half the veterans attending postsecondary education under the GI Bill went to the business, trade, and personal services schools that sprang up to serve them. More federal aid to proprietary school students became available in 1965 with the passage of the National Vocational Student

Loan Insurance Act, and in 1972 the Higher Education Act amendments made proprietary schools full partners in the receipt of federal student aid. By the late 1980s, proprietary school students were
receiving one-fourth of all Pell grants, one-third of all Stafford
loans, and more than one-half of all supplemental student loans.
The federal government was providing $4 billion per year to stu-
dents in those institutions.

The proprietary schools focus on specific job skills, usually
within a limited number of fields, often only one. Only a few offer
degrees similar to those awarded in the higher education sector;
most provide certificates of completion or other awards noting competence in narrow areas. Programs generally consist of a predetermined group of courses with few options. The faculty are hired and
fired by the schools' owners and administrators; tenure and academic governance are nonexistent. Enrollments are small, averaging
under four hundred. More than 40 percent of the total are in five
states: New York, California, Ohio, Illinois, and Texas.

To be eligible for federal student aid funding, the schools must
be licensed by the state and accredited by an agency recognized by
the U.S. Department of Education. Since the mid-1980s each state
has designated one or more agencies to license the institutions, and
there are eight national accrediting organizations. The schools have
been successful primarily because of the aid funds available to their
students and because they can develop programs rapidly for specific
occupational purposes, adjusting them as conditions of employment
change in a region. Whereas the staff in a public institution must
seek approval from numerous sources before developing a new curriculum, a process often taking eighteen months, the proprietary
school managers can have those same programs up and running
within a few weeks. However, charges of questionable business practices have been raised continually, especially regarding accounting
procedures and aggressive recruiting practices. Default rates on student loans have been considerably higher than for students in the
traditional sector, and federal agencies have continually tried to

bring the institutions under control. Between 1993 and 1997 the U.S. Department of Education revoked the eligibility to participate in federal aid programs for nine hundred proprietary schools, primarily because 25 percent or more of their students defaulted on their loans. States also questioned institutional practices, as in the case of a two-year business college that New York State charged was doubling tuition so that students could receive maximum awards, with the school then forgiving payment of the balance (Maldonado, 1998). Pell Grants received by students in proprietary schools dropped to 10 percent by 1997 (Weiss, 1997).

A set of even more marginal institutions has also taken form. These are the academic-degree-granting agencies that range from profit-making institutions offering non-campus-based degree programs to those that mail impressive-looking academic credentials upon the receipt of a fee, no questions asked. Some of these organizations have developed large followings overseas where employers might not be able to tell the difference between a doctorate from New York University and one from the University of Coney Island. And in the United States most municipal, state, and federal agencies advance staff members in grade and pay based on their presenting additional degrees, with little heed to where they were earned. When the market is there, businesses will arise to meet it.

The states typically have been able to exercise little control. California enacted a Private Postsecondary Education Act in 1977 in an attempt to monitor the institutions by developing a set of procedures under which licensure might be granted. However, they continued to grow, with those founded in the twenty years since the passage of that act representing 80 percent of the total. A 1986 directory listed 177 licensed in California: 40 granting the doctorate, 39 with a religious mission, 22 emphasizing psychology or family counseling, 13 teaching law, 5 offering courses in fine or applied art, and 58 offering specialized programs of other types (Weiner, 1989, p. 7). This was a heterogeneous group, with some of the institutions approved by paying a fee for a business license and others being authorized by passing a state Department of Education review. In general though, few states were exercising more than minimal oversight and typically did not take care to publicize the fact that most institutions had not been reviewed but were only licensed to function as businesses.

The System

By the end of the twentieth century, the higher education system that had evolved over the centuries since the colonies were formed had reached a stage of diversity, complexity, and comprehensiveness that could never have been foreseen. It had become a set of institutions related by a medium of exchange and arranged by principles of sequence loosely followed. Each institution maintained courses, curriculum, student and faculty relationships, and requirements that looked decidedly like those in similarly labeled activities in other institutions. Higher education had become, in effect, a national system that could not be described merely by examining its legal arrangements or the structure of its institutions. It was more a social system with its various parts standing in certain relationship to each other. It had rules of conduct, sets of shared beliefs, and expectations on the part of students, staff members, and the public.

The system's medium of exchange has been the degrees conferred and the transcripts recording student progress through the courses—the instruments by which activities in one institution can be recognized as those that go on in another. If these documents are not recognized by the majority of institutions within the system, the institution that issued them is not perceived to be part of the core group. Even though most of the students in proprietary trade schools are funded by the federal government, the certificates they earn carry no value within the graded system of higher education.

The system grows in certain standard ways. When the number of people wishing to attend increases, higher education either adds institutions or adds to the size of each unit. It often takes on functions that other social structures have been carrying out, as when it adds occupational and professional education formerly provided through apprenticeships. Recently it has added the function of furthering equity by adopting procedures designed to level distinctions between entire social groups. It sometimes relinquishes functions. For example, it has effectually abandoned responsibility for nurturing adolescents.

There is a relatively stable ratio between those who enter the system and those who exit holding certificates or degrees. Almost the same proportion of people enrolled in college in the 1960s received degrees as those who were there in the 1990s. In 1970, 8 million students were enrolled in all higher education sectors, and 1.27 million degrees were awarded. In 1994, 14.3 million students were enrolled, and 2.22 million degrees were awarded. The ratio was nearly the same in both years—1 degree for every 6.5 students. This happens, even though the number of people entering is so much greater, because some institutions graduate virtually everyone admitted whereas others maintain high attrition rates. It all has to do with selectivity: community colleges award degrees to only around 10 percent of their students, but Princeton and Pomona graduate practically all their matriculants.

This maintenance of a constant ratio exists also because standards are elastic across higher education and are protected within the academic system. A professor who gives a certain distribution of grades to one group of students tends to continue awarding that same distribution, even though over the years the students' absolute ability may have increased or decreased substantially; comparing grade distributions at colleges where there have been significant population shifts evidences this. It is a behavior peculiar to academics—an ideology that defends flexible standards. It suggests also that a dominant characteristic of professors is to sort their students.

The system is far from seamless. Its institutions are similar superficially, but each type of college posts its own rules regarding student admissions, instructional practices, scheduling, curriculum coordination, and faculty conduct. A college may or may not insist on its students' maintaining continuous progress. Some encourage part-time attendance and allow students to drop in and out at will. Others are decidedly opposed to sporadic attendance; their dropouts must justify their behavior before being allowed to return. The system's most stable feature is its allowing students to transfer among institutions; its most unstable feature is the variability of costs among institutions.

In common with other social structures, higher education institutions value self-perpetuation. They have become exceedingly skilled at sustaining themselves; their capital campaigns, legislative lobbying, and ability to deflect criticism are well refined. They solved the problem of access for the masses by erecting one thousand low-tuition community colleges, most of them in the years following World War II, even as they preserved every type of college that had ever been founded: residential and commuter, liberal arts and occupational, religious and secular. The institutions are engaged in basic and applied research, general education, professional development, high school make-up studies, job-entry skills development, career upgrading, and personal interest studies. The 2.1 million freshmen enrolling each year provide one measure of its success; the $190 billion it devours provides another.

Students

College enrollments continued growing as access broadened to include more older students, more part-time students, more female students, and students taking longer to complete degree programs. The entering students' proficiency changed little overall. While in college they changed programs; some fell out of popularity while others boomed. Costs increased; more financial aid was available.

Enrollment

The drive for more years of school can be seen in the data showing that between 1975 and 1994, undergraduate enrollment went up by 26 percent and graduate enrollment increased by 36 percent. Much of the increase was propelled by a rise in the percentage of people completing high school—from 83 percent in 1975 to 87 percent in 1996—and in the number of high school graduates who enrolled in college in the ensuing school term. The enrollment of recent high school graduates that had increased sharply for the first twenty years of the Mass Higher Education Era flattened out after 1965; for the next eighteen years the rate went from 51 to 53 percent. Beginning in 1984, a rapid increase brought the figure to 62 percent by 1995.

When subdivided by race and gender the percentage of high school graduates attending college and the enrollment of eighteen- to twenty-four-year-olds showed some different patterns. Under-graduate enrollments of women reached parity with those of men in the mid-1970s and increased by a considerably greater rate. Black student enrollment also increased but Hispanic enrollment did not, as that group's rate of college entry did not keep pace with its rise in high school graduation. (See Tables 5.2 and 5.3 for comparative enrollment figures.)

The increase in enrollments surprised many analysts who had viewed the precipitous drop in the number of eighteen-year-olds in the population that was obviously to occur between 1979 and 1992

Table 5.2. Percentage of High School Graduates Enrolled by Race/Ethnicity, 1975 and 1996.

Race/Ethnicity	1975(%)	1996(%)
White		
Enrolled the October following graduation	51	66
Enrollment of 18- to 24-year-olds	27	40
Black		
Enrolled the October following graduation	42	55
Enrollment of 18- to 24-year-olds	20	27
Hispanic		
Enrolled the October following graduation	58	51
Enrollment of 18- to 24-year-olds	20	20

Source: National Center for Education Statistics, 1997a, p. 62, 1997g, pp. 194, 196.

Table 5.3. Enrollment of Women, 1975 and 1995.

Program Type	1975 Total Enrollment	% Women	1995 Total Enrollment	% Women
Undergraduate	9,679,000	46	12,231,719	56
Graduate	1,263,000	45	1,732,470	56
First professional	242,267	21	297,592	42

Source: National Center for Education Statistics, 1996b, pp. 189–190, 1997g, p. 185.

and concluded that enrollments would drop as well. The Carnegie Council on Policy Studies in Higher Education (1980) had estimated a decline of from 5 to 15 percent in undergraduate enrollments between the mid-1970s and the mid-1990s. Along with others who had predicted enrollment declines, they did not anticipate the increased high school graduation rate and the increased rate of college attendance by younger and older students alike. For example, the percentage of twenty-two- to twenty-four-year-olds enrolled in college increased from 16 to 23 percent between 1975 and 1995 and enrollment of twenty-five- to twenty-nine-year-olds from 10 to 12 percent. During those same years the percentage of eighteen- to nineteen-year-olds enrolled went from 47 to 59 percent and of twenty- to twenty-one-year-olds from 31 to 45 percent. Some longitudinal data confirmed the cross-sectional numbers. Adelman (1994) analyzed the senior high school class of 1972 and found that within fifteen years, 56 percent of the group had entered college, and roughly two out of three had attended some form of postsecondary education, including proprietary or adult school, during that time. In brief, around 3 million people graduated from high school in 1972, and by 1986 over 1.8 million of them had gone to college or to trade school, or had participated in some form of additional education. The enrollment picture that had looked so dismal to observers watching the decline in the number of eighteen-year-olds turned out to be different than most had expected.

The increased enrollments led to more degrees being awarded at all levels. (See Table 5.4.) The fields in which degrees were awarded shifted also. The master's degrees awarded tended to follow the ratios for the bachelor's except in business, where they increased by 160 percent, and in engineering, where the 66 percent increases in bachelor's degrees were matched by a doubling in the number of master's degrees awarded. In the health professions the 50 percent increase in bachelor's degrees was paralleled by a 150 percent increase in master's degree awards. Some of the more notable shifts in degrees awarded by sex were in architecture, where women's share of the degrees awarded went from 20 percent to

Table 5.4. Changes in Earned Bachelor's Degrees by Selected Field, 1974–75 and 1994–95.

Field	1974–75 Total	1994–95 Total	% Change 1974–75 to 1994–95
Agriculture	17,528	19,841	+3
Architecture	8,226	8,756	+6
Biological/life sciences	51,741	55,984	+8
Business	132,731	234,323	+77
Communications	19,248	48,803	+154
Computer sciences	5,033	24,404	+385
Economics	14,046	17,673	+26
Education	166,758	106,079	−36
Engineering	46,852	78,154	+67
English	47,619	51,901	+9
Health fields	49,090	79,855	+63
History	31,470	26,598	−15
Mathematics	18,460	13,723	−26
Modern foreign languages	17,115	12,309	−28
Political science	29,126	33,013	+13
Physical sciences	20,778	19,177	−8
Sociology	31,488	22,886	−27

Source: National Center for Education Statistics, 1997g, pp. 306–315.

38 percent; in business where the master's degrees awarded to women increased from 8 percent to 36 percent of the total; and in engineering where master's degrees awarded to women increased from a minuscule 2 percent to 15 percent. (See Table 5.5.)

The National Center for Education Statistics survey for fall 1995 found 14,261,781 students enrolled in the 3,728 institutions classified as "higher education" and 850,262 in the 4,947 "other postsecondary institutions" (National Center for Education Statistics, 1997j, p. 6). The minority groups were overrepresented in the two-year colleges as well as in the "other postsecondary" sector (primarily proprietary trade schools). (See Table 5.6.)

Table 5.5. Total Number of Degrees Awarded and Percentage Awarded to Women, 1975 and 1994.

	1975		1994	
Degree Type	Number Awarded	% Women	Number Awarded	% Women
Associate	360,171	47	542,449	59
Bachelor's	922,933	45	1,169,275	54
Master's	292,450	45	387,070	55
First professional	55,916	12	75,418	41
Doctoral	34,083	21	43,185	39

Source: National Center for Education Statistics, 1996b, p. 253.

Table 5.6. Percentage of Enrollment by Race/Ethnicity, Fall 1995.

Race/Ethnicity	% of Total	% of Higher Education Institutions	% of Other Postsecondary Institutions
White	74.1	74.7	64.9
Black	11.0	10.7	16.5
Hispanic	8.2	7.9	12.7
Asian	5.7	5.8	4.3
American Indian	1.0	0.9	1.5

Source: National Center for Education Statistics, 1997j, p. 6.

More students were attending part-time, working off campus, and taking longer to complete their programs. Part-timers increased from 39 percent in 1975 to 43 percent in 1994. Of the students aged sixteen to twenty-four and attending full-time, 36 percent were working while in college in 1973, 46 percent did so in 1993 (National Center for Education Statistics, 1997a, p. 74), and 66 percent in 1996 (Basinger, 1998). The percentage of students who graduated within five years fell steadily between 1983 and 1996—at public institutions from 52 to 45 percent and at private institutions from 60 to 57 percent. Dropout rates changed relatively little over the thirteen-year period; they changed not at all in public institutions, and went up by 3 percentage points in the private institutions ("College Attrition Rates Are on the Rise," 1997, p. 4).

Job upgrading gained in popularity. In 1995, 32 percent of employed workers participated in skill improvement training for their current job; nearly half the people taking job-related courses were college graduates. Many of the students just out of high school who could not find work and many unemployed people who had been in the labor force matriculated at community colleges. The relationship had been observed decades earlier: "Community college enrollments rise and fall remarkably in phase with the ups and downs of unemployment" (Betts and McFarland, 1969, p. 749).

Proficiency

The proficiency level of students entering higher education has long been a matter of concern, and ways of estimating it have taken various forms. High school grade point averages and patterns of courses taken provide one measure, entrance test scores another. The number of entrants that colleges shunt to remedial instruction is an indicator of student ability, although the criteria on which colleges make those decisions are quite varied. Overall, comparisons over the years are not reliable because of the varying numbers of students taking the tests, the inconsistency in grades awarded, and the numerous subject areas in which students may be assessed.

The pattern of courses that students took in high school evidenced efforts to enhance proficiency. In state after state, graduation requirements were strengthened so that a considerably greater percentage of high school graduates in 1994 had taken core academic subjects as compared to students graduating in earlier years; 51 percent of the graduates had taken four units in English and three each in science, social studies, and mathematics. This compared with only 14 percent who had taken this array of courses in 1982. However, the percentage of college freshmen enrolled in remedial classes remained steady. In 1995, as in the 1980s, around 30 percent of the entrants took remedial courses in reading, writing, or mathematics.

If students were taking more units in core academic subjects in high school, why were colleges still maintaining sizable remedial efforts? Grade inflation was at least part of the problem. Between 1990 and 1994 the American College Testing Program collected data on around 530,000 students per year who were enrolled in more than five thousand public schools. Using only the students' grades in at least three courses in three of the four basic areas of mathematics, science, social science, and English, and comparing them with scores on all four tests of the ACT Assessment, relationships were drawn between grades and test scores. The average test scores remained constant across the five-year period, but the mean high school grade point average increased from 2.94 to 3.04. The analysts concluded that no significant improvement in average student achievement had occurred but that grades had improved, undoubtedly because "grading and the standards teachers use to award grades are relative" based on factors other than a student's knowledge of course content, factors "such as attendance, effort, discipline, etc." (Ziomek and Svec, 1995, pp. 6–7).

Gains are difficult to document also because of the larger proportion of the population staying in school. Since the mid-1970s the National Assessment of Educational Progress has been assessing student knowledge in several subject areas. Trends for seventeen-year-olds show the following: reading scores increased between 1971 and 1988 and then declined so that the 1996 scores were slightly ahead of 1971; mathematics achievement was about the same in 1996 as in 1973; science proficiency was lower in 1996 than it had been in 1969; the large gaps in achievement between whites and minorities narrowed, especially as the proficiency exhibited by black seventeen-year-olds improved relative to the whites in mathematics and science over the years prior to 1996 (Campbell, Voelkl, and Donahue, 1997, p. 4). The NAEP samples were drawn from a wide pool, and the averages flattened out differences among various groups and states.

The increased number of students interested in further education led to an increase in the number participating in the advanced placement (AP) program whereby high school students might gain college credit. "Between 1984 and 1995, the number of students taking AP examinations increased dramatically, rising from 24 students per 1,000 11th- and 12th-grade students to 66 per 1,000" (National Center for Education Statistics, 1997a, p. 78). Furthermore, the number of Graduate Record Exam takers went up from 265,000 in 1970 to 389,000 in 1985, but as a percentage of bachelor's degrees awarded, the number remained steady at around 33 percent. Scores on the verbal portion of the GRE fell from the mid-1960s to the end of the 1970s, then stabilized. Scores on the quantitative portion bottomed out in the 1970s and then began a climb that lasted through the 1980s. The biology subtest scores were stable for the thirty years after 1965. In education the scores bottomed out in 1980 and then climbed so that by 1995, they were approximately where they had been in 1965. Engineering and psychology scores remained stable but literature declined steadily. More academic courses taken in high school, more participation in AP programs, higher grades, stable test scores and percentages of students directed to remedial studies, and an increased percentage of young people matriculating—all these factors interacted. Some were reinforcing; others acted to negate the others. A consistent pattern in student proficiency was difficult to discern.

Access

Student access was enhanced not only by the increase in various forms of financial aid but also by laws and court decisions, most of which extended the trends that had been established earlier. Discriminatory policies reducing the likelihood that people of color, women, older people, and the disabled could attend were continually and successfully attacked. In the case of *Bob Jones University* v. *United States* (1983), the U.S. Supreme Court upheld an Internal Revenue Service decision that institutions discriminating on the basis of race would be denied tax-exempt status. In *Mississippi University for Women* v. *Hogan* (1982) a male applicant challenged the admissions policy of an all-female nursing school, and the Supreme Court ruled that public institutions could not discriminate on the basis of gender. Subsequent cases affecting private, single-sex colleges such as the Virginia Military Institute and The Citadel extended that ruling.

Rulings regarding disabled students were made in relation to the Rehabilitation Act of 1973 and the Americans with Disabilities Act of 1990—federal acts that protected disabled individuals who otherwise met academic and technical standards. In *Southeastern Community College* v. *Davis* (1979), the Supreme Court ruled that the college was within its rights in denying the admission of a severely deaf student to its nursing program because the student's disability would preclude her taking part in the clinical aspects of the nursing program and would create serious difficulties in practicing the profession. However, in other circumstances institutions might be required to provide sign language interpreters for deaf students. In *Doherty* v. *Southern College of Optometry* (1988), the federal appellate court ruled that applicants must be accepted in spite of their handicaps if they could become qualified to participate in the program with the aid of reasonable accommodations. This ruling reinforced the requirement that institutions build access ramps for physically disabled students and make accommodations in science laboratories so that visually handicapped students might participate.

The Age Discrimination Act of 1975 prohibited discrimination on the basis of age in programs or activities receiving federal financial assistance. In *Purdie* v. *University of Utah* (1978), the Utah Supreme Court ruled in favor of a fifty-one-year-old woman who had applied to the educational psychology department and had been rejected as too old. Earlier, a federal district court had ruled in favor of two sixteen-year-old plaintiffs who had sought entrance to Sonoma County Junior College in California. The court reasoned that the institution's requirement that students be eighteen years old was not rational in relationship to the state's interest in educating qualified students. Other cases brought under the Age Discrimination Act similarly related age distinction practices to issues of institutional operation and objectives. A medical school's policy of not admitting anyone over thirty-five years of age because of its goal of producing doctors who would have the most possible years of practice was rejected because maximizing length of practice was not part of the normal operations allowed by the Age Discrimination Act nor was it a basic objective of a medical school. However, when students were being selected for training for jobs that required a certain level of physical fitness, although a physical fitness test might have a disparate impact on older applicants, it was permissible because it had a direct and substantial relationship to the job.

Student residence has also been an issue. Most rulings have agreed that states have a legitimate interest in giving preferential treatment to their own residents, even if this has the effect of limiting access for out-of-state students. Challenges to a number of states' residence requirements have had differing outcomes. In *Starns* v. *Malkerson* (1970), the students argued that a one-year residency requirement was discrimination affecting the fundamental right to travel interstate guaranteed under the Fourteenth Amendment, but

the Court found that a one-year residency requirement did not have
sufficient impact on that right to be constitutionally impermissible.
However, courts have rejected other residency requirements as
unconstitutional, as in *Kelm v. Carlson* (1973), when a court of
appeals invalidated a requirement that a law student have proof of
employment in the state. The courts have also rejected statutes
mandating that the students' residency at the time of application
be considered their residency for their entire time as students.

Affirmative action rulings have evolved. In 1978 Bakke contended that the medical school at the University of California at
Davis was holding positions open for minority applicants and that
he, a white applicant, had been rejected unfairly; the Court ruled
that specific quotas violated the Civil Rights Act but that institutions could consider any number of student characteristics in their
admissions procedures. The U.S. Court of Appeals ruled that the
University of Maryland's program of awarding scholarships to black
freshmen was illegal because other students were equally needy, and
in 1995 the Supreme Court let stand the lower court's ruling. In
1996 the U.S. Court of Appeals ruled that the University of Texas
Law School was not within its rights in using race as a basis for
admissions, holding that the laws were designed to prohibit specific,
not general, discrimination. Kaplin and Lee (1995) reviewed the
major laws and court cases and interpreted them as follows: institutions must employ affirmative action to overcome the effects of
past discrimination; admissions procedures must apply uniformly to
all candidates and must not discriminate on the basis of race, sex,
or age; and "the institution must exercise special care in determining its objectives and relating its system to them" (p. 416).

Other issues have been raised in terms of student access. The
Supreme Court in 1977 ruled that New York State could not discriminate against resident aliens in granting scholarships, student
loans, and other forms of financial aid without showing a compelling
state interest. In this case New York's interest in protecting its citizens or in encouraging aliens to become citizens was considered not

sufficient. Students have also sued institutions on the grounds that documents such as school catalogues and regulations establish express or implied contracts. Sometimes they have prevailed in obtaining degrees after completing all prescribed courses. Questions of the legality of entrance examinations were raised when colleges were using exams to exclude students from college-level courses and restrict them instead to remedial classes. The California legislature passed a Matriculation Act in 1986 that was designed to assist entering students' reading, writing, and arithmetic through remedial courses. Suit was brought against institutions that barred low-ability students from college-level courses, and colleges subsequently were allowed only to *advise* students to first enroll in remedial classes.

By 1997 around half the states were requiring students to pass standardized exams to graduate from high school, but the movement was colliding with the doctrine of disparate impact, which was being extended to college admissions. In *United States* v. *Fordice* (1992), the Supreme Court ruled that Mississippi's use of ACT scores exclusively to restrict admission to certain of the state's public universities was perpetuating racial discrimination. If the tests that an applicant must take have a disparate impact on minorities (the most commonly used tests certainly do), and if the content of the tests is not expressly relevant to the requirements of the curriculum (a testable question), their use could be restricted. The colleges were being asked to show the relationships among admission tests, placement in courses and programs, grades attained, and graduation rates. If the concept of disparate impact were to achieve the force of law in adjudicating issues, not only of entrance requirements but also of graduation rates and curriculum content, it would have a greater impact on institutional autonomy than any other measure ever applied to higher education.

Behavior

In general, the body of law and court rulings continued the trend toward furthering the principle that students are entitled to be treated as adults not subject to any special supervision. Although many parents might have preferred that the colleges exercise greater control, the concept *in loco parentis* was virtually abandoned in most of higher education. Once the Twenty-Sixth Amendment, which lowered the voting age to eighteen, was ratified in 1971, the concept of adulthood dropped to that age, and in most states, eighteen-year-olds could enter into contracts, be held liable for debts, and enjoy the other privileges of full-fledged citizenship. In the case of *Beach v. University of Utah* (1986) the court summed up the prevalent position when it said that it is unrealistic to impose on a university the role of maintaining custody over its adult students; the institution would have to baby-sit every student, a task beyond its resources. Furthermore, such measures would be inconsistent with the relationship that institutions attempted to sustain with their students and would be inconsistent with the objectives of a college education. Nonetheless, there still remained the position that institutions had to maintain a safe environment and to protect students from undue risk.

The several thousand chapters of fraternities and sororities on college campuses caused special problems. A lower court decision, later reversed, held that a college was liable for damages because it failed to supervise a student who was paralyzed in an accident during a party at his fraternity house (*Whitlock v. University of Denver*, 1987). In a case brought by a student who had been injured during a fight between two fraternities at the University of Delaware, the trial court took the position that the school had a special obligation to prevent on-campus misconduct. There continued to be a strong undercurrent of opinion, especially in the lower courts, holding that institutions had some responsibility for what happened to their students, even though students were independent adults. The colleges were finding it better to enforce limited regulations stringently than to impose general guidelines and overambitious rules. They were supposed to educate, not police, students, but they still had to establish and enforce rules of conduct. For example, a number of states made fraternity hazing a criminal offense, but lower courts ruled that students injured during hazing activities might still name universities as defendants because the institution failed to enforce regulations preventing such activities. However, when students living off campus got in trouble with the local authorities, the institutions have been successful in divorcing themselves from the cases on the grounds that it was impossible to monitor the students' behavior.

Responsibility for student employees has also received some attention. In a case decided in Arizona in 1986, the court ruled that although Pima Community College was not exempt from state unemployment compensation laws, a former student who had been employed under the federal work-study program and was no longer working was not eligible for unemployment compensation because he had been a student, not an employee. A scholarship athlete at Indiana State University had been seriously injured in football practice and lost his scholarship because he could no longer play. In 1983 the Supreme Court of Indiana ruled that because there had been no attempt to enter into an employer-employee relationship in the awarding of the scholarship, the student did not meet the definition of employee and therefore could not receive workers' compensation benefits.

In comparison with the students of the 1960s, those attending in the Contemporary Era were docile in the extreme. No military draft loomed to threaten them; there was no war to protest. International tensions were markedly reduced, especially after the demise of the Soviet Union in 1991. What activism and protests there were centered for the most part on ethnic groups seeking favorable, or at least more equitable, treatment in admissions, curriculum, and recognition. As the institutions yielded gradually but steadily to minority-group demands, as stated in campus grievances but more effectively in the legislatures and courts, the reasons for campus protests withered. So did the interests of more than a minuscule number of students in pursuing them. Hate speech and sexual harassment engaged student attention, but as the institutions struggled to erect rules governing them, these issues also moved away from immediate concern. Few issues were so compelling that students across the land were ready to act in concert. Although a proposed fee increase might trigger a short-lived demonstration on one campus, it did not have the force of a Cambodian bombing that could ignite students everywhere.

Faculty

During the early years of the Contemporary Era, the faculty consolidated the gains in professionalism that they had made in the latter years of the Mass Higher Education Era. Faculty demographics shifted quite a bit, with numbers of women entrants increasing markedly. The percentage of faculty working as part-timers increased as well. A move toward modifying definitions of faculty productivity so that the staff would spend more time on teaching and less on research generated much press but was slow in modifying working conditions. Faculty preparation, in-service development, and evaluation standards changed little. Faculty salaries increased throughout the 1970s, dipped in the early 1980s, and turned up again in the 1990s, but overall they hardly kept pace with the rate of inflation. Protected by a lengthy history, court decisions, and state governments that with rare exception proved benign, institutions of higher education continued as desirable places of employment.

Demography and Salary

The major shift in faculty demographics was in the increased proportion of women. For the quarter-century preceding 1995 the total faculty doubled to 932,000, with the number of men employed increasing by 62 percent and the number of women by 240 percent. The proportion of women in faculty ranks increased from 23 percent in the earlier year to 40 percent, with most of that increase occurring in the early 1990s. The women professors were distributed unevenly across higher education institutions; they represented a lower-than-average percentage of the faculty at research institutions, higher than average at community colleges. However, the distribution overall was closer to parity than it had been at any time previously. As for ethnic distribution, a little less than 5 percent of the full-time faculty were black, 5 percent Asian, and slightly over 2 percent Hispanic. The gains for minorities were coming much more slowly than for women.

The aging of the faculty slowed on average, as early-retirement systems and a steady influx of new hires ensured that younger faculty remained highly represented. In 1992, 36 percent of the faculty were under age forty-five; 37 percent were between forty-five and fifty-four. The part-timers were somewhat younger—49 percent were under age forty-five. The ratio of full-time and part-time faculty changed considerably. In 1975, more than 70 percent of the professors were employed full-time; that figure dropped to below 60 percent by 1995. The increased hiring in the early 1990s was revealed in the length of time that full-time faculty members had been employed; in 1992 one-third were in the first seven years of their careers. Nearly 17 percent of the new professors were members of minority groups. Around one-fourth were not born in the United States. Women were well represented in the new hires, making up almost 41 percent of the group.

During the first twenty years of the Contemporary Era faculty salaries tripled; full-timers were averaging $15,622 in 1975 and $47,811 in 1995. But the salaries barely kept pace with inflation; the $15,622 in 1975 was worth $45,367 in constant 1995 dollars. In inflation-adjusted terms, salaries dipped in the early 1980s, rose in the latter part of that decade, and remained static through the first five years of the 1990s (National Center for Education Statistics, 1996b, pp. 242–243). The figures were affected by the increased numbers of women entering academe. They tended to be clustered in the earlier years of their careers and at lower academic ranks. In constant dollars their salaries averaged $39,120 in 1975 and $41,369 in 1995. (See Table 5.7.)

Table 5.7. Average Salary of Full-Time Faculty by Sex and Type of Institution, 1974–75 and 1995–96 (in Constant 1995–96 Dollars).

	1974–75	1995–96
All faculty	$46,601	$49,309
Women	40,184	42,871
Men	48,632	52,814
Public four-year institutions	48,539	51,172
Private four-year institutions	45,021	50,819
Community colleges	44,440	43,295

Source: National Center for Education Statistics, 1997g, p. 251.

Major changes by field were seen in business, where average salaries for full-timers increased, and in health and humanities, where they decreased. (See Table 5.8.) Salaries differed among types of institutions. In 1994–95 the average salary for a full-time faculty member on a nine-month contract was $42,101 in the community colleges, $53,444 in the public universities, and $63,280 in the private universities. The average salary for men and women showed little difference at the lower ranks, but a spread of around 13 percent existed at the full professor level, where men were likely to have been in their positions longer. For the academic year 1996–97 the faculty received an average raise of 3 percent, slightly less than the rate of inflation, which was 3.3 percent.

Academic salaries looked high in comparison with the average wage rate for all American workers but continued to lag behind those of professionals with comparable years of schooling in other fields. The AAUP estimated that professors earned 38 percent less

Table 5.8 Average Salary of Full-Time Faculty by Selected Fields of Instruction, 1987–88 and 1992–93 (in Constant 1992–93 Dollars).

Field	1987–88	1992–93
Business	$45,243	$49,223
Health	64,860	55,624
Humanities	42,420	40,972

Source: National Center for Education Statistics, 1997g, p. 249.

than lawyers, engineers, and health care professionals, "although the gap between our earnings and our professional peer group earnings has narrowed by 16 percentage points since 1979" (Magner, 1997, p. A8). Because many professors were staying on the job longer, some institutions were raising the top salary so that these faculty members did not hit the salary ceiling and remain stuck there until they retired. The community colleges especially were affected by sizable proportions of faculty members reaching the top of the salary scale. Accordingly, several created such categories as *master teacher* or *senior scholar,* so that their more productive professors could be paid more. The private universities typically had no such problem and could raise an individual professor's salary as much as the budget allowed. The public universities often had salary scales locked in systemwide or by union contract and had to make other arrangements. Many added salary steps. The University of California, which had phased in steps four, five, and six in the full professor ranks in the 1960s, added step seven in 1979 and step eight in 1988; by 1996 it was considering step nine (University of California . . . , 1996).

Labor Market

The sources of faculty remained as they had been. The doctoral degree was expected for people entering the faculty ranks at universities, and the master's degree for those joining community colleges. The number of doctoral degrees awarded annually, which had increased notably during the 1960s, topped out at 34,083 in 1975 and remained at that level through the 1980s. But the number moved up again after that from 35,720 in 1989 to 44,446 in 1995. Master's degrees similarly showed a precipitous increase in the 1960s and early 1970s, reaching 292,450 in 1975. The numbers flattened out, reaching 310,621 by 1989 and then turned up so that by 1995, 397,629 master's degrees were awarded. Nearly all of these degrees were awarded in the traditional models that had been established by the research universities and comprehensive institutions in earlier eras. The doctor of arts programs that had begun in the 1960s did not spread; few institutions were added to the two dozen or so that had begun such programs earlier. The master of arts in teaching fared little better. The traditional discipline-oriented graduate programs remained the primary source for college faculty members.

Faculty supply and demand remained in equilibrium. Various analysts had predicted an oversupply of doctoral degree holders or an undersupply of qualified staff, but the labor market remained constant. Salaries were not keeping pace with inflation, but the attractiveness of the academy remained high. For one thing higher education represented a stable career in an era of instability in the broader labor market, where corporations were dismissing long-term employees and where cutbacks in fringe benefits had become the norm. The supposed overproduction of Ph.D.'s relative to demand proved a myth, in large measure because a steadily expanding research enterprise absorbed large numbers of graduates as postdoctoral scholars and because, by 1994, 27 percent of the doctorates were being awarded to non-U.S. citizens, up from 11 percent at the start of the era.

Because the institutions were concerned that senior faculty, the highest-paid members of the academy, would stay on indefinitely, around 40 percent of them were offering early retirement incentives by the mid-1990s. These incentive plans were much more likely to be found at the research universities; 75 percent of them developed such incentives. Most of the plans were funded by the retirement systems that had become wealthy over the decades, which the large number of professors entering academe had funded, along with institutional or state contributions. But dollars alone were not sufficient to tempt sizable numbers of senior instructors who enjoyed their work, contact with students, and campus life in general. Furthermore, not every retirement led to a corresponding opening for a full-time instructor at a junior level. Frequently the position was collapsed and the professor's responsibilities spread among other staff members, or a part-timer was employed to take up the retiree's responsibilities.

Tenure, Academic Freedom, and Due Process

The concept of tenure has been part of higher education since 1915, when the AAUP began arguing that academic freedom and job security were linked. In its most basic form, tenure means only that after a probationary period, professors are entitled to continuous employment until they choose to leave or until the institution can show good cause for termination. The question of what constitutes good cause has been argued extensively as professors have been challenged for their views, capabilities, activities on or off the campus, and even their cost. Not all institutions have tenure systems, but job rights have been protected nonetheless under prerogatives such as an individual's property interest.

Various contractual relationships define a faculty member's association with the institution. Where there are collective bargaining agreements, the contract may be no more than a form filled in by the professor in which the employee agrees to abide by the terms of the agreement negotiated between the bargaining unit and the institution. Employee handbooks and oral promises made by administrators can sometimes create contracts. AAUP guidelines have been used as evidence of binding agreements. However, in case of dispute, clear contractual language usually prevails unless there are statutes contravening the agreement. Sometimes so-called academic custom and usage will be considered by a court when the statutes are not explicit about the behavior and when a contract or agreement is ambiguous.

The early years of the Contemporary Era saw an important case affecting the rights of faculty members to organize into bargaining units and have those units recognized by the governing board of their institution (see Table 5.9). In 1980, in *National Labor Relations Board* v. *Yeshiva University*, the Supreme Court ruled that full-time faculty at that private university had managerial

Table 5.9. Faculty Unionization by Institutional Type, Selected Years 1984–1996.

Year	Total Number of Institutions	Total Number of Faculty	Public Four-Year Number of Institutions	Public Four-Year Number of Faculty	Public Two-Year Number of Institutions	Public Two-Year Number of Faculty	Private Four-Year Number of Institutions	Private Four-Year Number of Faculty	Private Two-Year Number of Institutions	Private Two-Year Number of Faculty
1984	—	182,964	—	104,367	—	68,996	—	9,087	—	514
1986	—	195,570	—	110,029	—	76,297	—	8,502	—	742
1988	1,028	213,673	370	123,638	570	80,106	73	9,108	15	821
1990	1,007	217,398	350	119,752	572	87,347	71	9,742	14	557
1992	922	228,856	273	118,624	565	100,750	71	8,939	13	543
1994	1,057	234,570	332	123,655	639	101,017	72	9,331	14	567
1996	1,115	246,207	336	124,738	686	110,584	79	10,405	14	480

Source: National Center for the Study of Collective Bargaining in Higher Education and the Professions, 1984, 1986, 1988, 1990, 1992, 1994, 1996.

responsibilities such that they would not be covered as employees under the federal National Labor Relations Act. The Court said also that Yeshiva was a specific case; the exemption might not apply in other institutions where the faculty had few if any managerial responsibilities. Subsequent rulings applied the managerial exclusion in around half the cases that were brought forward. The controlling principle was that public institutions are subject to state law, whereas private institutions are under the jurisdiction of federal law, although the latter may come under state law if they receive significant state funding. In 1994, around 26 percent of all the faculty were represented in collective bargaining units; 96 percent of them were in public institutions. Thirty-one states had recognized the right of faculty to bargain collectively, but of the 246,000 unionized faculty members, 65 percent were in California and New York. Overall, the unionized faculty in ten states accounted for 83 percent of the total.

The concept of academic freedom was adjudicated in several cases. In *Bishop v. Aronov* (1991), a court of appeals ruled that a professor's First Amendment free speech and freedom of religion rights had not been violated when, in response to student complaints about his introducing religious commentaries in a physiology class, the university told him to desist. The court stated that administrators were entitled to exercise some control over style and content of speech in school-sponsored activities as long as their actions were reasonably related to legitimate pedagogical concerns.

In a second case regarding academic freedom, a court of appeals ruled that a philosophy professor at the City University of New York could not be stopped from publishing articles regarding the relative levels of intelligence among races. The students demonstrated against the professor, but despite their own rules prohibiting such disruption, school officials refused to ban the demonstrations. The professor's writings were considered to be protected expression, and they were on issues of public concern; the institution had produced no evidence to support its argument that it was acting to protect students from possible harm if they disagreed with the professor's controversial ideas (*Levin* v. *Harleston*, 1992).

In 1982 a court of appeals recognized a researcher's privilege to not disclose his research findings (*Dow Chemical* v. *Allen*). The Environmental Protection Agency had sought to use the researcher's notes and findings in ruling whether several herbicides manufactured by Dow should be taken off the market. The court ruled that the researcher had a right to not reveal his findings because in this case the interests of government were not strong enough to prevail over the concept of academic freedom.

Contractual language and rules governing due process have come into play in various cases. In one (*Welter* v. *Seton Hall University*, 1992) two instructors who had been terminated without the specified twelve-month notice were reinstated when the New Jersey Supreme Court found that their dismissals had been based on dissatisfaction with their performance. However, fraud by a faculty member, such as failure to disclose a second full-time job, can result in a rescission, which voids the contract and does not entitle the professor to a hearing prior to dismissal.

The diverse ways in which American colleges and universities are organized and managed lead to various interpretations. At religiously affiliated institutions the courts shy away from questions of church governance or policy because of First Amendment protection of freedom of religion. In a celebrated case concerning an institution closely connected to the Catholic Church (*Curran* v. *Catholic University of America*, 1989), a court ruled that the institution was within its right in revoking the professor's ecclesiastical license, without which he could not teach Catholic theology, because he had taken several public stands against the teachings of the church. The court decided that the professor knew that ecclesiastical faculties, which are licensed by the Vatican, are different in that they have an obligation to abide by the authority of the mother church. The court would not overturn the university's withdrawal of the professor's license to teach.

Federal laws prohibiting discrimination on the basis of age, sex, or disability have also been brought forward in adjudicating cases involving faculty members. In 1987 a federal district court applied the Equal Pay Act to require a salary adjustment for all female faculty after the plaintiffs presented evidence that the school president had said that male faculty should be paid more. Furthermore, the institution was unable to provide any legitimate reason for pay differences. Title VII's general prohibition against sex discrimination allowed claims to be brought alleging that although the female plaintiffs are not doing the same work, their jobs have comparable worth. However, in 1984 a court of appeals rejected a complaint brought by a faculty of nursing who said they were paid less because they were predominantly female. The court said that Title VII did not prohibit an institution from paying faculty members in different departments on different scales. The fact that one department had a predominance of female instructors was not in itself sufficient cause to bring the claim for equal pay.

The Age Discrimination in Employment Act enjoined employers from discriminating against persons forty or more years of age, who must be employed, retained, and paid on the same basis as all other employees unless the specific nature of the work can be shown to require the use of younger people. In a case adjudicated in 1983 (*Leftwich* v. *Harris-Stowe College*), the newly appointed regents of a college that had been taken over by the state college system determined to employ a new faculty. All prior instructors were invited to apply for positions at the institution, but when one professor who had scored higher on the regent's evaluation than the other two applicants was not retained, he sued, claiming discrimination on the basis of age. The facts showed that the tenured faculty at the same college before it had been taken over by the new board were older and better paid. The court of appeals rejected the regents' claim that hiring nontenured faculty was more cost effective and promoted innovation and quality, saying that if higher salaries could be used as an argument to justify discharging older employees, the purpose of the Age Discrimination Act would be defeated. Furthermore, the assertion that younger faculty would bring in new ideas assumed that older professors were necessarily stagnant— precisely the kind of stereotypical thinking that the act was designed to eliminate.

The issue of job rights took a different turn in 1994 when the Ohio Supreme Court ruled that tenure and promotion documents at the state's public colleges should be open to inspection by all interested parties. A review of tenure decisions at Ohio State University showed that research, publications, and extramural grants received still weighed heavily in promotion decisions. "In almost every negative tenure case, inadequate research was cited as the major reason" (Lederman and Mooney, 1995, p. 17). All claims that good teaching was to be accorded higher value seemed not to enter into the decisions; the academic reviewers were still applying the old standards of research. Even so, questions of the usefulness of tenure have accelerated, as laws ruling that mandatory retirement can no longer be imposed have led to fears that an aging, higher-paid faculty would bankrupt an institution in which budgets remained static. The argument has also been advanced that one of the reasons women and minority group professors have not advanced as rapidly as they might is that the upper echelons of the professoriate are still occupied predominantly by white male professors who will not step aside and make room for their junior colleagues.

Because promotions at research universities were still being based on publications and grants received, and because professors with tenure could not be removed regardless of their age, little other than persuasiveness, appeals to different standards of professionalism, and rewards for mentoring young faculty or taking on additional teaching responsibilities could be employed to change faculty behavior. Efforts to change the standards for awarding tenure or for allowing institutions to dismiss tenured professors were making little headway. Tenure might no longer be necessary to shield professors from discrimination on the basis of race, sex, or religion, but it has certainly been useful in protecting academic freedom. Grossly incompetent tenured faculty have always been subject to dismissal, but the criteria and process for determining incompetence have rarely been spelled out so that they could withstand challenges. In most cases the procedures have been so elaborate, the reviews so lengthy, that dismissals on the basis of incompetence have been exceedingly rare.

Because the procedures for dismissing instructors have been so complicated that they have rarely been used, a different procedure for helping faculty members maintain their currency and productivity has been tried. Called post-tenure review, this process involves a mandatory assessment of every professor's work at periodic intervals, even after tenure has been awarded. Because the process is supposed to identify any impediments to improvement and to assist the professor in modifying behavior as necessary, it is in accord with the best principles of faculty evaluation—a process that has never been of much use in determining who shall be terminated but rather in providing a mirror through which individuals might view their own activities. Overall though, the wave of dismissals that shook the job security of long-term employees elsewhere crashed against the walls of academe and receded with little apparent effect.

Productivity

Issues of faculty productivity, never far below the surface, arose once again in the 1990s. According to the National Survey of Postsecondary Faculty, full-time instructors worked an average of fifty-three hours per week, with 55 percent of those hours devoted to teaching. The range in percentage of time dedicated to teaching was from 35 percent at private research universities to 69 percent at community colleges. Two-thirds of the faculty teaching undergraduate classes exclusively met from two to four classes; when faculty teaching graduate classes were factored in, the modal number was two.

Multiplying the hours that faculty spent in the classroom by the number of students yielded an average of around 250 student-classroom-contact hours per week (National Center for Education Statistics, 1996b, p. 234). These figures had changed little in the preceding decades, leading to the charge that professors were being paid more for the same amount of work. Put in economic terms, their productivity had decreased.

However, a review of the ways faculty spent their time did not answer the question of productivity. Some commentators applauded the factory model: professors were expected to be on the job for specified periods of time and to deliver certain products. Others wanted the faculty to teach more. Because most colleges received at least a portion of their funds based on the number of students attending, the professors who taught bigger classes would be more productive. Publications might be counted, but their quality was difficult to assess, whereas the number of students within range of an instructor's voice was indeed measurable. But the basic issues remained: Should individual faculty members be assessed on the basis of productivity, or should the measure be applied to entire departments? To what extent should productivity standards differ in research universities, liberal arts colleges, and community colleges? Would productivity be enhanced if instructors had to stay in their offices for a specified number of hours per week? How does an hour spent speaking with a graduate student about a dissertation compare with an hour in which the instructor is lecturing, writing a grant proposal, or preparing a program to be broadcast to a wide audience?

The number of students relative to the number of faculty at an institution has long been a crude but favored index of gross productivity. If the most productive faculty teach the greatest number of students, then the instructors in community colleges, where the ratio of full-time equivalent (FTE) students to FTE faculty approximates twenty to one, are the most productive. Obviously, because conducting research or guiding advanced graduate students is not part of the mission of the community college, the instructors there would be expected to teach more students. But the student-faculty ratio in public four-year institutions, around fifteen to one, is higher than the twelve-to-one ratio in private institutions. Does that mean that private-college faculty are less productive?

The faculty at research universities had their own concern with definitions of productivity. From time to time someone would count the number of pages in published articles and suggest that the lengthier pieces indicated greater productivity. More often, the journal in which an article appeared would be considered, with higher productivity suggested by articles appearing in higher-prestige publications. The dollar value of extramural grants might be noted, leading inevitably to questions of whether a dollar received for a research project was the same as a dollar solicited for student support. And in all institutions questions of the value of committee service (How much more productive is the chair of the committee than the committee's members?) or of community service (Is chairing a United Fund drive worth as much as a series of speeches to local business and professional groups?) were pondered.

Productivity indexes simply conflict with too many variables. Within the same department some instructors work harder at classroom teaching, whereas others are highly entrepreneurial, bringing in grants for research or student support. One professor may turn out a half-dozen short papers a year, whereas another takes five years to complete a book. Some spend many hours counseling students, whereas others find the activity not worth the time they could better devote to preparing a distance education program. Add to all that the differences among academic departments or disciplines in the same institution, and the differences among institutions in the same higher education system, and it is easy to conclude that neither the faculty as a whole nor any enlightened administrators would accept an index of productivity applied indiscriminately across the board.

Even so, the faculty were forced continually to justify their activities. One of the most persistent challenges came from legislators,

state-agency officials, or members of governing boards who applied
the most simplistic measures of productivity, typically the number
of classes taught and the number of students in each class as related
to the professor's salary. Here the part-time faculty member, paid
considerably less and with few responsibilities outside the classroom,
appeared desirable. The salary and fringe benefits for full-time community college instructors in the mid-1990s totaled about $6,000
for each class taught, whereas a part-timer with similar professional
qualifications might be employed to teach a class for $2,000. In the
research universities, the $15,000 or more per class taught by a full-
time professor was viewed as excessive when a part-timer could be
employed at less than one-third the price. The unions and academic
senates fought incessantly against this line of reasoning, pointing
out that a college was a community of scholars engaged in a variety
of activities, not a factory employing pieceworkers. Neither they
nor the budget-balancers have ever been able to convince each
other of the meaning of productivity in their terms.

As distance learning and noncampus colleges expanded in the
1990s, the introduction of additional numbers of non- or quasi-
faculty threatened to further complicate issues of productivity. Technologists, media aides, archival specialists, site arrangers, production
designers, and a host of other people engaged in preparing instructional materials now had to be considered. Who are the faculty
when an army of technicians, each skilled in a specified area, has
produced an instructional program that is used in courses offered for
credit? Which union speaks for these people? To what index of productivity do they adhere? Who judges the quality of their work?

There are limits to viewing the workplace as a pure market in
which people are paid on the basis of their productivity. Outside
academe, piecework—paying employees on the basis of how much
they turn out—has all but disappeared in industries and professions
except for sales and the most routine occupations. Most staff members in most occupations use sets of skills applied more generally
and knowledge and attitudes that cannot be assessed exclusively by

viewing products; they are not paid according to the way they contribute at any given moment. Of all the fields, higher education
most depends on a broad array of potentialities, least on a measure
of products. Rewards for loyal service enter into the equation—thus
creating a bond between institution and individual. Regardless of
political persuasion, court-protected job rights, and faculty organizations, norms of fairness and trust built on a lengthy tradition
supersede questions of productivity.

Outside academe, the tendency in the 1990s was to reduce the
number of full-time staff who had rights to their jobs and to employ
temporary workers. The savings were enormous, as institutions and
corporations converted substantive portions of the workforce from
full-time staff members to part-time, fungible people with little loyalty to the enterprise. The ostensible reason was that the corporations were pruning the dead wood; the real reason was that they
could pay temporary staff considerably less for doing the same work.
The universities, school systems, and civil service were among the
last bastions of career security and norms of professionalism. Legislators with little understanding of or sympathy for higher education
as a stable institution or an enterprise with its own peculiar standards might have looked longingly at what was happening in the
rest of corporate America as they juggled funds among competing
agencies. But whether they proposed regulations mandating indexes
of productivity based on graduation rates, number of classes taught
per instructor, or time spent on campus, the results were invariably
crude measures that only a rare faculty member might think valid.
The professors' profession was too differentiated, too complex to be
captured with that type of net.

Academic Life

Just as the faculty in different disciplines and different types of institutions view productivity in various ways, the working conditions
surrounding the faculty differ according to the same variables. Overall, the American academic profession is concerned primarily with

teaching. Even though research has long been essential for promotion in the university sector, it takes up a relatively small amount of faculty time at other than doctorate-granting institutions. According to the 1993 National Survey of Postsecondary Faculty, around 90 percent have instructional responsibilities as their major assignment. And the overall average of fifty-three hours per week that full-time faculty members devote to their work differs little from the hours they reported in 1987 (National Center for Education Statistics, 1997k, p. 32). Within those norms the ways faculty spend their time vary considerably depending on discipline, institution, and even on the stage of a professor's career. Professional autonomy and academic freedom are most fully realized at the research universities; high levels of personal interaction with students at the liberal arts colleges; a high degree of reclusivity and an aversion to committee work in all sectors. As a corporate body the faculty value participation in governance; on the individual level most would prefer to have little to do with it.

During the Contemporary Era the percentage of time that faculty spent on various activities, broken out by academic rank and type of institution, further differentiated the group (see Table 5.10). Average class size remained at thirty between 1987 and 1992, but the mean number of classroom hours taught per week increased from 9.8 to 11 as community colleges captured more of the enrollment growth. Faculty at research universities averaged 6.9 classroom hours, up from 6.5, whereas those in community colleges were averaging 16.2, up from 15. Class sizes were largest at the research universities, smallest at the liberal arts colleges. The main differences among institutional types were that the faculty at research universities spent 39 percent of their time in teaching and 32 percent in research, whereas those at liberal arts colleges and community colleges spent around 66 percent of their time teaching and less than 10 percent on research (National Center for Education Statistics, 1997a, pp. 285–286). Several researchers (Finkelstein, 1984, for example) further separated faculty time according to gender and

Table 5.10. Percentage of Time Full-Time Postsecondary Faculty Spent on Various Activities, by Academic Rank and Type of Institution, Fall 1987 and Fall 1992.

		Academic Rank					Type of Institution			Liberal	
Activity	Total	Full Professor	Associate Professor	Assistant Professor	Instructor	Lecturer	Research	Doctoral	Comprehensive	Arts	Two-Year
Fall 1987											
Teaching	57	51	54	57	70	69	43	54	64	67	73
Research/scholarship	17	21	20	19	6	10	30	2	12	10	4
Professional growth	5	4	5	4	7	6	4	4	4	4	5
Administration	13	16	13	10	10	9	14	1	13	14	11
Outside consulting/ freelance work	3	3	3	2	3	4	3	3	3	2	3
Service and other	5	5	5	7	4	3	6	3	4	3	4
Total	100	100	100	100	100	100	100	100	100	100	100
Fall 1992											
Teaching	54	50	52	55	68	61	39	46	60	64	69
Research/scholarship	18	22	19	20	6	10	32	23	13	10	5
Professional growth	5	4	4	5	6	6	4	4	5	5	6
Administration	13	15	14	9	10	13	13	14	13	15	12
Outside consulting/ freelance work	2	3	3	2	3	2	3	3	3	2	3
Service and other	7	6	7	9	8	8	9	10	6	5	6
Total	100	100	100	100	100	100	100	100	100	100	100

Note: Columns may not add up to 100 percent due to rounding.

Source: National Center for Education Statistics, 1997a, p. 144.

race, as well as age and institutional type, and concluded that "faculty are as different from each other as they are from the population at large. . . . At the very least, both institutional type and prestige and academic discipline may be seen to differentiate among species of academics" (p. 225).

Many studies have considered the way faculty members spend their time and how well-satisfied they are with their choice of a career. Here again, the responses vary among institutional types, but one characteristic is consistent: faculty derive satisfaction from the work they do, the autonomy they enjoy, their own activities; dissatisfaction relates to extrinsic demands, administrative intrusions on their workspace, and the salary they receive. In brief, they confirm the Herzberg two-factor theory (Herzberg, Mausner, and Snyderman, 1959): personal satisfaction is related to the content of the work, whereas dissatisfaction arises from the environment surrounding the worker. Nearly all instructors feel that they are good teachers and enjoy interacting with students.

Finkelstein (1984) reviewed studies examining the relationship between teaching and research and concluded that to the extent that teaching effectiveness is related to intellectual competence, it is positively associated with research productivity; involvement with research does not detract from good teaching, but conducting research is not a necessary condition for good teaching. Competent, involved professionals apparently devote much energy to every area of their work that they deem important. However, except for the faculty who have willingly taken on the task of teaching underprepared students, most would prefer a brighter group of people to work with. They also want more opportunity to pursue professional development activities that they arrange for themselves: sabbatical leaves, grants for study in their own field, and allowances for travel. Salary is a separate indicator of satisfaction. In 1987 NCES found 59 percent of the full-timers indicating satisfaction with their pay—a figure that dropped to 55 percent in 1992 (National Center for Education Statistics, 1997k, p. 57).

Although faculty became increasingly differentiated among academic fields and institutions, the rise of the part-time faculty had the greatest influence on professionalism. In 1995, 41 percent of all instructional faculty were part-timers, up from 22 percent in 1970. Throughout higher education the part-timers were the migrant workers of academe: students earning extra money while working toward degrees of their own, recent graduates hoping eventually to find full-time positions, people with jobs elsewhere teaching for the extra pay, retired teachers wanting to stay involved, professionals in other fields being brought in because of their specialized knowledge. They helped institutions balance the budget, but at the same time they diminished faculty professionalization because they did not adhere to the traditional core values that included not only teaching but also research, public service, service to the institution, and commitment to a career in which they were judged by their peers. The group was most highly represented at the community colleges where a majority of the staff were part-timers distinguished by several characteristics in addition to their being paid less: they had less teaching experience, held lower academic credentials, had less choice in the selection of materials to be used in their courses, placed less emphasis on written assignments in determining student grades, were less likely to use instructional support services, had less out-of-class contact with students or colleagues, were little involved in departmental affairs or curriculum development, and were less likely to be members of professional associations (Cohen and Brawer, 1996).

The widespread use of part-timers evidenced a schism in the profession. If the part-timers had been reviewed and supervised by the career faculty, they might have been considered as the paraprofessionals, aides, or support staff employed by most other professional groups. But in most cases the part-time faculty were left to teach with the expectation that their students would enjoy the same kind of educational experience they would have if a full-time career professor were heading the class. Supervision of them typically was perfunctory; if they met their classes regularly and turned their grades in on time, few other demands were placed on them. The quality of learning manifested by their students was not likely to come under review.

This is not to say that the learning attained by students in classes taught by full-time instructors was a matter of review either. Faculty were being evaluated, but student learning was not. Evaluation of faculty across higher education was being made by students, peers, administrators, and professors themselves. Faculty were being judged on their apparent teaching ability, their scholarship, service to the institution, and colleagueship. But all attempts to tie student learning to the ministrations of an individual instructor had proved futile; the nature of institutions in which students chose the classes and instructors they would take, and in which specific measurable objectives and pre- and posttests were rarely used beyond the remedial or introductory level, made it impossible to control all the variables so that a measure of pure teaching effectiveness could be described. Even so, evaluation of faculty remained a topic for continual discussion. Marchese (1997) traced student evaluations of teaching and reported, "By 1973, 29 percent of all colleges employed student evaluations; by 1983, 53 percent did; today the practice seems all but universal." He concluded that the literature on student evaluations constituted "the largest single body of research in the world of higher-education studies" (p. 4). Well into the 1970s the faculty at many institutions had resisted adding student evaluations to their dossiers, but by the 1990s this resistance had almost totally collapsed. The question of whether these evaluations related to student learning remained open.

In the Mass Higher Education Era the faculty had made substantive gains in pay because of an expanding economy and a growing belief in higher education's importance to a technologically based economy. Also, they had won the right to bargain collectively. There was little incentive for them to change; faculty were protected by their own views of academic freedom. They considered teaching few students relative to the instructors in the lower-grade schools to be a well-deserved perquisite. Institutions might expand their mission, but the faculty did not have to respond to new demands; they were the arbiters of the beliefs guiding their own behavior.

In the 1990s, contentions that the faculty had become an arrogant group resistant to change were heard increasingly. The faculty were accused of operating in an insular environment, sustaining an elitist mentality. Scholarly recognition by one's peers was considered the highest goal regardless of whether one's own institution or students were benefiting. The peer review process began to be seen more as self-protection than self-policing. Boyer (1990), for example, accused professors of devoting less time to advising students and more time to pursuing their own research interests, which were not subject to accountability by outsiders. Data showing that the higher the faculty rank the fewer the hours in the classroom were used to point out how the professors felt little responsibility toward teaching in particular or to the goals of their institution in general. If the institutions were supposed to be for the purpose of helping students advance, why should the faculty use them as bases of self-protection? Why should they enjoy autonomy and job security in an environment of corporate downsizing? What gave them the right to create their own conditions of work? All were questions that might not have been raised at a time when the faculty were so underpaid that few cared what they did. None would be resolved until the faculty themselves developed and adhered to strict codes governing their work, especially those that demanded they provide evidence of student learning.

Curriculum

Curriculum continued changing by accretion. Colleges typically added more programs and courses than they dropped. Even if a college completely abandoned a set of courses, they usually remained in place at another institution. Vestiges of every prior curriculum were present somewhere.

Degrees

The shifting patterns of curriculum were reflected in the degree awards. By the middle of the 1990s, nearly 1.2 million students were earning bachelor's degrees each year. The trend toward vocationalism was led by business majors, who accounted for 20 percent of all the bachelor's awards, up from 15 percent at the start of the era. When added to the degrees in education, health professions, engineering, and other occupational fields, bachelor's degrees in career preparation studies made up 58 percent of the total awards, up from 54 percent. In addition to business, degrees in communications and protective (administration of justice) services increased notably, but those in education declined by one-third, as the master's degree became the more popular point of entry to the teaching profession. Bachelor's awards in computer and information sciences and in law and legal studies quadrupled, and those in engineering-related technologies and parks and recreation studies doubled.

Some popular undergraduate majors carried through to the graduate level, but others served as general education programs, with the graduates either leaving college with a degree suggesting preparation in the liberal arts or going on to graduate and professional schools to major in more specialized areas. Library science became almost exclusively a master's-level program, with few bachelor's or doctorate awards in that area. Education had practically the same number of bachelor's and master's degree awards. Bachelor's degrees in protective services totaled over 23,000, but fewer than 1,500 master's degrees were conferred in that field. Undergraduate studies in the liberal arts were dominated by majors in social sciences, history, English, communications, psychology, and the biological sciences.

The pattern of master's and doctoral degrees awarded reveals the spread of occupational studies in graduate schools. Business and education accounted for almost half of the 397,000 master's degrees conferred in 1995, down slightly from the percentage conferred in those fields at the start of the era. Altogether, vocationally oriented master's degrees totaled 80 percent of all awards, up from 76 percent. The increase resulted from a 150 percent rise in awards in the health professions, an 80 percent increase in engineering, and a 50 percent increase in public administration. At the doctoral level the same vocational fields accounted for 49 percent of the degrees conferred, up from the 40 percent awarded in those categories in 1976. However, nearly all of the doctoral degrees conferred should be considered occupationally relevant, as most of the students with doctorates in the liberal arts entered teaching or governmental service, and those gaining doctorates in the sciences either stayed on as postdoctoral research scholars and instructors or took employment in research laboratories outside academe.

The sciences changed somewhat. Even though bachelor's degrees awarded in engineering rose considerably, degrees in the biological and physical sciences and mathematics declined so that, overall, the sciences dropped slightly, from 15 to 14 percent of the undergraduate degrees. The situation was reversed at the graduate level. Science degrees represented 10 percent of the master's degrees awarded in 1975 and 12 percent in 1994—an increase accounted for primarily by the doubling in the number of engineering awards. The distribution of doctoral degrees also favored the sciences, rising from 22 percent of the total awards in 1975 to 25 percent by 1995, thanks largely to the health professions. Doctorates in the biological and physical sciences were up by one-third, and those in engineering were more than double the awards of the earlier year. The sciences clearly were strongest at the doctoral level; during those same years the number of awards in English, foreign languages, liberal arts and humanities, and social sciences and history all declined.

Differences in course-taking patterns by men and women reflected modifications in roles and opportunities. By 1994, women accounted for 59 percent of the associate degrees awarded,

54 percent of the bachelor's degrees, 55 percent of the master's degrees, and 39 percent of the doctorates. Women received well over twice as many associate degrees in business and five times as many in the health professions, whereas eight times as many associate degrees in engineering and engineering-related technologies were awarded to men. At the bachelor's level, awards in business were almost equally divided between men and women, but women continued their dominance of the health professions, receiving around four and a half times as many bachelor's degrees in those fields; 80 percent of the bachelor's degrees in engineering were conferred on men. In English, women received nearly twice as many bachelor's and master's degrees and more than one-third as many doctorates. Some dramatic shifts in degrees awarded to males and females appeared in the first-professional level. Whereas in 1976, 4 percent of the degrees conferred in dentistry were awarded to women, by 1994 the number had increased to 38 percent. For the same span of years medical degrees conferred on women increased from 16 percent to 38 percent of the total, and degrees in law from 19 percent to 43 percent (National Center for Education Statistics, 1996b, p. 281).

The students receiving bachelor's degrees took a much greater variety of courses, as graduation requirements continued shifting, with more courses being accepted for degree credit. By 1984 students could receive a bachelor's degree from 80 percent of the colleges without having taken a course in foreign language, from 42 percent of the colleges without a course in history, from 48 percent without a course in English or American literature, from 54 percent without a course in mathematics (Adelman, 1994, p. 195). Of the students receiving bachelor's degrees in the early years of the Contemporary Era, 74 percent had had at least one course in English composition and 70 percent a course in general psychology. But no discipline other than those two was represented on the transcript of as many as half the graduates. The integrative courses in Western or world civilization had been taken by fewer than 30 percent of the graduates and the venerable area of philosophy by less than 23 percent. The tug of war between proponents of free election and those arguing for a common core continued to be dominated by the former group, while the vocationalists made steady inroads.

Concerns about the length of time students were taking to obtain bachelor's degrees and the learning they attained—subjects of discussion for many decades—continued. The high cost of college attendance led some observers to argue that the requirements for the bachelor's degree should be reduced to three years of full-time study. But because most students were taking five or more years to complete their undergraduate work, this suggestion seemed fey. Mandates that students graduate or lose their financial aid after having completed a certain number of units gained ground. Some state systems also were threatening to reduce funding for courses taken by students who had completed at least 120 units and not received a bachelor's degree or, in the case of the community colleges, 60 units without obtaining the associate degree. The institutions resisted, primarily because they were providing remedial education that typically did not count toward degree requirements and because students who switched majors and thus had to obtain more than the minimum number of credits were being penalized. The imposition of exit tests that would preclude students from obtaining bachelor's degrees unless they could demonstrate certain minimum competencies made some headway. However, the measures used to determine which students should pass from sophomore to junior level within a state system were more widespread; Florida, Georgia, and Texas were leaders in establishing such tests.

Remedial Studies

Remedial studies, defined as "courses in reading, writing, or mathematics for college students lacking those skills necessary to perform college-level work at the level required by the institution" (National Center for Education Statistics, 1996e, p. iii), remained among the most intractable areas of the curriculum. Higher percentages of students were graduating high school, and the percentage of those going on to college continued increasing as well. But even with the supposed tightening of high school graduation requirements and the leveling of, or in some areas increase in, scores made by seventeen-year-olds on tests of basic skills, college-level remedial education continued to be as prominent as it ever was. In 1995 more than three-fourths of the colleges that enrolled freshmen offered at least one remedial reading, writing, or mathematics course. This ranged from 100 percent of the public community colleges to 63 percent of the private four-year colleges. State policies tended to either require or encourage public institutions to provide remedial education. Most colleges did not award degree credit for the courses but counted them toward institutional credit that allowed students to remain as full-timers receiving financial aid.

Remedial studies have brought forward debates reaching beyond the campuses, often to the systemwide level and to state legislatures. In 1995 the California State University Board of Trustees unanimously approved a resolution calling for the system to reduce the number of remedial classes offered. Similar concerns were raised by the state university systems in Florida, Texas, and elsewhere. Several state legislatures also questioned the amount of resources that the public universities were devoting to remedial education, and proposals were made continually to divert remedial studies to the community colleges. By the mid-1980s the San Diego Community College District was offering remedial English and math classes for both San Diego State University and the University of California at San Diego. And that was in addition to the remedial instruction that the district was maintaining for its own students.

Many other proposed remedies focused on the lower schools that in some states were directed to adopt core curriculum ranging from elementary through twelfth grade and to test all students for proficiency in the basic skills before granting high school diplomas. However, progress in these areas was slow. High school graduation requirements did increase during the 1980s, but so did the proportion of students taking longer to graduate. By 1993, 87 percent of the thirty-year-olds had received high school diplomas or equivalency certificates, up from 78 percent in 1972. Much of the increase came from people who completed high school while they were in their twenties—a group that scored lower on measures of basic skills. And they were finding their way into higher education.

Remedial education was sometimes used in attacks on open admissions by those who wanted to turn higher education back to a time when it enrolled a smaller percentage of the population and represented less of an expenditure of public funds. The experience of university systems that had begun accepting nearly all applicants and that had apparently been unable to produce a sizable number of well-qualified graduates was often cited. Soon after the City University of New York adopted open admissions in 1970, 70 percent of the English courses offered in its ten senior colleges were remedial, and nearly 90 percent of the matriculants required remedial writing instruction. By the mid-1990s, only around one-fourth of the students entering the system were graduating within eight years. CUNY became a poster child for those wishing to point to the failure of open admissions.

Multiculturalism

The area of the curriculum known variously as multiculturalism, diversity studies, or race-gender-class studies became one of the most fascinating areas for review. The essence of multiculturalism is that studying the culture of Western Europe is insufficient to understand modern America, that various other ethnicities, religions, and nations have a literature, history, and art that all people should learn in order to appreciate the contributions, background, and thinking of each. Portions of these programs had been introduced along with the rise in participation by women and members of ethnic minority groups in both the student body and the faculty. Throughout the first two decades of the Contemporary Era they had grown in magnitude so that by the early 1990s, approximately half the senior institutions were requiring students to take courses that treated history, literature, or other disciplines in the humanities and social sciences from a multicultural perspective. The community colleges were less involved with race and gender studies. In 1991, 9 percent had at least one ethnic studies course in their class schedule, down from 15 percent in 1975; women's studies courses had held steady at 3 percent; social and ethnic studies combined accounted for 3 percent of the humanities class enrollments in 1977 and less than 1 percent in 1991. Most community colleges had coopted multicultural studies by merging them with mainstream courses in history, literature, and interdisciplinary humanities.

Curriculum has always evolved; if it hadn't, students today would be absorbed with the trivium, quadrivium, and Greek and Latin texts read in the original. But multiculturalism engendered controversy far out of proportion to its actual effect. Some claimed that these studies violated the tradition of cognitive rationality because they were based more on a political or social service agenda than on the reasoned research that had become the hallmark of higher education. To others they demonstrated once again that higher education had no idea of the broad areas of knowledge its students should gain, that it was subject only to the political power that one or another group was able to muster. Some critics claimed that the institutions were doing students a disservice by allowing them to concentrate on multicultural studies and thus diminish their employability after graduation; the fact that just over one-tenth of 1 percent of the bachelor's degrees awarded in 1994 were in ethnic and cultural studies seemed not to reduce the heat in the arguments.

Not content with examining an expansion of the curriculum as a phenomenon following in the tradition of curricular evolution, proponents and opponents alike confounded multicultural studies with representativeness, affirmative action, and competition among the various ethnic groups. Demands for multicultural curriculum were often wrapped around calls for a more diverse faculty and student body, greater financial aid for low-income students, and the political power that goes with a defined academic department. Threats, marches, and sit-ins have been employed, leading one observer of a prolonged hunger strike to comment wryly, "Many things in this world are worth dying for, but an academic department?"

Many of the proponents insisted that the groups with which they were concerned had been victims throughout history, and it was their intention to reduce the imbalance by studying literature produced by women, along with the art, music, and culture of ethnic groups and the political oppression suffered by all of them. More reasoned views held that eventually multiculturalism would take its place along with everything else that higher education had adopted over the years. Others felt that the campuses were now generating and exporting hysteria in matters of race and gender relations, that "a genuinely academic discussion of multiculturalism—one that was analytical and informed by a knowledge of the experience of other multicultural societies, past and present—would . . . be close to impossible" (Ellis, 1997, p. 217). Accusations of debased standards, abandonment of traditions, patriarchies, Eurocentrism, lack of academic credibility, political agendas imposed on the past, truth in bondage to power, and other wondrous charges kept academic writings lively. But the families sending the more than two million freshmen to college each year seemed considerably more concerned that their children gain the knowledge and skills useful in advancing them in society. And few became exercised when an institution required an ethnic studies course or when an instructor built consideration of alternative viewpoints into a history class.

Academic Ethos

What is the essence of academe? Although the evolution of academic disciplines mandates that they continually revise methodology and topics of study, some types of changes are denounced as betraying higher education's heritage. In the 1960s, Nisbet (1971) noted that the essential dogma of academe—its commitment to reason and the advancement of rational thought—had been debased by its acceptance of a plethora of alternative viewpoints, especially those holding that there was no hierarchy of knowledge, that no method of inquiry, pattern of discourse, or area of study was inherently valid. Mills (1959) admonished the social scientists for their excessive interest in methodology and relative indifference to social problems. He found scholars shaped by an institutional bureaucracy that standardized scholarship and led social scientists toward imitating the approaches taken by natural scientists. Trilling (1972) extended Hofstadter's work of twenty years earlier, showing how both intellectuals and the public had lost confidence in rationality and how resentment of scholarship had become widespread. He perceived an adversary culture that had grown to conflict with the socially responsible criticism in which higher education had previously been engaged. The debates over whether the academy should be devoted to learning for its own sake were long over, but there was no agreement on what the central theme should be.

Curricular evolution continued. The social sciences turned toward attempts to solve social problems. Some of this move arose from student cries for a relevant curriculum, but more came from the faculty and the institutions' managers who saw funding and political power grow when they could convince the public and the supporting agencies that they were offering something of immediate value to the community. The disciplines were now serving multiple masters: the profession, the university, and the community—the latter having become the most demanding master of all, as the political and social climate of the time pulled the institutions in varying directions. Within the social sciences, vacillation between qualitative and quantitative methods pointed up the problem. The qualitative method had brought knowledge to bear on specific problems; the quantitative method had showed the magnitude of the problems. And yet the researchers were precluded from going too far toward the qualitative lest they be accused of engaging in mere reportage and backtracking away from the place they had won in the halls of scientific research.

The sciences faced a different type of criticism. The early twentieth century had seen science splitting away from metaphysics and theology, developing its own methods centering on the principle that testable theory was the goal. Scientific statements had to be made in terms of observation; measurement had to be subject to verification by repetition. The language of science centered on deductive arguments and rational statements. True science was empirical, logical, and positive. Mathematics and theoretical or mathematical physics were at the peak of the hierarchy of sciences because they most closely approximated the ideal model. Subsequently, antagonism toward science became more prevalent. Some of the attacks were based on what science had done to the environment by effecting industrial processes that caused pollution. Others held that science had yielded fearsome weaponry. And as reactions against Eurocentrism grew, a few extremists accused science of being merely a cultural choice.

The study of literature came under assault from many quarters. Shakespeare, Dante, Goethe, and Plato had been defended formerly by professors of literature on the grounds that studying the classic writers aided understanding of the human condition and raised fundamental questions of existence. Suddenly these authors were accused of being racist, sexist, homophobic, and contributors to the way the ruling groups maintained their power. Print itself was attacked, and an oral tradition was brought forward as a more valid form of communication. History was a biased story told by upperclass dissimulators and more properly viewed from the viewpoint of society's oppressed victims. Writing in 1997, Ellis observed, "Twenty years ago no one would have believed it possible that professors, of all people, would one day argue that the universities should have an overtly political function, work directly for social and political change, and inculcate a particular political viewpoint in their students" (p. 7). And who would have thought professors of literature would teach that writers do not know what they are writing, do not understand the implications of their words, and produce only works of unexamined assertions and prejudices? If the battle was between egalitarianism and elitism, egalitarianism was clearly winning. As an educational and cultural ideal, it was destroying the last quarters in the stronghold of exclusivity that higher education once was.

In the graduate schools the most prominent curriculum shifts occurred in the humanities and social sciences, where the race-gender-class enthusiasts were most effective. As Shils (1992) notes, some very distinguished traditional scholars were still there, but "they are living on the defensive, surrounded by very alien spirits. These alien spirits are at present in a self-indulgent delirium of destructiveness. They have broken with the traditions from which they have come and what they have to put in its place are things of only very small value" (p. 1273). Shils went on to point out how sociology was "riddled by the intellectual detritus of the radicalism of the 1960s and 1970s" and the work of the economists had become very technical (p. 1273). Historical studies too "are afflicted by some of the fashionable hostility to the belief that historical research aims to discover the truth about its diverse subject matters," and "anthropology has become infested with relativism and agnosticism" (p. 1274). The natural sciences had been immune to most of that form of disorder: "Even those who disparage science and regard it as part of a corrupt bourgeois society still want more scientific research to be done, and they want more governmental support for it" (p. 1274). In sum, the all-inclusive university was thriving on ever-finer specialties, doing well at scientific inquiry and technological development even as the ever-shrinking humanities were tasting the bitter gall of fewer students, attenuated resources, and civil war.

Instruction

"Good morning, students, and welcome to the first class meeting of the semester. During this term we will be studying the concepts of, reasons for, and ways of developing. . . . Your resources include my lectures, class discussions, your textbook, the library, and the programs in the learning laboratory. You will write two fifteen-page papers and take three exams—one essay and two multiple-choice. Each paper and exam counts equally in determining your grade."

Those introductory remarks, familiar to everyone who has ever taken a college class, serve several purposes. They establish a first connection between instructor and students—one that is so important that student evaluations of instructors at the end of the course correlate significantly with impressions gained in the first couple of minutes of contact. The instructor is also creating an environment for student learning by describing the course content, instructional aids, sequence of events, and measures of attainment to be employed. Whether the introductory remarks are delivered to a class of five or five hundred, whether they are presented by a professor in person or on television, whether spoken or written, the purposes and effects are the same. The conditions of learning are being described, and an implied contract is being negotiated, with the instructor saying, "These are the goals of the course; these are the ways I will help you attain them; and here is how I will determine the extent to which you have succeeded." Each student who remains in the class is, in effect, agreeing to the contract by participating according to the terms outlined. Reduced to its essence, this is the teaching-learning paradigm.

The teaching-learning transaction is amenable to observation, measurement, determination of effect. Its costs can be calculated along with the time it takes. And yet it has engendered endless commentary as questions of efficiency have been raised. Why should instruction cost as much as it does? Why are costs continually rising? How much are the students learning? How much of their learning is related to the cost of instruction? Are there more efficient ways of effecting learning?

The quest for efficiency in instruction has a long history. Most proposals center on having instructors teach more students by meeting more or larger classes or on paying instructors less, as when part-time teachers are employed or students become more responsible for their own learning. These patterns are tried continually. Failure to find the magic bullet that would yield a notable increase in efficiency is attributed variously to professors who stubbornly refuse to work longer hours, uncaring administrators and bean-counters who look only to the bottom line of passing more students through so that tuition and state reimbursements remain high enough to balance the budget, and apathetic students who refuse to apply themselves to their studies.

Many attempts to increase productivity have focused on reproducible media. Educators have long sought technology that would enrich the learning environment and reduce students' dependence on the live instructor. In summing this quest, Cuban (1986) commented that the "dream has persisted from the invention of the lecture centuries ago to the early decades of this century. . . . In the insistent quest for increased productivity and efficiency, the lecture, film, radio, television, and microcomputer are first cousins" (p. 3). He saw an ongoing paradox of stability in change. As each new technology was introduced, the literature was filled with claims of extraordinary improvements in student learning and promotional tactics devised by those who would add the innovation to the arsenal of instruction. Usually the calls for technological reform came from foundation executives, educational administrators, equipment manufacturers, and a few eager innovators from among the faculty. Academic studies followed that demonstrated the effectiveness of the device. Complaints then surfaced about the logistics of use or of slow adoption by the instructors. Administrators accused faculty members of clinging to antiquated techniques; professors charged administrators with attempting to destroy the personal relationship between teacher and student; costs of equipment soared considerably faster than its adoption. Cuban labeled the technology cycle "the exhilaration/scientific-credibility/disappointment/teacher-bashing cycle" (p. 5). As Oettinger (1969) had concluded even earlier, "The technology-there-is fails in the schools-as-they-are. No one can tell for sure how to marry the technology-that-could-be with the schools-that-might-be" (p. 219). Eventually each innovation took its place as another aid to instruction, never to disappear, never to supplant what had gone before.

A review of a few of the technological aids illustrates the point. Film-oriented college courses appeared in the 1920s along with research supporting the use of film as a valuable teaching tool. In the 1930s, radio was to bring the world to the classroom, to make the finest teachers available to everyone; classroom broadcasting spread rapidly once the hardware bugs were worked out and commercial stations and universities provided programming. Instructional television, introduced in the 1950s, was supported initially by The Ford Foundation, then by the federal government through the National Defense Education Act. Predictably, research found little difference in the amount of information that students could learn from television and that obtained in the conventional classroom. Autoinstructional programming was next, using self-paced workbooks either printed or presented through so-called teaching machines and eventually computers. Multimedia instruction followed, combining film, television, and audiotape with workbooks and drill. Most recently, E-mail and the Internet have been introduced—one used in communication between faculty and students, the other promising to serve as a worldwide infinite library making information available to anyone, anyplace, at any time. Will these be the technologies that will burst the bounds of the campus, freeing students to learn on their own, changing the role of the faculty?

The computer was the key to the new media. First applied to self-paced, prepackaged instructional programs, it then became a more flexible tool, especially as it provided access to the Internet. Whereas radio, television, and film had demanded programmers producing materials on one end and passive listeners or viewers on the other, the computer allowed for interaction among both groups. Like the telephone it could be employed to bypass the authorities.

Television, radio, books, and film were selective in what they deployed, but the Internet knew no such bounds. It promised ultimate freedom. Anyone could introduce materials to it; anyone could retrieve information from it. Its most sanguine advocates showed how users could re-create materials, rewrite texts, reorganize information continually. Ultimately there would be no history, no authoritative statements, only evolving knowledge. Meantime, it opened a world of resources. To the extent that students knew how to judge the value of the information they derived from this infinite resource, their studies could be as broad as they wanted to make them. The resources of the campus, the faculty, libraries, and laboratories were no longer a limitation.

College staff members proceeded as though they still had a role to play. At bottom was the firmly held belief that students needed guidance. If they did not, there would be no reason for schools at any level; young people could merely park themselves in front of computers and search the world's databases, learning anything they wanted to know. And indeed that was a fanciful dream long before the Internet existed. Illich (1970) felt that schools as institutions led away from the development of self-reliance and created a form of social reality divided between that which is academic (institutionalized education) and that which is not. His view of an ideal learning forum for society would be to "provide all who want to learn with access to available resources at any time in their lives; empower all who want to share what they know to find those who want to learn it from them" (p. 108). This pattern of thought reached back to the romantic naturalists of the eighteenth century, who contended that social institutions were corrupting, that people could learn what they needed to know without bureaucratic intervention. A counterview held that schools aided in the development of logical thought, rationality, commonly held understandings, and the kind of humanistic values that the Enlightenment held as its highest standard, that without instruction designed according to the best principles of a democratic society, people would tend toward irrationality, tribalism, intellectual laziness, and social disintegration.

Meantime on the campuses, the staff attempted to integrate the new technology with the instructional forms and content that they were committed to pursuing. The first application was to provide logistical support to conventional instruction. Faculty members used the computer to prepare lecture notes and overhead transparencies, send E-mail messages to their colleagues and students, develop colorful classroom presentations, and otherwise replace the typewriter and blackboard. These seemed limited uses of the nearly $2 billion that higher education was spending annually for instructional support. But they were the most prevalent because they fit the existing college form: teachers and students interacting with each other within the confines of scheduled classes held on college campuses.

Most applications of distance learning have been developed in similar fashion. An instructor presents lectures on television, uses interactive video to sustain discussions with students irrespective of where they are, reacts to student work through E-mail, and prepares and sends materials for student use. The instructor is the designer and conductor, and the students are involved to the extent that they participate on the instructor's terms. Content is predetermined, outcomes are specified, student progress is tallied, and records are maintained.

These applications of technology have dominated because they keep intact the roles of professors and students. It is rather like the early automobile makers putting the engine in front because that was the position held by the horse when it pulled the carriage. The lag in full-scale application of technology to human learning is not the result of a cabal led by professors who want to keep their jobs, institutional managers wanting to protect the physical plant, or funding agencies preferring to perpetuate the familiar. It is society's way of changing incrementally, adapting the new to the former. In education the staff and students merge all the earlier technologies into the existing forms, so much so that the campuses and classrooms of the 1990s would be familiar to the people of the 1890s.

Integrated collegewide plans for converting sizable numbers of courses into multimedia applications suitable for presentation on or off campus have not been widespread. More often, applications of instructional technology have centered on piecemeal approaches. Some colleges have found funds for particular types of hardware and made them available to any who wanted to use them. Others have effectually separated the applications of technology from the mainstream faculty and built technologically oriented divisions or separate entities dedicated to providing distance learning; many of these colleges without walls have a history stretching back to the time when open-circuit television was their centerpiece. But across the system, few reasoned observers believed that if only technological aids to instruction were introduced more rapidly, higher education's fiscal problems would end.

The quest for saving money through increasing productivity, with technology as the centerpiece, has merged with the desire to make people more responsible for their own education and with the changes in hierarchical systems in the workplace. Industry has moved into team production based on organic systems operating from the bottom up. New businesses are developed by entrepreneurs working in ad hoc association with producers, suppliers, customers, and financiers across the land. Flexibility is the rule of thumb. Educational systems, never known for their rapidity of response to societal change, are considered laggards. But technology does not operate itself; instructional programs are not self-generating. Shunting the faculty aside in the search for autoinstructional materials does not solve the problem. Learners might be free to purchase computers and search the Internet, but if sequenced, designed instruction based on defined goals and content remains important, it must still be developed and maintained.

By no measure has information technology resulted in greater instructional productivity. For that matter few industries have enjoyed increased per capita output sufficient to justify the billions spent on it. Nonetheless, higher education has been compelled to install it because it is an essential component of student literacy. The graduates will enter a world where all forms of information technology are basic tools. Expenditures on technology are like expenditures on laboratory equipment. The biological sciences could be taught in a classroom with chairs and a chalkboard, but the students would not learn the way scientists function. The colleges have to install technology and their staff has to use it, even if it adds to the cost of instruction.

The effort to bring about more learning for less money was becoming a battleground. One group was trying to convince the faculty to teach more students or to create or adopt aids to instruction. Another was committed to cutting costs by employing contingent instructors. A third wanted to bypass the faculty or, at best, use only the committed innovators who would work in teams along with support groups to develop the instructional software, or those who would bypass the campuses entirely and rely instead on virtual universities with instructional materials picked up from innumerable sources. However, they all agreed that the rising number of college-age students and the limited budgets were forcing changes as far-reaching as those effected at the start of the University Transformation Era.

Governance

The steady progression toward secularization and extramural influences on higher education continued. State-level activities were particularly pronounced as calls for accountability and outcomes assessment spread from one capital to another. Accrediting bodies furthered the calls, adding to the burden of college administrators who were forced to respond. Membership associations such as the national organizations subscribed to by various types of institutions played a coordinating role. Hovering over all was the federal government, which assumed regulatory power in particular areas. As federal and state regulations multiplied, the word *compliance* entered the vocabulary of higher education. Institutional research and affirmative action offices expanded as more types of data and documentation were needed. The self-governing campus was a fading memory, as the big business of higher education became ever more subject to extramural management.

Federal and State Government

Governmental influences on higher education have always been bottom-heavy; that is, the states more than the federal government have funded institutional development and continuing support. But the federal government has played a role, its influence shifting over the years. First, land grants stimulated new institutions; then funds for special buildings, student financial aid, and program research were made available. Overall, the proportion of higher education revenue contributed by the federal government decreased from 16 percent in 1975 to 12 percent by 1994, but governmental pressure for student access continued, and a new area—institutional accountability for educational effects—opened.

Federal student aid led to governmental oversight. The U.S. Department of Justice brought suits against a number of institutions for discrimination and price fixing. The Student Right-to-Know and Campus Security Act, passed in 1990, required colleges to provide information about graduation rates and to submit reports on crime on campus. The Americans with Disabilities Act of 1990 and the Rehabilitation Act Amendments of 1991 tightened requirements for educating people with disabilities. Federal-level concern with regard to discrimination was seen further in the Civil Rights Act of 1991. The act amended earlier acts pertaining to employment-related testing, among other things. In 1994 Congress passed the Goals 2000, Educate America Act, which furthered the move toward state and local educational standards and assessments. Even so, the states carried the major responsibility for broadening access and maintaining the basic programs.

State governments have broad powers that are limited only by the federal Constitution, each state's own constitution, and powers that the federal government has preempted. The extent of state control on higher education differs from state to state, but rules cover a wide range: licensing, funding, and administration of institutions, along with general laws concerning labor relations, contracts, and liability. State-level boards of governors may enjoy autonomy from the state legislatures if they are noted in the constitution, but in half the states the governing agency is created by statute that is easier to amend.

A few cases reveal how these differences are manifest. When the state legislature voted to close a campus of the University of South Dakota and turn it over to the state prison system, a suit challenged its power to do so (*Kanaly v. State of South Dakota*, 1985). The state supreme court ruled that although the university was statutorily created and therefore the legislature had the power to transfer its assets, the legislature had also created a trust fund for the university, which would have to be reimbursed for the loss of its assets. The regents of the University of Michigan brought suit against the state in 1975, alleging that the legislature's way of appropriating funds had violated the state constitution. In 1990 the Michigan Supreme Court ruled that the legislature could attach conditions to its funding of the university but only to the extent that they would not interfere with the management and control of the institution because those powers were constitutionally reserved for the university. In California the constitutionally created university was ruled exempt from a section of the State Education Code stating that the board of regents must take the prevailing wages in different parts of the state into account when establishing salaries. In Ohio a court ruled in favor of laid-off employees who sought reinstatement on the grounds that they had been dismissed under misapplied rules, finding that the university was a state agency and therefore required to follow the state's administrative procedure code. A court rejected the University of Florida's argument that because the search committee that was screening candidates for dean of its law school was only advisory, the state's open-meeting statute did not apply.

State governors were becoming more influential. In Maryland, Oregon, and West Virginia, the state coordinating boards were reorganized to become part of the governor's cabinet. In several other states the governors actively sought to influence the composition of the coordinating boards. The governors of the fifty states adopted a series of recommendations calling on higher education to clarify the missions of the various institutions, emphasize access and undergraduate education, implement assessment of student learning, and provide incentives to improve quality. In 1989 the first national education summit brought the governors together with the president to discuss these types of issues.

The power of the states to license private education was questioned. Traditionally, courts have ruled that state legislatures can license colleges just as they license any other business entity, provided that the qualifications of the schools in question are spelled out and examined. In 1967 the New Jersey Supreme Court responded to a college's challenge of the state board of education's denial of a license, upholding both the board's decision and the empowering statute, concluding that the state could regulate private postsecondary institutions. And in 1982 the same court ruled that a fundamentalist Presbyterian college was not exempt from a state statute requiring degree-granting institutions to have a state-issued license. The state's interest in regulating education was deemed greater than its alleged threat to the free exercise of religion. But the states were also enjoined from regulating the activities of colleges that were chartered in other states on the grounds that the federal government had the power to regulate interstate commerce, including interstate educational activities.

The trend toward consolidating governance of public institutions continued as Massachusetts and Maryland established statewide multi-institution boards during the 1980s. In several other states, coordinating boards were given increased authority, functioning more as governance entities. Marcus (1997) reports that forty-nine restructuring proposals had been brought forward in twenty-nine states between 1989 and 1994. Legislatures initiated about half of them, and governors and state-level higher education authorities brought forward the others. The desire to reduce costs was integral to most of the proposals, but improving accountability and coordination and increasing the governor's legislative authority also ranked high. Half the states conducted studies of higher education effectiveness in the late 1980s, with twelve increasing centralization. In the 1990s the trend toward centralization found Minnesota and Montana merging governance of their two-year and four-year colleges. Kentucky's community colleges and technical schools were placed under a new governing board. Texas merged university systems, and New Hampshire consolidated its technical colleges. Florida's board of regents increased its control over all public higher education in the state. And other centralizing reforms took place in North Dakota, Utah, Colorado, and Tennessee.

However, not all was in the direction of super boards. Connecticut authorized the institutions to submit budget requests directly to the governor and the legislature, bypassing the board of governors. Oregon permitted its higher education institutions to make purchases, enter into contracts, and manage their personnel outside the state government's central agencies. Hawaii, Virginia, and South Carolina also allowed the institutions to perform several functions that had been carried out by state bureaus. The New Jersey Board of Higher Education was replaced by a commission on higher education that had less responsibility; institutional governing boards were given more power, although the governor gained the authority of appointing trustees of the state colleges. And the governor of Illinois was given power to appoint the board of trustees of the University of Illinois.

On the one hand the legislatures wanted the state-level boards to control the institutions' ambitions and to keep their representatives from working directly with legislators to gain approval for favored activities and programs. The institutions, on the other hand, wanted the state boards to represent them to the legislature, seek increased funds, and keep the legislatures from looking too closely into institutional affairs. But the various institutions in every state's higher education system had different missions, responsibilities, and goals. Any action on the part of a state board, even an across-the-board increase in funding, gained the ire of one or another institution and invariably yielded the comment, "We deserved more than the others." Although the boards insulated the legislators to some degree, in most states the leading individual institutions had their own lobbyists, and the boards often found themselves under legislative pressure to take action favoring a single institution or institutional type.

The flurry of restructuring occurred because higher education in all states was experiencing the same problems: budgets insufficient to keep up with costs, mandates to maintain open access, frequent clashes between institutional representatives and governing boards, and unclear distinctions among responsibilities. Each of the many plans was designed to help distinguish between the decisions that should be made at the state or system level and at the level of the institution. The complex, multilevel, combined centralized and decentralized system that was higher education in the fifty states was under continual review, with no indication of a slowing in the process. The Education Commission of the States concluded that states should decentralize where feasible but also should redefine their central structures so that responsibilities were clearly delineated. It concluded also that "higher education structures from one state should not and cannot be transferred to or imposed on another state" because each state has its unique history (McGuinness, 1995, p. 13).

Associations

The numerous voluntary interinstitutional associations and consortia—some statewide, some regional, some national—exert a form of influence. The broadest is the eighty-year-old American Council on Education (ACE), with 1,600 institutional and associated members. ACE's broad-scale agenda includes furthering women and minorities in higher education, developing leaders, and expanding higher education's adult and distance-learning activities. Other associations include the Council of Independent Colleges, with a membership of 400 and a mission to advance funding for private institutions; the American Association of State Colleges and Universities, enrolling more than 90 percent of the comprehensive public colleges and universities in the nation; the Association of Catholic Colleges and Universities, and perhaps 400 others.

Each association has an agenda representing either a consensus of what the leaders in the member institutions deem important or what the association heads consider to be the cutting-edge issues. In the 1940s and 1950s the American Association of Junior Colleges promoted occupational education, urging its member colleges to expand that area of the curriculum. Under different leadership in the 1960s and 1970s, the association issued numerous statements on behalf of adult education, distance learning, and programs to serve the broadest possible constituency. More recently, the group—renamed American Association of Community Colleges—has lined up with the forces promoting outcomes assessment and urged its member institutions to provide information routinely on the number of people served, the number who graduate, transfer, or obtain employment, and the contribution of the college to its local economy.

In addition to its special agenda each association tries to enhance public perception of its member institutions and to influence federal legislation that benefits its colleges. Each has a publications program through which information on national issues affecting the institutions is disseminated. Many have staff members who speak with congressional aides and monitor the progress of pending legislation. Frequently an association newsletter will suggest that institutional leaders contact their local congressional representative and speak in favor of or in opposition to a pending bill that might affect programs or students in that sector. The groups function much as the trade and business associations do, gaining funding for their efforts from institutional dues and from the sale of products and services. The extent to which they influence activities at the institutional level is unclear, but the groups' carrying messages, sharing ideas, and suggesting policies can certainly bolster local leaders who wish to move their institutions in particular directions.

Accreditation

Accreditation is another force affecting the conduct of institutions. The process of accreditation has evolved so that it rests now on complex relationships between federal and state governments and the voluntary members in the various accrediting groups. This involved system includes six regional accrediting associations with eight higher education commissions within them, eight national associations, and around seventy-five specialized and programmatic accreditors that are "recognized by the U.S. Secretary of Education as reliable authorities" (Rodenhouse, 1997, p. vi). The regional associations accredit each institution as a whole. The national associations also accredit institutions but are more specialized, such as associations accrediting Bible colleges. Programmatic accrediting bodies have been established for numerous fields of study: music, engineering, nursing, law, optometry, and so on.

Each accrediting agency establishes standards for the institutions or program for which it has oversight. The group seeking accreditation prepares a self-study that indicates how it meets the accrediting association's standards. The association sends a team of volunteers from like programs or institutions to visit the group being accredited. The team reports back to the association. Institutional accreditation normally applies to the entire structure, whereas programmatic or specialized accreditation refers to programs, departments, or schools within a larger institution. The accrediting associations themselves have a national coordinating group called the Council for Higher Education Accreditation, which is funded by the colleges and universities.

The entire process of accreditation is peculiar to the United States because there is no national ministry of education or any other official body setting standards and assessing compliance. Although the U.S. Department of Education scrutinizes the accrediting bodies, it does not review institutions. However, although the voluntary membership associations have no legal status their functioning has the effect of making them quasi-official bodies. An institution typically is chartered by a state, and the state also licenses individuals to practice in many occupations and professions. When the licensing of individuals is associated with graduation from an accredited program, "membership in the involved, specialized professional associations, supposedly voluntary, becomes almost obligatory" (Harcleroad, 1996, p. 326). Regional accreditation might be considered in restraint of trade if it is the only option for an institution's gaining a cachet. Furthermore, the federal government expects these voluntary consortia to determine which institutions are eligible to receive funding, particularly student aid. Therefore an institution's eligibility for federal funding is based on membership in voluntary associations that, by the nature of government reliance on them, have become voluntary in name only.

The standards set by the accrediting bodies affect institutional conduct, in some ways compromising institutional autonomy. An institution that does not comply with the standards runs the risk of being denied accreditation; its students in turn risk being denied not only federal aid but also eligibility to practice their profession. Criticisms of the accreditation system include the inconsistent expectations on the part of those doing the evaluations, the inappropriate comparisons made between unlike institutions, and the tendency for uniform criteria to limit creativity and instead effect homogeneity. The standards themselves have been criticized for attending more to process and input measures than to outcomes. The accreditation process has been cited as good at detecting problems such as financial trouble, inadequate facilities, or incompetent leadership but not very good at determining the quality of instruction or student learning. Some institutional leaders have complained that when the standards shift, as they did when the Western Association of Schools and Colleges proposed adding the criterion of ethnic diversity to its standards, the freedom of institutions to select students according to their own criteria is compromised.

During the 1990s, accreditation standards tilted in the direction of institutional outcomes. Their criteria became considerably more specific, with recommendations containing the word *should* giving way to those saying *must*. Institutions were expected to display planning and evaluation processes that covered all aspects of their operations: fiscal accountability, curriculum development, student performance, facilities maintenance. Specifications for general education curriculum became more pointed, and students were to be computer competent. It was no longer enough to specify the size and type of library holdings; student use of learning resources must be documented. Faculty must teach only those courses for which they were credentialed, and a minimum number of faculty must hold the doctorate. These standards were not uniform across regional or programmatic associations, and they have not yet been strictly enforced, but enough of them were set in place so that they suggested a trend in intent if not in substance. The accreditation process was a powerful shadow government.

Institutional

The roles of trustees and administrators changed little as the Contemporary Era opened. Officially the trustees were supposed to appoint, support, and evaluate the president, review the mission of the institution, approve long-range plans, oversee the educational program, ensure financial solvency, maintain the physical plant, preserve institutional autonomy, enhance the public image, serve as a court of appeal, and assess their own performance. This list of responsibilities had been stated with little deviation in several books and papers dating to the 1950s. The forty thousand or so trustees serving on American college and university boards have been expected to understand their responsibilities and adhere to them. Why do they serve? They gain little pay but they are involved in public service, which itself can be gratifying. They also gain an audience for their occasionally extreme views.

All trustee activities do not follow the script. Trustees have used their positions to publicize their own wishes to attain higher public office; board meetings offer a forum for them to make pronouncements on controversial topics. Trustees have also used their office to steer contracts in the direction of friends, even though such activities are considered breaches of public trust. Another area where trustees let their personal biases influence their work enters when those who are affiliated with or sympathetic toward extremist groups make decisions regarding educational programs sponsored by such groups. The trustees of a California community college district in 1997 argued in favor of a course teaching that the Holocaust never happened, even though several members of the board were also affiliated with the group that had sponsored the course.

Trustees and administrators may jeopardize their institutions if their actions overstep the bounds of responsibility with which they are charged. In the case of public institutions the state constitution or statutes describe their authority, and in the case of private institutions the articles of incorporation and the state license covers it. In addition, statutes and court decisions and state corporation or trust laws bound liability. Kaplin and Lee (1995, p. 77) summarize the various types of authority, saying it may be express, implied, or apparent. Express authority is within the language of a written document. Implied authority is necessary for exercising express authority and can therefore be inferred. Apparent authority describes a situation where someone acting for the institution leads other people to believe that authority exists when in fact it does not.

Numerous cases have been brought challenging the authority of trustees and administrators on various grounds. In a 1992 case a custodian challenged his termination by the university chancellor on

the grounds that the trustees did not have the authority to delegate
hiring and firing power to the chancellor. The Louisiana Court of
Appeals determined that the delegation was proper. In a 1977 case
the trustees of a private college were sued on the grounds that they
had attempted to amend the bylaws of the college. The Missouri
state court ruled that the board lacked the power to do so because
the college's original articles of agreement had dealt with the specific issue, and the trustees therefore did not have the authority to
change them (Kaplin and Lee, 1995, pp. 81–82).

The issue of institutional liability for the acts of others finds its
way into court frequently. Negligence and defamation are the two
most common torts whereby an institution might be held liable for
acts committed by its trustees, administrators, or other employees
within the scope of their relationship with the institution. To determine if a duty exists, courts often use the standard of whether the
risk of harm to the individual is foreseeable and unreasonable. A
student who fell on a slippery floor in a university building on her
way to class sued on the grounds that the institution had a duty to
exercise reasonable care to keep the premises in a safe condition.
The Louisiana Court of Appeals held that the university, through
the actions of its janitors who were acting within the scope of their
employment, had breached that duty of reasonable care and was
therefore liable for the student's damages. In 1993 a court ruled that
a school had a special relationship with students who participated
in intercollegiate sports. Thus when a student died of heart failure
during a practice, the school had a duty to have medical care available; the failure to do so made the school liable for damages. But a
Florida district court in 1980 ruled that the on-campus abduction
and murder of two students was not foreseeable, hence the school
had no liability. Similarly, a New York court ruled that the drown-
ing deaths of two students during a school-sponsored canoe trip was
caused by the terribly severe and unforeseen weather conditions and
not by the breach of any duty of the university (Kaplin and Lee,
1995, pp. 103–111).

Other cases have been brought on the grounds of defamation. In 1991 a graduate of Indiana University sued on the grounds that an apparently candid letter of reference from a professor assessing her strengths and weaknesses was defamatory. The Indiana Court of Appeals ruled that a qualified privilege protected the professor and the institution if the communication in question was made in good faith on matters in which the letter writer had an interest or duty. Therefore, because the university was involved with teacher training, the letter was protected by the qualified privilege. Similarly, a court ruled that although a statement about an assistant professor by her department head at a public university was admittedly libelous, the qualified privilege applied because the communication referred to the plaintiff's work.

A trustee, administrator, or any other employee may be personally sued along with the institution. If so the individual may not be protected by the same immunity that covers the institution itself. Kaplin and Lee (1995) explain that for this defense to apply, the individuals must have been acting within the scope of their authority and the act must have been discretionary, involving policy judgment as opposed to acts in which the person has little or no discretion with regard to choices being made. In a ruling issued by the Supreme Court of Mississippi in 1989, a dean was adjudged to have immunity against a defamation suit brought by a faculty member who argued that he was libeled by a letter from the dean recommending denial of tenure. The court held that evaluation of the faculty member was within the scope of the dean's authority, thus he was immune as a public official. Similarly, faculty members who evaluate their colleagues are immune because they are acting within the scope of their official responsibilities. People seeking promotion within universities know that their colleagues and administrators will be evaluating them and hence have no basis for claiming defamation. In sum, individuals are rarely liable for acts committed as part of their official responsibilities, and institutions are rarely liable if the conditions in question are considered necessary and reasonable for the conduct of institutional affairs.

The role of the president remained all-purpose. In addition to being responsive to the institution's board of trustees, presidents also had to be attentive to the faculty, students, alumni, and local community. Presidents have always been involved with fundraising and campus politics; the 1990s were no different. Student activism was still present, not to the degree of disruptiveness that marked the 1960s and 1970s but enough to gain a considerable amount of attention as demands for ethnic-related programs and departments remained prominent. Boards of trustees tended to take a more active role in managing campus affairs. Frequently, when students, alumni, or people from the surrounding community wanted to speak out on issues, instead of the president's sorting out the messages and presenting summary statements and alternative positions to the board, the petitioners addressed the board directly. In many instances the governing boards seemed to treat the president as only one voice among many.

The larger the institutions became, the more they began to look like business corporations. Presidents were being selected less because of their scholarly accomplishments, more for their ability to manage large-scale enterprises. When the California State University system sought a new chancellor in 1997, the search was marked by a reduced emphasis on academic credentials. The board removed from the list of criteria the statement, "Significant academic accomplishments of the character to command the professional respect of the academic community . . . and experience sufficient for the rank of full professor." One of the trustees pointed out that "the element of business experience is more than just a plus, it's a necessary ingredient" (Wallace, 1997, p. A18). The temblor that was felt soon after was not a California earthquake, it was Veblen, an early-century antagonist to businessmen in university governance, rolling over in his grave.

The role of the faculty in academic governance underwent some changes as well. The tradition of faculty governance through committee and through rotating administrative leaders drawn from within faculty ranks was thrashing like a lion in winter. It could not be sustained in large-scale institutions with their manifold purposes and sizable enrollments and physical plants. Within very broad limits, the faculty retained the privileges of selecting and promoting their colleagues, choosing curriculum, and sustaining their preferred instructional practices. But growth in enrollments, development of new programs, and expansion into various areas of service were controlled by trustees and administrators. Decisions about undergraduate admissions were made by administrators in the context of resources available. Decisions about faculty appointments were made largely by the faculty within the context of positions allocated by administrators. The 1966 "Statement on Government of Colleges and Universities," issued and endorsed by the major institutional and governance associations, had delineated areas of concern and still reflected the principles guiding governance, including "the faculty has primary responsibility for such fundamental areas as curriculum, subject matter and methods of instruction, research, faculty status, and those aspects of student life which relate to the educational process." The governing board and the president should review faculty decisions in those matters but take a counter position "only in exceptional circumstances" (The Carnegie Foundation, 1982, p. 18). By the 1990s those exceptional circumstances were appearing more frequently, as various other constituent groups exerted more pressure on the board and administrators.

Except on a few tiny private campuses, collegial governance was a distant memory, replaced now by shared governance—the concept that every constituent group should have a part in deciding every issue. A 1988 California legislative act required the governing board of each community college district to consult with the faculty, administrators, support staff, and student representatives whenever policies or procedures on academic and professional matters were under review. College governance structures and institutional planning and budgeting—matters that formerly were discussed and decided by the governing boards—were now being reviewed by all the constituencies. One of the results was gridlock;

decision making was delayed by the necessity of consulting with representatives of the faculty union or academic senate (or both), the clerks, the building-maintenance people, and the students. In the larger institutions the political forces given sanction by recognition caused delays in deciding anything. The astute practitioners had to maneuver within the thicket—bypassing, persuading, using loopholes, and otherwise finding ways of getting their work done. The processes described in the organization charts and procedures manuals by no means told the true story of academic management and decision making.

Conflicting Demands

Much of the writing about higher education in the 1990s has been concerned with problems of declining resources. And most of the responses have been to recommend various forms of redesign or restructuring so that the institutions will function more efficiently. The basic problem has been that higher education has had no way of determining relative value. The premises that all knowledge is of equal worth and that the professionals in specialized areas can alone determine the value of their work, have led to the conclusion that all comparisons among institutional missions or academic departments are odious. Accordingly, programs may be duplicative, outmoded, or excessively expensive, but there are no easy ways to reallocate funds within institutions or to shift resources from one institution to another.

Institutional decision-making structure is both hierarchical and decentralized—hierarchical because the funds are allocated by a central administration, decentralized because each unit makes its own decisions. All the schools, colleges, departments, research units, and other elements in the system make their own internal allocations based on the resources they can command. The relative merits of these various decisions cannot be adjudicated because no one has a picture of the institution that reaches across units at the level at which these decisions are made. Information systems typically have not been designed to provide uniform data for every program.

Extrinsic demands create other complications. Funding comes from many sources, and some funding agencies specify how their monies shall be allocated. Accrediting agencies influence expenditures on laboratories, libraries, and work stations. State legislatures impose programs. The federal government supports some activities and withdraws when those activities are no longer popular. The budget allocation process brings all these issues to the fore, but for the most part higher education's leaders can do little except petition for more resources. The existing institutional mechanism cannot ensure that necessary decisions about what to promote and what to cut will be made. There are few national guidelines for minimum qualifications, few interinstitutional plans, few ways of combining comparative data. Institutional autonomy and the autonomy of each group within institutions have been so cherished that it has been practically impossible to move rational decision making to a structure different from the form it took when the enterprise was one-tenth the size.

Because comparative value is impossible to assess, when budget reductions become necessary the typical pattern has been to share the pain uniformly by taking equivalent funds proportionately from each unit. When that proves insufficient, an institution may collapse the school or department that has the least political force, that is too weak to protest effectively, that has the least amount of support within or outside the institution. Another favored approach has been responsibility-centered management, giving the authority for budget allocations to the individual units. This acknowledges that no central authority can compare relative worth, that each individual department can adjudicate allocations more efficiently. And institutions have reduced expenses by implementing voluntary early retirement programs in which staff members make their own determination of whether to leave based on their own personal considerations. The best faculty may go along with the least productive members. Because the central administration has no way of knowing who the best and worst staff members are and, if it has such information, no way of mandating that the worst leave, it is helpless in guiding the process.

Still open are questions of value to the broader community. How many professional practitioners does society need in each area? What is the worth of an archive of the culture, a housing for classicists? No governance structure can even begin to address these issues, yet they are fundamental to the conduct of higher education. The recurrent budget crises have forced a flurry of activity, but changes in the direction of more purposeful or efficient functioning are quite doubtful. By its nature higher education is inefficient if measured in the sense of inputs and outputs. Its various units stagger along, as messy as democracy, and perhaps as valuable.

Finance

The unprecedented increase in revenues and expenditures of the 1960s ended in the 1970s. In the decade between 1957 and 1967, expenditures rose from around $3.5 billion to $18.5 billion. The doubling of enrollments during that time did not alone account for this manifold increase. Government-sponsored research expenditures nearly tripled, and state funds coming into higher education went up more than fourfold. Educators became accustomed to annual budget increases for rising salaries, funds for equipment and special projects, and capital improvement money. Those who had become staff members during the surge in employment of the prior fifteen years had never known privation. Those who had been around for a longer time forgot how poverty-stricken they had been.

Several publications appeared in the mid-1970s cautioning that the trend was turning and that people who were employed to build the institutions during the period of rapid growth were now out of date. The new administrators would have to know how to negotiate reductions, as both public resources and the eighteen-year-old population would steadily decline. However, the voices of a few analysts and the projections on a population graph were not sufficient to change practice. Higher education does not reinvent itself easily; its traditions run deep, and by far the greater proportion of its expenditures are as entrenched as though they were entitlements fixed by law. Nor could the institutions respond to the double-digit inflation of the late 1970s that boosted the price of everything from utilities to library books. They still had to buy the computers that were becoming essential for modernizing management systems and supplying data to the demanding state and federal agencies. They had to award raises to the staff to at least partially offset the effect that inflation was having on their personal budgets. And they had to hope that somehow they would muddle through, finding the funds they needed even though projections were dire.

The changes in funding were less dramatic in the overall per-institution or per-student category than they were in the variations in sources of income. Federal aid to students shifted away from grants in the direction of loans. State funds did not increase sufficiently to accommodate the rise in enrollments. Tuition went up rapidly so that students and their families bore an ever-increasing proportion of the total cost of instruction. Grants from philanthropic foundations moved from general awards to those given for specific purposes. Funds received from corporations became more likely to be attached to contracts for specific services. The dollars that could be used for discretionary purposes dropped. Fortunate was the institution whose leadership was able to accommodate to these shifts.

Revenue

One note before tracing the sources of revenue: colleges are *always* short of money. The nature of their financial structure dictates that. The public institutions cannot run a surplus. The administrators know that failing to spend one year's appropriation may mean commensurate cuts in the next year's funding. However, if they spend all their money, their institution is at risk if its appropriation is cut. In sum, it is a no-win game; the institution can only break even or fall short. In a private institution, surplus funds can be added to the endowment only if they are so earmarked or if all campus groups are first satisfied—the latter an unlikely occurrence. If a college gains an unrestricted donation, all the staff immediately seek raises, every department suddenly needs an additional faculty member, the number of tuition discounts that the institution can give is increased, and there is always a building that needs painting. Public or private, the net effect is the same; colleges do well to break even.

A view of the current-funds revenue of institutions of higher education between 1976 and 1995 displays changes in source (see Table 5.11). Federally supported student aid is included in the figures on tuition. The table shows how tuition became increasingly prominent as the share of other revenue from governmental sources declined.

The percentage differences between public and private sector institutions are shown in Table 5.12.

Because the state governments were the largest single source of revenue coming into public institutions, the decline in the proportion of state support was most hurtful. The sizable change in ratio resulted from tax-limitation initiatives, beginning with California's in 1978, and continued with increased demands for funds by other state agencies. State prisons proved a major competitor. California's "Three Strikes and You're Out" bill, which passed in 1994, mandated that anyone convicted for a second felony would receive double a normal sentence; for a third felony, if the other two were for violent or serious crimes, the perpetrator would receive triple the normal sentence, with a minimum of twenty-five years. This added dramatically to the prison population and to mandatory state spending on corrections. The concomitant decrease in funds available for other state services forced major reductions in state funding for

Table 5.11. Revenue of Institutions of Higher Education by Source of Funds, 1975–76 and 1994–95 (in Current Dollars).

	1975–76		1994–95	
Source of Funds	Revenue (in thousands of $)	% of Total Revenue	Revenue (in thousands of $)	% of Total Revenue
Tuition and fees	8,171,942	21	$51,506,876	27
Federal government	6,477,178	16	23,243,172	12
State governments	12,260,885	31	44,343,012	23
Local governments	1,616,975	4	5,165,961	3
Endowment earnings	687,470	2	3,988,217	2
Private gifts and grants	1,917,036	5	10,866,749	6
Sales and services	7,687,382	19	43,039,561	23
Other	884,298	2	6,967,023	4
Total	39,703,166	100	189,120,570	100

Source: National Center for Education Statistics, 1997g, p. 343.

Table 5.12. Percentage of Current-Fund Revenue by Source, Public and Private Sector Institutions, 1994–95.

Source	Public Institutions	Private Institutions
Tuition and fees	18 %	42 %
Federal government	11	14
State governments	36	2
Local governments	4	1
Private gifts, grants, and contracts	4	9
Endowment income	1	5
Sales and services	23	22
Other sources	3	5

Source: National Center for Education Statistics, 1997e, pp. 4, 6.

colleges. In the early 1980s, higher education in California received about 9 percent of the state's general fund, whereas just over 2 percent went to corrections; by 1997 the funding for prisons had *surpassed* that going to higher education.

The situation in other states was little better. In the states in the Southern Regional Education Board area, per capita personal income grew from 79 percent to 90 percent of the national average during the years following 1960, but the college-going rate was still the lowest in the nation, and the share of state and local government budgets going to higher education fell. In terms of inflation-adjusted dollars, higher education funding in the middle 1990s was equal to what it had been in 1984, yet enrollments had increased by 16 percent. State funding as a percentage of public institution revenue decreased by a greater percentage than the overall decrease in the United States. And here the differences among the states were most pronounced: Georgia was awarding some type of aid, including non-need-based aid, to practically all of its undergraduates, but one-third of the states in the region were allocating no funds to that category. Nationwide, although state spending on student aid had been increasing through the early 1990s, by the middle of the decade that too had leveled off. Overall though, the strong economy allowed states to boost institutional support by 6 percent per year in 1996 and 1997 (Nespoli and Gilroy, 1998).

Federal Support

Federal funds, a second major source of revenue, also declined as a percentage of overall income. In 1980 federal support accounted for 18 percent of higher education expenditures; by 1997 it had dropped to under 14 percent. After adjustment for inflation, federal funding declined by 28 percent. Funds for research at universities increased by 41 percent in constant dollars, but most of that increase occurred in the 1980s; between 1990 and 1997, federal research funds increased by only 3 percent. Moreover, the category of "off-budget support" should be added to these figures. Almost all the funds in this category consist of loans and work-study monies that demand matching funds paid by participating institutions. These funds tripled between 1980 and 1997 when measured in constant dollars, an indication of the continuing shift from grants to loans. Federally subsidized or guaranteed loans were being made through several programs: Federal Family Education Loans, in which the federal government subsidized the loans by paying interest to the lender while the borrower was in school and guaranteed the loans against default; Federal Direct Student Loans, accounting for one-third of the new-loan volume generated in the mid-1990s, which made it possible for students to borrow directly from the government instead of through an intermediary bank; State Student Incentive Grants, which were matched dollar for dollar by state contributions; and Supplemental Educational Opportunity Grants, providing funds to undergraduates who demonstrate financial need (Hoffman, 1997, pp. 12–13).

Several other acts affected finances either by adding funds or by increasing expenses. The Tribally Controlled Community College Assistance Act of 1978, reauthorized in 1990, provided funds for community colleges for Indian students. In 1978 the Middle Income

Student Assistance Act modified financial assistance programs to include middle-income as well as low-income students. The Challenge Grants Amendments of 1983 set up funds for which institutions might apply on a matching basis. In 1984 the Carl D. Perkins Vocational Education Act replaced the Vocational Education Act of 1963 and continued federal assistance for vocational education. In 1985 the GI Bill was renewed for veterans entering military duty after that year. A 1990 act established additional mathematics, science, and engineering scholarship programs, and in that same year the Student Right-to-Know and Campus Security Act required institutions to provide information about their graduation rates and also to certify that they had a campus-security policy. The Civil Rights Act of 1991 amended the Americans with Disabilities Act along with the 1964 Civil Rights Act and the 1967 Age Discrimination Act. And every few years the Higher Education Act of 1965 was revised and reauthorized in various ways. For example, in 1994 the date for penalizing colleges that had excessively high rates of student loan default was delayed for historically black colleges and universities and for tribally controlled community colleges.

Many of the federal acts were designed to broaden access not only for students who had previously benefited from grants and loans but also for groups that might have suffered from discrimination in the past. Research in higher education continued to be subsidized on the grounds that although the Cold War had ended, the United States was in an unending economic war with the rest of the world. On the micro-level the federal government threatened to cut off financial aid to students in institutions that banned military recruitment on campus. Higher education and the federal government were not only indelibly wed, they continued renewing their marriage vows even as they engaged in periodic spousal disagreements. Those who opposed governmental regulation and those who opposed egalitarianism—often the same groups—were unable to overturn the sanctity of the relationship.

The federal government's funding of research increased as a percentage of institutional revenue from 8.7 percent in 1987 to 9.3 percent in 1995. The augmentation went to the public sector, whereas the proportion actually declined in the private sector, even though the top five recipients were private universities: Cal Tech, Johns Hopkins, Chicago, MIT, and Stanford. Those five were receiving more than one dollar in every six that the federal government was contributing to higher education in the United States. By contrast, the top five public institutions—the Universities of Washington, Michigan, Wisconsin, California at San Diego, and California at Los Angeles—were receiving about one dollar in every sixteen. Overall, the top twenty-five recipients were about evenly split between public and private institutions. Federal funds, mainly for research, averaged around $340 million per institution per year in the research universities and were augmented by grants and contracts from philanthropic foundations and other donors. The funds were concentrated; one hundred universities received 80 percent of the money. Funds for medical research and research in the biological and physical sciences dominated the awards, but research in astronomy, oceanography, and social sciences was also supported. Research in education—never a large proportion of the federal government's research effort—declined between 1980 and 1997, whereas research programs administered by the Department of Defense increased by 19 percent. The most sizable percentage increase was in research funded by NASA, which tripled during those years, most of the increase coming in the 1980s. The percentage of federal funding for research in the life sciences increased, whereas engineering's share decreased. But five of every eight dollars that the federal government put into research and development was dedicated to defense, with health and space following as a distant second and third.

Programmatic emphases were the rule. The National Science Foundation funded fourteen Engineering Research Centers by 1987, with the idea of cultivating interdisciplinary research in association with industry. The Department of Defense steadily decreased its support for basic research, even as it doubled its overall funding for academic research in the five years between 1978 and 1983. Private donors similarly became more likely to award funds for specific activities. Geiger (1993) reports that "whereas in 1970 about one-third of gifts were unrestricted, less than 20 percent were in the late 1980s. For research universities the proportion was closer to 10 percent" (p. 314). The largest increase in voluntary support was enjoyed by schools of business and engineering.

University leaders strove continually to increase their proportion of extramurally derived funds, even to the extent of developing elaborate research parks. By 1995, twenty-five additional research parks had been formed, adding to the ten that had existed in 1975. Business incubators that assisted in the growth of new enterprises and organized research units cutting across several fields were established. The institutions developed procedures regarding the licensing of intellectual property rights, although for several years income from this source rarely exceeded the expense of administering the activity.

The spread of the funding base for research fit with the growing importance of economic development and technology transfer. The federal government could not be relied on as a source of steadily increasing funds in all areas. Annual funding for university-based research increased from $3.4 billion to $9 billion between 1975 and 1996, but this was not evenly distributed across agencies. The Departments of Housing and Urban Development, Justice, and State reduced funding over the twenty-year span, and other agencies displayed peaks and valleys: Education dropped from $160 million to $29 million in one year (1984–85) and took eight years to recover to the higher figure; Department of Commerce funds dropped from $62 million to $36 million between 1986 and 1988 and by 1991 had regained the earlier figure; Department of Defense funds reached a high point in 1994 and two years later had declined by 18 percent; Department of Transportation funding decreased by

28 percent between 1995 and 1996. The Department of Health and Human Services was the most consistent agency, showing increases every year from a starting point of $1.3 billion to $6.8 billion (National Center for Education Statistics, 1996b, pp. 390–391). But even within those figures the types of research supported varied considerably, as one or another disease or social crisis captured the legislators' attention.

Tuition

College tuition charges have come in for a considerable amount of examination, especially as they accelerated in public institutions in the 1990s. From the beginning of the Mass Higher Education Era through the 1970s, tuition increases were averaging slightly more than the rate of inflation, but family income was going up as well so that college remained affordable for most people. During the same period, student aid programs expanded along with the lower-tuition public colleges, so that both the private and the public sector were able to attract sizable numbers of students. By the 1980s, however, the situation had changed. Tuition was increasing much more rapidly than either inflation or family income—about 10 percent per year at both private and public institutions. For the decade the median family income increased by 50 percent, but tuition by almost 90 percent. When adjusted for inflation, family income went up around 6 percent, and tuition more than 30 percent. Even when the figures were adjusted to account for family size, disposable personal income, age of the head of household, or any other reasonably relevant measure, tuition costs still increased considerably more rapidly.

For the three years beginning in 1991, tuition at public four-year colleges increased by 12, 10, and 8 percent, respectively, and at public two-year colleges by 13, 10, and 10 percent. The latter figures were influenced by the tripling of fees in California—the state with by far the greatest number of community college students. For the nation, the average figure for all institutions went from $924 in

1977 to $4,312 in 1996; for the public colleges the increase was from $479 to $2,176; for the private colleges it went from $2,467 to $11,858 (National Center for Education Statistics, 1996d, pp. 320, 321). The public two-year colleges, which had long prided themselves on policies of maintaining extremely low tuition and which averaged under $500 a year as recently as 1983, passed the $1,000 mark ten years later.

The rapid rise in tuition led several institutions and states to organize prepayment plans that allowed families to pay for four years of college at the time of matriculation and thus avoid tuition increases while the student was enrolled. Another type of prepayment was introduced in 1985, when Duquesne University announced that a family could prepay tuition for a child who would attend some years later; if the child were not admissible the payment would be refunded, but without interest. Duquesne suspended the plan less than three years later, but a number of other institutions introduced versions of it. The public sector got involved as well when, in 1986, Michigan began allowing families to pay into a state-managed investment fund with the understanding that their payments would cover tuition at any public institution in the state when the child was ready to matriculate. If the child chose to attend a private institution or go out of state, the fund would pay the equivalent of what would have been received if he or she had attended a public college in Michigan. Investments in the fund were deductible from state income tax, and the Internal Revenue Service ruled that income from the trust could be spread over four years and taxed at the child's rate of taxation. "By November 1988 some 27,000 families had actually signed up, investing nearly 200 million dollars" (Hauptman, 1990, p. 23).

Other states developed different types of incentives. Missouri allowed state income tax deductions for contributions to college savings accounts. Illinois sold several million dollars' worth of zero-coupon bonds; if a family held a bond for five years and used the proceeds to pay for college expenses, the state would make a supplemental interest payment. By 1998, twenty-five states had passed legislation allowing prepaid tuition or savings plans whereby families might receive state tax deductions for contributions to college savings accounts. Federal tax deferrals were available on interest earned in the accounts. All the plans were designed to encourage families to save for their children's education. The wealthiest families—those most likely to prepay tuition—were in effect buying an insurance policy covering them against tuition increases, whereas the lower-income families (who were less likely to participate) would have to take their chances, hoping that higher tuition would not price their offspring out of college.

The federal government has had various types of tax exemptions, such as allowing parents to give up to $10,000 per year per child with the income from those funds taxed at the presumably lower child's rate. Other tax-based initiatives encountered difficulty because any plan connected to income tax payments invariably benefited the wealthier families more. As a way around the problem, a provision in the Taxpayer Relief Act of 1997 granted tax deductions for up to $1,500 of tuition paid by lower- and middle-income families. It was designed particularly to aid students in their first two years of college.

Student Aid

Student aid stemming from federal, state, and institutional sources continued the increases that had been accelerating since the late 1960s (see Table 5.13). Aid from all sources, less than $550 million in 1964, climbed to $4.5 billion by 1971, $10.5 billion by 1976, and more than $26.6 billion by the end of the 1980s. Even when viewed in constant dollars, the aid increased more than tenfold over the twenty-five-year span. Much of the increase was the result of student borrowing. Overall, grants accounted for 83 percent of all aid in the mid-1970s, but by the end of the 1980s this percentage had shrunk to 51 percent. Grants accounted for 80 percent of federal aid in 1976, a figure that dropped to 61 percent by 1980.

Table 5.13. Aid Awarded to Postsecondary Students, 1975–76 to 1994–95 (in Millions of Constant 1994 Dollars).

Type of Aid	1975 to 1976	1977 to 1978	1979 to 1980	1981 to 1982	1983 to 1984	1985 to 1986	1987 to 1988	1989 to 1990	1991 to 1992	1993 to 1994	1994 to 1995 (Estimated)
Federally guaranteed loans (including Perkins, Family Educational, Ford Direct, and other specially directed loans)	$4,604	$5,508	$8,565	$12,106	$12,091	$13,523	$16,033	$15,671	$16,345	$22,784	$25,683
Federally supported grants (including Pell, SEOG, SSIG, CWS, Social Security, veterans aid, military aid, and other specially directed grants)	17,888	15,222	13,363	10,789	7,964	8,160	7,775	8,425	9,149	8,948	8,926
Total federal aid	22,492	20,730	21,928	22,895	20,055	21,683	23,778	24,096	25,494	31,822	34,609
State grants	1,273	1,558	1,463	1,410	1,566	1,788	1,926	2,008	2,112	2,408	2,628
Institutional and other grants	3,036	2,825	2,710	2,674	3,229	4,040	4,878	5,784	7,166	8,349	8,929
Total federal, state, and institutional aid	26,801	25,113	26,100	26,979	24,850	27,511	30,582	31,888	34,772	42,579	46,166

Source: Gladieux and Hauptman, 1995, pp. 10–11.

Aid patterns differed according to types of students and institutions. Full-time students were more likely to receive aid than part-timers, four-year college students more than those in two-year colleges, graduate students more than undergraduates, students in the private sector more than those in public institutions, and students in proprietary schools more than any others. By 1992, 52 percent of the students in public institutions, 70 percent in the private nonprofit sector, and 76 percent in proprietary schools were receiving some form of aid (National Center for Education Statistics, 1996b, p. 325). At the graduate level, 68 percent of the students received aid.

The fluctuation in sources in types of aid had a long history. Guaranteed Student Loans (GSLs) began in 1965. By the end of the 1980s, when more than $100 billion had been loaned, they accounted for by far the largest amount of aid. The GSL program provided federal guarantees for loans that banks made to students using the funds for college expenses. The program stemmed from several premises: college is a profitable investment both for individuals and for society; would-be students typically are poor credit risks, hence cannot readily borrow funds to finance that investment; default rates on loans to students would likely be such that banks would not make such loans except at exorbitant rates of interest to cover losses. Not least, by guaranteeing loans to students who could then give the money to any college that would accept them, the issue of aid to parochial institutions would be circumvented.

As older students began attending in larger numbers, and as the ratio of part- to full-time students increased, the complexities of the various aid programs increased as well. The Education Amendments of 1972 created the Basic Educational Opportunity Grant program (Pell Grants), retained the Educational Opportunity Grant program (adding the word "supplemental" to it), authorized State Student Incentive Grants that provided matching funds for state scholarship programs, and created the Student Loan Marketing Association—a government-sponsored corporation designed to provide the funds for student loans. As need testing was introduced, the program grew ever more complex. Students attending proprietary schools benefited greatly, as a program originally established in 1965 was merged with the GSL program in 1968 and in 1972 was tucked into the programs covering all of higher education. By 1989, students attending the profit-making schools received 26 percent of all Pell Grants and 35 percent of all GSLs.

Amendments to the program in 1978 brought about further changes. The most significant was the removal of need testing, thus allowing all students, regardless of income, to be eligible for Guaranteed Student Loans. Because interest rates on student loans were lower than commercial rates—considerably lower in the environment of extremely high interest rates in the early 1980s—"any family with a student in college would have been irrational not to have borrowed the full amount available. . . . Not surprisingly, annual loan volume jumped from roughly $1.7 billion in 1977 to nearly $7.2 billion in 1981" (Breneman, 1991, p. 9). And because the GSL program was not subject to direct control through annual congressional appropriations but operated as an entitlement, the volume of such loans grew sharply as all other federal programs such as work study and state incentive grants declined. Still, the states had not been remiss. Their grant programs in 1976 totaled less than $500 million, but by 1989 they had exceeded $1.6 billion and in 1995 reached nearly $2.5 billion. Higher education in the United States had become dependent on grants and loans made to all types of students at all levels and in all sectors.

A view of grants and loans awarded tells only part of the story. They must be placed in the context of tuition charges and living expenses in order to arrive at the net cost of college attendance (see Table 5.14).

In 1993, full-time undergraduates in public four-year institutions were receiving grants totaling 30 percent of the average tuition and fees charged—a percentage that had been constant for the preceding decade. In comparison, funds that students received from all

Table 5.14. Pell Grants and Stafford (GSL) Loans as a Proportion of College Costs of Attendance, Selected Years, 1975–1987 (in Current Dollars).

Year	Maximum Award	Average Award	Maximum Award as Percentage of Average Cost		Average Award as Percentage of Average Cost	
			Public	Private	Public	Private
Pell grants						
1975	1,400	761	61.8	32.8	33.6	17.8
1980	1,750	882	53.2	27.4	26.8	13.8
1985	2,100	1,279	43.4	20.9	26.4	12.7
1987	2,100	1,350	39.7	18.2	25.5	11.7
Stafford loans (GSL)						
1975	2,500	1,312	110.3	58.6	57.9	30.8
1980	2,500	2,086	76.0	39.1	63.4	32.7
1985	2,500	2,307	51.7	24.8	47.7	22.9
1987	2,625*	2,466	49.6	22.7	46.6	21.4

*For first- and second-year students. For upperclassmen, the maximum loan is $4,000.

Source: Hauptman, 1990, pp. 12–13.

sources prior to the opening of the Mass Higher Education Era had approximated less than 10 percent of the total cost of attendance and the 40 percent of cost—a figure inflated by Vietnam War veterans attending under the GI Bill—that students were receiving at the beginning of the Contemporary Era. This aid included grants, loans, various work-study and campus-based aid, and fellowships, along with tuition discounts provided by most private sector institutions. During the 1980s the proportion of student aid received in the form of loans increased. By the late 1980s, grant money had fallen to around 13 percent of the cost of attendance, whereas veterans' aid along with college work-study programs, which accounted for 20 percent in 1975, had dropped to 2 percent. At the same time, loans jumped from 7 percent of the total cost of attendance in 1975 to more than 15 percent in the early 1980s and continued rising.

For the public sector the increases in tuition offset decreases in funds received from state governments. Tuition increases in the private sector offset the decline in revenue received from the federal government. Overall, the annual percentage change in tuition was greatest in the latter 1980s and early 1990s, when tuition in the public sector went up by more than 10 percent for every year from 1988 to 1993, including a 14 percent increase between 1991 and 1992. The private institutions increased tuition by relatively modest amounts, surpassing 10 percent for only two of those years. But of course they were starting from a much higher base.

Some of the tuition rate increases at public institutions were truly phenomenal. Between 1987 and 1994, the University of California fees for in-state resident undergraduates went up from less than $1,500 to more than $4,000—a rate of increase nearly matched by the public universities in Michigan and Washington. Furthermore, the differential fees paid by students in graduate and professional schools increased even more markedly, as the states were reluctant to support students who were in training for what were perceived to be lucrative careers. The fee override for students in law, medical, and business schools in public universities often amounted to a doubling of the regular graduate school tuition. Students who had been willing to pay more for their undergraduate education at prestigious colleges because they thought it helped their chances of gaining entrance to highly selective professional schools were paying more again after they were admitted.

Expenditures and Cost Controls

Institutional expenditures reflect the inflation of the time. Between 1976 and 1994, expenditures per student increased by 30 percent in terms of constant 1994 dollars. The four-year institutions were most affected; their per-student expenditures went up by 34 percent, whereas those in the two-year institutions rose by 18 percent. And whereas public four-year institution expenditures increased by 27 percent per student in constant dollars, in the private sector they went up by 40 percent. Much of the latter increase was a result of scholarships and fellowships that private institutions made available—a sum that surpassed 11 percent of expenditures by 1995. The Higher Education Price Index, which in 1960 was 4 percentage points lower than the Consumer Price Index, had reached parity in 1966. At the beginning of the Contemporary Era, it was 2 points greater, and by 1994, 17 percentage points higher. Clearly, higher education costs were rising more rapidly than consumer prices in general throughout the era.

Cost cutting became a watchword. In a time of rising income, programs can be added, and even though individual unit budgets may not go up as much as the program directors desire, accommodations can be made for the most part. But when income increases more slowly than costs, whole programs may be put on the block. Which ones should be cut? Higher education has never been able to assess relative worth. A federal mandate for State Postsecondary Review Entities was supposed to provide guidelines that would direct institutions to expand or cut back programs on such criteria as the number of graduates relative to entrants. However, the higher education community could not abide a set of federal regulations that purported to distinguish between worthy and less-worthy programs. Their complaints led to the demise of the ruling before it could be implemented.

State-level initiatives had somewhat greater success. Some states provided additional funds for programs demonstrating an increased percentage of graduation and job-getting rates. Others imposed restrictions, holding forth the stick instead of the carrot. In those cases a specific limit was imposed whereby the state would not subsidize course enrollments beyond 60 units for the associate degree and 120 units for the bachelor's. Courses that students took beyond the minimum requirements would be reimbursed at a lower level. Institutional leaders did not like that either, claiming that it squelched flexibility and penalized colleges that provided sizable amounts of non-degree credit-bearing remedial instruction.

Several unique characteristics make costs difficult to control. One of the intractable cost inflators is faculty salaries as related to productivity. With higher salaries being paid to professional practitioners outside the academy, university salaries must increase unless higher education is to revert to a time when professors were among the lower-paid professional workers. But unless the student-faculty ratio is increased—a proposition typically resisted by faculty in power to do so—real teaching costs go up. Costs in higher education increase also because there are no universally agreed-on measures of productivity. Prestige—arguably the highest institutional value—usually increases when more resources are acquired. And adding prestigious professors and handsome buildings contributes to spiraling costs. The fixed salary schedules whereby faculty who teach large numbers of students are paid the same as those who teach few also make it difficult to control costs. And even the research monies that faculty members attract to the institution do not help budgets; faculty members who spend more time on research do not reduce the need to have classes taught. Expansion in the number of courses that an institution offers (a continuing phenomenon for several decades) represents another cost factor that is difficult to control. The more courses in the class schedule, the more specialized the faculty needed to teach them, and the fewer students available to take them. And yet which of the many new courses is unworthy of being retained?

Efforts to control costs during the era led institutions in all sectors to take some rather obvious steps. Better building utilization was one of them, as institutions expanded summer-session course offerings and extended the hours of instruction. Offering voluntary early-retirement programs to long-term employees was another measure. Between 1990 and 1994, three such programs at the University of California led to around two thousand faculty retirements and a savings of $200 million in salary. Even though two-thirds of the retirees were replaced, most of the new hires were at the junior level.

Other courses of action included increasing class size, especially in community colleges where the average size went from twenty-seven to thirty-one in the decade prior to 1994. Library budgets typically took a cut, even as the cost of books and journals escalated. The proportion of funds spent on research increased because that activity usually was funded by extramurally generated monies earmarked for the purpose. Funds for instruction decreased as a percentage of the whole, as lower-paid faculty were employed and as low-enrollment classes were cut. But higher education's ability to control costs has been considerably less effective than its ability to increase its resources.

Philanthropy

Although raising money from corporations and individuals could not generate revenue sufficient to replace the diminishing state funds, the institutions had no choice but to continue seeking more from that source. Private giving declined by 20 percent between 1968 and 1974 after considering the rate of inflation, but by the end of the 1970s it had increased and was well up in the 1980s. By the 1990s, around 80 percent of such funds were restricted to certain uses, typically applied research or buildings. Schools of business and engineering were especially successful in attracting support because they tended to have alumni and friends in the corporate sector. Museums, endowed chairs, and galleries also received funds from private donors. These types of facilities by no means enhanced institutional productivity, but they added prestige to the campuses fortunate enough to receive them, along with an endowment sufficient to pay for their continuing maintenance. An overall breakout showed that in the mid-1990s, private support was received in the following proportions: 27 percent from alumni, 23 percent from other individuals, 21 percent from corporations, 20 percent from foundations, 2 percent from religious organizations, and 7 percent from other sources. The total amounted to more than $11 billion (Eaton, 1995).

The increased emphasis that public universities gave to private fundraising put them in direct competition with their counterparts in the private sector. Early in the 1990s, 70 percent of the institutions affiliated with the Association of American Universities were either conducting or planning campaigns seeking at least $100 million in private funds. By 1994 the public institutions were collecting $4.5 billion in private gifts and grants, as compared with the $5.7 billion received by private institutions. Public research universities were doing particularly well. The Universities of Michigan, Minnesota, and California, along with Ohio State and Penn State, became aggressive fundraisers. The University of California alone received more than half a billion dollars in private donations in 1994.

In public and private institutions alike, the drive to increase funding from the private sector led to sizable investments in staff. It was not unusual for a major university to have three hundred people working in the development office. The institution's president had to be involved, along with numerous people skilled in fundraising. The development officers proceeded with deliberate plans, targeting wealthy donors and establishing personal relationships with them where possible; they emphasized the prestige of their institution, the scope of its programs, and the way it was serving the public. They were careful to tailor their requests to purposes identified as being favored by particular donors. Fundraising in both the public and private sector had become so important that the issue dominated presidential selection; individuals with unattractive lifestyles or mannerisms might well be rejected regardless of their academic credentials. Presidents who could relate well personally with private donors and with corporation and foundation officials were much more desirable.

College endowments prospered in the strong economy of the late 1990s. Two hundred and thirty-five institutions had endowments worth more than $100 million each in 1997 ("Fact File," 1998). Although a few public university systems had broken into the top ranks, the list was still dominated by those in the private sector. Of the twenty-five institutions with endowments valued at more than $1 billion, nineteen were private universities. Only thirteen public institutions—headed by the Universities of Texas, California, and Virginia, along with Texas A&M—were numbered among the top fifty. The rising stock market led to college endowments' earning double-digit incomes. In fact, the income from Harvard's nearly $11 billion endowment contributed more to its budget than it was receiving from the tuition it charged. For the five years prior to 1996, endowment income was led by Emory University, with earnings exceeding 22 percent, thanks to its sizable holdings in Coca-Cola stock. But Yale's 17 percent earnings, Harvard's 16 percent, and the 15 percent earned in the endowment portfolios of a half-dozen other universities were not far behind ("Harvard's Men," 1996).

The resource base was shifting, and many institutions were struggling to stay afloat, but the ability of higher education to control costs remained limited. Its major problem was that the distribution of resources within the system was operating to define it, with the magnitude of resources coming in exercising the most control. That is why most funding formulas fall back on the non–educationally related practice of allocating resources on the basis of program cost. By that line of reasoning, the higher the cost of offering the program, the more resources will be devoted to it, regardless of its social or educational merit. It is politically nearly impossible for educators to discuss in open forum the rationale for differential allocation within the system, but they can band together and argue for more resources coming in from the outside. That is also why for every hour that national associations spend giving their members specific guidelines for cutting budgets, they devote ten more to petitioning Congress, state legislatures, and the public for increased support.

Thus the first twenty years of the Contemporary Era saw several shifts in sources of revenue but few changes in the ways funds were allocated within institutions. Tuition remained relatively stable throughout the 1970s, but after 1980, accelerated at a rate of between 3 and 6 percent per year in constant dollars. During that same time, median family income actually fell in constant dollars, so that the gap between the cost of college and the average individual's ability to pay kept widening.

Revenue per FTE student increased, so that by 1992 it exceeded $30,000 at private universities. Comparable figures at other institutions were $17,000 at public universities, $15,000 at private four-year colleges, $12,000 at public four-year colleges, and less than $6,000 at public two-year colleges. Tuition as a proportion of that revenue reached 45 percent at the private universities and 69 percent at the other private four-year colleges. All types of institutions in the public sector were deriving around 22 percent of their income from tuition. In constant dollars, tuition revenue as a percentage of total revenue had gone up across the board by from 5 to 8 percent, evidencing the transfer of the cost of higher education to individuals and their families. Even so, 47 percent of the undergraduates at four-year institutions and all of those attending two-year colleges in the nonprofit sector were paying tuition of less than $3,000 per year (National Center for Education Statistics, 1997a).

Student financial aid offset much of the cost of college attendance. The average grant given to full-time dependent students was around 29 percent of tuition charges, and because students from low-income families received higher awards, the financial aid represented a much greater percentage of tuition costs for them. Internal institutional expenditures for scholarships also increased, doubling at private universities and four-year colleges between 1980 and 1992 as expressed in constant dollars.

In general, higher education was still being provided largely in the same way it was when the nation was founded. Despite the increased tuition, students paid less than the cost of their education. They seemed to prefer high-spending institutions, feeling that they were receiving more for their money whether it came from their pockets or from a subsidy. Their cost of attending college

included foregone earnings, which in all but the highest-cost institutions were greater than the amount of tuition that a student paid.
But higher education had grown so important that young people
who did not attend jeopardized their earnings; they were locked out
of the many professions and occupations that demanded certification. More than ever, to paraphrase a popular advertisement, they
dared not leave home without it.

Outcomes

Each era has been marked by modified goals, which in turn have led
to changed practices. And each goal shift has engendered cries of
degradation, betrayal of the fundamentals, destruction of the rock
on which the system was founded. Two generations after the University Transformation Era began emphasizing research, professional
schools, and support for business, many academics were still deploring the turn away from an emphasis on the classics, religion, and
hierarchical beliefs. The Mass Higher Education Era growth in the
size and number of institutions, along with rapid expansion of occupational programs, yielded commentaries that many of the new students were not qualified, the colleges should not be trade schools,
and the intimacy of the small campus was lost. During the Contemporary Era, system goals shifted toward more diversity in the student body, the inclusion of everyone who could be enticed to attend
on the grounds that anyone without a college degree faced a bleak
future, and an increased dependency on tuition as a source of revenue in both public and private institutions.

Critiques and Commentaries

Even though higher education could not deliver on all its pledges, it
has never known how to back away from them. It had made too
many promises. If the billions devoted to research on social issues
seemed to yield no reduction in social ills, instead of reducing their
claims, the institutional representatives typically said only that they

needed more money or that other institutions were at fault and
should change. Never able to say merely, "Send your young people
here and we will teach them to be good citizens and more productive workers," it promised also to ameliorate social problems, cure
diseases, enhance the economy, relieve unemployment, and show
people how to be nice to one another. In addition it set itself the
moral stance of criticizing other institutions and ideas that seemed
less worthy. Were students unprepared for collegiate studies? Blame
the lower schools. Were college dropout rates too high? Students
had to quit school and take jobs because not enough extramural
financial aid was available. And open access—a goal throughout
the Mass Higher Education Era—was modified so that a diverse student body, rationalized as reflecting society, itself became a goal.

Higher education expanded its involvement with the broader
community in many ways. The research enterprise became ever
more tied to economic development and industrial ventures. The
professional schools expanded their direct community service
through cooperative professional care ventures; hospitals opened to
broader segments of the population; legal aid was provided, and
attempts were made to influence governmental policy on everything
from the environment to the economy. The content of collegiate
studies grew to encompass a greater variety of outcomes. Few new
degrees were offered, but more ways of satisfying the requirements
for existing degrees were developed.

Criticisms of higher education flowed from within and outside
the academy, just as they had for the preceding century. At the
beginning of the era several issues seemed clearly defined. Some
thought the universities should turn inward and dedicate themselves
to learning and research for their own sake, benefiting society only
indirectly through advances in basic knowledge and the education
of able students. Obviously, this was not going to happen; higher
education was far too compromised already. On the other side of
the spectrum, critics contended that higher education had remained
neutral, thereby endorsing the status quo in society, especially the

social-class hierarchy. No matter how much the institutions did to support low-income students in attending, the gap in income between social groups continued growing wider. Why was higher education not devoting more of its resources to narrowing the gap? Higher education was castigated for not devoting its energies to moral education. Some laid at its door the breakdown in ethics as evidenced by scandals in government, drug use, sexual promiscuity, and a general lack of respect for authority. No matter what the universities did to attempt to ameliorate unemployment, racial tensions, and urban problems in general, it was never enough. The staff might conduct research, consult, organize legal aid activities, provide health and dental clinics, and send students to work in poor communities, but the problems persisted.

Ernest Boyer, president of The Carnegie Foundation for the Advancement of Teaching, and Derek Bok, president of Harvard—two of the more respected critics—contended repeatedly that higher education should increase its relationships with and efforts on behalf of the broader community. Boyer (1996) argued that higher education reached its finest moments when it served larger purposes, as when it participated in "building of a more just society" and in making the nation "more civil and secure" (p. 13). He deplored the scholars who viewed the campus "as a place where students get credentialed and faculty get tenured, while the overall work of the academy does not seem particularly relevant to the nation's most pressing civic, social, economic, and moral problems" (p. 14) and argued for a variety of types of scholarship: conducting research that continues to expand human knowledge, participating in integrated or interdisciplinary activities, sharing knowledge by communicating it not only to students and colleagues but also to the broader community, and applying knowledge that actually assists in solving social problems.

Boyer echoed Bok (1982), who had said that society needed much more from higher education than it was getting. The institutions should work directly to solve basic social problems; prepare more and better teachers; act to reduce poverty, homelessness, drug abuse, and chronic unemployment; prepare students for careers in international trade; and be more heavily engaged in moral development for everyone. And still the institutions remained opportunistic: they followed the money and took on whatever projects an agency was willing to fund. They indulged themselves in internecine warfare over student admissions, curricular emphases, and faculty promotion criteria. The idea that higher education could reform itself or even that it maintained consistency in its goals and processes was outstandingly archaic in a system as large as this one had become.

Research

Research remained a major function, and the amount spent on it continued the dramatic rise that had begun in the 1950s. Between 1975 and 1994 the funds devoted to organized research increased fivefold. To these figures should be added collaborative efforts with other organizations and the funds devoted to faculty time on research, which typically were accounted for in other budget categories. Even so, research funding remained steady at 9 percent of overall current-fund expenditures, as instructional costs kept pace.

The relationship between private industry and research in the universities shifted. The two systems had interacted for many decades as industry looked to the universities to train the scientists who would staff their laboratories and to conduct the basic studies that would enhance their work. Well into the Mass Higher Education Era, industry was doing most of its product development in its own setting. During the 1980s, industry's investment in university-based research increased notably, fueled by a change in expectations that had been growing for the previous two decades. The federal government had been so supportive of research that the universities did not have to expand liaisons with industrial corporations. But as federal support was cut back in the 1970s, industry was once again looked on as a patron. Furthermore, the nature of programmatic research shifted as the federal government put increasing funds into such areas as the war on cancer and on social programs designed to ameliorate the pernicious effects of poverty, race, and environmental degradation. The separation between basic and applied research grew increasingly blurred. In biotechnology, for example, genetic engineering, immunology, and other cross-disciplinary efforts opened up various possibilities, but because it took so long for the experiments and development of products to reach a commercial stage, support for research had to be continued over many years.

One of the ways that industry and universities participated in research and development in both biotechnology and electronics was for new corporations to be founded, with industry, venture capitalists, and universities all participating. University staff members did not have to leave their positions, funds from many sources could be tapped, and all groups could share in the proceeds of whatever products might be developed. According to Geiger (1993), "Approximately 200 biotech firms were founded between 1980 and 1984," many effected by combinations of venture capitalists and university scientists, both of whom sought out each other as a way of developing products and extending basic research (p. 303). In molecular biology departments, affiliation with a company was considered a normal state of affairs because of the long timelines and sizable funds that product development in that area demanded. The leaders of large drug companies realized that if they were to keep up, they needed to gain access to scientific developments both through the universities and through the biotech firms that were being founded. In the early 1980s, contracts for research in biotechnology were being negotiated routinely. "By one estimate, industry support for biotechnology in universities totaled $120 million in 1984" (p. 304).

The relationships between industry and the universities were symbiotic. Cooperative ventures were seen as a way for the universities to build their scientific research programs through gaining additional resources and for corporations to gain access to the latest in scientific study. The federal government assisted by amending patent law so that universities could retain title to inventions developed under federal research funding. Other federal government legislation supporting the research efforts and the collaborators included tax incentives, relief from governmental regulation, and outright financial support. Many states increased the tax credits that industry could claim for investing in cooperative research projects with universities. Even small firms that derived no immediate benefit from tax breaks because they had not yet generated profits were assisted when state university researchers collaborated with them on research proposals and on joint funding. These types of arrangements also yielded support for graduate students who were then expected to remain within the state and contribute to technology transfer.

The arrangements between universities and industrial corporations were criticized by those who felt they took the universities into areas antagonistic to the academic norms developed over the prior century. Some held that the universities were "too ready to allow a Trojan horse inside the walls of learning," that the "flow of research money undermines the university's independence, increases the dominant status of research relative to teaching, . . . promotes some disciplines unfairly above others, and represents a state-sponsored intellectual policy the consequences of which may be as damaging to scholarship as state-sponsored industrial policies have so often been to economies" (David, 1997, p. 12). However, two things proved certain: first, most students or faculty members on campus were unaffected by the relationships with industry, as the vast majority of institutional effort went on as before; second, industrial competitiveness was considered essential for America to hold its position at the head of world markets in biotechnology and microelectronics. Regardless of whether the rank and file of students and faculty approved of these types of relationships, the top institutional administrators almost invariably did, and most of the leading universities organized administrative divisions precisely to solicit contracts with industry.

The research collaborations with industry involved the universities in what Kaplin and Lee (1995) summarize as "complex legal problems concerning contract and corporation law, patent ownership and patent licenses, antitrust laws, copyright and trademark laws . . . and conflict-of-interest regulations" (p. 946). The courts tended to view research agreements as the basic documents governing the relationship between the universities and private business. In cases of dispute they focused on the express language of the contract, highlighting the importance of giving careful consideration to the research agreements' spelling out rights to inventions or patents, ownership of equipment, and what constituted substantial performance. Issues of what was patentable had to be clarified. In two cases adjudicated in 1980 and 1981, the Supreme Court ruled first that a newly developed strain of bacteria was patentable because, although it was a living thing, it was a man-made product. Second, the Court ruled that a process for creating cured rubber products from uncured synthetic rubber was patentable because it was a process rather than a mathematical formula, which had been ruled nonpatentable. Other issues arose regarding ownership of patents on inventions created by employees in the course of their employment. In most states, if the employment contract made no provision for the assignment of patent rights, the employee owned the patents but the employer retained royalty-fee rights for business uses. In 1996, 131 universities earned $336 million from licenses and patents, up 23 percent from the prior year. Half the total went to six institutions: California, Columbia, Stanford, Michigan State, Wisconsin, and Chicago (Blumenstyk, 1998).

The connections with industry were exerting a centrifugal force on the universities. The arts and sciences, once considered the intellectual core of the university, had been shrinking anyway as the proportion of students in professional schools increased. By the 1980s, research in engineering and the sciences took a further toll, as organized research units were built in numerous areas that demanded collaboration across disciplinary lines. These units involved faculty from more than one department, maintained their own budgets, and had specially designated leaders; often they had their own facilities. They employed sizable numbers of graduate or postdoctoral students along with part-time faculty members or full-time researchers paid by the separate funds that the unit controlled. The center directors typically had greater authority than the department chairs, and the centers operated with little control from the central university administration. Stahler and Tash (1994) conclude that in the major research universities these centers accounted for over one-fourth of the expenditures on research and that their budgets averaged over $15 million.

Research in the United States moved steadily ahead. The nation's share of the world's scientific literature grew close to 40 percent, surpassing the combined totals for Germany, Britain, France, and Japan. Ideas and people moved from academe into business much more smoothly in the United States than elsewhere. Research universities in America generated economic growth by spawning patents and entrepreneurs. The graduates and faculty from the leading research universities created companies, some of which grew into sizable enterprises. David (1997) cites a study finding that "if the 4,000 or so companies founded by MIT graduates and faculty were turned into an independent nation, the income they produced would make it the 24th richest in the world. These firms account for annual revenues of some $230 billion and employ more than 1m people" (p. 14).

Access and Degrees

The purposes of higher education have expanded since the colleges were founded as agencies of personal mobility and community pride and were associated with the dominant churches in the colonies. In the nineteenth century, the institutions added research and professional training, and in the twentieth, several additional functions:

providing general education beyond that which young people could receive in the lower schools, enhancing the economy by developing products and human capital, providing opportunity for lifelong learning, and expanding the scope of research and professional training. Higher education was able to do all that without relinquishing any of its other purposes because of the lack of any central authority imposing restrictions. The competition among colleges and their ability to respond to market forces or consumer-driven desires enabled them to continually seek yet additional groups for which they could provide an expanding list of services.

Higher education's most obvious benefits begin with its enhancing of personal mobility and individual development. As documented in numerous studies summarized by the National Center for Education Statistics, alumni get better jobs, earn more money, change their attitudes, have better health habits, and are more involved in civic affairs. A growing area of inquiry has attempted to estimate higher education's contribution to the economy, not only through developing human capital but also by yielding products and processes, as when business start-ups and the development of entire industries can be attributed to higher education's involvement. A third area includes higher education's effects on society generally, that is, the extent to which it assists in ameliorating social problems and in changing the conditions of national life.

Higher education's contribution to individual mobility begins with the proportion of the population that it enrolls. Between 1975 and 1995 the percentage of high school graduates aged sixteen to twenty-four who matriculated in college immediately after leaving high school increased notably, from 51 to 62 percent. To those numbers must be added the students who delayed entry to college but who showed up years later; two-thirds of the 1980 high school sophomores had enrolled by 1992 (Adelman, 1994). Higher education was absorbing people from all walks of life. The enrollment rates for students from every socioeconomic group increased, with the most dramatic gain made by those from the highest-income families: 83 percent attended college, compared with 65 percent twenty years earlier. Male enrollments increased from 53 to 63 percent, and the enrollment of females from 46 to 61 percent. Of the 191 million people aged eighteen and over, 38 million had been to college; more than 27 million had obtained a bachelor's degree, nearly 9 million the master's degree, 2.4 million a first professional degree, and 1.7 million the doctorate.

These enhanced participation rates kept the United States at the top of the world's nations in terms of the intake and graduation of young people. The average for all countries reporting data went up from 14 to 17 percent between 1985 and 1991, but the 29 percent of the age group enrolled in the United States kept it far ahead of the others (National Center for Education Statistics, 1996d). Because many American students enrolled part-time and took longer to complete their degrees, the 30 percent of twenty-two-year-olds who had received degrees was behind Canada's 33 percent and Norway's 31 percent (Organisation for Economic Co-operation and Development, 1993, p. 179). The relationship between expenditures and graduation rates was apparent, as those countries with the highest growth in public funds given to higher education experienced the greatest increase in graduation rates. In the United States, expenditures for higher education as a percentage of all public spending increased by two-tenths of a percent from 1985 to 1991, and graduation rates by about 5 percent.

Degree production in the United States changed somewhat in terms of field of study and time to degree. Between 1976 and 1994 the proportion of students receiving bachelor's degrees in humanities, computer and information sciences, engineering and engineering technologies, business management, health sciences, and other technical and professional fields increased, and the proportion in social and behavioral sciences, life sciences, physical sciences, mathematics, and education decreased (National Center for Education Statistics, 1997a, p. 104). These fluctuations were the result of many forces, most of them extramural. For example, the requirements for teacher certification in many states changed, so that a bachelor's degree with an education major would no longer suffice, hence the proportion of degrees awarded in that field showed a precipitous decline. At the other extreme the employment possibilities for students majoring in business increased so that degrees awarded in that field showed the greatest gain, moving the business majors from fourth place to first in total bachelor's degrees awarded.

Between 1976 and 1993 the total time it took for a student to complete a doctorate degree increased in all fields of study. The interval between completion of the baccalaureate and of the doctorate rose from 8.8 to 11.2 years. Students in the natural sciences took the least time to degree but even there, the number of years increased from 6.8 to 7.8. For education the increase in time was from 12.8 to 19.7 years. Other fields in which students took 10 or more years between completion of the baccalaureate and the doctorate included humanities, social and behavioral sciences, and other technical and professional fields.

Some concern was raised that more Ph.D.'s were being produced than were needed. In the sciences the rise in the number of postdoctoral appointments was used to contend that graduates had no positions available to them except for temporary research assignments. However, as Geiger (1997) points out, expenditures for academic research had grown even faster than the proportion of postdoctoral appointments; thus postdoctoral researchers' staying on within higher education should not be viewed as indicating that there were no research jobs available. Furthermore, the number of graduate degrees conferred to foreign students increased by two-thirds between 1977 and 1994, whereas those awarded to U.S. citizens increased by only 15 percent. In 1994, foreign students earned 12 percent of all master's degrees and 27 percent of all doctorates (National Center for Education Statistics, 1997f). Nearly half the foreign graduates left the United States, and those who remained represented an economic windfall from a human capital perspective.

Personal Benefits

The benefits that individuals derive from going to college have been traced for many decades, with psychological studies the most prominent area of inquiry. Feldman and Newcomb (1969) summarized many of the studies conducted during the Mass Higher Education Era, and Bowen (1977) attempted to put a dollar value on the changes experienced by individuals in the college years. Pascarella and Terenzini (1991) summarized the 2,500 or so studies that were conducted after Feldman and Newcomb's work. Astin (1993) studied various types of college effects, concentrating especially on full-time students just out of high school. Accordingly, a rich literature is available that traces what happened to individuals from various groups who attended all types of colleges.

The intended outcomes of college include various goals, many achieved, many standing as ideals. Bowen (1977) lists them in taxonomic order: cognitive learning, made up of ten outcomes ranging from verbal and quantitative skills to intellectual tolerance and a desire for lifelong learning; emotional and moral development, made up of six goals, from personal self-discovery to refinement of taste, conduct, and manner; practical competence, including seven goals, among which are citizenship, health, and economic productivity; direct satisfaction and enjoyment from college education; and avoidance of negative outcomes (pp. 55–58). Astin's list (1993) includes eleven affective and eight cognitive outcomes, and his measures relate both to college and postcollege attitudes and behavior (pp. 10–11).

In summarizing findings from the thousands of studies they reviewed, the analysts found certain consistencies:

- College has a substantial cognitive impact, with students gaining most in verbal ability.

- Students gain in substantive knowledge in specific academic areas.

- Smaller gains are shown in the areas of rationality and critical thinking.

- Substantial increases in intellectual tolerance are made, as are modest increases in intellectual integrity, understanding of truth, wisdom, aesthetic sensibility, and creativity.

- Religious orientation decreases except for students in religious institutions.

- Psychological well-being shows moderate increases, especially in the areas of confidence and self-sufficiency.

- College-educated people tend to have a stronger future orientation and are better able to delay gratification.

- Seniors are more likely than freshmen to be in favor of civil liberties and individual autonomy and more opposed to discrimination on the basis of race, gender, and age.

- College graduates are less likely to be unemployed and more likely to work longer hours, but are not necessarily more satisfied with their jobs.

- College-educated parents devote more time to their children and enhance tendencies toward further education among them, thus effecting an intergenerational outcome.

- College-educated adults are healthier and take greater advantage of health services.

These consistent findings point to socially desirable outcomes of college attendance. They vary by student age, ethnicity, pattern of college attendance, and numerous other characteristics and situations, but when all are aggregated, the evidence for the value of college-going is quite clear. The most powerful cognitive effects are in oral and written communication, abstract reasoning, and ability to deal with conceptual complexity. Attitudinally, students tend to move away from authoritarian, dogmatic thinking as they gain in aesthetic sophistication. The magnitude of the changes shows little relationship to the typical measures used to estimate the quality of an institution, certainly not to dollars spent, size of library, or degrees held by the staff. After controlling for the characteristics that students bring to a college when they matriculate, the effects of institutional type prove very modest. Pascarella and Terenzini (1991) conclude that the characteristics of an institution have "a small, perhaps trivial, net influence" (pp. 108–109). Astin (1993) shows how the extent of student involvement in college life is most significant, especially when students reside on campus and participate in both sponsored and ad hoc activities.

Income and Employment

The economic value of education has also been traced for many decades, with the findings showing consistently that one's income rises with years of schooling. The penalties of not finishing high school are severe, and as people grow older, the disadvantage of not having a high school diploma persists: 86 percent of the male high school graduates aged twenty-five to thirty-four were employed, compared with 75 percent of those who did not complete high school; among females in that age group, less than half the high school dropouts were employed, compared to 66 percent of the graduates. The median annual salary of males who did not complete high school was 74 percent of the salary of the high school graduates; female high school dropouts earned 62 percent of the wages paid to female high school graduates.

The rewards for attendance are also positively related to college graduation. Male and female graduates aged twenty-five to thirty-four were more likely to be employed than their counterparts who had not been to college; 92 percent of the males and 84 percent of the female graduates were employed versus 86 and 66 percent, respectively. Males who had completed a bachelor's degree earned more than their counterparts who had only a high school diploma, and the premium was even greater for females with bachelor's degrees. Less unemployment and higher wages were the most obvious benefits of schooling.

These earnings advantages have been consistent (see Table 5.15) (National Center for Education Statistics, 1997a, p. 111). The economic benefit of college-going for males remained steady from the early 1970s through the mid-1990s; more than 92 percent of those with bachelor's degrees or higher credentials were employed. And the employment rate of females with college degrees increased substantially, from less than 60 percent to nearly 84 percent (National Center for Education Statistics, 1997a, p. 118). The wage premium for females was greater as well; although females overall earned less than males, the spread between the earnings of those with bachelor's degrees and those with high school diplomas widened (see Table 5.16). In 1976 a female with a bachelor's degree earned $1.58 for every dollar earned by a female with a high school diploma; by 1995 the ratio was $1.91 to one dollar. For males the spread widened from $1.19 per dollar to $1.52.

Differences in median starting salaries for male and female college graduates and for those who had majored in various fields

Table 5.15. Median Annual Earnings of Wage and Salary Workers Aged 25–34, 1975 and 1995 (in 1996 Constant Dollars).

Highest Educational Level	1975		1995	
	Women	Men	Women	Men
Grades 9–11	$ 9,258	$24,493	$ 8,581	$16,229
High school diploma	14,405	31,269	13,916	21,965
Some college	17,853	33,422	17,866	24,366
Bachelor's degree or higher	24,828	36,527	26,611	33,367

Source: National Center for Education Statistics, 1997a, p. 281, 1997b, 1997c, 1997d.

Table 5.16. Ratio of Median Annual Earnings of Wage and Salary
Workers Aged 25–34, 1976 and 1995.

| | 1976 | | 1995 | |
Highest Educational Level	Women	Men	Women	Men
Grades 9–11	0.61	0.78	0.62	0.74
High school diploma	1.00	1.00	1.00	1.00
Some college	1.14	1.03	1.28	1.11
Bachelor's degree or higher	1.58	1.19	1.91	1.52

Source: National Center for Education Statistics, 1997a, p. 120.

showed some changes in the first twenty years of the Contemporary
Era. In 1996 constant dollars, the 1993 college graduates earned
$23,600; the starting salary for males was $26,122 and for females
$21,990—a 16 percent difference for those who were working full-
time. Graduates in the humanities, social and behavioral sciences,
natural sciences, and education earned less than the median,
whereas those in computer sciences and engineering, business and
management fields, and other professional or technical areas earned
more. However, the gap in earnings narrowed for most fields; for
example, graduates in the humanities earned 20 percent less than
the median in 1977 but only 11 percent less in 1993 (National
Center for Education Statistics, 1997a, p. 122). The earnings differential displayed by graduates in the various areas of study was
considerably greater than the difference in earnings between graduates in the same field of study in different colleges. Once people
obtained college degrees, especially the bachelor's degree, it mat-
tered little whether they began at a community college or whether
it took them four, five, or six years to complete a program; the
degree was the cachet.

    In pure economic terms the cost of obtaining a degree—tuition
plus foregone earnings—was an investment in a person's future
income. Bowen (1977) figured the value of a bachelor's degree at
between 8 and 9 percent per year over a lifetime, and Pascarella and
Terenzini (1991) calculated the rate of return at between 9 and

11 percent. In an extension of the belief that a scarcity of degree-holders results in a premium for those who hold degrees, the penalty for not having a degree was growing as more people gained them. Green (1980) had anticipated this situation in his comment that when nearly everyone has attained a certain level of schooling, those who have not done so suffer a disaster. When there are only a few dropouts, schooling becomes defensive for the individual, "compulsory in ways that it was never compulsory before" (p. 101). The presence of many high school graduates created the compulsion for the few people without high school diplomas to obtain them; the same held true for degrees all along the system.

Although having a bachelor's degree was the means by which people's earnings increased the most, students earning associate degrees also gained. Sanchez and Laanan (1997) reviewed studies of the earnings of graduates with vocational certificates or associate degrees from community colleges. Looking at both short-term and long-term effects, they found that from 1975 to 1994, those who entered the workforce with a bachelor's degree increased their earnings by 202 percent, whereas those with an associate degree or some college education showed an earnings increment of 165 percent. An Illinois study of short-term effects found individuals' average earnings increasing by 10 percent for the first two quarters following completion of an occupational education program. A North Carolina study found a 12 percent increase for a similar group over a one-year period. Students gaining occupational certificates in California made a 47 percent gain in wages between their first and third year out of community college. Nationally, men with a college education nearly managed to keep pace with inflation between 1976 and 1995; those with some college but no degree experienced a decline of 27 percent; those with a high school diploma lost 30 percent; and the real wages of high school dropouts declined by 34 percent.

The percentage of college graduates going into various fields has shifted considerably from one decade to the next. Bok (1993) points out how the number of graduates entering teaching and business increased by two and one-half times in the latter nineteenth century, whereas those entering medicine and the ministry decreased. This does not mean that medicine and the ministry were less valued, merely that opportunities for greater numbers of graduates were opening elsewhere. During the 1960s, when the professions were relatively stable and earnings were rising steadily, "the supply of talented young university graduates entering each occupation seemed to stay reasonably related to demand" (p. 40). The rising proportion of undergraduates and graduates alike majoring in business between 1970 and 1990 was phenomenal, but the number of law graduates grew at a similar rate.

Although institutions have been accused of ignoring the employment market when they admit students, the market is not predictable. When a sizable number of graduates are available, various business, industries, and agencies ramp-up the qualifications they expect in new employees, and after short periods of dislocation the surplus is absorbed. At the bachelor's-degree level 78 percent of the recent graduates who were employed in 1994 had jobs related to their fields of study, and 60 percent reported that their jobs required a college degree. The number of new doctoral recipients increased substantially, even as the percentage finding positions in higher education fell from 68 to 52 percent between 1970 and 1993. Most of the graduates in physical science and engineering were employed in industry, and opportunities in public service and governmental agencies opened for those with humanities or social science degrees. But no one seemed able to refute the human capital thesis: everything else being equal, those with more and better education earn more and enjoy higher standards of living. The link between these variables is far from perfect, but the concept of overeducation is considerably less valid.

The kaleidoscope of influences on higher education included a widespread belief that higher education had the most powerful effect on what became of a person, that education was the primary if not the sole route to success. The conflict between this notion and the belief in egalitarianism that was proceeding contemporaneously led to some inconsistent conclusions. One set of commentators deplored a cognitive elite, that is, a set of high-IQ people who had maneuvered their way through the most prestigious institutions to gain power. However, a sizable proportion of high-income people achieved their wealth through routes other than the professions. In fact the MBA typically led its holders to middle-level positions in business or banking, not to the boardrooms or chief executive officer ranks in corporations. And education, still the most popular master's degree, certainly did not contribute to an individual's gaining great wealth. The fields of business and education, which accounted for half the master's degrees awarded, were entered by risk-averse students—people whose approach to life rarely led them into the ranks of the superwealthy (Lemann, 1996). Education was egalitarian in its most basic form: it led to higher income—not the *highest* income but a higher income for an ever-wider sector of the population. Never a path to riches, it had become a broad road leading toward middle-income employment, one that everyone except the most entrepreneurial, the luckiest, or those with the prenatal intelligence to be born into wealthy families had to travel.

The numbers of people choosing different professional schools is based on many factors, including the hope for future income, the expectation of obtaining a position at all, and the general prestige and lifestyle anticipated. The higher education system has seemed able to adjust to the demands placed on it by schools and departments that are competing for the best students and faculty and the highest budgets and by the individual students who are deciding on which program to enter according to their own perceptions. No experience in the United States or elsewhere suggests that mandates and quotas stemming from extramural agencies can do a better job of allocation.

Issues of income differential are frequently brought up in discussions of opportunity for education. Enabling everyone to go to an equally efficient school would not materially affect the spread of income, but that remains a goal. As for higher education, even if colleges were as free to the individual as elementary schools are, all people would not attend. In the mid-1970s, around one in five individuals was dropping out of secondary school after the age of compulsory attendance, and around half the high school graduates were not enrolling in college, even in states where tuition at the public institutions was minimal. Twenty years later the secondary school dropout rate had declined to around one in eight, and more than 60 percent of the high school graduates were matriculating in college. Opportunity to go to college was becoming more equalized, and more people were taking advantage of it. But it was not ubiquitous, and because students are not all equally talented, ambitious, or hardworking, some succeeded in achieving their goals and others failed, even though everyone had the same chance. Equal opportunity never ensures equal results. Accordingly, those who perceive unequal results and conclude that opportunity must have been unequal cannot be satisfied. They view the unequal results and seek the minutiae of unequal opportunity, finding discrimination a pervasive force.

Most of what happens to people in their lifetime is not amenable to intervention by the broader society. Equalizing the amount of schooling that people get would have little effect on the traits that lead some to have higher income than others. In a competitive economy some people work harder or longer or are more valuable to their employers. Others establish and sustain their own businesses. The type of school they attend has little to do with equalizing those traits. Educational credentials are far from being the only thing—probably they are not even the most important thing—that determines a person's future. People with more education tend to make more money, in large measure because many lucrative occupations are closed to those with less schooling. But talent is unevenly distributed, and two people graduating from the same program with the same GPA will still progress differently in their careers. As Henry (1994) concludes, "We are an elitist society because nothing else is logical. . . . We are egalitarian, because nothing else is diplomatic"

(p. 31). Schools are elitist to the extent that they move some people toward better positions in society. They organize to rank young people hierarchically and to further the idea that knowing more is better than knowing less. That in itself is elitist.

Societal Benefits

Support for education has been justified on the grounds that it is in the compelling interest of the state. During the Cold War, arguments for federal funding turned on that rationale. More recently, contentions have been made that higher education assists in the maintenance of civic order, reduces the crime rate, and increases community physical and mental health as well as enhances the human capital needed for a growing economy. Researchers have sought ways of measuring these broad social effects. Welfare recipiency has been tracked. Not surprisingly the percentage of persons aged twenty-five to thirty-four who receive public assistance shows a negative relationship with years of schooling; in 1992, 17 percent of all persons with nine to eleven years of school were receiving welfare—a figure that dropped to one-half of 1 percent for those with sixteen years or more of schooling (National Center for Education Statistics, 1995). However, community service and volunteerism increased with educational levels; adults with some postsecondary education were twice as likely to volunteer their time and make charitable contributions (National Center for Education Statistics, 1996a). To the well-documented higher income and employment enjoyed by professional school graduates can be added the contention that they directly improve social conditions through the work they do. Professionally trained people have always been highly represented in the ranks of civic leaders. The values associated with academe—social responsibility, concern for the environment, and decrease in prejudice—all become part of a community's tone.

Still, it is not logical to expect expenditures on higher education or the percentage of people enrolled to continue increasing indefinitely. No studies have shown that people who have been to college are less productive or that it is socially undesirable to have a high proportion of college-educated people in a community. But some economic analysts find merit in efforts to cap enrollments and limit expenditures, holding that at some point the cost of educating marginal students becomes greater than the economic benefit they deliver. For much of the workforce, motivation and work habits are considerably more important than advanced training. Furthermore, the argument goes, the nation's productivity might be better enhanced by investing in technology. If higher education's main benefit is to enhance individual income, let the individual pay for it.

Higher education's requests for continually increased funding rest on a combination of premises: direct contributions to the economy, enhanced productivity yielded by trained workers, and progress toward an equitable society by providing everyone with opportunity to advance. Its weakest arguments from an economic perspective are that it should be supported because of the intrinsic educational value that its students gain. Education for its own sake is perceived as a consumption item. Institutions and programs showing measurable economic and social benefits are much easier to defend than are those claiming to have value in and of themselves. Many scholars have contended that higher education is more than an engine of economic activity, that it is the home of ideas, the archive of a people's culture. But those arguments have few friends in the legislatures. Cultural archive, pleasurable experience, learning for its own sake, and contributor to social equity—all represent a strong current but one that has been essentially diverted to an eddy by a flood of economic concerns. Still, as economists have concluded, "If future income and job-benefit returns to the student were all that education had to offer, there would be little reason for governments to subsidize it as they do" (Baumol, Blackman, and Wolff, 1989, p. 199).

Assessment

The need to justify budgets by measuring tangible contributions has grown and shows no signs of abating. Commissions in every state have been formed, with each seeking ways of controlling costs and demonstrating the value of higher education. Whether or not institutional leaders perceive these as debasing the institutions and compromising their autonomy is irrelevant. The commissions study, the state boards gain authority, and the institutions, often grudgingly, comply.

A review of a few of these state plans of the 1990s reveals their tone and consistency. The boards governing education in New York challenged the institutions to be accountable for results and to measure progress using performance indicators that among other things, revealed graduation rates and employer satisfaction (The University of the State of New York, 1996). The Kentucky General Assembly mandated a higher education accountability process, including an undergraduate alumni survey, graduating student survey, remedial follow-up analysis, indication of pass rates on licensure examinations, and persistence and graduation rates (Kentucky Council on Higher Education, 1996). The West Virginia legislature created a Higher Education Report Card revealing annual data in several categories, including student outcomes, economic and workforce development, campus security, and graduation rates (State College and University Systems of West Virginia, 1997). In many of the states where centralized government was less evident, the universities themselves reported data on similar goals; the University of Arizona set its own standards for student persistence, graduation rates, and the average number of years to complete bachelor's degrees, along with some institutionally specific goals such as integration of undergraduates in research and the proportion of lower-division courses taught by ranked faculty (University of Arizona, 1996).

A few nationally constituted groups also developed taxonomies of educational outcomes. The Center for the Study of Higher Education at the Pennsylvania State University prepared a listing of policy issues using the input-environment–outcomes model popularized by Astin. They defined input as access, affordability, financial support, and student preparation. Environment or process issues included institutional accountability, campus climate and facilities, faculty productivity, and technology. The outcomes had to do with lifelong learning, public service, educational effectiveness, graduate and professional education, and workforce preparation and retraining (National Center for Education Statistics, 1997i, p. 5). However, these institutionally dominated groups were advisory at best. The National Center for Education Statistics continued its widely reviewed data efforts, and the state agencies proceeded with their own outcomes-assessment indicators.

In the broad sense the flurry of outcomes assessments was generated by higher education's success. When it enrolled but a small proportion of the population and laid claim to only a few dollars in public resources, it was not the subject of much attention. But when it aided the founding of industries and kept the United States competitive in new technological areas, while at the same time enrolling an ever more diverse set of students, it began to be viewed as a major utility. The public had great expectations; practically every state wanted to have a world-class university within its boundaries, and most of the young people wanted to be prepared for higher-status employment. Furthermore, the time lines shortened; institutions were not to have the luxury of developing greatness over a span of centuries. Nor could they reject governmental initiatives. In the forty years prior to the mid-1990s, federal support for research grew fiftyfold in current dollars, and institutional capacity to produce Ph.D.'s by more than ten times. The percentage of gross domestic product that the United States spent on higher education was greater than that of any other country except Canada (National Center for Education Statistics, 1997a, p. 176). Even though that percentage had increased little since the start of the era, the dollar figure was large enough to capture public attention.

Much of higher education did not take kindly to attempts to convert its processes into quantifiable outcomes. Many analysts insisted that a college could not be measured in terms of outcomes, impacts, or tangible benefits because of the nature of learning and the human experience. Many of the effects of college-going on individuals are subtle, not easily quantified; causal connections of social benefits are even more difficult to assess. But those arguments, reasonably raised regarding the effects of any educational program, were convincing few people outside the academy. If the staff wanted to return to a time when they were paid as poorly as church parsons and their college matriculated a few students housed in poorly heated buildings, they may have been able to step aside from the demands for accountability, productivity, and results. However, they had become captives of their own success. For decades they had promised that if only enough funds were forthcoming, they could equalize opportunity, produce better citizens, ameliorate social problems, train workers for any emergent field, enhance the development of industry, and enrich the culture of the broader community. By the end of the century it was payback time.

Conclusion

Trends and Issues for the Future

This book has recounted the major trends in higher education since the Colonial Era: institutions growing larger and more varied; students gaining access; faculty becoming professionalized; curriculum expanding, especially toward occupational studies; governance moving toward secularization and comprehensive, state-level units; finance becoming based on diversified, predominately public funds; and research and outcomes moving toward the service of the individual, the public, the professions, and the economy.

Which of the trends might have been predicted when the nation was formed? Large multipurpose institutions? No. The plethora of professions that would demand years of schooling prior to practice, and an economy that would allow young people to delay entry into the workforce until they were well into their twenties were not on the horizon. Student access? Yes, because it embodies the egalitarian, democratic ideal on which the nation was founded. Faculty professionalization? No. That had to await the nineteenth-century German concept *Lehrfreiheit* and the professionalizing of several other occupational groups. A curriculum more directly related to occupations? Perhaps. The trend was imminent in the last few years of the Colonial Era, as the newer colleges attempted to provide curriculum beneficial to a variety of commercial interests. Diversified financing? Yes, because from the start the colleges relied on combinations of public funds, tuition, and donations, although the eventual magnitude of state contributions was not foreseeable. Secular governance? Yes, because governance was interdenominational in several institutions, and attempts were made early on to involve civic leaders. But state-level governance and multi-institutional systems would have been hard to visualize because the early colleges functioned independently in scattered locations. Expectations that higher education would ameliorate social problems and enhance the economy? No. The early colleges were influential in developing men of public affairs, but the economy did not depend on college-spawned inventions or a workforce trained in postsecondary institutions.

Which trends will remain intact into the next century? The growth of new institutions slowed considerably in the Contemporary Era, and few new campuses will be built in coming years. State, federal, and private-philanthropic funds will be available to expand campus facilities but not sufficient to establish entire institutions except for non-campus-based structures such as virtual universities. The concept of open access, well grounded in the Mass Higher Education Era, cannot be feasibly altered. However, smaller percentages of students will have full-time, on-campus experience. A more highly professionalized faculty is not likely because the desire to save money by employing part-time staff will remain strong. Curriculum will continue broadening, as academic inquiry sustains its pattern of generating new subspecialties and as additional occupational groups seek higher education's cachet. Effectually, all the external pressures on curriculum favor vocationalism. Secular governance has become dominant, and the only private groups able or inclined to overturn it will be those managing a growing proprietary school sector. State-level control is certain to grow; the independent public college has already become an oxymoron. Higher education's contributions will continue in the service of individual mobility, economic development, and research designed to assist industry.

This chapter provides a summary of contemporary issues with a modest peek toward the next few years. Only the most powerful trends are apparent because unforeseeable events convert specific projections into little more than informed guesses. Will the national economy sustain its 1997 year-end pattern of low inflation, low unemployment, and a balanced budget? Within a year or two that set of circumstances could be totally altered. Inflation, depression, any number of catastrophes can affect the funds available for higher education's support. However, the place of the colleges and universities as institutions essential to the society is secure. Regardless of variations in the economy they will remain intact because of what they mean to individuals seeking a step up in social or economic status. They have performed that function since they were founded, and except for the armed services, no other social institution comes close to what they do. Of course they do more, especially as they associate with government and private industry to conduct the research, train the workers, and invent the products basic to a modern economy. Their less quantifiable social and cultural benefits are nonetheless valuable as well.

One clue to the viability of the system is afforded by the way it appears to the rest of the world. European influence on American higher education came in two stages. First was the college form, especially the curriculum and the residential pattern, imported from England. Subsequently, the German model of research, academic freedom, and public service was appended. But all that happened over one hundred years ago. Now, the Europeans look to the United States as a point of reference for reforming their higher education. They admire the American system's ability to charge tuition as it opens access to all education seekers and its ability to combine research and service, academic and vocational curriculum, and graduate and undergraduate studies, all within the same set of institutions. The diversity of forms and the students' ability to transfer among them seems desirable, along with the capacity to modify structures and reassign responsibilities with minimal restraint from civil service bureaucracies. The Europeans know that their future has to include many aspects of America's complex, highly successful system.

Societal Context

The context for higher education includes a continuation of various groups' seeking to redress injustices. The long-standing efforts to bring about a more equal economic society, that is, to reduce the gap between the poor and the wealthy, have been superseded by competition among ethnic groups for a greater share of benefits. Classifying people by race or ethnicity is particularist. Those categories should have been minimized in higher education, especially in the universities dedicated to cosmopolitanism and universalism. Instead, they are stronger there than in most social institutions. This has generated conflict within higher education and between it and much of its constituency but, curiously, has served the system well by forcing it to become cognizant of social injustice—something not prominent in its conduct over most of its history. And it has brought additional resources, both in the form of funds to establish programs for special groups and in people with fresh attitudes and ideas.

Affirmative action was set up originally to remedy the effects of discrimination but has expanded into different realms. Because the courts have been ruling that claims of discrimination are valid only when specific individuals can show that they were harmed, the proponents of affirmative action have broadened its purposes so that diversity, that is, the proportional representation of various subgroups on the campuses, has become a goal. But even when minority students are admitted in proportional numbers, they are not found in equivalent ratios in all programs. And subgroups keep clouding progress; black males have fallen behind in comparison with black females, Filipino Americans in comparison with Chinese Americans, Mexican Americans when compared with Cuban

immigrants. The targets keep shifting. Which groups must be represented in relation to what? The idea that every identified group
and every subset within it be represented in every college program
in proportion to that group's numbers in the population is prepos-
terous on its face. If affirmative action can be adjudged a success
only when that is achieved, it is doomed to failure in perpetuity. But
as long as each group continues exerting pressure, college counsels,
institutional research directors, and curriculum planners, along with
civil rights attorneys and U.S. Department of Education compliance specialists, can depend on being fully employed.

Although the calls for equity according to race, gender, and ethnicity are supported by politically aware groups and federal legislation, they will not continue forever at the same volume. Women
have attained parity in the student body, and their proportionate
representation in all faculty ranks is imminent. Pressure from that
quarter will subside. And the categorizations themselves may
change as other ways of stratifying people gain appeal. Two hundred
years ago an observer of higher education might have commented
on the different benefits accruing to certain religious groups. By the
mid-nineteenth century, immigrants would have been found
excluded. One hundred years ago the gap between participation
rates of wealthy and poor was being deplored. Fifty years ago the loss
of talent was a major issue, and programs were organized to enable
all the bright young people to go to college. Twenty years ago people with disabilities became prominent. All stratifications are con-
text-specific, constructed according to what seems important at the
time. They ebb and flow in the eyes of the public. None are
immutable.

Students and Staff

Several demographic factors keep the number of potential students
growing. The National Center for Education Statistics projects
enrollments for ten-year periods by calculating the number of

eighteen-year-olds in the population (a relative certainty) and (less certainly) by estimating rates of immigration, high school graduation, college-going, and the participation of adults. And then, depending on the weights it assigns to each, it displays high, middle, and low estimates. For 2008, its middle projection shows 16 million students, an increase of just over 1 percent per year for ten years. The higher tuition charges, shift in financial aid from grants to loans, and competition from the broader postsecondary sector can upset those figures. But one effect is certain: 350,000 more eighteen- to twenty-four-year-olds per year will put pressure on the system somewhere, especially in the West and South where population growth is highest. Most will want to attend college, if not the bucolic, residential campus then the urban commuter institution. Throughout their career as pupils, they have been told, stay in school, study, make good grades so that you can go to college. Their great-grandparents stood aside while a fortunate few had the campus experience in the first half of the twentieth century. This generation will not accept being shunted off to take lessons via computer.

Forecasting the demand for faculty is less certain because in addition to enrollment projections, other variables enter. The number of faculty leaving was easier to estimate when most institutions had a mandatory retirement age. However, beginning in 1994, federal law prohibited that imposition, and its effects have not yet been fully realized. The 1993 National Survey of Postsecondary Faculty (National Center for Education Statistics, 1996c) found that around 6 percent of all full-time faculty and staff left the institutions at which they were employed a year earlier, and of those, 37 percent retired. But that figure was in line with the ratio prevalent for many years. No one knows if those numbers will continue. Furthermore, how much would faculty-student ratios change if the size of the average class continued growing and if the efforts to have professors teach more classes began to bear fruit? In the middle 1990s, estimates were ranging from fifteen thousand to forty thousand new hires per year for the ensuing ten or fifteen years. Schuster (1995), who has studied the academic labor market for a number of years, considered a wide range of variables and arrived at a figure of eighteen thousand new hires per year—a number that could be comfortably accommodated by the people receiving graduate degrees and seeking faculty employment.

In large measure the demand for professors will depend on the relative strength of faculty organizations that contend teaching positions should be filled by full-timers and of the opposition, that is, managers who prefer employing lower-cost part-timers. Because evidence of the effectiveness of one or the other type of instructor is unconvincing, the issue will continue to be decided in local and state-level political arenas. Where an institution's leaders see the necessity for rapid response to new demands and where they have problems balancing the budget, they will extol the virtue of a fungible faculty, claiming that it is easier to deploy especially trained instructors to teach new types of courses than to retrain permanent staff. Where the faculty groups are able to counter those moves, the managers will build new types of units modeled on contemporary extension divisions and employ the needed faculty off book, as it were. At any rate, the so-far fruitless attacks on tenure will subside along with the proportion of full-time staff. Between 1991 and 1995, the full-time higher education staff decreased by 1 percent and the part-time staff increased by 18 percent (National Center for Education Statistics, 1998, p. iii). As the rise in employment of part-time and non-tenure-track instructors has revealed, there is no need to make a frontal assault on the professors. Institutions can merely stop replacing them as they leave.

Curriculum

Curriculum evolves continually, usually incrementally and with little attention from people outside the affected programs. But controversy has raged over multiculturalism as a curriculum organizer.

Some commentators have observed that studying other cultures undermines American unity, that the slogan *E Pluribus Unum*—from many, one—is being supplanted by *Ex Uno Plura*—from one, many. They deplore what they see as efforts to set aside reason, rational discourse, and logic—traits reaching to the roots of our civilization—and assert, "Our students are today being taught that such categories as 'African-American,' 'female,' or 'person of color' are in effect more fundamental than the category of American, let alone of rational man" (Glynn, 1993, p. 24). Such arguments seem overwrought, but not when they are placed alongside the hyperbolic claims of the more extreme proponents of ethnic identity, who claim that a curriculum based on the Western experience and the contributions of dead white males is a tool of oppression, along with the language and premises that higher education uses to conduct its discourse. The threats and accusations are considerably more impassioned than those raised at the turn of the century when the classics lost their place at the core of the curriculum, more so than those put forward subsequently when vocational studies were said to be squeezing out the liberal arts.

Drawing a pall over issues of multiculturalism in the curriculum has been the determined effort by some extremists to deny the validity of all literature, history, art, and science. Usually termed *deconstructionism*, this nihilistic philosophy—known since early in the century—rests on the argument that all literature is in fact only opinions, or feelings, of the people who wrote it and cannot be studied for what it says but only for what it reveals about the motives of the author. Similarly, history is subject to constant revision depending on the temper of the times; therefore it can be studied only from the point of view of who wrote it and when it was written. All art is made up of individual emanations and political statements; there are no schools of art, only personal expression. Science, too, is political and individualistic; the experimentation, theory generation, and verification upon which it has rested for three centuries should be viewed only as styles, not as yielding truths.

Multiculturalism and deconstructionism make odd bedfellows, but they come together in their denunciation of a core curriculum centering on Western thought. Penetration has been greatest in the humanities, where questions of what constitutes the canon can be debated interminably. Some social scientists too have seen error, if not evil, in all assertions of universal principles, making claims about the origins of scientific thought and progress that would put to shame the most prodigious assertions of Stalinist and Nazi pseudoscience. Few debates centering on logic and rationality have resulted. Instead the protagonists tend to draw outrageous conclusions, not least the contention that rational argument is itself a tool of oppression. Adelson (1974) was on the mark when he predicted that the irrationalism and anti-intellectualism that were conspicuous during the period of student activism "may yet turn out to be the most sorrowful legacy of the sixties" (p. 57).

The extreme multiculturalists will find their victories evanescent. They must confront the counterweights in the broader society and the waves of young students arriving annually expecting conservative collegiate forms, not controversy. Even though the defenders of religion in the eighteenth century and of a curriculum based on study of the classics in the nineteenth had institutional history on their side as they fought intensive rear-guard actions, they were eventually overtaken by contemporary ideas. With no such base the multiculturalists are warring from outside tradition and in opposition to the spirit of the times. Research in every area of human endeavor exposes the sophistry of group identity; within-group differences are greater than between-group averages on every intellectual and attitudinal measure. However, the debate will remain volatile because it questions the scientific ethos—the foundation of knowledge on which the modern university was built.

Some analysts have attempted to reconcile the current polar positions. Kellner (1998) links multiculturalism with media literacy and critical pedagogy to form what he calls "critical media literacy," a "new frontier" in education (p. 115). Edward Wilson

(1998) has postulated "consilience" as a way of reconciling the philosophies underlying science, the humanities, and other ways of constructing knowledge. He views postmodernism, the belief that nothing can be known, as "the ultimate antithesis of the Enlightenment," and argues that "to the extent that philosophical positions both confuse us and close doors to further inquiry, they are likely to be wrong" (pp. 58–59). Consilience would unify the natural sciences, drawing disparate disciplines into comprehensive areas of study and bringing humanities together with the creative arts as "the two great branches of learning in the twenty-first century. Social science will split . . . with one part folding into or becoming contiguous with biology, and the other fusing with the humanities." The college curriculum cannot feasibly continue separating into increasingly minor specializations. If students are to be worthily educated, "the consilience of science with the social sciences and the humanities in scholarship and teaching" will guide reform (p. 62). Wilson has suggested a return to general education—the elusive goal of reformers since the elective principle became popular at the turn of the twentieth century. This time the attacks launched by postmodernists, deconstructionists, and multiculturalists have stimulated the call. It may or may not be heeded.

Other types of curricular changes will proceed on track. The undergraduate programs in research universities will shrink in relative influence and magnitude as expansion continues in professional schools, extension divisions, hospitals and auxiliary services, and liaisons with industry. The comprehensive universities will persist in magnifying their professional education and community service activities. In the community colleges, occupational education will remain strong along with programs in business and entrepreneurship, which are often established in association with community agencies. The future for remedial studies is less certain, not because more students will be well prepared for college but because proprietary enterprises will compete aggressively for that function.

A broad view of the directions for curriculum sees workforce preparation and recurrent retraining continuing as major influences, and programs designed to prepare and upgrade students for an ever-increasing number of occupations growing. Courses with content that can be used in a greater number of different occupations will be especially prized. The new technologies of the so-called information age have created a demand for flexible, highly educated knowledge workers, the "symbolic analysts" (so styled by Reich, 1992). An increasing number of jobs will be created by self-employed entrepreneurs who depend on their knowledge of communication, interpersonal relations, and economics. Curriculum as a consumption item will be set back; as students are forced to borrow more to finance their studies, they will concentrate on completing their educational programs. The pleasurable experience of being in a campus environment has already become too expensive for most. If esoteric courses designed by professors with a particular interest in a narrow area are to survive, especially those courses that cannot draw more than a handful of students on any one campus, they will tend increasingly to be presented through the electronic media so that a critical mass of students can be engaged.

Some areas of the curriculum are more vulnerable than others. Journalism, speech, physical education, and home economics declined precipitously in the 1960s and 1970s. Social welfare, public health, library studies, and urban planning did not fare well in the 1980s and 1990s. The forces squeezing them came from several directions. Universities aspiring to be seen as research institutions tended to diminish their community service schools. Labor markets and student interests shifted. Student need for basic literacy studies absorbed institutional resources. Straitened budgets limited the number of programs that could be sustained. However, most institutions reform curriculum at glacial speed, and the enterprise is large enough to contain areas long past their prime. The classics, Greek, and Latin still represented a significant proportion of the curriculum for generations after the mainstream of American thought had moved in a completely different direction.

Instruction

Many analysts have watched enrollments growing more rapidly than budgets and have devised strategies for saving money on instruction. Having the faculty teach larger classes and more hours has been a popular suggestion because it fits the most simplistic model of gross productivity. Other recommendations range widely. Reconceptualize the faculty role to include less emphasis on research and more time spent with students. Eliminate duplication in curriculum by establishing statewide or regional compacts through which an institution strong in one area would attract students from other colleges that could not afford to offer those programs. Have public and private institutions in a state share staff and faculties. Increase productivity through accelerated graduation rates, including those based on shortened time to degree.

But instructional technology has held the most allure. Its proponents viewed the expansion of technology in industries, workplaces, and homes and concluded that higher education could service more students, save money, and effect better learning if only it adopted automated ways of teaching. Their hopes were fueled by the colleges' use of information technology. The 1997 survey of campus computing found one-third of all college courses using E-mail, one-fourth using the Internet, and one-eighth using "some form of multimedia resources" (Green, 1997a, p. 3), all up considerably from prior years. Two-fifths of the colleges required computer instruction or information technology competency for their undergraduates.

Money might eventually be saved through greater use of distance education, defined as "courses delivered to remote (off campus) locations via audio, video, or computer technologies" (National Center for Education Statistics, 1997k, p. 3). In 1995 one-third of all colleges and universities provided a total of more than 25,000 different courses to over 750,000 students—5 percent of the total higher education enrollment. Sixty-one percent were undergraduate courses, 29 percent graduate, 7 percent continuing education for professionals. The courses were beamed to students' homes and to other branches of the institutions primarily using two-way interactive video, one-way prerecorded video, and various computer-based technologies. Expansion along those channels is certain, especially if it could be shown to save the costs of bringing students to campus. But saving enough to put more than a tiny dent in the budget seems well in the future.

The vision of higher education's replacing its instructional forms with a paradigm centered on student learning has gained numerous adherents. Although the concept has a long history, it never made much headway until new developments in instructional technology made it more feasible. Can students be led to construct knowledge for themselves? Will faculty become facilitators for students who design their own goals and learning paths? Will higher education be funded on the basis of the value it adds to its students, whether measured by cognitive learning or enhanced progress in the workplace? O'Banion (1997) concludes that as more problems appear (high enrollments, reduced budgets, competition from the for-profit sector) that cannot be solved within the old paradigm, the probability of higher education's shifting toward becoming a learning-centered institution grows. That, too, remains to be seen.

The most intriguing issues in instruction center on autodidacticism. To what extent can young people guide themselves to knowledge? For the last several hundred years, more and more people have been gaining access to more information through all forms of print and sound media, from books and newspapers through radio, television, and the Internet. No sentient human can now be considered information-deprived; the quantity, if not the quality, is overwhelming. Even so, only the most romantic observer believes that providing a person with a computer and a modem can result in a complete education. Most have little doubt that instruction designed deliberately to effect understanding and analytical ability will continue being essential, if only because people are not born with the ability to distinguish the meritorious from the meretricious.

The context, way of certifying, and mode of payment will shift, but the need is a constant.

Several forces will influence developments in curriculum and instruction overall. A major issue in curriculum is the power of tradition that has kept the liberal arts intact at the core of undergraduate education. The extent to which familiarity with the canon remains important depends on its value in the broader community. The type of cultural literacy it suggests has always served several purposes: sharpening critical awareness, providing an adornment of manners and knowledge, enhancing communication and interpersonal relations, and leading to tendencies to make better life decisions. Other ways of gaining these understandings may override the advantage that studying the liberal arts has provided. Or literacy itself may be devalued in a society that has turned further from intellectualism.

Higher education was dipping its toes into the same water that engulfed health care. In the 1970s, more expensive tests, hospitals, and physicians led to an alarming percentage of the gross domestic product going to medicine. In the 1980s, managed care grew rapidly, and costs were contained; for most patients hospital stays and visits with physicians became shorter. Attempts to slow the increased costs of higher education and to accommodate the rising number of college-seekers may similarly lead to most students having less time with professors, more technology, more self-paced learning. But in the meantime, as Green (1997b) concludes, "The genie will not go back into the bottle: adult enrollments will expand, not decline; demand for technology will continue, not diminish; the opportunities for distance and online education will grow, not recede" (p. J9).

Institutions, Governance, Finance

Virtual universities and proprietary schools were the only institutional types to expand by sizable numbers during the Contemporary Era. The traditional sector absorbed enrollment increases by providing courses on branch campuses and during more hours of the day and week. The most telling example of the paucity in institutional expansion came from the states where community colleges were central to higher education. Few opened from the 1960s to the 1990s, even in Florida, Arizona, and California, where the population more than doubled.

Distance education has continued as the compelling vision, with programs and organizations to deliver it established in single states (Maine, Colorado, Iowa, Oregon, California, Kentucky, Wisconsin), regions (Western Cooperative for Educational Telecommunications), and consortia (Committee on Institutional Cooperation, consisting of twelve large institutions in the East and Midwest). The governors of fifteen states plus Guam were developing Western Governors University, designed to absorb the imminent increase in student demand through degree-credit distance education. Although fewer than 3,500 degrees and 2,000 certificates were awarded to distance-education students in 1995, those numbers are certain to expand.

The proprietary sector was deep into innovative educational forms. The University of Phoenix claimed 60,000 students in 1997—all attending part time in classes taught by hourly-rate instructors in office buildings and other rented quarters in thirty-one states. DeVry, Inc., provided business and technical education to 48,000 students, Strayer Education, Inc., to 9,400. Education Management Corp. specialized in arts and culinary classes. Those four plus several others were listed on the stock exchange, collecting part of the "$3.5-billion spent on proprietary postsecondary education in 1995" (Strosnider, 1998, p. A36).

The more that distance education and proprietary schools grew, the more blurred the lines between higher education and the postsecondary sector became. The Jones Education Connection, another for-profit enterprise, delivered college courses through cable television and satellite transmission to students all over the world. In most applications, the traditional colleges in which the courses were developed received royalties from the fees paid to the proprietary schools. But what of the professors who saw courses that they developed broadcast widely? Heretofore, patents and copyrights have been treated differently. The former had value, and the university claimed the major share of it, but professors were free to hold copyright to their own products. Now course materials are increasingly being marketed, not only by the institution where the producer works. Controversy over intellectual property rights is certain to grow.

New forms of information technology, competition from non-traditional schools, distance education provided by colleges acting in concert with corporations, and on-campus applications of new instructional designs were leading to a kaleidoscopic vision of the future for financing instruction. The billions that institutions were spending for technology were not helping budgets. Half the colleges and universities were imposing mandatory user fees to ameliorate some of the costs, suggesting that technology was not only failing to reduce instructional costs, it was increasing them. On average the institutions were spending 40 percent of their information technology budgets on academic computing, and rapid obsolescence meant that costs would remain high for the foreseeable future.

It is easy for policy analysts to applaud the variety of proprietary schools, corporate learning centers, and distance learning opportunities that have arisen to accommodate more students with diverse interests without taxing state budgets. Questions of quality control and intellectual property rights are less readily resolved. Accrediting associations in particular will continue to be under pressure. Their history of concern with process is laboriously shifting toward insistence that institutions measure product. When an education provider has no campus, library, laboratories, or permanent faculty, other indicators of worth must be generated. Accreditation standards will emphasize testing and engage educators in protracted battles over the types of tests and the criterion scores that institutions prefer employing. State-level accreditors will also have to deal with the thorny problems engendered by distance educators that have no campus or office within the state, hence over which the accreditors have no jurisdiction. It is possible that where the same course is taught on campus or on-line by any provider, students will receive college credit—a development already ensured by a bill passed by the Texas legislature in 1997 (Gallick, 1998).

The main issues in overall finance were that demands for budget balancing at the federal level and for reduced taxes and more funds for social services in the states have limited gains in public financing of higher education. The sizable increases in public sector tuition in the early 1990s may slow but will show no sign of reversing. A tone of "let those who use it pay for it" will be prevalent as heightened charges for toll roads, state and national parks, and public facilities of all types spread. Although some students complain of debt burdens and many observers deplore the potential for limiting access, government-guaranteed loans and out-of-pocket funds will shoulder more of the costs.

The precedent had been set not only by the shift from grants to loans that marked the 1990s but as far back as the pattern of financing homes that began in the 1930s. When the Federal Housing Administration started guaranteeing loans, people were able to purchase homes with small down payments, low interest rates, and extended repayment terms. The same principle was being applied to college attendance. Even though Pell Grant funds available increased from $5.9 billion in 1997 to $7.3 billion in 1998, and the maximum award increased from $2,700 to $3,000, higher tuition charges and the greater number of students made the loan pool grow even more. Sixty percent of the 1996 graduates of public four-year institutions had taken out at least one loan. Their average debt was $11,500, up from $8,500 for those who graduated three years earlier. For professional school graduates the average debt was nearly $60,000 (Basinger, 1998).

The proportion of federal aid going to individuals instead of institutions seems certain to grow. Even more certain is that higher education will not receive public funds sufficient to provide an on-campus educational experience for all who seek it. Many will learn in different contexts, perhaps setting up a new pecking order contrasting those who have taken classes on campus with those who have not. As Astin (1993) has documented extensively, there is a qualitative difference in learning and experiences between students who participate in college life and those who do not. Those who have attended traditional colleges will try to exploit it.

Higher education began with private institutions, added public colleges built by the states, and evolved so that federal funds paid an increasing share of the costs in both sectors. The direction now is for reprivatization of institutions through the for-profit sector. As long as employers and governmental agencies stand ready to grant or loan funds to students, and as long as the trend toward making the consumers bear the costs remains intact, proprietary schools will expand. Business licenses are easy to obtain, and short courses for particular job entry and retraining can be built readily.

Different issues are opening in association with massive technology corporations, for example, Microsoft, GTE, and Hughes Electronics. Some have contracted to provide standardized technology to college campuses—an extension of the sales or donations of computer equipment that had been undertaken in prior years but this time designed to augment continuing sales of their proprietary products. Some are developing distance education networks together with traditional universities whose leaders see chances to reach more students without having to create their own networks. Complaints that the developments are not all salutary, especially because they put higher education in the hands of corporate managers uninterested in faculty oversight, have little effect. The trend is intact.

Outcomes

The drive to establish outcomes indicators proceeded fitfully throughout the 1990s. The federal government's *Goals 2000* opened the decade. Most states tried to encourage institutions to develop their own measures, but the data were inconsistent and difficult to aggregate. Next, the colleges were to provide uniform data to agencies that would report statewide information, especially about degrees awarded and the cost of instruction. By the mid-1990s these efforts had become widespread, with most states developing systemwide indicators within several broad areas. As summarized by the Education Commission of the States (*Charting Higher Education Accountability*, 1994) these were:

- *Instructional inputs:* test scores of entering freshmen; number and performance of remedial students

- *Instructional processes:* time to degree; class size; faculty workload

- *Instructional outcomes:* graduation rates; student performance on licensure examinations

- *Efficiency:* student-faculty ratios; program costs

- *Condition:* research activity; proportion of accredited programs; campus facilities

- *Access:* enrollment, persistence, and graduation rates subdivided by students' ethnicity

- *Articulation:* student transfer rates

- *Relation to state:* employment rates and salaries for graduates

Despite the gradual codification of these types of indicators, procedures for applying the data to higher education reform were still sparse. However, the mandates to supply information will remain prominent. Most interesting to watch will be the attempts to tie outcomes to funding and the effect they have on institutional functions.

The gain in earnings displayed by people at various levels of education has continued as a prominent measure of higher education's effects. In 1997 the Council for Aid to Education concluded that the gap in earnings, which had widened in the prior twenty years, would widen even more in the ensuing twenty years. The highest-paid workers would show a modest growth in real earnings, but those in the middle of the distribution, who lost about 14 percent in real wages between 1976 and 1995, by 2015 would be earning 25 percent less than they had in 1976. And for workers in the lowest 10 percent of the wage group, earnings would drop by 44 percent. Put another way, in 1976, "families at the 90th percentile enjoyed income levels nine times greater than those of families at the 10th percentile. By 1993, the disparity was twelvefold. At this rate, the ratio will exceed sixteen to one by 2015" (p. 5). The level of schooling attained thus becomes increasingly important.

In summation, by the most widely used measures, higher education continues yielding benefits such as the following to individuals and to society at large:

- It helps individuals move between social classes. Education or the level of schooling attained is a major determinant of a person's social-class placement.

- It widens social divisions. The type of institution that students attend and the experiences they share serve as inputs to class differentiation. In other words, even if the students who graduate from a law school each year began life in a poverty-ridden community, that community does not change; in fact the social-class division has been widened, because the graduates have moved away from their origins.

- It yields better products and intellectual capital through research.

- It enhances community welfare. College graduates are less likely to engage in health-damaging activities, more likely to support cultural events, and be active in civic affairs.

- It develops the economy. A region's industry relates not only to its trained workforce but also to the multiplier effect of businesses and entire industries started by university staff in collaboration with entrepreneurs.

- It enhances personal income. The more schooling people receive, the more money they make, and the less likely they are to be unemployed or the recipients of social welfare.

- It develops literacy. The community colleges and comprehensive institutions especially have been engaged in direct language training for immigrants and in enhancing the basic skills of students who completed high school without mastering these abilities.

- It is an economic engine, employing over two million people and spending $190 billion per year.

- It develops human capital, increasing the skills, energy, abilities, and tendencies in the population that lead to greater productivity and less deviant behavior.

- It enhances personal development. Young people are assisted toward maturity. They broaden their outlook; they learn to delay gratification and to appreciate differences among individuals. They gain access to a society that welcomes them as worthy citizens.

Analysts have long tried to place a dollar value on each of these outcomes but have been frustrated by all the contaminating variables. Stimulated by state-level calls for indicators of higher education's value, they try continually to ascribe worth. But higher education's spirit is too mercurial to be captured in the crude measures available. It serves many functions, provides something for anyone seeking it, and is a national asset of incomparable value.

The funds spent to support higher education represent a greater share of the nation's gross domestic product than they did fifty years ago, but they have not grown as much as the proportion of the population that the system serves. By this global measure, higher education has increased its productivity.

Cost-saving measures seem destined to make little progress, as established patterns of expenditures remain set. The price of introducing instructional technology is so high and its immediate applications so limited that rapid savings from that quarter cannot be expected. Furthermore, productivity is not merely a matter of increasing the number of graduates. Values enter into the equation. Wallhaus (1996) points up the difference: "The implied analogy between a college graduate and widget is viewed as a shocking lack of understanding of the values of the academy, its culture and its role in society. . . . The outcomes of higher education are much more difficult to define and measure than products of manufacturing processes and other service industries" (p. 3). The ultimate in efficiency would be students learning everything they need to know on their own, but that illusion contradicts the history of human learning. The older generation has always had to instruct the young, and it will continue doing so even as more of the cost reverts to the beneficiaries.

Higher education's position in the life of the nation is secured by its traditional value and power. Perhaps most important now is its ability to adapt to changing conditions. No one knows what higher education will look like in coming years. The only certainty is that an open system will continue experimenting with forms and content, learning and revising as it goes, even while retaining the strengths it has developed over the past 350 years. The American people deserve no less from institutions that are part of the fabric of their society and manifestations of the nation's self.

References

Adams, J. T. *The Epic of America*. New York: Blue Ribbon Books, 1931.

Adelman, C. *Lessons of a Generation: Education and Work in the Lives of the High School Class of 1972*. San Francisco: Jossey-Bass, 1994.

Adelson, J. "Looking Back." *Daedalus*, 1974, *103*(4), 54–57.

Ambrose, S. E. *Undaunted Courage: Meriwether Lewis, Thomas Jefferson, and the Opening of the American West*. New York: Simon & Schuster, 1996.

American Council on Education. *The Student Personnel Point of View: A Report of a Conference on the Philosophy and Development of Student Personnel Work in the College and University*. American Council on Education Studies, 1937, Series I, *1*(3). Washington, D.C.: American Council on Education.

Angelo, T. A., and Cross, K. P. *Classroom Assessment Techniques: A Handbook for College Teachers*. (2nd ed.) San Francisco: Jossey-Bass, 1993.

Astin, A. W. *Four Critical Years: Effects of College on Beliefs, Attitudes, and Knowledge*. San Francisco: Jossey-Bass, 1977.

Astin, A. W. *What Matters in College? Four Critical Years Revisited*. San Francisco: Jossey-Bass, 1993.

Astin, A. W., and Chang, M. J. "Colleges That Emphasize Research and Teaching: Can You Have Your Cake and Eat It Too?" *Change*, Sept.–Oct. 1995, *27*(5), 44–49.

Basinger, J. "GAO Reports Big Jump in Student Loans." *Chronicle of Higher Education*, Feb. 1998, *44*(25), A37.

Bate, W. J. *Samuel Johnson*. Orlando: Harcourt Brace, 1975.

Baumol, W. J., Blackman, S.A.B., and Wolff, E. N. *Productivity and American Leadership*. Cambridge, Mass.: MIT Press, 1989.

Betts, J. R., and McFarland, L. L. "Safe Port in the Storm: Impact of Labor Market Conditions on Community College Enrollments." *Journal of Human Resources*, Fall 1969, *30*(4), 741–765.

Bledstein, B. J. *The Culture of Professionalism: The Middle Class and the Development of Higher Education in America*. New York: Norton, 1976.

Bloom, A. "The Failure of the University." *Daedalus*, 1974, *103*(4), 58–66.

Blumenstyk, K. G. "Royalties on Inventions Bring $336-Million to Top U.S. Research Universities." *Chronicle of Higher Education*, Feb. 1998, *44*(25), A44.

Bok, D. *Beyond the Ivory Tower: Social Responsibilities of the Modern University*. Cambridge, Mass.: Harvard University Press, 1982.

Bok, D. *The Cost of Talent*. New York: Free Press, 1993.

Boorstin, D. J. *The Americans: The Colonial Experience*. London: Sphere Books, 1991.

Bowen, H. *Investment in Learning*. San Francisco: Jossey-Bass, 1977.

Bowen, H. *The Costs of Higher Education*. San Francisco: Jossey-Bass, 1980.

Bowen, H., and Schuster, J. *American Professors: A National Resource Imperiled*. New York: Oxford University Press, 1986.

Boyer, E. L. *Scholarship Reconsidered: Priorities of the Professoriate*. Princeton, N.J.: The Carnegie Foundation for the Advancement of Teaching, 1990.

Boyer, E. L. "The Scholarship of Engagement." *Journal of Public Service and Outreach*, 1996, *1*(1), 11–20.

Breneman, D. W. *GSLs: Great Success or Dismal Failure?* Fishers, Ind.: United Student Aid Funds, May 1991.

Breneman, D. W. *Liberal Arts Colleges: Thriving, Surviving, or Endangered?* Washington, D.C.: Brookings Institution, 1994.

Broome, E. C. *A Historical and Critical Discussion of College Admission Requirements*. New York: Columbia University Press, 1903.

Brubacher, J. S., and Rudy, W. *Higher Education in Transition: A History of American Colleges and Universities, 1636–1976*. (3rd ed.) New York: Harper-Collins, 1976.

Burke, C. B. *American Collegiate Populations: A Test of the Traditional View*. New York: University Press, 1982.

Butts, R. F. *The College Charts Its Course*. New York: McGraw-Hill, 1939.

Campbell, J. R., Voelkl, K., and Donahue, P. L. *Report in Brief: NAEP 1996 Trends in Academic Progress*. Washington, D.C.: National Center for Education Statistics, Sept. 1997.

Carnegie Commission on Higher Education. *A Classification of Institutions of Higher Education*. Berkeley, Calif.: Carnegie Commission on Higher Education, 1973a.

Carnegie Commission on Higher Education. *The Purposes and Performance of Higher Education in the U.S.: Approaching the Year 2000. A Report and Recommendations*. New York: McGraw-Hill, 1973b.

Carnegie Council on Policy Studies in Higher Education. *A Summary of Reports and Recommendations*. San Francisco: Jossey-Bass, 1980.

The Carnegie Foundation for the Advancement of Teaching. *Missions of the College Curriculum: A Contemporary Review with Suggestions: A Commentary*. San Francisco: Jossey-Bass, 1977.

The Carnegie Foundation for the Advancement of Teaching. *The Control of the Campus: A Report on the Governance of Higher Education*. Lawrenceville, N.J.: Princeton University Press, 1982.

The Carnegie Foundation for the Advancement of Teaching. *A Classification of Institutions of Higher Education*. Princeton, N.J.: The Carnegie Foundation for the Advancement of Teaching, 1994.

Chapman, G. "Will Technology Commercialize Higher Learning?" *Los Angeles Times*, Jan. 19, 1998, pp. D1, D6.

Charting Higher Education Accountability: A Sourcebook on State-Level Performance Indicators. Denver, Colo.: Education Commission of the States, 1994.

Clark, B. R. *Places of Inquiry: Research and Advanced Education in Modern Universities*. Berkeley: University of California Press, 1995.

Clark, B. R. Substantive Growth and Innovative Organization: New Categories for Higher Education Research. *Higher Education*, 1996, *32*, 417–430.

Clark, B. R. "The Modern Integration of Research Activities with Teaching and Learning." *Journal of Higher Education*, May–June 1997, 68(3), 241–255.

Cohen, A. M., and Brawer, F. B. *The American Community College*. (3rd ed.) San Francisco: Jossey-Bass, 1996.

"College Attrition Rates Are on the Rise." *Activity*, Winter 1997, *35*(1), 4.

Committee on the Objectives of a General Education in a Free Society. *General Education in a Free Society: A Report of the Harvard Committee*. Cambridge, Mass.: Harvard University Press, 1945.

Committee on Veterans Affairs, United States Senate. *Final Report on Educational Assistance to Veterans: A Comparative Study of Three G.I. Bills*. Senate Committee Print No. 18. Washington, D.C.: U.S. Government Printing Office, 1973.

Council for Aid to Education. *Breaking the Social Contract: The Fiscal Crisis in Higher Education*. New York: Council for Aid to Education, May 1997.

Cuban, L. *Teachers and Machines: The Classroom Use of Technology Since 1920.* New York: Teachers College, Columbia University, 1986.

David, P. "The Knowledge Factory." *Economist,* Oct. 1997, *345*(8037), 1–22.

Dexter, F. B. *Biographical Sketches of the Graduates of Yale College with Annals of the College History.* Vol. 2. *1745–1763.* New York: Henry Holt, 1986.

Eaton, J. S. *Investing in American Higher Education: An Argument for Restructuring.* Paper prepared for the Commission on National Investment in Higher Education, Jan. 5, 1995. (Available from Council for Aid to Education, 342 Madison Avenue, Suite 1532, New York, N.Y., 10173.)

Eiseley, L. *The Firmament of Time.* New York: Athenaeum, 1970.

Ellis, J. M. *Literature Lost: Social Agendas and the Corruption of the Humanities.* New Haven, Conn.: Yale University, 1997.

Emerson, R. W. *An Oration Delivered Before the Phi Beta Kappa Society at Cambridge, August 31, 1837.* (2nd ed.) Boston: Munroe, 1838.

"Fact File: 495 College and University Endowments." *Chronicle of Higher Education,* Feb. 1998, *44*(24), A49.

Feldman, K. A., and Newcomb, T. M. *The Impact of College on Students.* San Francisco: Jossey-Bass, 1969.

Finkelstein, M. "From Tutor to Academic Scholar: Academic Professionalization in Eighteenth and Nineteenth Century America." *History of Higher Education Annual,* 1983, *3*, 99–121.

Finkelstein, M. *The American Academic Profession: A Synthesis of Scientific Inquiry Since World War II.* Columbus: Ohio State University Press, 1984.

Flexner, A. *The American College: A Criticism.* New York: Century, 1908.

Flexner, A. *Medical Education in the United States and Canada: A Report to The Carnegie Foundation for the Advancement of Teaching.* New York: The Carnegie Foundation for the Advancement of Teaching, 1910.

Flexner, A. *Universities: American, English, German.* New York: Oxford University Press, 1930.

Franklin, B. *Benjamin Franklin's Proposals for the Education of Youth in Pennsylvania.* Philadelphia.: University of Pennsylvania Press, 1931. (Originally published 1749 as *Proposals Relating to the Education of Youth in Pensilvania.*)

Freire, P. *Pedagogy of the Oppressed.* New York: Continuum, 1970.

Gallick, S. "Technology in Higher Education: Opportunities and Threats." *UCLA Faculty Association Newsletter,* Feb. 1998, pp. 1–6.

Garbarino, J. W., with Aussieker, B. *Faculty Bargaining: Change and Conflict.* Report prepared for the Carnegie Commission on Higher Education and the Ford Foundation. New York: McGraw-Hill, 1975.

Garbarino, J. W. "State Experience in Collective Bargaining." In *Faculty Bargaining in Public Higher Education: A Report and Two Essays*. San Francisco: Jossey-Bass, 1977.

Geiger, R. L. *Private Sector in Higher Education: Structure, Function, and Change in Eight Countries*. Ann Arbor: University of Michigan Press, 1986a.

Geiger, R. L. *To Advance Knowledge: The Growth of American Research Universities, 1900–1940*. New York: Oxford University Press, 1986b.

Geiger, R. L. *Research and Relevant Knowledge: American Research Universities Since World War II*. New York: Oxford University Press, 1993.

Geiger, R. "The Ten Generations of American Higher Education." In P. T. Altbach, R. O. Berdahl, and P. T. Gumport (eds.), *American Higher Education in the 21st Century: Social, Political, and Economic Challenges*. Chestnut Hill, Mass.: Boston College, Center for International Higher Education, School of Education, 1996 (preliminary edition). (Also, Johns Hopkins Press, 1998.)

Geiger, R. L. "Doctoral Education: The Short-Term Crisis vs. Long-Term Challenge." *Review of Higher Education*, Spring 1997, *20*(3), 239–251.

Giele, J. Z. "Two Paths to Women's Equality." *Temperance, Suffrage, and the Origins of Modern Feminism*. New York: Twayne, 1995.

Gladieux, L. E., and Hauptman, A. M. *The College Aid Quandary: Access, Quality, and the Federal Role*. Washington, D.C., and New York: Brookings Institution and College Board, 1995.

Glynn, P. "The Age of Balkanization." *Commentary*, July 1993, *96*(1), 21–24.

Goodchild, L. F., and Stanton, C. M. (eds.). "History of Higher Education Newsletter." *History of Higher Education*, Spring–Fall 1987, *8*(1–2). (ED 303 974)

Goodchild, L. F., and Wechsler, H. S. (eds.). *ASHE Reader on the History of Higher Education*. (2nd ed.) Needham Heights, Mass.: Simon & Schuster Custom Publishing, 1997.

Grant, G., and Riesman, D. *The Perpetual Dream: Reform and Experiment in the American College*. Chicago: University of Chicago Press, 1978.

Green, K. C. *Campus Computing 1997*. Encino, Calif.: Campus Computing, 1997a.

Green, K. C. "Drawn to the Light, Burned by the Flame? Money, Technology, and Distance Education." *ED, Education at a Distance*, 1997b, *11*(5), J1–J9.

Green, T. *Predicting the Behavior of the Educational System*. Syracuse, N.Y.: Syracuse University, 1980.

Hamlin, A. T. *The University Library in the United States*. Philadelphia: University of Pennsylvania Press, 1981.

Handlin, O., and Handlin, M. F. *Facing Life: Youth and the Family in American History*. Boston: Little, Brown, 1971.

Hansen, W. L., and Weisbrod, B. A. "The Distribution of Costs and Direct Benefits of Public Higher Education: The Case of California." *Journal of Human Resources*, Spring 1969, 4(2), 176–191.

Harcleroad, F. F. "The Hidden Hand: External Constituencies and Their Impact." In P. T. Altbach, R. O. Berdahl, and P. T. Gumport (eds.), *American Higher Education in the 21st Century: Social, Political, and Economic Challenges*. Chestnut Hill, Mass.: Boston College, Center for International Higher Education, School of Education, 1996 (preliminary edition). (Also, Johns Hopkins Press, 1998.)

Harris, S. *A Statistical Portrait of Higher Education*. Report prepared for the Carnegie Commission on Higher Education. New York: McGraw-Hill, 1972.

"Harvard's Men." *Barron's*, Dec. 2, 1996, pp. 31, 38.

Hauptman, A. M. *The Tuition Dilemma*. Washington, D.C.: Brookings Institution, 1990.

Henry, W. A., III. *In Defense of Elitism*. New York: Doubleday, 1994.

Herbst, J. "The Institutional Diversification of Higher Education in the New Nation: 1780–1820." *Review of Higher Education*, Spring 1980, 3(3), 15–18.

Herbst, J. "Church, State and Higher Education: College Government in the American Colonies and States Before 1820." *History of Higher Education Annual*, 1981, 1, 42–54.

Herbst, J. *From Crisis to Crisis: American College Government 1636–1819*. Cambridge, Mass.: Harvard University Press, 1982.

Herzberg, F., Mausner, B., and Snyderman, B. D. *The Motivation to Work*. New York: Wiley, 1959.

Hesburgh, T. M. "The 'Events': A Retrospective View." *Daedalus*, 1974, 103(4), 67–71.

Hoffman, C. M. *Federal Support for Education: Fiscal Years 1980 to 1997*. National Council for Educational Statistics, 97–383. Washington, D.C.: U.S. Department of Education, Sept. 1997.

Hofstadter, R. *The Development and Scope of Higher Education in the United States*. New York: Columbia University Press for the Commission on Financing Higher Education, 1952.

Hofstadter, R., and Smith, W. (eds.). *American Higher Education: A Documentary History*. 2 vols. Chicago: University of Chicago Press, 1961.

Hutchins, R. M. *The Higher Learning in America*. New Haven, Conn.: Yale University Press, 1936.

Illich, I. *Deschooling Society*. New York: HarperCollins, 1970.

Jencks, C. *Inequality*. New York: Basic Books, 1972.

Jencks, C., and Riesman, D. *The Academic Revolution*. New York: Doubleday, 1968.

Jordan, D. S. *The Call of the Twentieth Century: An Address to Young Men*. Boston: American Unitarian Association, 1903.

Jordan, W. D., and Litwack, L. F. *The United States*. (7th ed.) Upper Saddle River, N.J.: Prentice Hall, 1994.

Kaplin, W. A. *The Law of Higher Education: A Comprehensive Guide to Legal Implications of Administrative Decision Making*. San Francisco: Jossey-Bass, 1985.

Kaplin, W. A. *The Law of Higher Education: A Comprehensive Guide to Legal Implications of Administrative Decision Making*. (2nd ed.) San Francisco: Jossey-Bass, 1990.

Kaplin, W. A., and Lee, B. A. *The Law of Higher Education: A Comprehensive Guide to Legal Implications of Administrative Decision Making*. (3rd ed.) San Francisco: Jossey-Bass, 1995.

Kellner, D. "Multiple Literacies and Critical Pedagogy in a Multicultural Society." *Educational Theory*, Winter 1998, *48*(1), 103–122.

Kentucky Council on Higher Education. *Annual Accountability Report Series for Kentucky Higher Education*. [http://www.che.state.ky.us/brochure.htm]. 1996.

Kerr, C. *The Uses of the University*. The Godkin Lectures at Harvard University. Cambridge, Mass.: Harvard University Press, 1963.

Kett, J. F. *Rites of Passage: Adolescence in America, 1790 to the Present*. New York: Basic Books, 1977.

Kreger, J. L. "An Industrial Designer in Academe: Albert Kahn and the Design of Angell Hall." *LSAmagazine*, Spring 1998, *21*(2), 4–12.

Kuttner, R. *Everything for Sale*. New York: Knopf, 1997.

Ladd, E. C., and Lipset, S. M. *The Divided Academy: Professor and Politics*. New York: McGraw-Hill, 1975.

Lederman, D., and Mooney, C. J. "Lifting the Cloak of Secrecy from Tenure." *Chronicle of Higher Education*, Apr. 1995, *41*(31), 17–18.

Lemann, N. "The Great Sorting." *Atlantic Monthly*, Sept. 1995, *276*, 84–100.

Lemann, N. "A Cartoon Elite." *Atlantic Monthly*, Nov. 1996, *278*, 109–112, 114–116.

Lovett, C. M. "American Professors & Their Society." *Change*, July–Aug. 1993, *25*(4), 26–37.

Lucas, C. J. *American Higher Education: A History.* New York: St. Martin's Press, 1994.

Lyman, R. W. "In Defense of the Private Sector." *Daedalus*, 1975, *104*(1), 156–159.

MacDonald, G. B. (ed.). *Five Experimental Colleges.* New York: HarperCollins, 1973.

MacIntyre, A. *Whose Justice? Which Rationality?* Notre Dame, Ind.: University of Notre Dame Press, 1988.

Magner, D. K. "Increases in Faculty Salaries Fail to Keep Pace with Inflation." *Chronicle of Higher Education*, July 1, 1997, *43*(43), A8–A9.

"Making America Rich." *Wall Street Journal*, Mar. 26, 1998, p. A22.

Maldonado, C. *SYRIT Computer School Systems.* Office of the State Comptrollers Audit Report 95-T-8. New York, Office of the State Comptrollers, Feb. 5, 1998.

Marchese, T. "Student Evaluations of Teaching." *Change*, Sept.–Oct. 1997, *29*(5), 4.

Marcus, L. R. "Restructuring State Higher Education Governance Patterns." *Review of Higher Education*, Summer 1997, *20*(4), 399–418.

McGuinness, A. C., Jr. *Restructuring State Roles in Higher Education: A Case Study of the 1994 New Jersey Higher Education Restructuring Act.* Dec. 1995. (Available from Education Commission of the States, 707 17th Street, Suite 2700, Denver, CO 80202–3427.)

McKeachie, W. J. "Research on Teaching at the College and University Level." In N. L. Gage (ed.), *Handbook on Teaching.* Skokie, Ill.: Rand McNally, 1963.

McLachlan, J. "The Choice of Hercules: American Student Societies in the Early 19th Century." In L. Stone (ed.), *The University in Society.* Vol. 2. Princeton, N.J.: Princeton University Press, 1974.

McMaster, J. B. *A Brief History of the United States.* Sacramento: California State Series, 1909.

McPherson, M. S., and Schapiro, M. O. *Keeping College Affordable: Government and Educational Opportunities.* Washington, D.C.: Brookings Institution, 1991.

Meriwether, C. *Our Colonial Curriculum, 1607–1776.* Washington, D.C.: Capital, 1907.

Miller, M. T., and Nelson, G. M. (eds.). *Graduate Programs in the Study of Higher*

Education: Selected Syllabi. Lincoln: Nebraska University, Lincoln Department of Educational Administration, 1993. (ED 363 238)

Mills, C. W. *The Sociological Imagination.* New York: Oxford University Press, 1959.

Moynihan, D. P. "The Politics of Higher Education." *Daedalus,* 1975, *104*(1), 128–147.

Nash, G. B., Crabtree, C., and Dunn, R. E. *History on Trial: Culture Wars and the Teaching of the Past.* New York: Knopf, 1997.

National Center for Education Statistics. *Digest of Education Statistics.* Washington, D.C.: U.S. Department of Education, 1992.

National Center for Education Statistics. "Welfare Recipiency, by Educational Attainment." In *Indicator of the Month.* NCES 95–787. Washington, D.C.: U.S. Department of Education, July 1995.

National Center for Education Statistics. "Community Service and Volunteerism." In *Indicator of the Month.* NCES 96–795. Washington, D.C.: U.S. Department of Education, Mar. 1996a.

National Center for Education Statistics. *Digest of Education Statistics.* Washington, D.C.: U.S. Department of Education, 1996b.

National Center for Education Statistics. "Institutional Policies and Practices Regarding Faculty in Higher Education." In *Statistical Analysis Report.* NCES 97–080. Washington, D.C.: U.S. Department of Education, Nov. 1996c.

National Center for Education Statistics. *International Education Indicators: A Time Series Perspective.* Washington, D.C.: U.S. Department of Education, 1996d.

National Center for Education Statistics. "Remedial Education at Higher Education Institutions in Fall 1995." In *Statistical Analysis Report.* NCES 97–584. Washington, D.C.: U.S. Department of Education, Oct. 1996e.

National Center for Education Statistics. *The Condition of Education.* Washington, D.C.: U.S. Department of Education, 1997a.

National Center for Education Statistics. "The Condition of Education 1997—Supplemental Table: Table 33–2." [http://nces.ed.gov/pub/ce/c9733d02.html]. 1997b.

National Center for Education Statistics. "The Condition of Education 1997—Supplemental Table: Table 33–3." [http://nces.ed.gov/pub/ce/c9733d03.html]. 1997c.

National Center for Education Statistics. "The Condition of Education 1997—Supplemental Table: Table 33–4." [http://nces.ed.gov/pub/ce/c9733d04.html]. 1997d.

National Center for Education Statistics. *Current Fund Revenues and Expenditures of Institutions of Higher Education: Fiscal Years 1987 Through 1995*, NCES 97–441. Washington, D.C.: U.S. Department of Education, Sept. 1997e.

National Center for Education Statistics. "Degrees Earned by Foreign Graduate Students: Fields of Study and Plans After Graduation." In *Issue Brief*, NCES 98–042. Washington, D.C.: U.S. Department of Education, Nov. 1997f.

National Center for Education Statistics. *Digest of Education Statistics*. Washington, D.C.: U.S. Department of Education, 1997g.

National Center for Education Statistics. "Distance Education in Higher Education Institutions." *Statistical Analysis Report*, NCES 98–062. Washington, D.C.: U.S. Department of Education, Oct. 1997h.

National Center for Education Statistics. *Enhancing the Quality and Use of Student Outcomes Data*, NCES 97–992, prepared by Patrick Terenzini for the Council of the National Postsecondary Education Cooperative Working Group on Student Outcomes from a Policy Perspective. Washington, D.C.: U.S. Department of Education, Sept. 1997i.

National Center for Education Statistics. *Enrollment in Higher Education: Fall 1995*, NCES 97–440. Washington, D.C.: U.S. Department of Education, 1997j.

National Center for Education Statistics. *Instructional Faculty and Staff in Higher Education Institutions: Fall 1987 and Fall 1992*, NCES 97–441. Washington, D.C.: U.S. Department of Education, 1997k.

National Center for Education Statistics. *Fall Staff in Postsecondary Institutions, 1995*, NCES 98–228. Washington, D.C.: U.S. Department of Education, Mar. 1998.

National Center for the Study of Collective Bargaining in Higher Education and the Professions. *Directory of Faculty Contracts and Bargaining Agents in Institutions of Higher Education*. Vols. 1–22. New York: National Center for the Study of Collective Bargaining in Higher Education and the Professions (annual), 1974–1996.

National Education Association of the United States. *Salaries Paid and Salary Practices in Universities, Colleges, and Junior Colleges, 1957–58, Third Biennial Study*. Research Report 1958–R1. Washington, D.C.: National Education Association of the United States, May 1958.

Nespoli, L. A., and Gilroy, H. A. "Lobbying for Funds." *Community College Journal*, Feb.–Mar. 1998, 68(4), 10–14.

Nevins, A. *The Origins of the Land-Grant Colleges and State Universities*. Washington, D.C.: Civil War Centennial Commission, 1962.

Nisbet, R. A. *The Degradation of the Academic Dogma: The University in America, 1945–1970.* New York: Basic Books, 1971.

O'Banion, T. *A Learning College for the 21st Century.* Phoenix, Ariz.: American Council on Education and Oryx Press, 1997.

Oettinger, A. G. *Run, Computer, Run: The Mythology of Educational Innovation.* Cambridge, Mass.: Harvard University Press, 1969.

Organisation for Economic Co-operation and Development. *Higher Education and Employment: The Case of Humanities and Social Sciences.* Paris: Organization for Economic Cooperation and Development, 1993.

Orlans, H. *The Effects of Federal Programs on Higher Education: A Study of 36 Universities and Colleges.* Washington, D.C.: Brookings Institution, 1962.

Ortega y Gasset, J. *Misión de la Universidad* [Mission of the university]. (Translated with an introduction by H. L. Nostrand.) Princeton, N.J.: Princeton University Press, 1944.

Pace, C. R. *Measuring Outcomes of College: Fifty Years of Findings and Recommendations for the Future.* San Francisco: Jossey-Bass, 1979.

Park, R. "Some Considerations on Higher Education of Women." In H. Astin and W. Z. Hirsch (eds.), *The Higher Education of Women: Essays in Honor of Rosemary Park.* New York: Praeger, 1978.

Pascarella, E. T., and Terenzini, P. T. *How College Affects Students: Findings and Insights from Twenty Years of Research.* San Francisco: Jossey-Bass, 1991.

Peters, W. E. *Legal History of the Ohio University, Athens, Ohio: Compiled from Legislative Enactments, Judicial Decisions, Trustee's Proceedings, etc.* Cincinnati, Ohio: Press of the Western Methodist Book Concern, 1910.

Rashdall, H. *The Universities of Europe in the Middle Ages.* (New ed.; M. Powicke, and A. B. Emden, eds.) Oxford: Clarendon Press, 1936.

Reich, R. B. *The Work of Nations: Preparing Ourselves for 21st Century Capitalism.* New York: Vintage Books, 1992.

Rodenhouse, M. P. (ed.). *1997 Higher Education Directory.* Falls Church, Va.: Higher Education Publications, 1997.

Rogers, C. *Freedom to Learn.* Columbus, Ohio: Merrill, 1969.

Rothstein, W. G. "Medical Education." In B. R. Clark and G. Neave (eds.), *The Encyclopedia of Higher Education.* New York: Pergamon Press, 1992.

Rudolph, F. *The American College and University: A History.* New York: Knopf, 1962.

Rudolph, F. *Curriculum: A History of the American Undergraduate Course of Study Since 1636.* San Francisco: Jossey-Bass, 1977.

Sanchez, J. R., and Laanan, F. S. "Economic Returns to Community College Education." *Community College Review,* Winter 1997, 25(3), 73–87.

Schneider, H., and Schneider, C. (eds.). *Samuel Johnson: His Career and Writings.* New York: Columbia University Press, 1929.

Schuster, J. H. "Whither the Faculty? The Changing Academic Labor Market." *Educational Record,* Fall 1995, *76*(4), 28–33.

Shils, E. "Universities: Since 1900." In B. R. Clark and G. Neave (eds.), *The Encyclopedia of Higher Education.* New York: Pergamon Press, 1992.

Shores, L. *Origins of the American College Library, 1638–1800.* Nashville, Tenn.: George Peabody College, 1966.

Sinclair, U. *The Goose-Step: A Study of American Education.* (2nd ed.) Pasadena, Calif.: Upton Sinclair, 1923.

Sloan, D. "Harmony, Chaos, and Consensus: The American College Curriculum." *Teachers College Record,* 1971, *73*(2), 221–251.

Snow, L. F. *The College Curriculum in the U.S.* New York: Teachers College, 1907.

Snyder, T. D. (ed.). *120 Years of American Education: A Statistical Portrait.* Washington, D.C.: National Center for Education Statistics, Jan. 1993.

Stahler, G. J., and Tash, W. R. "Centers and Institutes in the Research University: Issues, Problems and Prospects." *Journal of Higher Education,* Sept.–Oct. 1994, *65*(4), 540–555.

State College and University Systems of West Virginia. *West Virginia Higher Education Report Card.*
[http://www.scusco.wvnet.edu/www/reportcr.htm]. 1997.

Strosnider, K. "For-Profit Higher Education Sees Booming Enrollments and Revenues." *Chronicle of Higher Education,* Jan. 1998, *44*(20), A36–A37.

Ten Brook, A. *American State Universities, Their Origin and Progress; A History of Congressional University Land-Grants.* Cincinnati, Ohio: Robert Clarke, 1875.

Thelin, J. R. *Foundations/History/Philosophy.* Prepared as part of the ASHE-ERIC Clearinghouse for Course Syllabi in Higher Education Project. Washington, D.C.: ERIC Clearinghouse for Higher Education, 1986.
(ED 272 124)

Thiederman, S. "Creating Victims to Compensate Victims." *Los Angeles Times,* Nov. 27, 1996, p. B9.

Thurow, L. C. "One World, Ready or Not: The Manic Logic of Global Capitalism." *Atlantic Monthly,* Mar. 1997, *279*(3), 97–100.

Thwing, C. F. *A History of Education in the United States Since the Civil War.* Boston: Houghton Mifflin, 1910.

Tollett, K. "Community and Higher Education." *Daedalus,* 1975, *104*(1), 278–297.

Trilling, L. *Mind in the Modern World.* New York: Viking Press, 1972.

Trow, M. A. "The Public and Private Lives of Higher Education." *Daedalus*, 1975, *104*(1), 113–127.

Trow, M. A. "American Higher Education: Past, Present, Future." *Studies in Higher Education*, 1989, *14*, 1, 5–22.

U.S. Office of Education. *Annual Report, Federal Security Agency*. Washington, D.C.: U.S. Government Printing Office, 1945.

University of Arizona. *Measurable Goals for Undergraduate Education*. [http://pubrec.oir.arizona.edu/daps/pubrec/reports/measgoals_rptcrd.htm]. 1996.

University of California Academic Senate Academic Council. "Senate Committee Proposes Adding Step IX to Professor Scale." *Notice*, Apr. 1996, *20*(6), 2.

The University of the State of New York. *Leadership and Learning*. [http://www.nysed.gov/regents/strategy.html]. 1996.

Veblen, T. *The Higher Learning in America: A Memorandum on the Conduct of Universities by Businessmen*. New York: Sagamore Press, 1957. (Originally published 1918.)

Veysey, L. R. *The Emergence of the American University*. Chicago: University of Chicago Press, 1965.

Vine, P. "The Social Function of 18th Century Higher Education." *History of Education Quarterly*, Winter 1997, *16*, 409–424.

Wallace, A. "Search for CSU Chief to Be Done in Secrecy." *Los Angeles Times*, Aug. 5, 1997, pp. A3, A18.

Wallhaus, R. A. *Priorities, Quality and Productivity in Higher Education: The Illinois P-Q-P Initiative*. Denver, Colo.: Education Commission of the States, Sept. 1996.

Wayland, F. *Report to the Corporation of Brown University on Changes in the System of Collegiate Education*. Providence, R.I., Mar. 28, 1850.

Weiner, S. S. *The Tangled Thicket: Sham Academic Degrees in California and the Problem of State Regulation*. Oakland, Calif.: Western College Association, Mar. 1989.

Weiss, K. R. "Loan Defaults Fall Amid Crackdown." *Los Angeles Times*, Nov. 26, 1997, p. B2.

Wessel, D. "The Wealth Factor." *Wall Street Journal*, Apr. 2, 1998, p. A1.

Wilson, E. O. "Back from Chaos." *Atlantic Monthly*, 1998, *281*(3), 41–62.

Wilson, R. "A Subversive Sympathy." *Atlantic Monthly*, 1997, *280*(3), 108–110, 112.

Wolfle, D. *America's Resources of Specialized Talent. Report of the Commission on Human Resources and Advanced Training*. New York: HarperCollins, 1954.

Wolfle, D. *The Home of Science: The Role of the University*. New York: McGraw-Hill, 1972.

Ziomek, R. L., and Svec, J. C. "High School Grades and Achievement: Evidence of Grade Inflation." ACT Research Report Series, 95–3. Iowa City, Iowa: American College Testing Program, Nov. 1995.

Index